Abortion to Save m

ABORTION

A Reference Handbook

Second Edition

ABORTION

A Reference Handbook

Second Edition

Marie Costa

CONTEMPORARY WORLD ISSUES

ABC-CLIO

Santa Barbara, California
Denver, Colorado
Oxford, England

Library of Congress Cataloging-in-Publication Data

Costa, Marie, 1951–
    Abortion : a reference handbook / Marie Costa. — 2nd ed.
      p. cm. — (Contemporary world issues)
    Includes bibliographical references and index.
    1. Abortion—United States—Handbooks, manuals, etc.
I. Title. II. Series
    HQ767.5.U5C67   1996   363.4'6—dc20   96-12251

ISBN 0-87436-827-8 (alk. paper)

02 01 00 99 98 97 96   10 9 8 7 6 5 4 3 2 1 (cloth)

ABC-CLIO, Inc.
130 Cremona Drive, P.O. Box 1911
Santa Barbara, California 93116-1911

This book is printed on acid-free paper ∞.
Manufactured in the United States of America

*This book is gratefully dedicated to those who
search for common ground in human conflicts,
wherever and whenever they arise.*

Contents

Preface

Abortion, a word once rarely spoken out loud, has over the last three decades become synonymous with controversy and conflict. Many of those involved seem to feel that they are at war with an enemy that strikes at the heart of their values and beliefs, at the whole order by which they organize their lives. "We are pro," claims each camp, "and they are anti"—anti-baby, anti-woman, anti-family, anti-choice, anti-life, anti-everything we and the country stand for.

Common to participants in a debate such as this is the belief that, "If people really understood what this is all about, they would agree with us (and do what we want them to.)" But such is not necessarily the case. People can understand one another and still disagree. A pregnant woman may understand that an abortion means the death of a living human being and still choose to abort. A "sidewalk counselor" may understand that continuing a pregnancy will disrupt or even devastate a woman's life and still urge her to have the baby. By the same token, a woman who always believed that if she got pregnant she would have an abortion may be unwilling to carry through with her plan, and a

xiii

woman who has picketed an abortion clinic may find herself a patient at that very clinic. When the abstract becomes real and personal, what seemed clear and indisputable can become murky indeed. Yet each side continues to hurl its slogans and images at the other and at anyone in the vicinity, as if shouting louder and harder, telling the most poignant stories, or displaying the most riveting images will somehow convince everyone to see it their way.

Although abortion has been a source of conflict throughout history and throughout the world, the battle as it is being fought in the United States today is distinctly American. Laurence Tribe (1990) compares American attitudes about abortion with those in more repressive societies such as Stalinist Russia, Nazi Germany, and Communist China. In these countries, he writes, "neither those advocating abortion nor those opposing it use the language of 'rights' that characterizes the abortion debate in the United States. Scant attention is paid either to the rights of the woman to have her child or to her right to terminate her pregnancy—or to any right of the fetus to be born. Rather, the conflict is structured almost wholly in terms of corporate groups, like the state and the family, and centers on the needs of and the duties owed to such groups" (p. 63).

But the United States was largely founded on the concept of rights, so that here even moral issues—and almost no one would disagree that abortion is a moral issue—are framed in the language of rights. Few issues, however, place such cherished, and in many minds, fundamental rights in direct conflict—the right to live versus the right to choose how to live, including whether or not to become a parent. Other rights, too, are involved in the struggle over abortion, such as the right to speak out versus the right to exercise a legal option. Values are also at issue in the American battle over abortion. Some see the conflict as one between traditional family values and self-expression and fulfillment, between Judeo-Christian ethics and the more amorphous "situational ethics," between selflessness and selfishness. Others see it as a conflict between those who would stop change and those who would pursue a vision of a new world.

Can such a conflict ever be resolved? Some, such as sociologist Kristin Luker, say no, because those holding "pro-choice" and "pro-life" opinions also hold worldviews that are diametrically opposed. Others believe a resolution is possible by adopting a compromise solution that would please neither side but that "most people" could live with—allowing abortions only in the first 12 weeks, for example, or only for specific reasons. Still others believe the issue will eventually become moot, as mifepristone (RU 486) or other abortifacient drugs become readily available in the United States.

Perhaps in anticipation of this time, or simply through a realization that the old tactics have brought about a stalemate, some activists, at least, are changing their strategies and goals. The battle for safe, legal abortion has expanded, in large part due to the efforts of women of color, into a call for full reproductive freedom, including the right to have, as well as not to have, children. Such a movement seeks access not only to contraceptives and safe abortion, but to prenatal care, child care, and help for women and families. At the same time, many of those opposed to abortion have chosen to focus on making the alternatives more attractive and feasible, by providing housing, medical care, jobs, education help, financial assistance, parenting classes, and compassionate adoption services to women facing unplanned pregnancies.

The publicity given to the loud voices, the demonstrations and the violent acts of a radical few, obscures the fact that many people on both sides share a common goal: to make "choice" a reality where little choice existed before. In the past, a woman with an unwanted pregnancy usually "had no choice" but to continue being pregnant, often at the price of social disgrace. Then she "had no choice" but to relinquish her baby to strangers, or to enter a too-hasty marriage, or to struggle as a single parent of a child branded as illegitimate. Today, thousands of women have abortions because they feel they "have no choice"—because they lack financial resources, family support, or a loving partner, because their education or their career is at stake, or because they have too much to cope with already. As Mary Cunningham Agee, founder of the Nurturing Network, says, "Both the 'pro-life' and 'pro-choice' movements—characterized most often by their emotionally-charged legislative battles, rhetorical debates and judgmental protests—often overlook the imminent needs of the woman about whom they are arguing." What's more, Agee says, she believes that "there *does* exist, between the two groups, a *common ground* (not necessarily a "middle" ground) which would provide both groups with an opportunity to serve the woman faced with an unwanted pregnancy."

Such efforts would bring both sides into closer alignment with the majority of Americans, most of whom regard the issue with profound ambivalence. Nonetheless, the battle over abortion will no doubt continue to rage for some time to come—in the media, on the sidewalks before abortion clinics, in state and national legislatures, in the courts, in the churches, within the medical profession. For this reason, it is important for Americans, whether they are deeply involved in the conflict or simply concerned observers, to understand what the battle is about. Though understanding may not bring agreement, it can bring compassion, empathy, and a willingness to talk. And with these come the possibility of finding the common ground that does exist. As Faye Ginsburg (1989) discovered in her study of abortion activists in Fargo, North Dakota, "Whether pro-life or pro-choice, activists express their motivation for social action as a desire to alter the meaning and circumstances of procreation in order to make conditions better for the next generation. In other words, they are concerned, as female activists, with their role in reproducing the culture, but in terms different from the present."

It is just possible that the struggle over abortion presents a greater opportunity than is at first apparent amidst the smoke and fire of passionate debate. Perhaps it represents an opportunity that can only be discovered on the common ground where lies the hope for a better world; one in which each child—each person—is loved, welcomed, and respected, in which all life is valued, and in which everyone has the opportunity for fulfillment and self-expression, however they define it. It is to the search for that common ground that this book is dedicated.

About This Book

The purpose of this book is to provide access to the available information, as well as the full spectrum of thought, on abortion. It does not attempt to promulgate any view, except the view that all voices should be heard and listened to. As objectively as possible, it presents historical and factual background information, along with resources for further exploration into the social, psychological, legal, medical, political, and moral aspects of abortion. By pulling together a wide array of information not available in any other single source, this book may prove of service to many different people—students, researchers, writers, journalists, historians, and activists, as well as individuals who are interested in clarifying their own thoughts and feelings about abortion. Be warned, however—the more you know, the less clear those thoughts and feelings may become. Such is the nature of this complex, troubling, and endlessly fascinating topic.

Organization

Like others in the Contemporary World Issues series, this book is meant to serve both as a "one-stop" resource and as a guide to further research. Chapter 1 sets the historical context with a chronology that includes significant legislation, court decisions, medical developments, trends, political events, religious proclamations, and other relevant occurrences. Chapter 2 contains biographical sketches of some of the current key players in the debate, including activists, doctors, lawyers, and politicians. Chapter 3 contains statistical and factual information about abortion, including laws and policies; statistics; information on access to abortion services and harassment of abortion providers; public opinion about abortion; abortion techniques, complications, and risks; and embryonic and fetal development. Chapter 4 is an annotated directory of organizations, including activist groups, research organizations, educational organizations, legal defense funds, political lobbying groups, and support services, including alternatives to abortion. Chapter 5 is an annotated bibliography of print resources, including bibliographies, anthologies, books and monographs, and periodicals. Chapter 6 is an annotated listing of nonprint resources, including a computer database search service, films, and videos. A glossary of important terms and an index complete the volume.

About the Language Used in This Book

Language has become a major sub-issue in the abortion debate, with people on each side employing different terms to describe themselves and their opponents. It is difficult for a writer not to get caught up in the cross fire or to be accused of taking sides based on her or his terminology. In an effort to be both balanced and descriptive I have adopted the following approach: when describing specific individuals or organizations I have tried to use the terms they would use themselves, most often "pro-life" or "pro-choice." In more general contexts, however, I have used terms that describe the participants in relationship to their specific stance on abortion; for example, "abortion rights supporters" or "advocates of legal abortion" on the one side, and "antiabortion groups" or "opponents of legal abortion" on the other. I hope most readers will find this acceptable.

About the Second Edition

A great deal has happened since the first edition of *Abortion: A Reference Handbook* was published in 1991. Change has taken place in the courts, in the legislatures, and on the front lines of abortion clinics and activist organizations. The controversy, however, is no closer to being resolved. If anything, the debate has become more divisive and bitter than ever.

This new edition reflects both the changes and the enduring sameness of the issue. The basic organization of the book remains the same. The chronology in chapter 1 has been updated through 1995. Additions and deletions to the biographical sketches in chapter 2 reflect changes in the cast of players, as some activists have retired or moved on to other things, while others have come to take their places and reshape the debate. The statistical information in chapter 3 has been updated to reflect the most recent data available, and other information has been added, including an update on mifepristone (RU 486), expanded sections on public opinion on abortion and the psychological impact of abortion, and a new section on abortion-related Supreme Court cases. The entire chapter has also been reorganized to make it easier to understand and use. The directory of organizations in chapter 4 has been updated with current (as of mid-1995) addresses, phone numbers, and descriptions; several new organizations have been added, while a few have been deleted because they are no longer in existence, were not traceable, or are not national in scope. Chapters 5 and 6 have been expanded to include books, periodicals, and videos issued since the first edition; selections considered outdated or no longer useful were deleted. Chapter 6 also includes a brief list of abortion resources on the Internet. The video distributors in chapter 6 have been consolidated into a single list at the end of the chapter.

As before, I have made every attempt to keep the information in *Abortion* as factual and objective as possible, so that readers and researchers may draw their own conclusions.

References

Agee, Mary Cunningham. No date. *Unique and Differentiating Characteristics of the Nurturing Network*. Descriptive paper.
Ginsburg, Faye D. 1989. *Contested Lives*. Berkeley: University of California Press.
Luker, Kristin. 1984. *Abortion and the Politics of Motherhood*. Berkeley: University of California Press.
Tribe, Laurence H. 1990. *Abortion: The Clash of Absolutes*. New York: W. W. Norton.

Chronology 1

Classical Greece

Abortion is legal, although an abortion provider can be punished for failing to inform the father. In *The Republic*, Plato states that women who become pregnant after the age of 40 should be compelled to have abortions. Aristotle believes that the state should determine the number of children a married couple can have and that any woman becoming pregnant after reaching the allotted number should have an abortion. He proposes that the fetus first has a vegetable soul, which is succeeded by an animal soul and finally, when the body is fully developed, by a human soul. An early abortion is not therefore the killing of a human being. Hippocrates, however, disapproves of abortion and includes a clause against it in his medical oath.

Roman Empire

Despite official pro-natalist policies promoting at least three children per couple among the upper classes, abortion and contraception are frequent and widespread among those who can afford it (among the poor, nfanticide and abandonment are common). According to Roman law, the "child in the belly of its mother" is not a person, and abortion, therefore, does not constitute murder. Such legal regulation of abortion as exists in the Roman Empire at this time is aimed at protecting the rights of fathers, not of fetuses. A wife who procures an abortion without her husband's consent is subject to exile. References are made to abortion in the writings of Ovid, Juvenal, Seneca, and Pliny, who lists abortifacient drugs.

Beginning of Christian Era
(First through Seventh Centuries)

From the first century onward, Christian thought is divided as to whether early abortion is murder. An early church document, the *Didache*, condemns abortion, saying "You shall not kill the fetus by abortion or destroy the infant already born" (Hurst 1989, 6). Many early documents indicate that abortion was considered a sin if it was used to conceal evidence of the sins of fornication or adultery. St. Augustine, while condemning birth control and abortion because they break the proscribed connection between the sexual act and procreation, does not hold abortion to be homicide if it occurs before hominization of the fetus. Hominization, also referred to as formation, animation, vivification, or ensoulment, is thought to occur at 40 days for a male embryo and 80 days for a female embryo. In questions of ambiguity the embryo is considered female.

Middle Christian Era
(Eighth through Sixteenth Centuries)

According to Hurst (1989), throughout this period abortion is treated as a serious sin of a sexual nature, but it is not considered homicide. The *Irish Canons,* written around A.D. 675, specify one penalty for abortion before hominization and a different and more serious penalty after hominization. Writing around A.D. 1100, church scholar Ivo of Chartres, while condemning abortion, states that abortion of an "unformed embryo" is not homicide. This stance will be reiterated 40 years later by Gratian, whose writings on the subject form the basis of canon law for the next 700 years.

In practice, particularly because of the uncertainty as to when pregnancy actually began, the concept of delayed hominization means that early abortions are not considered criminal acts. There is some debate as to whether even late abortions were actually prosecuted under common law.

In his writings on the subject, St. Thomas puts forward the concept of hylomorphism, which says that human beings are a unity of two elements: primary matter, or the potentiality of the body, and substantial form, or the actualizing principle of the soul. Both elements are necessary for a human being to exist, implying that the embryo must have a fully human body—one developed beyond the early stages of pregnancy—before it is capable of receiving the soul and becoming human. St. Thomas, however, believes both contraception and abortion to be vices against nature and sins against marriage; his views are adopted as the official doctrine of the Roman Catholic Church.

1588   Pope Sixtus V issues a papal bull declaring that abortion at any state of pregnancy is homicide. The bull calls abortion both a moral sin and a secular crime, punishable by excommunication.

1591   Pope Gregory XIV issues a papal pronouncement reinstating the concept of delayed hominization and recommending that church penalties for abortion of an unanimated fetus be no stricter than civil penalties.

1621   Paolo Zacchia, a Roman physician, publishes a treatise proposing that a rational soul is present in humans from the moment of conception, a concept that will gradually gain acceptance and influence.

Seventeenth and Eighteenth Centuries

In colonial America and the early United States, abortions are not explicitly prohibited in any written law, nor are they prosecuted under common law. Abortion is generally regarded as both legal and moral if it occurs prior to "quickening," or the first perception of fetal movement by the mother. Prior to quickening, the embryo is believed to be inanimate.

Nineteenth Century

From 1800 to 1900, the fertility rate for white American women (the only statistics available) will drop from 7.04 to 3.56 children, largely due to increased use of abortion. During the first half of the century, abortion becomes increasingly visible in the United States; by 1850, abortionists are advertising openly in newspapers, magazines, popular health manuals, and religious publications, which also carry ads for abortifacients and home remedies for "menstrual blockage." Most home medical manuals contain sections explaining how to release "obstructed menses" as well as lists of things to avoid during a suspected pregnancy because they were thought to bring on abortion.

Prior to 1840, most observers believe that the vast majority of American women seeking abortions are unmarried. As the century progresses, however, an increasing number of married women—primarily native-born, upper and middle-class white Protestants—seek abortions in order to limit the size of their families and/or to space their children.

1803   As part of an omnibus crime bill known as Lord Ellenborough's law, the English parliament passes a law making abortion by any method before quickening punishable with exile, whipping, or imprisonment, and abortion through the use of poisons after quickening a capital offense. In the United States, however, the distinction between quick and unquick remains "virtually universal" through the early 1800s, and common law continues to treat prequickening abortions as legal.

1812   The Massachusetts Supreme Court dismisses charges levied against Isaiah Bangs for preparing and administering an abortifacient potion, on the grounds that the indictment against him did not state that the woman was "quick with child" at the time the potion was given. This ruling confirms the generally accepted belief that abortion early in pregnancy is beyond the scope of the law and therefore not a crime. *Commonwealth v. Bangs* will remain the ruling precedent for abortion cases through at least the first half of the century.

1821   Connecticut passes a law prohibiting the inducement of abortion through "dangerous poisons." The law, which seems primarily intended to protect women from dying as a result of taking potions meant to induce abortions, applies only to abortions after quickening. The maximum penalty is life imprisonment for the person who administered the poison; the woman herself (if she survived) was not considered guilty of any crime (Mohr 1978, 22).

1825   Missouri passes an abortion statute that, like Connecticut's, is primarily an antipoison measure.

1827   Illinois passes an abortion poison control measure on the model of Connecticut's 1821 statute.

1828   England's 1803 antiabortion statute is revised to make instrumental abortion after quickening a capital offense and thus equal to abortion through the use of poisons.

New York passes a bill outlawing abortion by any means after quickening. The statute only includes successful abortions—either the woman or the fetus must die in order for an offense to have occurred. The maximum penalty for the person performing the abortion is one year in jail and/or a fine of $500. The bill sets an important legal precedent by explicitly permitting abortion to save the life of the mother. The bill will be signed into law in 1829 and take effect in 1830. In reality, however, it will have little impact on abortion practice, largely because of popular resistance to the regularization and regulation of medicine.

1830   Following the English lead, Connecticut revises its statute to outlaw instrumental abortion, as well as the use of poisons, after quickening. Under the new law, a person who attempts to perform an abortion can be punished by seven to ten years in prison.

1838   Great Britain modifies its abortion law to remove the concept of quickening and to eliminate the death penalty for abortion.

1834   Ohio passes a law making attempted abortion a misdemeanor, without reference to quickening. The law also makes the death of either the mother or the fetus after quickening a felony.

1840   By this time 10 of the 26 states have some statutory restrictions on abortion. Most of the laws apply only after quickening, but the Maine code makes attempted abortion of any pregnant woman by any method a crime, "whether such child be quick or not." The Maine law also includes an exception for therapeutic abortions in the event the mother's life is threatened.

In practice, most of the early antiabortion laws are enforced laxly, if at all. All of them were passed, not on their own, but as parts of major revisions of criminal codes or of omnibus crime bills. As Mohr (1978) says, "This was significant because it indicates that there was no substantial popular outcry for antiabortion activity; or, conversely, no evidence of public disapproval of the nation's traditional common law attitudes. . . . The first wave of abortion legislation in American history emerged from the struggles of both legislators and physicians to control medical practice rather than from public pressures to deal with abortion per se" (pp. 42–43).

Mohr also points out that a major loophole in all of the laws "was the necessity to prove intent, which was simply impossible to do, given the tolerant attitude of the American courts toward abortion when an irregular physician treated an unquickened woman for something he claimed he thought was not pregnancy" (p. 41). Further, the laws were designed to punish only the person who administered a potion or performed the surgery; none of them punished the woman involved.

1845   Massachusetts passes the first state law to deal separately and exclusively with abortion. The law makes attempted abortion a misdemeanor punishable by 1 to 7 years in jail and a fine of $2,000. If the abortion leads to the woman's death, the crime is elevated to a felony punishable by 5 to 20 years in the state prison. By midcentury, eight more states—New York, Michigan, Vermont, Virginia, California, New Hampshire, New Jersey, and Wisconsin—will have enacted initial antiabortion statutes, and Massachusetts will have strengthened its law by making it a crime to advertise abortion services or products.

1847   The American Medical Association is founded. The impetus behind the birth of the AMA is a drive to professionalize the practice of medicine and to gain control of a market served not only by schooled physicians (called "regulars") but by midwives, local healers, homeopaths, and abortionists. The campaign to criminalize abortion, carried on through the latter half of the nineteenth century, will be a key component in the physicians' successful struggle to gain a monopoly in the medical marketplace. According to Mohr (1978), the physicians do not seek to unconditionally outlaw abortions. Instead, they want laws giving them the exclusive power to determine a woman's need for a "therapeutic" abortion. Thus, the doctors will lobby against attempts by legislatures to define specific circumstances where abortion is or is not justified.

1857   Dr. Horatio Storer, obstetrician and gynecologist, launches what will become a national drive to end legal abortion. The campaign has two primary goals: to turn public opinion against abortion and to persuade state legislatures to pass specific legislation making abortion a crime.

1859   Dr. Storer succeeds in persuading the AMA to pass a resolution condemning induced abortion, including those performed before quickening, and urging state legislatures to pass laws forbidding it. The AMA drive includes a large-scale media and lobbying campaign that focuses on the fetus's right to life. Another aspect of the campaign aims at awakening fears of "race suicide" among the Protestant middle and upper classes, based on declining birth rates among native-born whites (due in part to abortion) compared to high fertility among predominantly Catholic immigrants.

1861   England passes the Offenses against the Person Act, which states that anyone procuring an "unlawful abortion" (which is not defined), including the woman herself, is subject to life imprisonment. A person aiding or abetting an abortion can be sentenced to three years in prison.

1864   The AMA establishes a prize to be awarded to the best antiabortion book written for the lay public.

1865   The AMA antiabortion prize committee, which is made up of prominent Boston physicians and chaired by D. Humphreys Storer, gives its first gold medal to Storer's son, Dr. Horatio R. Storer, for "The Criminality and Physical Evils of Forced Abortion." Expanded into book form, the paper is published by the AMA under the title *Why Not? A Book for Every Woman*.

1867   Dr. Edwin M. Hale, a homeopathic physician, publishes *The Great Crime of the Nineteenth Century*, in which he claims that "two-thirds of the number of conceptions occurring in the United States . . . are destroyed criminally"—undoubtedly a gross exaggeration (Mohr 1978, 78). In two earlier volumes, *On the Homeopathic Treatment of Abortion* (1860) and *A Systematic Treatise on Abortion* (1866), Hale had defended abortion, which he believed to be common (he estimated the rate at one out of five pregnancies), often advisable (as in cases of seduction or threat to the health or life of the mother), and quite safe. Along with Hale, most homeopaths will soon join the regular physicians in condemning abortion.

1868   Doctors Horatio R. Storer and Franklin Fiske Heard publish *Criminal Abortion: Its Nature, Its Evidence, and Its Law*, a "careful large-scale and systematic attempt to calculate midcentury American abortion rates" (Mohr 1978, 78). The book, which is intended to substantiate more general claims made by Storer and other antiabortion physicians, is aimed primarily at lawyers and legal scholars rather than at the general public. It estimates the ratio of abortions to live births in New York and elsewhere in the nation as being about one to four. Later estimates will put the number of abortions as high as one out of every three pregnancies.

1869   Pope Pius IX issues the papal enactment *Apostolicace sedis*, which abandons the previously existing limitation that excommunication was to be imposed only for abortions of "ensouled" fetuses. By implication, the enactment lays the groundwork for the church's subsequent position that all abortion is murder.

1871   A report by the AMA Committee on Criminal Abortion describes women seeking abortions as "unmindful of the course marked out for [them] by Providence" and characterizes them as selfish and immoral, "[yielding] to the pleasures—but [shrinking] from the pains and responsibilities of maternity . . ." (cited in Tribe 1990, 33). Mohr (1978) notes that along with the doctors' campaign against abortion, "most doctors were bitterly and stridently condemning what one of them called the '*non-infanto* mania' that afflicted the nation's women and desperately decrying the unwillingness of American wives to remain in their 'places' bearing and raising children" (p. 168).

1873   The Comstock Laws are passed and signed into law. The laws prohibit sending "obscene" materials through the mails, including contraceptives and abortifacients or any information about them. Section 211 of the federal Criminal Code provides a maximum of five years' imprisonment and a fine of $5,000 for sending through the mail any "paper, writing, advertisement or representation that any article, instrument, substance, drug, medicine or thing may, or can be, used or applied, for preventing conception" or for abortion, or any "description calculated to induce or incite a person to so use or apply any such article, instrument, substance, drug, medicine or thing" (Fryer 1966, 117). A clause exempting physicians from the law is omitted when the bill is presented to Congress; it passes on the first vote with no debate. Anthony Comstock, the major force behind the law's passage, becomes a special agent of the Post Office Department, which is empowered with enforcing it. From 1873 to 1880, he will be responsible for indicting more than 55 persons he identifies as abortionists, among them the infamous Madame Restell.

1878   April. Anthony Comstock arrests Madame Restell, New York's most successful, wealthy, and famous abortionist, after purchasing abortifacient preparations from her. Restell, whose real name is Ann Lohman, will make international headlines by committing suicide the day before her trial.

1879   Helgar dilators are invented. These are metal rods of progressively larger diameter, used to dilate the cervix so that instruments may be inserted to remove the embryo or fetus and placenta.

1880   By this time, 40 states have passed antiabortion statutes, making induced abortion at any stage of pregnancy a criminal act. Most of the laws contain exceptions for therapeutic abortions, which are permitted when in the opinion of a physician they are necessary to save the woman's life. Enforcement of the laws is sporadic—in Michigan, for example, there will be 156 indictments and only 40 convictions from 1893 to 1932. In Minnesota there will be 100 indictments and 31 convictions between 1911 and 1930. Although they will be struck down by the *Roe v. Wade* ruling of 1973, versions of these nineteenth-century laws will remain on the books in 16 states and the District of Columbia in 1995 (National Abortion Rights Action League 1995).

Also by this time, nearly all home health manuals specifically condemn abortion and avoid any discussion of procedures that might be used to induce abortion, in marked contrast to manuals published earlier in the century.

During the next decade, obstetrical textbooks begin to recommend use of antiseptic techniques for abortion (which most states still permit for therapeutic reasons) as well as for childbirth. This will reduce but not end deaths from puerperal fever, which continues to be a major and often fatal complication of abortion well into the second half of the twentieth century.

1892   Canada makes it a crime to possess "obscene" materials, including contraceptives and abortifacients.

1899   Abortion becomes a crime in Japan.

Twentieth Century

1920   The government of the Soviet Union issues its first abortion decree, calling abortion a necessary "evil" and suggesting its causes are rooted in social illnesses left over from the czarist regime. The purpose of the legalization is to protect public health and help keep women in the labor force, not to give women control over their reproduction.

1929   England enacts the Infant Life (Preservation) Act, stating that termination of pregnancy, particularly with a viable fetus, is unlawful. Excepted are abortions done in "good faith" to protect the life of the woman. According to Tribe (1990), the law "raised more questions than it answered, requiring women and doctors to negotiate the murky waters of good faith, viability, and necessity" (p. 67).

1936   Frederick J. Taussig publishes a study in which he estimates, on the basis of vital statistics and medical questionnaires, that more than 500,000 illegal abortions are being performed annually in the United States.

In the U.S.S.R., Joseph Stalin outlaws abortion, declaring that motherhood is not a private matter but one of "great social importance" (Tribe 1990, 57). The unavailability of contraceptives, a long-standing tradition of using abortion as birth control, and the problems of obtaining housing and other necessities ensure that illegal abortion will remain common, however, and two decades later the government again legalizes abortion for "public health reasons" (ibid., 58).

1938   In England, obstetrician Aleck Bourne is tried under the 1861 statute for performing an abortion on a 14-year-old who had been raped by two soldiers. Bourne is acquitted, on the basis that in certain situations doctors may act to safeguard a woman's mental or physical health as well as to save her life; the judge further states that in some circumstances a doctor may have an "affirmative duty to terminate a woman's pregnancy" (Tribe 1990, 67).

1941   In Germany, the Third Reich bans the production and distribution of contraceptives as part of a policy that includes forced impregnation of "suitable women" and treatment of abortion as a criminal offense. By 1943, the penalty for performing an abortion on a "genetically fit" woman is death, and allowing one's premises to be used for an abortion merits a prison sentence. By contrast,

1941   abortions are encouraged among Jewish and other "un-
cont.   fit" women, as a complement to a program of mandatory
       sterilization of "genetically inferior" persons begun in
       1933.

1942   Switzerland becomes the first Western European nation
       to liberalize abortion laws, permitting abortion in cases
       of rape, incest, danger to the woman's health, or likeli-
       hood of fetal defect. Because of the relatively broad inter-
       pretation of "health," women from countries with more
       restrictive laws, including the United States, sometimes
       come to Switzerland seeking abortions.

1948   Japan passes the Eugenic Protection Laws, which permit
       abortions "to prevent the increase of the inferior descen-
       dants from the standpoint of eugenic protection and to
       protect the life and health of the mother" (Tribe 1990, 60).
       A year later the act is amended to include economic hard-
       ship as a health consideration; effectively, the act makes
       abortion available on demand.

1950s U.S. hospitals begin creating abortion committees to me-
       diate requests for abortions, which are still illegal except,
       in the judgment of the physician (and the committee), to
       "save the life of the mother."

1953   Kinsey releases his report on the sexual behavior of Ameri-
       can females. Among other findings, he reports that among
       the women he surveyed, nine out of ten premarital preg-
       nancies had been ended by abortion. Among married women,
       22 percent had had at least one abortion by the age of 45.

1958   The vacuum aspiration technique for early abortions is
       pioneered in Communist China.

1959   The American Law Institute (ALI) proposes legalizing
       therapeutic abortions in cases that would "gravely im-
       pair the physical or mental health of the mother," where
       the child would be born "with grave physical or men-
       tal defects," or where the pregnancy was the result of
       rape or incest. The ALI code will provide a model for
       the liberalized abortion laws passed in several states
       beginning in 1967.

1960 May 9. The federal Food and Drug Administration (FDA) approves commercial distribution of oral contraceptives ("the pill"). By 1966, an estimated 6 million women—one-fifth of those of childbearing age—are using the pill.

1962 Abortion makes national headlines in the case of Sherry Finkbine, an Arizona mother of four who decides to have an abortion after learning of the possible effects of thalidomide, which she had taken in early pregnancy. The day before her scheduled abortion, Mrs. Finkbine seeks publicity to warn other pregnant woman of the dangers of thalidomide. As a result, the hospital refuses to perform the abortion (despite a judge's recommendation) out of fears of legal prosecution. Mrs. Finkbine eventually obtains an abortion in Sweden; the embryo is severely deformed.

The United Presbyterian Church becomes the first major religious organization to urge uniform laws for therapeutic abortions. It will be joined a year later by the American Lutheran Church Executive Committee and the Unitarian Universalist Association.

 In Grove, Oklahoma, Dr. W. J. Bryan Henrie is convicted of performing abortions and sentenced to jail in a case that Lawrence Lader (1973) will call "the first time that a licensed doctor had become a cause célèbre after conviction for abortion" (p. 6). After serving his two-year sentence, Dr. Henrie begins a solo campaign to change the abortion laws, traveling by bus to speak at conferences, meetings, and legislative hearings around the country and publishing a magazine called *Destiny, Voice of the Silent Ones.* In one issue he writes, "I am ashamed of a law that must be broken to save the honor and respect of many women."

1962–ㅤAn outbreak of German measles (rubella) leads to births
1965ㅤof 15,000 congenitally abnormal babies. In some states, physicians who perform abortions on pregnant women with the disease risk losing their licenses. The rubella outbreak adds impetus to the medical profession's growing shift toward favoring liberalized abortion laws.

1963 March. Pope John XXIII institutes a commission to study the question of birth control.

1963   Also in 1963. The Eleventh All-Union Congress of Gyne-
cont.   cologists includes a presentation on the use of vacuum
       aspiration for early abortion. The technique soon spreads
       worldwide, particularly to Eastern Europe and Japan.

1964   In response to pressure from Dr. James McNulty, a Catho-
       lic physician on the California State Medical Board, the
       board conducts an investigation of nine San Francisco
       physicians who performed abortions on pregnant women
       who had had rubella. The experiences of the "San Fran-
       cisco Nine" will deter other California doctors from per-
       forming such abortions and help bolster efforts to pass
       reform measures in that state.

1965   June 7. In *Griswold v. Connecticut*, the Supreme Court
       strikes down a state law banning the use of contracep-
       tives by married couples, overturning an individual's con-
       viction for providing a married person with contraceptives
       and information about their use. The opinion, written by
       Justice William O. Douglas, cites the "zone of privacy cre-
       ated by several fundamental constitutional guarantees."
       The ruling will serve as a critical precedent to the 1973
       Roe v. Wade decision.

       Also in 1965. The first National Right to Life Committee is
       formed, essentially as an information clearinghouse. Local
       organizations in states provide the group's political power.

        In California, Patricia Maginnis founds the Society for
       Humane Abortion, calling for repeal of all laws restricting
       abortion.

1966   March 30. The Association for the Study of Abortion is
       incorporated in New York. The ASA is primarily an edu-
       cational organization that will refrain from direct politi-
       cal action in order to keep its tax-exempt status; however,
       according to Lader (1973), the board of prominent law-
       yers, doctors and theologians "gave abortion the prestige
       and authority that was invaluable at the start" (p. 58).

       July. In California, Patricia Maginnis announces a series
       of free, public classes to teach women self-abortion tech-

niques that she has twice used on herself. The classes also cover contraception, abortion referrals overseas and in the United States, after-abortion care, and police tactics. The classes are a deliberate attempt to mount a public challenge to restrictive abortion laws and to dramatize the refusal of hospitals and doctors to assume responsibility for fighting the laws.

1967   February 20. Patricia Maginnis and Rowena Gurner are arrested in Redwood City, California, for holding public classes on abortion techniques and referrals. At their trial, their defense claims abridgement of their constitutional rights of free speech and press; the judge finds in their favor.

April. Colorado becomes the first state to pass a liberalized abortion law, following the guidelines proposed by the American Law Institute (ALI) in 1959. North Carolina and California soon follow suit. By 1972, 11 other states (Arkansas, Delaware, Florida, Georgia, Kansas, Maryland, Mississippi, New Mexico, Oregon, South Carolina, Virginia) will pass legislation to permit therapeutic abortions based on the ALI guidelines. In reality, the Colorado law does not make abortion much more available than before. The requirements are very strict, and abortions cost at least $500. During the first 14 months the law is in effect, only 338 abortions are performed, 100 of them on women from outside Colorado.

April. In California, Dr. Leon Belous is arrested for providing a woman with the phone number of another doctor, who performed an abortion on her. Determined to test and overthrow the state's restrictive abortion laws, Dr. Belous insists on basing his defense on constitutional grounds [see 1969].

April 6. At a lecture at Boston University, activist Bill Baird publicly challenges the constitutionality of the Massachusetts "crimes against chastity" statute, under which only married couples can receive birth control information or materials and then only from physicians. Before an audience of 1,500, Baird offers to distribute packages of

1967
cont.
contraceptive foam and reads the names of Tokyo clinics specializing in abortion. When 12 single women step forward to take the foam, Baird is duly arrested; his case will eventually reach the Supreme Court [see 1970].

May. Reverend Howard Moody of the Judson Memorial Church in Greenwich Village organizes the Clergy Consultation Service for Abortion. On May 27, Moody and 21 Protestant ministers and Jewish rabbis announce that they will refer women to doctors that they know perform safe and legitimate abortions. The announcement is reported on the front page of the *New York Times*. At its peak, the service will include some 1,200 clergy members in more than 20 states, including Protestant ministers, Jewish rabbis, and even some Catholic priests. The members refer women to doctors in Puerto Rico, Great Britain, and even the United States.

May. The recently formed National Conference of Catholic Bishops (NCCB) launches a nationwide antiabortion education campaign directed at both Catholics and non-Catholics, with an initial budget of $50,000. The campaign is part of the NCCB's fight against "coercive" use of birth control.

July. The vacuum aspiration method for early abortions reaches the United States with the publication of two articles in *Obstetrics and Gynecology*.

Also in 1967. At the 1967 conference of the one-year-old National Organization for Women (NOW), the "Right of Women To Control Their Reproductive Rights" is included in the organization's Women's Bill of Rights, despite the reservations of mainstream professional women who fear that focusing on the abortion issue will take attention away from their economic goals.

The British Parliament passes the Abortion Act, permitting abortion until viability as long as two doctors certify that the pregnancy poses a greater risk than abortion to the life or mental or physical health of a woman or to her existing children—in essence making early abortion available on request. Viability, as set by the Infant Life (Preservation) Act of 1929, is set at 28 weeks of gestational age. The act, which applies only to Great Britain and not to Ireland, serves as a model for legislation in a number of countries. In the years following the bill's passage, England will maintain a fairly high rate of legal abortion. A significant number of abortions will be performed on non-English women who come from countries with more restrictive laws, especially Ireland, where abortion is illegal, and Spain, until that country legalizes abortion in 1985. During the next two decades, the law will survive numerous attempts by antiabortion groups to pass new restrictions.

1968   March. The American Civil Liberties Union issues a statement calling for the repeal of all criminal abortion laws in the United States, saying that such laws restrict women's rights and are unconstitutionally vague.

May 1. In Washington, D.C., Dr. Milan Vuitch is arrested for performing an abortion on "Mrs. Donald R.," a secretary at the Navy Munitions Building whose husband had deserted her and impregnated two other women before impregnating her during a temporary reconciliation. When she refused to live with him or bear his child, Mr. R. went to the police and offered to cooperate in the arrest of Dr. Vuitch. The Serbian-born Dr. Vuitch has performed hundreds of low-cost abortions since 1966, mounting what was in effect an open challenge to restrictive laws. In his trial, Dr. Vuitch challenges the constitutionality of the abortion laws, asserting that, as Mrs. R.'s doctor, only he had the right to decide whether her health was threatened by her pregnancy and whether an abortion was necessary [see 1969].

July 29. Pope Paul VI issues *Humanae Vitae*, an encyclical that reaffirms the doctrine that Catholics may not use any form of birth control other than the rhythm method or abstinence.

Also in 1968. President Lyndon Johnson's Presidential Advisory Council on the Status of Women, chaired by former Oregon Senator Maurine Neuberger, releases its report, calling for repeal of all abortion laws.

1969   February. The First National Conference on Abortion Laws, held in Chicago, establishes the National Association for the Repeal of Abortion Laws (NARAL), which will become the National Abortion Rights Action League in 1973. NARAL's sponsors include feminists, radical clergy, liberal lawyers and politicians, health professionals, population control and welfare rights advocates, and more conservative groups such as Church Women United, the Young Women's Christian Association, and the Commission on Uniform State Laws.

 March. The Redstockings, a radical women's liberation group, holds an "Abortion Speak Out" at the Washington Square Methodist Church in New York City. Hundreds of women attend the meeting, where individual women stand to describe publicly their experiences with illegal abortion.

June 12. Rev. Robert Hare of Cleveland is indicted in Massachusetts for violation of antiabortion statutes for referring a woman to a Massachusetts physician, Dr. Pierre Brunelle, as part of his work for a clergy counseling service. The indictment is dismissed, but the prosecutor appeals, and the case is still dragging through the courts in January 1973, when the *Roe v. Wade* decision strikes down all state antiabortion laws. Rev. Hare is the only American clergyman to be indicted on an abortion charge. Dr. Brunelle is convicted and sent to prison.

 September 5. In the case of Dr. Leon Belous, the California Supreme Court, by a vote of four to three, declares the state law restricting abortion unconstitutional and exonerates the doctor, saying that the "fundamental right of a woman to choose whether to bear children follows from the Supreme Court's and this court's repeated acknowledgment of a 'right of privacy' or 'liberty' in matters related to marriage, family and sex." The decision, which is the first state supreme court decision to declare any antiabortion statute unconstitutional, sets a precedent for numerous forthcoming challenges to state laws (Lader 1973, 109–110).

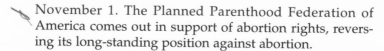 November 1. The Planned Parenthood Federation of America comes out in support of abortion rights, reversing its long-standing position against abortion.

November 10. Citing the recent Belous decision in California, Judge Arnold Gesell of the U.S. District Court of the District of Columbia reaches a verdict in the case of Dr. Milan Vuitch that exonerates the doctor and declares the District's law unconstitutional. It is the first time a federal court has overthrown an abortion law. The government immediately appeals the case to the Supreme Court, which agrees to hear it [see 1971]. Dr. Vuitch reopens his clinic a few blocks from the White House; he is soon taking 100 abortion cases per week.

December. In Dallas, Texas, attorneys Linda Coffee and Sarah Weddington meet with Norma McCorvey, a pregnant woman who has been trying unsuccessfully to get an abortion, to ask her to be the plaintiff for what they hope will be a landmark case challenging the constitutionality of Texas's restrictive abortion laws. Coffee and Weddington, both recent graduates of the University of Texas Law School (where they were two of the five women in their class), have been seeking a plaintiff for their suit for several months; McCorvey agrees to participate even though they tell her that the time involved will make it virtually impossible for her to get the abortion she seeks. For ten years, until she herself comes forward, McCorvey will be known to everyone but Coffee and Weddington as "Jane Roe."

Also in 1969. In Chicago, members of the Chicago Women's Liberation Union begin the illegal feminist abortion collective known as "Jane," which grows out of an abortion referral and counseling service on the University of Chicago campus. Originally the collective steers women to safe and relatively cheap illegal abortions. Gradually, however, members learn how to perform the abortions themselves. Over its four years of operation, Jane will provide more than 11,000 abortions, most of them done in members' own homes. Although the nominal charge is $100, the average payment is $40, and no women are turned away because of inability to pay. The collective's safety record compares favorably with legal abortion clinics in New York and California—its single death is a woman already suffering from a severe infection, probably from an attempt at self-induced abortion, when she arrives at Jane. The collective places

1969
cont. special emphasis on intensive and caring counseling as "the heart of the procedure," in the belief that the medical and counseling components of abortion should not be separated and in the attempt both to provide sisterly support and to demystify the abortion experience. Of the dozens of activists involved in Jane, only seven members are arrested during its existence; the charges against them will be dropped in 1973.

Canada adopts a law allowing abortions in hospitals that have an appointed committee of three or more physicians when the committee determines that continuing a pregnancy will threaten the life or health of the pregnant woman.

 In Ashland, Pennsylvania, Dr. Robert Spenser dies at the age of 80. According to Lader (1973), for more than 40 years Dr. Spenser "had handled more abortions than anyone on the East Coast," charging between $10 and $50 dollars until the 1960s, when he raised his price to $100 (p. 4). Dr. Spenser, who often let women from out of town stay free at his clinic, performed some 30,000 abortions with only one death—of a woman who was bleeding when she arrived at his clinic—for which a jury exonerated him. Considered a leading citizen of his community, Dr. Spenser counted the mayor, the police chief, and most county officials among his close friends. "He became a legend," Lader writes, "not by challenging the law, but by ignoring it. The community protected him. He treated unwanted pregnancies as well as pneumonia for over 40 years because the community wanted it that way" (p. 5).

Senator Robert Packwood (R-OR) introduces legislation to legalize abortions in the District of Columbia and the entire United States; he will reintroduce the legislation in the 1971–1972 session of Congress, but no action will be taken on either bill.

 By the end of this decade, estimates of illegal abortions in the United States range from 200,000 to 1.2 million annually.

1970   March. In Austin, Texas, attorneys Sarah Weddington and Linda Coffee file class-action lawsuits in federal district court challenging the constitutionality of the Texas abortion law, which prohibits abortion except to save the life of the woman, and ask for an injunction to stop district attorney Henry Wade from enforcing the statute.

March 11. In response to pressure from a growing abortion rights coalition, Hawaii becomes the first state in the union to repeal its abortion law, legalizing abortions performed in the first 20 weeks of pregnancy. The bill, which does contain a residency requirement, is signed into law by the Catholic governor.

April. New York repeals its abortion law and passes a bill permitting abortion on demand up to the twenty-fourth week of pregnancy. The bill is passed with a dramatic last-minute vote change by Assemblyman George Michaels. Michaels was convinced by his wife and his son, an intern who had seen firsthand the effects of illegal abortion, to vote against the wishes of his conservative, mostly Catholic constituents. The vote will cost him his political career. During the first six months after the bill is signed into law by Governor Nelson Rockefeller, 69,000 legal abortions are performed in New York City, half on women from out of state. Within nine months, the number of legal abortions passes 100,000.

June 17. In the case of *Roe v. Wade*, the federal district court rules that the law is indeed unconstitutional but refuses to grant the injunction. Both sides appeal to the Supreme Court.

June 25. The House of Delegates of the American Medical Association votes to support physicians' right to perform nontherapeutic abortions if, in their judgment, a woman's social and economic circumstances justify terminating her pregnancy.

Also in 1970. In *Baird v. Eisenstadt*, the Supreme Court rules that the Massachusetts "crimes against chastity" law is

1970
cont.
unconstitutional, thus legalizing access to birth control for single persons. The Baird decision will provide a strong precedent for the *Roe v. Wade* decision three years later.

Following Hawaii's and New York's lead, Alaska and Washington repeal their abortion laws, the latter as a result of a popular referendum. Efforts to pass liberalized laws fail, however, in 31 other states.

The Family Planning Services and Population Research Act, passed by Congress to fund family planning services abroad, includes a provision that states, "None of the funds appropriated under this title shall be used in programs where abortion is a method of family planning."

Dr. Jane Hodgson, a Minnesota physician, becomes the first doctor in U.S. history to be convicted of performing an abortion in a hospital, on a 23-year-old woman who had contracted rubella. Hodgson performed the abortion in a deliberate attempt to challenge Minnesota's restrictive abortion laws, but the Supreme Court will refuse to hear her case. Her conviction will be reversed by the Minnesota Supreme Court after the 1973 *Roe v. Wade* decision.

1971
April 21. The Supreme Court issues its decision in the case of *United States v. Vuitch*. On a five-to-two vote, with two justices not voting, the Court upholds the constitutionality of the Washington, D.C., law prohibiting induced abortions except "as necessary for the preservation of the mother's life or health." Although the case is remanded to the federal district court, the Justice Department decides not to pursue the charges against Dr. Vuitch [see 1968 and 1969]. Following the decision, Washington's abortion facilities, which include the Preterm Clinic (owned by a nonprofit coalition of prominent citizens), an outpatient clinic at Washington Hospital Center, and a number of private physicians performing in-office abortions, soon are among the country's busiest. The Preterm Clinic uses suction machines and a simplified procedure that bypasses the need for a sterile operating room and for prepping, shaving, and scrubbing patients. Its carefully kept records on more than 20,000 patients, with no deaths and few complications, demonstrate the safety of freestanding clinics.

June. New York passes a law outlawing commercial abortion referral services.

December 13. The Supreme Court hears arguments in two abortion cases, *Roe v. Wade* and *Doe v. Bolton*. *Roe v. Wade* is a Texas case challenging a typical nineteenth-century anti-abortion statute. The other case, *Doe v. Bolton*, questions the constitutionality of a Georgia law allowing therapeutic exceptions based on the ALI code. By this time, more than 70 criminal and civil abortion cases are pending in 20 states; the *Roe* and *Doe* cases are the first the Court has agreed to hear.

Also in 1971. The March of Dimes, as part of a comprehensive birth defects program, begins making grants for genetic services programs, including amniocentesis, a move that will be strongly opposed by antiabortion groups and the Catholic Church.

Dr. Jack Willke, a Cincinnati physician, and his wife, Barbara, publish *Handbook on Abortion*. The book, which will later be called the "bible of the pro-life movement," is the first to show color pictures of aborted fetuses.

India passes the Medical Termination of Pregnancy Act, permitting abortions in the likelihood of birth defects or if the birth threatens a woman's physical or mental health. Broad latitude in interpreting the law means that legal abortions are generally readily available, despite opposition to abortion from a number of Hindu and Muslim religious groups. Over the next two decades, a disturbing trend in use of abortion for sex selection and a decline in the proportion of women to men leads several Indian state governments to restrict access to amniocentesis and other sex determination tests and adds fuel to the ongoing abortion debate.

1972   February. The American Bar Association (ABA) calls for a federal law permitting abortion on demand through the twentieth week of pregnancy.

March 16. President Nixon's Commission on Population Growth and the American Future issues its report. The

1972
cont.

report calls on the federal government to ensure the avail-ability of birth control counseling, devices, and oral con-traceptives to all Americans, especially teenagers and the poor, and recommends that the nation follow New York's lead in making abortion available on demand. The report is immediately attacked by the National Conference of Catholic Bishops and others. Nixon rejects the section of the report dealing with abortion, and later writes a letter to Cardinal Terence Cooke of New York expressing his support for the repeal of the New York law.

May 13. New York Governor Nelson Rockefeller vetoes an attempt by the state legislature to repeal the state's liberal 1970 abortion law.

July. Delegates to the Democratic National Convention reject an attempt to include a plank in the party platform affirming a constitutional right to abortion.

October 11. The Supreme Court hears rearguments in the cases of *Roe v. Wade* and *Doe v. Bolton*.

Also in 1972. The Centers for Disease Control (CDC) be-gins its Abortion Surveillance division, which publishes annual statistical reports on abortions and the characteris-tics of women obtaining them.

In response to pressure from antiabortion and Catholic groups, the March of Dimes agrees to adopt a policy for-bidding the use of any of its funds for abortion.

Michigan voters turn down a referendum that would have legalized abortion in the first 20 weeks of pregnancy. The campaign against the referendum includes distribution to over 2 million households of a glossy color brochure, *Life and Death*, which contrasts a photograph of a child alleged to have been born at 22 weeks of pregnancy with one of a saline-aborted fetus. The referendum is defeated 62 per-cent to 38 percent, despite preelection polls showing 59 percent support for the measure. A similar campaign in North Dakota helps defeat a referendum in that state.

Connecticut passes a law allowing abortion only to save the life of the pregnant woman and imposing a maximum five-year prison term for abortionists. An amendment to allow abortions in the case of rape or incest is voted down during the debate. Although the law is declared unconstitutional, it is allowed to remain in effect pending the decision in the *Roe v. Wade* case currently before the Supreme Court. During the latter part of 1972, about 100 women travel from Connecticut to New York each week in search of legal abortions.

1973   January 22. The Supreme Court rules on *Roe v. Wade* and *Doe v. Bolton*. In a seven-to-two ruling, the Court declares Article 1196 of the Texas abortion statute to be unconstitutional on the grounds that it makes no distinction between abortions performed earlier or later in pregnancy and that it does not permit legal abortions for any reason other than to save the life of the mother. Because ruling that one article unconstitutional would leave Texas with a law prohibiting all abortions for any reason, the whole statute is overturned. In *Doe v. Bolton*, the Court also upholds a lower federal court ruling that Georgia's abortion law is unconstitutional. A major effect of the two decisions, unforeseen by abortion rights advocates who hail them as the beginning of the end of their fight, will be to galvanize the antiabortion, or right-to-life, movement into action. During the next decade, the movement mounts a broad-based campaign to prevent women from exercising the court-declared right to an abortion. Fought mostly at the state level, the campaign seeks to enact restrictions in the "gray zone of constitutionality" (Tribe 1990, 144). Examples of such restrictions include 24-hour waiting periods, stringent record-keeping requirements, and spousal and parental consent laws. The activists also campaign intensively around the country to elect politicians who are opposed to legal abortion and to vote supporters of legal abortion out of office.

February. The National Conference of Catholic Bishops announces that any Catholic involved in any phase of abortion will be subject to immediate excommunication.

April. Representative Angelo Roncallo (R-NY) introduces a measure to ban fetal research. The measure passes in the House but does not become law. Instead, a Senate compromise places a temporary moratorium on fetal research

1973
cont.

and forms the National Commission for the Protection of Human Subjects to study the issue. The commission-appointed study group will report that past fetal research provided great benefits and that the need for future research is even greater. However, fetal research restrictions modeled on the Roncallo proposals pass in 15 states.

June. The National Right to Life Committee (NRLC) is founded in Detroit. The organization has two board members from each state. These directors are elected from boards at the state level; representatives to the state board are elected by committees of leaders from local affiliates. The NRLC receives initial support from the United States Catholic Conference Family Life Division, but soon cuts its ties in order to allow the church to maintain its tax exemption.

June. Senator James Buckley (R-NY) and six other senators introduce a bill for a constitutional amendment that would overturn *Roe v. Wade* and outlaw abortion except where the mother's life is threatened. The amendment would extend the legal category of "person" to all "human beings, including their unborn offspring at every state of their biological development, irrespective of age, health, function or condition of dependency." By September, no fewer than 18 proposed constitutional amendments will have been introduced in Congress in response to *Roe v. Wade*. Some of these, like Buckley's, seek to extend the legal definition of "person." Others, such as one sponsored by Congressman Lawrence Hogan (R-MD), seek to ensure that due process and equal protection under the Fourteenth Amendment be extended to all individuals "from the moment of conception." Still others are "states' rights" amendments that seek to restore the regulation of abortion to the individual states. A number of bills are also introduced that attempt to accomplish the same ends through simple statute.

August. In response to intense lobbying spearheaded by the United States Catholic Conference, 38 CBS affiliates decide not to air reruns of two episodes of the television comedy *Maude* in which Maude decides to have an abortion. The campaign serves to demonstrate the considerable political clout of antiabortion activists.

November 13. The National Conference of Catholic Bishops issues a resolution calling on Catholics to "embark on a political crusade" at the grassroots level, with the goal of passing a constitutional amendment outlawing abortion.

Also in 1973. Planned Parenthood and NARAL hold nationwide seminars on how to set up clinics to offer safe and low-cost abortions, modeled on New York clinics set up after that state's repeal of its restrictive abortion law in 1970. The groups soon develop a national network of clinics to complement hospital-based services. The freestanding clinics can provide abortions at a generally much lower cost than hospitals (an average first trimester abortion costs $200 to $300). Many clinics also provide other reproductive health services such as contraception, pap smears, and sterilization. The clinics set an important precedent, and by the end of the 1980s, outpatient services for a wide variety of surgical procedures will be commonplace. Nonetheless, many women, particularly those in rural areas or in areas with mostly Catholic hospitals, will have difficulty obtaining legal abortions.

1974   January 22. About 6,000 demonstrators come to Washington, D.C., to participate in a March for Life on the anniversary of the *Roe v. Wade* decision. The march will become an annual event.

November. Pope Paul VI approves a document specifying that abortion cannot be justified by any extenuating circumstances, not even the threat to the pregnant woman's life.

Also in 1974. Congress passes legislation prohibiting use of U.S. funds for direct support of abortion services overseas; private family planning services may still receive U.S. aid if they use a separate, non-U.S.-funded account for abortion services.

Congress passes a "conscience clause" bill permitting any individual or hospital opposed to abortion to refuse to

1974
cont.

perform the procedure. The application of the bill to hospitals poses a serious threat to abortion availability in locales where a single hospital serves a large geographic area. Partly as a result of the conscience clause, as of 1975 only 17 percent of public hospitals and 28 percent of private, non-Catholic hospitals will perform abortions.

Congress passes an amendment to the Legal Services Corporation Act, which provides free legal aid to low-income individuals. The amendment prohibits legal services lawyers from providing representation on some abortion-related matters. The restriction will later be tightened to prohibit any representation by legal services attorneys in abortion-related cases.

The National Science Foundation Authorization Act passed by Congress includes a provision prohibiting the use of federal funds for fetal research. Also, the National Research Service Award Act of 1974 reauthorizes the National Commission for the Protection of Human Subjects of Biomedical and Behavioral Research and places a moratorium on fetal research.

The Missouri legislature passes an antiabortion bill that includes a spousal consent requirement for married women and a parental consent requirement for women under 18, and that outlaws saline abortions after the twelfth week of pregnancy—provisions that will be declared unconstitutional by the Supreme Court in 1976. The legislature also becomes the first to call for a constitutional convention to draft a human life amendment.

During this first year of legal abortion, 763,476 abortions are reported to the Centers for Disease Control. In the initial period of legality, women who qualify for assistance under the Medicaid program receive federal and/or state funding to pay for their abortions, a situation that outrages abortion opponents.

1975

January. In Massachusetts, Dr. Kenneth Edelin goes on trial for manslaughter in a case that garners national attention and generates public controversy. He is accused of not attempting to preserve the life of a fetus he had removed from a teenager during a hysterotomy (a technique used for late abortions, in which the uterus is cut open and the fetus removed). Witnesses for the prosecution include several prominent antiabortion physicians, including Fred Mecklenberg and Mildred Jefferson. The mostly Catholic jury convicts Edelin and he receives a one-year suspended sentence. In December 1976, the state supreme court will overturn the conviction on appeal.

January 22. The second March for Life draws an estimated 25,000 people to Washington, D.C. Featured speakers include Senator James Buckley (R-NY), author of the original human life amendment.

March. Senator Birch Bayh's (D-IN) Senate Judiciary Subcommittee on Constitutional Amendments holds extensive hearings on proposed constitutional amendments to reverse the 1973 Supreme Court decisions. The hearings include an unprecedented appearance by four Catholic cardinals who testify in favor of an amendment that would convey legal personhood to an unborn child from conception onward and that would allow no exception to the ban on abortion. Testimony is also heard from numerous pro-life and pro-choice leaders, as well as religious groups, doctors, and constitutional law experts. Six months later, the subcommittee votes not to report a number of the proposed constitutional amendments to the full Judiciary Committee.

April. The U.S. Commission on Civil Rights issues a 101-page report opposing efforts to enact a constitutional amendment outlawing abortion and opposing any ban on the use of federal funds to pay for abortions for the poor. The report states that such an amendment would violate the separation of church and state by "establishing one view (of when a fetus becomes a person entitled to legal protection) and thus inhibiting the free exercise of religion by others" (U.S. Commission on Civil Rights 1975). In response, abortion opponents in Congress threaten to cut off the commission's appropriations.

August. The Department of Health, Education, and Welfare (HEW), following recommendations of the National

1975
cont.

Commission for the Protection of Human Subjects [see 1973], lifts most restrictions on funding for fetal studies. The regulations also give women the right to consent to the use of their aborted fetal material for research and establishes safeguards to prevent research on potentially viable fetuses.

October. A National Institutes of Health report finds amniocentesis to be a safe and effective procedure for detecting fetal defects such as chromosomal abnormalities, metabolic disorders, and structural malformations of the brain and spinal cord.

November. The Family Life Division of the National Conference of Catholic Bishops (NCCB) outlines the "Pastoral Plan for Pro-Life Activity," a plan to gain support for a constitutional amendment that would recriminalize abortion. The plan spells out specific roles for the bishops in Washington, Catholic regional and diocesan officials, parish priests, and Catholic laymen. The NCCB gives unanimous approval to the plan.

Also in 1975. In Congress, both the Senate and the House defeat amendments to the 1976 HEW-Labor appropriations bill barring the use of Medicaid funds for abortions.

Justice William O. Douglas retires from the Supreme Court. President Gerald Ford nominates John Paul Stevens, aged 55, to take his place. Over the next 15 years, Justice Stevens, a moderate Republican, will vote consistently in favor of legal abortion.

In France, a law is passed guaranteeing "the respect of every human being from the commencement of life," except "in cases of necessity and under conditions laid down by this law" (Tribe 1990, 73). The law prohibits abortion as a means of birth control, but permits abortion up to the tenth week for a woman who believes that being pregnant "place[s] [her] in a situation of distress" (ibid.). The abortion must be preceded by counseling that encourages the woman to keep the child. If she still decides on abortion, social security will cover 70 percent of its cost.

1976   June 24. Freshman Congressman Henry Hyde (R-IL) proposes an amendment to the HEW-Labor Department appropriations bill banning federal funds "to pay for abortion or to promote or encourage abortion." The amendment is adopted in the House and defeated in the Senate, but in September agreement is reached on language that bans HEW funds for abortion "except where the life of the mother would be clearly endangered if the fetus were carried to term." Some observers suggest that Senate willingness to go along with the amendment reflects a belief that the Supreme Court will find it unconstitutional—a belief that seems to be well founded when U.S. District Court Judge John F. Dooling issues a restraining order and a preliminary injunction blocking its implementation [see 1977].

July 1. The Supreme Court rules on *Planned Parenthood of Central Missouri v. Danforth.* This class-action suit, filed on behalf of physicians performing or desiring to perform abortions and pregnant women seeking to terminate their pregnancies, sought relief from a Missouri abortion law enacted in 1974. The ruling strikes down provisions requiring minors to obtain parental permission and married women to obtain spousal permission for abortions, as well as a prohibition of saline infusion abortions after the first trimester and a requirement that physicians "exercise professional care to preserve the fetus's life and health" under penalty of a manslaughter charge. The Court upholds Missouri's statutory definition of viability, provisions requiring a woman's consent to abortion, and requirements for abortion reporting and record keeping with reasonable confidentiality requirements.

On the same day, the Supreme Court also rules on *Bellotti v. Baird,* a case challenging the parental consent clause in a set of abortion restrictions passed by Massachusetts in 1974. The clause required a minor to have the consent of both parents before obtaining an abortion but allowed the

1976
cont.
parents' veto to be overridden by a judge. The law included provisions that the parents be notified and allowed to present their side of the dispute in court. The Supreme Court remands the case to federal district court for certification to the Supreme Judicial Court of Massachusetts, citing unresolved questions about the state legislature's intent and the meaning of several provisions; it will reach the Supreme Court again in 1979.

Also in 1976. Right-to-life activist Ellen McCormack, a housewife from Merrick, Long Island, succeeds in entering or being listed as a Democratic candidate in presidential primaries in 19 states, as well as qualifying for federal matching funds and Secret Service protection. By September, she has won more than 267,000 votes and gained significant percentages in Massachusetts, Pennsylvania, Indiana, California, Wisconsin, New Jersey, and Florida. The McCormack candidacy sparks the beginning of the drive for a constitutional convention that would enact an amendment barring abortion. It also leads to antiabortion planks being considered at both the Democratic and Republican conventions. The Democrats reject the move, but the Republicans adopt a plank favoring "the continuance of the public dialogue on abortion and supporting the efforts of those who seek enactment of a constitutional amendment to restore protection of the right of the unborn child."

1977
January 15. Ruling in *Harris v. McRae,* a class-action suit brought on behalf of women needing Medicaid abortions, U.S. District Court Judge John Dooling states that the Hyde amendment, in excluding most medically necessary abortions from covered services, violates the First Amendment guarantees of the free exercise of religion or conscience and the Fifth Amendment rights of privacy, due process, and equal protection of the laws for poor women eligible under the program. The right of a poor woman to obtain a medically necessary abortion paid for by Medicaid, the judge wrote, is "nearly allied to her right to be" (Jaffe et al. 1981, 194). The federal government appeals the case to the Supreme Court, which refuses to stay Judge Dooling's

order. Pending a final decision, HEW resumes Medicaid payments for medically necessary abortions and notifies states they are required to pay their share.

June 20. The Supreme Court rules, in *Beal v. Doe* and *Maher v. Roe*, that states can deny Medicaid funding for nontherapeutic abortions for indigents. Prior to this, between 1973 and 1975, 13 states had adopted laws or administrative policies limiting Medicaid funding for abortions, but most of the laws had been thrown out by federal courts. Following these rulings and the passage of the 1977 Hyde amendment [see below], most states move to restrict abortion funding. By the end of 1979, amidst a storm of lobbying by both antiabortion and abortion rights forces, 40 states have restricted Medicaid funding for abortions either by legislation or by executive or administrative decree. At the federal level, funds are restricted not only for Medicaid recipients but for Peace Corps volunteers, military dependents, and working women who depend on employment-related pregnancy disability benefits.

Also in 1977. Representative Henry Hyde (R-IL) again introduces an amendment to the 1978 HEW-Labor appropriations bill, calling for a total ban on abortion funding in order to prevent "the slaughter of innocent, inconvenient unborn children." The amendment, which is supported by President Jimmy Carter, passes in the House, but it becomes the focus of a six-month debate in the Senate and heavy lobbying by Catholic and other antiabortion groups. A compromise amendment passes on December 7, barring federal funds for abortions except in cases of promptly reported rape and incest, where the life of the mother is endangered, or where "severe and long-lasting physical damage to the mother would result if the pregnancy were carried to term when so determined by two physicians." Judge Dooling subsequently lifts his temporary injunction blocking implementation of the amendment.

During 1977, the federal government pays $90 million for approximately 300,000 abortions under Medicaid.

1977   The March of Dimes announces that it will phase out
cont.   its genetic services program, which was largely respon-
          sible for the development of amniocentesis techniques.
          Antiabortion forces claim credit for the decision, due
          to years of pressure that included calls to Catholics to
          boycott the organization's fund drives.

          Father Charles Fiore founds the National Pro-Life Po-
          litical Action Committee (NPL-PAC). At about the same
          time, Paul Brown forms another PAC, the Life Amend-
          ment Political Action Committee (LAPAC). Both PACs
          favor a no-exceptions human life amendment, in con-
          trast to the version favored by the NRLC, which would
          allow abortions to save the life of the mother. Both
          groups also have strong affiliations with the New Right
          and the "pro-family" movement. Over the next few
          years, the PACs will target senators and representatives
          who disagree with their stance and succeed in driving
          several out of office.

1978   Abortion opponents in Congress succeed in barring the
          U.S. Commission on Civil Rights from conducting fur-
          ther abortion studies [see 1975]. Congress also passes
          legislation denying health insurance coverage for abor-
          tions to Peace Corps employees.

          Partially in response to pressure from the National Con-
          ference of Catholic Bishops (NCCB), the House and Sen-
          ate pass an antiabortion amendment to a broadly
          supported bill designed to mandate inclusion of preg-
          nancy-related conditions in employee fringe-benefit
          plans such as health insurance, sick leave, and tempo-
          rary disability plans. The compromise amendment gives
          employers discretion in covering abortions under health
          insurance plans (except where the woman's health is
          endangered), but requires them to pay medical pay-
          ments and earned sick leave or disability benefits for
          the treatment of abortion complications. Dissatisfied
          with the compromise, the NCCB files a class-action suit
          to halt implementation of the bill's abortion provisions,
          but the suit is dismissed on technical grounds.

In California, Dr. William Wadill is tried for delivering a live baby during a saline abortion and strangling it. Dr. Wadill is tried twice, with both trials resulting in hung juries. The trials spur antiabortion protests.

1979   January 9. In *Colautti v. Franklin*, by a six-to-three vote, the Supreme Court overturns a Pennsylvania law requiring a doctor to make efforts to sustain the life of an aborted fetus, if, in his professional judgment, the fetus is viable or might be viable, as long as such efforts did not adversely affect the mother. Grounds for overturning the law are that it is "impermissibly vague."

January 22. An estimated 60,000 people participate in the annual March for Life in Washington, D.C. At the same time, abortion rights activists announce the establishment of a fund to aid low-income women who are unable to get Medicaid funding for abortions because of the Hyde amendment. The fund is named in honor of Rosie Jimenez, a 27-year-old Texas mother who died from an illegal abortion after failing to get government funding for a legal abortion. "Rosie" will become a symbol of the abortion rights movement's fight to restore government funding for abortions.

July 2. In *Bellotti v. Baird*, by a seven-to-one vote, the Supreme Court overturns a Massachusetts law requiring minors seeking abortions to get the consent of both parents.

1980   January 19. Senator Jesse Helms (R-NC) introduces the Human Life Bill. The bill would define "person" to include an embryo from the moment of conception, thus, argue its supporters, having the same effect as a constitutional amendment extending constitutional protection to fetuses. On the same day, Representative Henry Hyde (R-IL) introduces a similar bill in the House. About the same time, Senator Orrin Hatch (R-UT) introduces the Hatch Human Life Federalism Amendment, which would override *Roe v. Wade* by a constitutional amendment that would let the states or Congress decide whether or not to outlaw abortion. The two approaches spark conflict among antiabortion groups, with the Catholic Church

1980
cont.

and mainstream groups like the NRLC supporting the Hatch Amendment while the New Right and its supporters back the Helms-Hyde bill.

January 20. An estimated 50 people representing 12 organizations meet in Washington, D.C., for the first annual Respect Life Leadership Conference to discuss common issues and concerns, prominent among them the passage of a human life amendment. The same week, abortion rights activists in 35 states launch a lobbying and political action campaign aimed at countering the political efforts against abortion.

June 30. In *Harris v. McRae* [see 1977], the Supreme Court, by a one-vote majority, affirms the constitutionality of the Hyde amendment in its most restrictive version, rejecting Judge Dooling's opinion that the amendment violates the Fifth Amendment rights of poor women. The ruling effectively shuts off any further litigation of the amendment and eliminates virtually all federal funding for abortion. In a companion decision, *Williams v. Zbaraz*, the Supreme Court holds that Illinois is not required under Title XIX of the Social Security Act to pay for abortions for which federal funds are unavailable under the Hyde amendment, and that Illinois funding restrictions do not violate the Equal Protection Clause.

Also in 1980. The Republican Party platform includes strong support for a human life amendment and advocates appointing federal judges on the basis of their demonstrated opposition to abortion. The party nominates Ronald Reagan, an avowed antiabortionist who had reluctantly signed California's liberalized abortion law in 1967.

1981

January 22. An estimated 50,000 people come to Washington, D.C., for the annual March for Life.

March 23. In *H.L. v. Matheson*, the Supreme Court upholds a Utah statute requiring physicians to notify the parents of unemancipated minors living with and dependent on their parents prior to performing abortions, on the grounds that since the law does not give parents "veto power" over the abortion, it is not unconstitutional.

Also in 1981. In the Senate, the Hatch Amendment and the Helms Human Life Bill are debated in Judiciary Committee subcommittees. Antiabortion groups are split in their support for the two bills. This fragmentation contributes to the inability of the bills' sponsors to move either legislation to the Senate floor.

Congress moves to make the Hyde amendment more restrictive by removing funding for abortions for victims of rape and incest.

Congress decides that public health service clinics receiving federal funds must notify parents of minors for whom contraceptives have been prescribed.

Justice Potter Stewart, one of the *Roe v. Wade* majority, retires, and President Ronald Reagan appoints Sandra Day O'Connor, aged 51, to take his place. In the first abortion ruling in which she takes part, *City of Akron v. Akron Center for Reproductive Health* [see 1983], Justice O'Connor will side with the minority.

1982   January 22. The annual March for Life in Washington, D.C., draws an estimated 25,000 demonstrators.

March. Senator Jesse Helms introduces an expanded version of the Human Life Bill (S. 2148), which includes a provision that would permanently prohibit virtually all federal funding for abortions except when a woman's life is threatened. The bill would also restrict abortion coverage under federal employees' health insurance policies, referrals for abortion, and training in abortion techniques.

August 15. Hector and Rosalie Zevallos, the owners and operators of an ob-gyn clinic in Granite City, Illinois, disappear. Two days later a man identifying himself as a member of the "Army of God" calls the FBI office in nearby St. Louis, saying that he is holding the Zevallos and demanding that President Reagan publicly denounce abortion and

1982
cont.
call for an end to it. He threatens to kill the couple if the demand is not met within three days. Reagan declines comment, and an FBI search is unsuccessful, but a few days later the Zevallos are released unharmed. The Zevallos incident is one in an increasing number of violent acts against abortion clinics since the mid-1970s, including arson, bombings, vandalism, and threats to clinic personnel and directors and their families. The kidnapper, Dan Anderson, will later be sentenced to 30 years in prison.

August 16. Senator Jesse Helms (R-NC) introduces an antiabortion amendment to the resolution to extend the debt ceiling, but Senator Robert Packwood (R-OR) and 12 colleagues defeat the amendment by conducting a filibuster that lasts nearly a month.

1983
January 22. An estimated 26,000 demonstrators rally in Washington, D.C., in the annual March for Life. At the same time, abortion rights activists hold rallies, fundraisers, and news conferences to mark the end of a decade of legal abortion.

June 15. In a mixed decision on *Planned Parenthood of Kansas City, Missouri v. Ashcroft*, the Supreme Court rules unconstitutional Missouri's requirement that abortions after 12 weeks of pregnancy be performed in a hospital. The Court upholds the state's requirements for pathology reports for each abortion performed, the presence of a second physician during post-viability abortions, and parental or judicial consent for unemancipated or unmarried minors seeking abortions.

June 15. In *City of Akron v. Akron Center for Reproductive Health*, the Supreme Court rules that the government cannot impose a fixed waiting period on any woman seeking an abortion. The six-to-three ruling also strikes down a parental consent requirement for minors under the age of 15, a requirement that second trimester abortions be performed in hospitals, specific requirements for disposal of fetal tissue, and a requirement that a woman seeking an abortion must receive detailed descriptions of fetal development as well as information on particular physical and psychological risks associated with abortion and be reminded that assistance is available from the father or social services should she choose to have the baby.

June 15. In *Simonopoulos v. State of Virginia,* the Supreme Court upholds a Virginia requirement that second trimester abortions be performed in a licensed hospital because the statute defines "hospital" to include outpatient clinics.

June 28. After two days of debate, by a 49-to-50 vote, the Senate defeats a revised version of the Hatch Amendment, which states simply, "A right to abortion is not secured by this Constitution."

November. Congress passes a continuing resolution prohibiting federal employee health insurance programs from paying for abortions.

Also in 1983. By a two-thirds vote in a popular referendum, the 1861 English law banning abortion is incorporated into the Irish constitution. Thereafter, about 4,000 Irish women annually travel to Great Britain to obtain legal abortions.

1984   January 23. A crowd of 30,000 to 50,000 people rally against abortion in Washington, D.C., joined by thousands in other cities around the country. Abortion rights activists hold smaller rallies of their own.

August. At the Mexico City International Conference on Population, the United States declares that it will deny funds to any private organization that performs or promotes (as through counseling) abortion as a method of family planning. Further, countries where abortion is legal can only receive U.S. population assistance through segregated accounts. The "Mexico City Policy" also threatens the United Nations Fund for Population Activities (UNFPA) with a cutoff of funds if it supports abortion or coercive family planning programs in any member nations.

October. A full-page ad appears in the *New York Times,* containing a declaration of support for Democratic

1984 vice-presidential candidate Geraldine Ferraro, who has
cont. been condemned by the Catholic Church for her support
of legal abortion. The declaration, signed by 24 nuns and
more than 70 religious leaders, testifies to the diversity of
opinion regarding abortion among Catholics. Church leaders warn the participating nuns that they must recant or
be dismissed. A year later, a second ad appears, declaring
support for the original signatories and attesting to the
right of Catholics to disagree with church teachings.

Also in 1984. For the first time, abortion becomes a key
issue in a presidential election.

1985 January 22. President Ronald Reagan addresses the annual March for Life in Washington, D.C. Although he has
met with leaders of earlier marches, this is his first address to the group as a whole. More than 70,000 people
cheer as the president expresses his solidarity with their
struggle. The same day, movement leaders preview *The
Silent Scream*, a film produced by former abortionist Dr.
Bernard Nathanson, which will generate a storm of criticism and controversy among abortion rights supporters
while galvanizing opposition to abortion.

Also in 1985. Despite the legality of abortion, services are
still not available in many areas, particularly rural areas
and small towns. According to the Alan Guttmacher Institute, the number of abortion providers has actually declined since 1982, from 2,908 to 2,680. During the same
period, the number of hospitals providing abortion services has decreased 15 percent, from 1,570 to 1,405, and 20
percent of public hospitals stopped providing abortions.
In 1985, only 2 percent of abortions will be performed in
rural communities or small towns. Freestanding clinics,
the vast majority of them in metropolitan areas, provide
over 87 percent of all abortions. Further, more than one-
half of all abortion providers now refuse to perform abortions after the first trimester.

1986 January 22. An estimated 36,000 people in Washington,
D.C., hear President Reagan address the annual March
for Life for the second time.

April. More than 100,000 people answer a call from the National Organization for Women to join in a March for Women's Lives in Washington, D.C.; another 20,000 march in Los Angeles in support of abortion rights.

June 11. In a hotly debated decision on *Thornburgh v. American College of Obstetricians and Gynecologists*, the Supreme Court, by a five-to-four vote, strikes down "extreme" reporting requirements that would make detailed information about the woman, the doctor, or the circumstances of an abortion available to the public. The ruling also declares unconstitutional an "informed consent" clause and holds that a physician is not required to try to preserve the life of a "viable" fetus if doing so poses any additional risk to the health of the pregnant woman. In separate dissenting opinions joined by Chief Justice Rehnquist, Justices White and O'Connor harshly criticize the "opposition" and the Court itself, not only for this ruling but for nearly all its abortion rulings since *Roe v. Wade*.

Also in 1986. Supreme Court Chief Justice Warren Burger retires. President Reagan appoints William Rehnquist, the most conservative sitting justice, to take his place, and appoints Antonin Scalia, age 50, to fill the vacancy.

In *Diamond v. Charles*, the Supreme Court rules that, in the absence of an appeal by the state, a physician's status as a pediatrician, parent, or "protector of the unborn" does not give him standing to challenge an Illinois abortion law.

1987   January 25. Five thousand demonstrators gather in a driving snowstorm for the annual March for Life, the smallest gathering since the march's inception.

December 14. In *Hartigan v. Zbaraz*, the Supreme Court splits four to four, thus invalidating an Illinois law that would have required parental notification and a 24-hour waiting period before teenagers could have abortions.

Also in 1987. Supreme Court Justice Lewis F. Powell retires. President Reagan nominates Judge Robert Bork to replace him, but the nomination goes down to defeat in

1987 the Senate after a heated and often bitter debate. The presi-
cont. dent then nominates Judge Douglas Ginsberg, who is
forced to withdraw the nomination after it is revealed he
smoked marijuana in college. The president's final nominee is Anthony Kennedy, a California law school professor with no expressed opinion on abortion. Of the sitting
justices, only four remain who have previously expressed
a commitment to abortion rights.

President Reagan directs Surgeon General C. Everett Koop
to prepare a comprehensive report on the health effects of
abortion on women.

1988 January 22. An estimated 50,000 demonstrators gather for
the annual March for Life in Washington, D.C.

July. The Binghamton, New York–based group Operation
Rescue receives national media attention when it mounts
a blockade of Atlanta abortion clinics during the Democratic National Convention. During the next two years,
thousands of people participate in "rescues" in New York,
Illinois, Pennsylvania, California, Connecticut, Colorado,
and other states. Thousands of the demonstrators are arrested; many elect to serve jail sentences rather than pay
their fines.

September 16. In Indiana, 17-year-old Becky Bell dies
in a Marion County hospital. The cause of death is listed
as "septic abortion with pneumonia." Becky soon becomes
a cause célèbre of the abortion rights movement, which
claims that she died because of Indiana's parental consent laws. Because she was unwilling to disappoint her
parents by telling them she was pregnant, Becky had
an illegal abortion and died from its complications. Following their daughter's death, Becky's parents become
national spokespersons arguing against parental consent laws; they also participate in the filming of a video
that they hope will lead to repeal of parental consent
legislation. The facts of the case are disputed by some
antiabortion groups, which claim that Becky actually
had a spontaneous abortion (miscarriage) and that, had
her parents known of her pregnancy, they would have
been able to seek medical help in time.

September 23. The French government approves the marketing of an "abortion pill" developed by a research team headed by French biochemist Dr. Etienne-Emile Baulieu. When taken orally during the earliest stage of pregnancy, the drug, mifepristone (RU 486), blocks the fertilized egg from implanting in the uterus. In later stages (up to about seven weeks since the last menstural period), it can be combined with prostaglandin to induce abortion.

October 26. Roussel-Uclaf, the pharmaceutical company that makes mifepristone, announces cancellation of plans to distribute the drug in France, citing pressure from French and American antiabortion groups. Two days later, French Health Minister Claude Evin orders the company to resume distribution of the drug, saying, "From the moment governmental approval for the drug was granted, RU 486 became the moral property of women, not just the property of the drug company" (Klitsch 1989, 1). By mid-1990 mifepristone will have been used in more than 50,000 abortions in France and elsewhere.

Also in 1988. Secretary of Health and Human Services Louis Sullivan issues new rules for distribution of family planning funds under Title X of the 1970 Public Health Service Act. About $200 million per year is currently distributed under the program, which began in 1970 and serves nearly 5 million low-income women annually. Under the "gag rule," as the new rules become known, physicians and counselors at clinics receiving Title X funds are prohibited from providing any information about abortion to patients. Women who ask about abortion are to be told that "this project does not consider abortion an appropriate method of family planning." The regulation further stipulates that all pregnant women are to be given lists of providers of prenatal care "that promote the welfare of mother and unborn child." In order to provide abortion counseling, clinics must maintain physically separate facilities, with separate personnel, accounting, and record keeping, and fund those facilities privately.

In a related action, the Defense Department issues a directive banning abortions at U.S. military facilities unless the woman's life is in danger.

1988   A growing number of state courts hear "fathers' rights"
cont.   cases, where men have sought to block their wives or part-
        ners from having abortions. Some of these cases have been
        appealed to the Supreme Court, which as of early 1996
        has refused to hear any of them.

        In the case of Dr. Henry Morgentaler, a Quebec physician
        who provided easy access to abortions in violation of the
        1969 Canadian statute, the Canadian Supreme Court in-
        vokes *Roe v. Wade* and holds that the 1969 law imposed an
        impermissible restriction on a woman's right to have an
        abortion, in effect making abortion available on request in
        Canada. Over the next two years abortion will continue to
        be a major issue in Canadian politics as antiabortion groups
        attempt to gain passage of laws restricting abortion.

1989   January. Surgeon General C. Everett Koop decides not to
        release a report commissioned by President Reagan in 1987
        on the health effects of abortion. In his letter to the presi-
        dent, Dr. Koop writes that "in spite of a diligent review
        on the part of many in the Public Health Service and in
        the private sector, the scientific studies do not provide
        conclusive data about the health effects of abortion on
        women."

        January 22. An estimated 67,000 people rally in Washing-
        ton, D.C., in the annual March for Life. The event takes on
        special significance because of anticipation surrounding
        the pending Supreme Court decision in the *Webster* case
        [see below].

        February. The Reproductive Health Equity Act is intro-
        duced in the House. The bill would restore full federal
        funding for abortion in all federal programs, including
        Medicaid, Indian Health Service, federal and military em-
        ployee health benefit programs, the Peace Corps, and fed-
        eral penal institutions.

        April 9. Abortion rights activists gather to march in Wash-
        ington, D.C., in one of the largest demonstrations ever held
        in the capital. Organizers of the demonstration hope to
        influence the pending Supreme Court decision in the

Webster case [see below]. Police estimate the crowd at 300,000, though some organizers claim the demonstrators number twice that.

April 28. In response to the earlier abortion rights march and also in an attempt to influence the pending *Webster* decision [see below], the National Right to Life Committee holds a national Rally for Life in Washington, D.C. Organizers estimate the crowd at 350,000; police and media estimates, however, are smaller.

July 3. In *Webster v. Reproductive Health Services*, in a fragmented, no-majority decision, the Supreme Court upholds a Missouri statute that prohibits the use of public facilities (including private facilities built on land leased from the state) or employees to perform abortions, requires physicians to test for fetal viability, and bans the use of state funding for "encouraging and counseling women on the abortion procedure." In their opinions, four justices indicate their desire to overturn the fundamental privacy right to choose abortion established in *Roe v. Wade*. During the months before the announcement, both sides viewed the *Webster* case as a potential challenge to *Roe v. Wade*, prompting numerous groups to file amicus curiae briefs and thousands of individuals to send letters to the justices. While not explicitly overturning *Roe v. Wade*, the decision continues to erode that earlier ruling and sets the stage for legislative activity at the state level. Both sides interpret the decision as a victory for the antiabortion movement, setting off a wave of abortion rights activity. In the following months, bills restricting abortion are introduced in several state legislatures.

August. The House of Representatives defeats an amendment preventing the District of Columbia from using local tax revenues to provide funding for abortions—the first time since September 1980 that an abortion-spending restriction has been defeated in the House. The Senate also passes an appropriations bill permitting the district to fund abortions with its own tax money, without a separate vote on the issue. The bill and a slightly modified later version are both vetoed by President Bush.

1989   October. For the second year in a row, the Senate approves
cont.   a Department of Labor and Health and Human Services
appropriation containing a provision requiring Medicaid
funding for abortions for rape and incest victims. The
House follows suit, voting after intense debate to approve
the funding amendment 216 to 206. President Bush vetoes
the measure, and an override attempt fails in the House
by a vote of 231 to 191.

November. By narrow majorities, Congress restores U.S.
funding to the United Nations Population Fund (UNFPA),
but is forced to remove the provision when President Bush
vetoes the entire Foreign Assistance Appropriation because
of it.

November. Representatives Don Edwards (D-CA),
Patricia Schroeder (D-CO), and Bill Green (R-NY) and
Senators Alan Cranston (D-CA), Robert Packwood (R-
OR), and Howard Metzenbaum (D-OH) introduce the
Freedom of Choice Act (FCA). The purpose of the FCA
is to codify the *Roe v. Wade* decision into federal law as
a means of protecting legalized abortion nationwide. It
would prohibit states from restricting the right of a
woman to choose abortion "before fetal viability or at
any time, if such termination is necessary to protect the
life or health of the woman," and would allow states
only to "impose requirements necessary to protect the
life or health of women." In addition to the 50 states,
the bill would apply to the District of Columbia, Puerto
Rico, and any other U.S. possessions or territories, including Guam.

November. The Reproductive Health Equity Act (RHEA)
is introduced in the Senate [see February 1989]. Because
the bill involves a number of federal programs, it is sent to
several committees in the House and the Senate, including Post Office and Civil Service and Government Affairs,
Armed Services and Foreign Affairs, and Judiciary.

November 12. In their second major demonstration this
year, hundreds of thousands of abortion rights supporters
gather in Washington, D.C., to protest the *Webster* decision and show support for keeping abortion legal.

Also in 1989. Operation Rescue protests and civil disobedience at abortion clinics lead to more than 20,000 arrests.

1990   January 22. A crowd estimated by police at 75,000 turns out for the annual March for Life in Washington, D.C.

March. The territory of Guam passes the most restrictive abortion law in the United States, outlawing abortion except to save the life of the mother. Under the law, abortion providers would receive third-degree felony prison terms, and persons who obtain or "solicit" abortions would be punished with up to one year in jail. The law is signed by the governor but is immediately challenged by Janet Benshoof of the American Civil Liberties Union's Reproductive Freedom Project. In the resulting court hearings the law is enjoined by U.S. District Court Judge Alex Munson.

March. The Idaho state legislature passes a bill that prohibits abortions except in the case of rape, incest, severe fetal deformity, or danger to the pregnant woman's life or health. Under threats of a potato boycott by abortion rights supporters, Governor Cecil Andrus vetoes the bill.

March. In Romania, thousands of women seek abortions and contraceptives, newly legalized after the downfall of Nicolae Ceaucescu's repressive government. Under the Communist regime, women were required to bear four children apiece—reportedly, women were even subjected to monthly pregnancy tests to ensure that they had not had illegal abortions. Some of the children born under this policy were sold by Ceaucescu, many developed AIDS, and hundreds of thousands are growing up in government orphanages.

April. In a widely publicized and controversial decision, the National Conference of Catholic Bishops awards a $5 million five-year contract to the public relations firm of Hill & Knowlton and the Wirthlin Group, a Republican polling organization, to develop a campaign to end public support for legal abortion. Several weeks later, the Catholic fraternal group Knights of Columbus announces that it will provide $3 million for the campaign.

1990
cont.

April 30. Doctors at the University of Colorado Health Sciences Center announce that a transplant of brain tissue from an aborted fetus produced "substantial improvement" in a patient with Parkinson's disease. Because of the federal ban on funding for fetal tissue research, the project is funded completely from private sources. Despite the lack of federal money, privately funded research also continues on the use of fetal tissue transplants to treat diabetes, immunodeficiency disorders, and several metabolic diseases. Other conditions that may someday be treated with fetal tissue transplants include leukemia, Huntington's disease, and Alzheimer's disease.

June. The Louisiana state legislature passes a bill that would prohibit abortion in all cases and impose a sentence of ten years' hard labor on any doctor convicted of performing an abortion. After Governor Buddy Roemer vetoes the bill, a second bill is hastily passed with provisions for rape and incest, but Roemer vetoes it as well.

June 5. New York Cardinal John O'Connor issues a public warning to Roman Catholic politicians that they risk excommunication if they persist in supporting legal abortion. A few weeks later Rachel Vargas, administrator of the Reproductive Services Clinic in Corpus Christi, Texas, becomes the first U.S. Catholic to be formally excommunicated because of her activism on reproductive rights issues, an action that garners national publicity.

June 25. In *Hodgson v. Minnesota*, the Supreme Court upholds a 1981 Minnesota statute requiring that both parents of a minor be notified 48 hours prior to performance of an abortion. Five justices vote to uphold the two-parent notification requirement, while six uphold the 48-hour waiting period. By a five-to-four vote, with Justice O'Connor voting with the majority, the Court strikes down an alternative portion of the statute that would have eliminated a judicial bypass option and required "absolute notice" of both parents except in specific contingencies.

June 25. In a companion decision, *Ohio v. Akron Center for Reproductive Health*, the Supreme Court upholds by a six-to-three vote a 1985 Ohio statute requiring an abortion provider to notify one parent 24 hours before performing an abortion on a minor; the statute includes a judicial by-pass option. In writing their opinions for these cases, the majority of the Court now holds that a woman's interest in obtaining an abortion is a "liberty interest." This is a significant departure from the "fundamental right" wording of earlier decisions and means that, in order to regulate abortion, states need show only a "rational basis" for their restrictions, as opposed to a "compelling interest," which is much more difficult to prove. Accordingly, the two decisions are hailed as victories by the antiabortion movement and decried by abortion rights supporters. At the time of the rulings, 38 states have parental notification or consent laws on the books, but the laws are being enforced in only 14 states.

July. Supreme Court Justice William Brennan, considered the Court's most liberal member, retires. His departure leaves only two sitting justices, both of whom are over 80, from the original *Roe v. Wade* majority, along with Justice John Paul Stevens, who has consistently voted in favor of abortion rights since his 1975 appointment. President George Bush nominates David Souter to take Brennan's place, asserting that no "litmus test" for abortion was applied in the nomination. Despite protests from abortion rights groups, Judge Souter wins easy confirmation in the Senate and takes his place on the Court a week after the opening of the 1990 session. The first abortion-related case to be heard by Souter will be *Rust v. Sullivan* [see 1991].

August. A federal judge strikes down portions of Pennsylvania's restrictive abortion law, ruling that requirements for spousal notification, a 24-hour waiting period, and parental consent or a court order for a minor are unconstitutional. The ruling is quickly appealed in a case abortion opponents hope will reach the Supreme Court.

October. Minnesota passes a law requiring hospitals and clinics to arrange for the burial or cremation of aborted fetuses. Also in October, the House of Representatives defeats a bill that would have permitted taxpayer financing

1990   of abortions in the District of Columbia, and the Senate
cont.   passes an amendment requiring organizations receiving
         federal funds to notify the parents of minors seeking abor-
         tions before performing the procedure.

         November. Abortion becomes an increasingly visible is-
         sue in gubernatorial elections and in legislative races at
         both the state and national levels.

         December 10. The Federal Food and Drug Administration
         approves distribution of Norplant, the first contraceptive
         to be approved in the United States in 30 years. Norplant
         consists of five small silicone rods that can be implanted
         in a woman's upper arm and that release small amounts
         of hormones over a five-year period; the implants may be
         surgically removed at any time to restore fertility.

1991   January. Senator Alan Cranston (D-CA) and Representa-
         tive Don Edwards (D-CA) reintroduce the Freedom of
         Choice Act, which would codify the 1973 Supreme Court
         Roe v. Wade decision by allowing women unrestricted ac-
         cess to abortions prior to viability. The law would pro-
         hibit states from passing restrictions such as parental
         notification or consent requirements or requirements that
         abortions be performed in a hospital.

         May 23. The Supreme Court announces its decision in *Rust
         v. Sullivan*. By a five-to-four vote, the Court upholds the
         legality of the "gag rule" instituted by the Reagan admin-
         istration and continued under President Bush. Under the
         gag rule, family planning clinics that receive federal fund-
         ing under Title X are forbidden from discussing abortion
         with their clients [see 1988]. The Court's newest justice,
         David Souter, votes with the majority to uphold the regu-
         lation. In response to the ruling, abortion rights groups
         mount a campaign to persuade Congress to pass a law
         nullifying the decision before the regulations can take ef-
         fect in the next 30 to 60 days.

         June 3. The Supreme Court announces that it will not con-
         sider a Planned Parenthood challenge to the Mexico City
         Policy, which bans U.S. foreign aid to overseas organiza-

tions that provide abortion information or promote abortion rights.

June 27. Justice Thurgood Marshall, age 82, announces his retirement from the Supreme Court. Four days later President George Bush nominates Clarence Thomas, a Washington, D.C., appellate judge and former head of the Equal Employment Opportunity Commission (EEOC), to replace him. Although the generally conservative Thomas insists that he has never expressed any opinion about *Roe v. Wade*, abortion rights activists see him as a threat and testify against his confirmation in the Senate. Before Thomas can be confirmed, he is accused of sexual harassment by another former EEOC employee, law professor Anita Hill. The subsequent nationally televised Senate hearings on the matter stir intense controversy and debate before Thomas is confirmed on October 15 in a 52-to-48 vote.

July 13. Breaking ranks with its party, the Young Republican National Federation votes to remove the antiabortion plank from its platform.

July 15. Operation Rescue begins its "Summer of Mercy" campaign in Wichita, Kansas. Over the next six weeks, thousands of abortion opponents from around the country participate in protests and blockades against the city's three abortion clinics. The three clinics remain closed for the first week of demonstrations, but face blockades when they reopen the second week. Two of the clinics appeal to federal courts for injunctions against the protestors, and on July 23 U.S. District Court Judge Patrick Kelly issues the injunction, stating the plaintiffs' rights have been violated under the Ku Klux Klan Act. The judge also declares a fine of $50,000 per day for anyone violating the order and asks Operation Rescue leaders to post a $100,000 bond against damages. Six days later federal marshals are called in to enforce the injunction. On August 6, the Bush administration joins Operation Rescue in requesting a stay of Judge Kelly's ruling, but the appeal is turned down by the Tenth Circuit Court of Appeals. In September, faced with heavy fines and flagging public support, Operation Rescue will declare the siege at an end. The demonstrations

1991
cont.
result in more than 3,000 arrests and cost the city hundreds of thousands of dollars in police overtime and court costs.

December. In New York City, Dr. Abu Hayat is charged with performing an illegal abortion in which the arm of an eight-month fetus was ripped off. The abortion was not successful, and the child was born two days later, at 32 to 34 weeks' gestation (New York law bans abortions after 24 weeks except to save the mother's life). Although Planned Parenthood and other clinics offer safe, legal abortions during the first trimester at an average cost of $250, Hayat charged Rosa Rodriguez $1,500 for the illegal abortion. His is one of a number of small, fly-by-night abortion clinics that operate in New York virtually unsupervised by city, state, or federal licensing authorities. The operators place small ads in foreign-language newspapers such as *El Diario* or the *Haiti Progres*, promising low-cost abortions and 24-hour service, luring poor women who are ignorant of their legal options and who speak little or no English. Defending criticism of its slow response to medical misconduct complaints such as those against Hayat, a state health department spokesperson says that the department gets numerous complaints and that most of them are unfounded. In the Rodriguez case, Dr. Hayat will be convicted of assault, performing an illegal abortion, and a related offense, and be sentenced to up to 29 years in prison.

1992
January 22. An estimated 70,000 people gather at the Mall in Washington, D.C., for the annual March for Life.

February. The Irish Supreme Court, in a four-to-one decision, overrules a court order barring a 14-year-old girl from leaving the country in order to have a legal abortion in England. The girl, who said that she had been raped by a friend's father, had threatened to kill herself if she had to go through with the pregnancy. Under a constitutional amendment approved by a referendum in 1983, Irish law forbids abortions except to save the life of the mother. However, an estimated 4,000 women a year travel to Britain to obtain abortions. In its ruling, the court declares that the girl's suicide threat constituted a "real and substantial risk" to her life that could only be avoided by terminating the pregnancy. The decision is widely regarded as opening the door to a greater number of abortions in Ireland.

April 5. In one of the largest demonstrations ever held in Washington, D.C., abortion rights supporters participate in a "March for Women's Lives" to protest the erosion of abortion rights in the United States and to urge passage of the Freedom of Choice Act, which would turn the 1973 *Roe v. Wade* decision into federal law. Organizers claim the crowd numbers more than 750,000; Washington authorities put the number at 500,000.

April 22. As the Supreme Court hears arguments in *Planned Parenthood v. Casey* [see June 29], demonstrations both for and against legal abortion take place outside the Court and in various places around the country. In suburban Buffalo, New York, nearly 200 antiabortion demonstrators are arrested following a confrontation with abortion rights supporters outside an abortion clinic.

May. Dr. Trent MacKay, of the University of California at Davis, announces the results of his study of abortion training in hospital residency programs for obstetrics and gynecology. Dr. MacKay surveyed 286 programs during the fall of 1991. Of these, 31 percent did not provide any abortion training, 12 percent required residents to learn how to perform first trimester abortions, and 7 percent provided training in performing second trimester abortions. Abortion training was optional in the remaining programs.

June 29. The Supreme Court issues its ruling in *Planned Parenthood v. Casey*. The case involved a challenge to Pennsylvania's strict abortion law, which required a 24-hour waiting period, a parental consent requirement for minors, and a spousal notification requirement for married women. In a fragmented, no-majority decision, the Court upholds an earlier appeals court ruling that left intact the waiting period and parental notification requirements but found the spousal notification requirement unconstitutional.

1992 July 1. In a move orchestrated by abortion rights groups,
cont. California social worker Leona Benton challenges the U.S.
ban on mifepristone by publicly attempting to enter the
country with a supply of the pills, which she plans to use
to end her pregnancy. When the pills are confiscated by
the U.S. Customs Service, Benton appeals to a federal judge,
who orders them returned to her because of a Food and
Drug Agency (FDA) policy allowing unlicensed drugs to
be brought into the country under some circumstances.
An appeals court stays the order, and Benton appeals to
the Supreme Court. On July 18, by a seven-to-two vote,
the Court rejects her plea to have the pills returned. Following the decision, Benton has a surgical abortion.

July 25. The German parliament votes to adopt a compromise version of East Germany's liberal abortion law. The
law allows women to obtain abortions on request through
the third month of pregnancy, with the stipulation that they
receive counseling at least three days before having an
abortion. The vote takes place minutes after Parliament
defeated a proposal to adopt the more restrictive law that
existed in West Germany prior to reunification.

October. A study published in this month's *American Journal of Public Health* reports that more than 10,000 women
died from illegal abortions and about 200,000 children were
placed in orphanages during a period when abortion and
contraception were outlawed in Romania. The study is
based on the statistics of births and maternal deaths between 1966 and 1989, when Romanian president Nicolae
Ceaucescu introduced policies criminalizing abortion and
contraception and actively prosecuted doctors who performed unauthorized abortions.

1993 January 13. The Supreme Court issues its ruling in *Bray v.
Alexandria Women's Health Clinic*. In a six-to-three decision,
the Court rules that federal judges and law enforcement
agencies cannot use the Ku Klux Klan Act to stop protesters who attempt to block women's access to abortion clinics. The law, enacted in 1871, banned conspiracies aimed
at violating the constitutional rights of a "protected class"
of people, such as African Americans. In its ruling, the

Court states that pregnant women seeking abortions do not constitute such a protected class.

January 22. Newly inaugurated, President Bill Clinton signs five directives that (1) revoke the administrative "gag rule," the Reagan and Bush administrations' ban on abortion counseling or referral by federally funded clinics; (2) lift the ban on fetal tissue research; (3) lift the ban on abortions in overseas military hospitals; (4) call for a review of the ban on importing RU 486; and (5) restore foreign aid to international family planning agencies that support abortion rights.

March 17. Antiabortion activist Michael Griffin shoots and kills Dr. David Gunn, an abortion provider, at the Ladies' Clinic in Pensacola, Florida. Griffin will later be convicted of first-degree murder and sentenced to life in prison.

March 19. Supreme Court Justice Byron White announces that he will retire this summer, after 31 years on the Court.

June 14. President Clinton nominates Ruth Bader Ginsburg, a federal appeals court judge who supports abortion rights, to the Supreme Court to replace Justice White. She is easily confirmed and is sworn in in August.

August 19. Rochelle Shannon shoots and wounds Dr. George Tiller, operator of an abortion clinic in Wichita, Kansas. Shannon had previously written letters of support to Michael Griffin [see March 17; see also October 1994].

August 20. Dr. George Patterson, who owns four abortion clinics, is murdered in Mobile, Alabama; it is unclear whether the killing is related to his abortion practice.

December. Congress passes the Freedom of Access to Clinic Entrances (FACE) Act, which makes it a federal crime to block access to a reproductive health facility or to use force or threats against people using the facility. The bill's supporters include a number of abortion opponents, who feel compelled to act against clinic violence and who are convinced of the bill's constitutionality.

1994   April. In Chicago, about 80 militant activists meet to work out a common strategy for combating abortion. Participant Paul Hill, a defrocked Presbyterian minister, brings a petition calling the 1993 murder of Pensacola doctor David Gunn justifiable homicide; the petition was signed by more than 30 activists. Over the next two days the delegates hold heated debates over whether violence is justified in their efforts to stop abortion. When the session is done there will be a permanent schism between those who advocate violence, such as the Portland, Oregon, group Advocates for Life and the Houston-based Rescue America, and those who decry it, such as Operation Rescue, which requires participants to sign a nonviolence pledge. One result of the meeting is the formation of a new group called the American Coalition of Life Activists (ACLA); it represents about a dozen groups around the country who support the use of deadly force against abortion providers. Three months after the Chicago meeting, Paul Hill will shoot three people, killing two of them, at a Pensacola clinic [see July 29].

April 6. Eighty-five-year-old Supreme Court Justice Harry Blackmun, who wrote the majority *Roe v. Wade* opinion in 1973, announces that he will retire from the Court at the end of the current session.

May 13. President Clinton nominates Stephen Breyer to replace Justice Blackmun. Judge Breyer appears to have a mix of liberal and conservative views. His position on abortion, along with other topics such as the death penalty, is unknown, as he has a limited record in such cases.

May 16. Roussel-Uclaf, the French manufacturer of the "abortion pill" mifepristone (RU 486), announces that it is donating its U.S. patent rights to the Population Council, a nonprofit organization. Clinical trials are set to begin in the fall.

May 26. President Clinton signs the Freedom of Access to Clinic Entrances (FACE) Act. The law stipulates a maximum punishment for first-time offenders of $100,000 and a year in prison.

June 31. In *Madsen v. Women's Health Center*, by a six-to-three vote, the Supreme Court upholds a Florida state court injunction creating buffer zones around abortion clinics and doctors' homes. The ruling validates the use of a 36-foot buffer zone around a Melbourne, Florida, clinic to keep protesters away from the clinic entrance and parking lot and off of a public right-of-way.

July 29. Paul Hill, a 40-year-old former minister, shoots and kills Dr. John Bayard Britton and his volunteer bodyguard, retired Air Force Lt. Col. James Barrett, outside the Pensacola, Florida, abortion clinic where Britton worked. Barrett's wife, June, is wounded in the attack. Hill will be tried twice, once under Florida law and once as the first person to be tried under the new federal clinic protection law (FACE). In both trials he will act as his own defense attorney, claiming that the murders were justified to prevent Britton from killing babies. In the state trial, a jury will take just 20 minutes to convict Hill of first-degree murder; he will be sentenced to die in the electric chair. In the federal trial, he will be convicted and sentenced to two life sentences, plus ten years for wounding June Barrett and five years for a weapons violation.

August. Attorney General Janet Reno orders the FBI to conduct an investigation to determine whether some anti-abortion activists have engaged in a criminal conspiracy to shut down or block access to abortion clinics and drive doctors who perform abortions out of business. The FBI will be joined in the investigation by agents of the Bureau of Alcohol, Tobacco, and Firearms.

October. Dr. Janet Daling, a scientist at the Fred Hutchinson Cancer Research Center in Seattle, Washington, announces the results of a ten-year study on abortion and breast cancer. The researchers found that women who had had an induced abortion had a 50 percent greater risk of developing breast cancer before the age of 45, which represents an average increase in risk from one case per 100 women to almost two cases per 100 women.

October. Rochelle ("Shelley") Shannon is indicted on federal charges that include setting fire or injecting noxious

1994
cont.

acid into nine abortion clinics in four states over two years, in addition to shooting Dr. George Tiller at his clinic in Wichita, Kansas, in August 1993. When federal agents search Shannon's home in Grants Pass, Oregon, they recover an operational manual by a group calling itself the "Army of God." The manual lists 65 ways to destroy, damage, or disrupt abortion clinics, along with such tips as how to block water and sewer lines with cement and how to use homemade plastic explosives. Shannon will eventually plead guilty and be sentenced to 20 years in prison. She is slated to begin serving the sentence after completing the remainder of the sentence she received for shooting Dr. Tiller.

November. The congressional election that gives Republicans a majority in both houses for the first time in decades also swings the balance in favor of abortion opponents. In the House, abortion opponents number 318, up 39 from the previous session, while abortion rights advocates hold 146 seats, with 71 in the middle. The number of senators who oppose abortion is 45, compared to 38 who call themselves pro-choice and 17 in the middle. Although abortion does not figure in the Republicans' "Contract with America," legislators and observers predict that it will became a significant issue once Congress passes its first 100 days.

November 8. In Vancouver, British Columbia, abortion provider Dr. Garson Romalis is shot and seriously wounded while eating breakfast in his home. It is not clear whether the shooting is related to his work, and no arrests are made.

December 15. Criminal charges are filed against a Washington state trooper who stopped a couple for speeding and, on learning they were en route to an abortion clinic, detained them for 45 minutes and then took them to a counseling session at a church camp. The trooper, Lane Jackstadt, is charged with unlawful imprisonment and official misconduct.

December 30. A gunman opens fire at an abortion clinic in Brookline, Massachusetts, killing Shannon Lowney, a receptionist, and wounding three other people. He then goes to a second Brookline clinic, where he kills Leanne Nichols, the receptionist, and wounds two others. The next day a 22-year-old hairdresser, John Salvi, is arrested after firing shots at a clinic in Norfolk, Virginia. Salvi, the son of devout Catholics, is known to acquaintances as a Scripture-spouting loner given to fits of rage. Although a handful of abortion opponents applaud the deaths, most condemn them in the strongest possible terms, including the National Right to Life Committee and Cardinal Bernard Law of Boston, who calls for a moratorium on clinic protests to give passions a chance to cool. Abortion rights activists contend that the Boston shootings, along with the earlier shootings in Pensacola, Florida, are part of a national conspiracy orchestrated by right-wing opponents of abortion.

1995   January. The American Coalition of Life Activists [see April 1994] releases a list of abortion providers it calls the "deadly dozen." Interpreting the release as a hit list, the Justice Department quickly notifies the named doctors and dispatches U.S. marshals to protect them.

January. Rev. Michael Bray, a fundamentalist Christian minister who spent nearly four years in prison for bombing ten clinics and related facilities, publishes *A Time To Kill*. The book allegedly explores the biblical and historical justification for using deadly force to stop abortion doctors, whom Bray compares to serial killers.

February. The Federal Bureau of Investigation confirms that it has been investigating death threats against abortion opponents under the Freedom of Access to Clinic Entrances (FACE) Act.

March 11. Ireland's lower house of Parliament passes a bill allowing doctors and other professionals to give women information on abortion, including addresses and phone numbers of clinics abroad.

March 13. The family of Dr. David Gunn files a wrongful death suit against John Burt, the regional director of the Houston-based group Rescue America. The suit accuses Burt of recruiting and inciting Michael Griffin, who shot

and killed Gunn outside a Pensacola, Florida, abortion
clinic in March 1993.

March 30. Pope John Paul II, in his eleventh encyclical, issues his strongest condemnation to date of abortion, contraception, and euthanasia, which he decries as part of a
"conspiracy against life" and a "culture of death." The encyclical, called "The Gospel of Life," deplores the modern
mentality that regards laws permitting abortion and euthanasia as necessary for individual freedom and com-
mands all Catholics to fight such laws. The encyclical also
reaffirms that any Catholic involved in procuring, performing, or receiving an abortion is subject to immediate excommunication, while at the same time calling on women
who have had abortions to repent in hopes that God will
forgive them.

May 30. The Supreme Court refuses to hear a New Jersey
case in which antiabortion protestors argued that "buffer
zones" around clinics and doctors' homes unconstitutionally restricted their free speech rights. The case stemmed
from a 1991 protest at a doctor's home, after which the
doctor and his family obtained a court order creating a
300-foot buffer zone around their house. After the June
1994 Supreme Court ruling upholding buffer zones, the
New Jersey court reduced the restriction to 100 feet, but
the protesters argued that any such restraint was unconstitutional without evidence of violence or threats against
the doctor or his house.

June. In a harbinger of future moves, House Republicans
approve an amendment to a 1996 defense spending plan
that would reinstate the ban on abortions in overseas military hospitals. Since President Clinton lifted the ban
through an executive order shortly after taking office in
1993, ten abortions have been performed in the affected
facilities.

June 20. Without comment, the Supreme Court leaves intact an appeals lower court ruling stating that the Freedom of Access to Clinic Entrances (FACE) Act does not
infringe on anyone's freedom of expression. Antiabortion
activists in Virginia had challenged the act, claiming that

it went beyond its stated goals of stopping violence and intimidation and restricted their right to peaceful protest as well.

June 23. After a bitter five-month battle, the nomination of Dr. Henry Foster for Surgeon General is killed on the Senate floor when supporters fail by three votes to stop a filibuster led by declared presidential candidate Phil Gramm (R-TX). Dr. Foster's supporters, including President Clinton, claim that the doctor was defeated simply because he performed abortions during his 40-year career as a gynecologist and obstetrician. His opponents, including Gramm and majority leader Robert Dole (R-KS), also a presidential candidate, assert that their opposition stemmed from problems with the doctor's honesty and credibility—he first said that he had performed 3 abortions, but later amended the figure to 39. Foster was also accused of knowing about and failing to stop a government experiment in which African-American men were not treated for syphilis; the accusation was never proven.

June 29. Continuing its bid to reverse President Clinton's loosening of abortion restrictions, House Republicans attach a provision to a $12 billion foreign aid appropriations bill cutting off aid to organizations that perform legal or illegal abortions abroad or that lobby to change other countries' abortion laws. In the following weeks, the House will approve other legislation denying federal workers insurance coverage for abortions; the House Judiciary Committee will vote to impose a two-year prison term on doctors who perform late-term abortions except to save the mother's life; and the House Appropriations Committee will approve measures to outlaw federal funds for fetal tissue research, allow states to deny payment for abortions for poor women who become pregnant as a result of rape or incest, bar the Legal Services Corporation from participating in abortion-related litigation, and cut off federal funds for the government's main family planning program. All of the legislation is being tied to spending bills that must clear Congress and be signed by the president to keep the government functioning; thus, a presidential veto on one or more of the bills could bring the government to a standstill.

1995
cont.

July 13. In Colorado, a state appeals court rules unanimously that the state's "bubble law" is constitutional. The law, passed in 1993, prohibits protestors from coming closer than eight feet to people entering or leaving abortion clinics. Three "sidewalk counselors" had argued that the law was a sweeping violation of their First Amendment right to free speech. The court disagreed, saying that the statute does not burden free speech more than is reasonably necessary and that it advances a significant government interest in protecting the safety of and providing unobstructed access for clinic patients and staff. The protestors plan to appeal and predict that the case will reach the Supreme Court.

July 14. The German parliament passes a law that makes abortion illegal but in practice allows almost anyone to obtain one. Under the new law, abortion is allowed only when the pregnancy is the result of rape or poses a threat to the mother's life. In all other cases, women must obtain counseling from a doctor, who is required to stress "the protection of unborn life." However, doctors and women who ignore the counseling and carry out an abortion will not be punished, and health insurance will cover the cost of abortions for poor women. Both sides praise the hard-won compromise, which ostensibly ends a battle that has divided Germany for decades and that threatened to derail reunification.

August 2. A federal appeals court strikes down three provisions of a controversial Utah abortion law, leaving intact the law's parental notification and informed consent requirements. The ruling declares that a provision banning experimentation on "live, unborn children" is unconstitutionally vague, that a provision requiring a physician to use an abortion method that would give the fetus the best chance of survival violates a woman's right to privacy, and that a ban on abortions after 20 weeks too closely resembles the legislature's original intent to ban most abortions.

August 8. In New York, Dr. David Benjamin is found guilty of second-degree murder for performing an illegal abortion and allowing the patient to bleed to death in a recovery room. The jury agreed with the prosecution that Benjamin showed "depraved indifference to human life" in the 1993 death of a Honduran immigrant at his clinic in Queens. The prosecution had charged that Benjamin knew that Guadalupe Negron was five months pregnant when he attempted to perform a "hasty and inappropriate" abortion on the mother of four, then left her unattended in a recovery room after puncturing her uterus and cervix during the surgery. Benjamin is believed to be the first physician in state history to be charged and convicted of murder involving a medical procedure. His license had already been revoked for "gross incompetence and negligence" in five previous cases. Benjamin will be sentenced to 25 years to life—the maximum possible sentence.

August 10. Norma McCorvey, who was the plaintiff "Jane Roe" in the 1973 Supreme Court case, announces that she has quit her job at a Dallas abortion clinic, been baptized, and joined Operation Rescue. McCorvey, who in the past served as a spokesperson and an icon for the abortion rights movement, states that she still supports legal abortion through the first trimester, but not beyond that. McCorvey's surprise move makes national headlines, but representatives on both sides of the debate downplay its significance, saying that they expect it to have little effect on the continuing controversy over abortion.

August 31. *The New England Journal of Medicine* publishes a study showing that a combination of two drugs currently available in the United States can be used to safely induce abortion early in pregnancy. The drugs are methratraxate, a tissue growth inhibitor used for treating cancer, arthritis, psoriasis, and ecoptic pregnancies, and misoprostol, a prostaglandin used in the prevention and treatment of gastric ulcers. Because the drugs are already approved in the United States for other uses, doctors can legally prescribe them for abortions.

October 2. On the first day of its new term, the Supreme Court refuses, without comment, to hear a challenge to the Freedom of Access to Clinic Entrances (FACE) Act. The

1995
cont.

Court's decision leaves in place lower court rulings that the law does not infringe on anyone's freedom of expression or religion.

October 16. In another defeat for abortion opponents, the Supreme Court refuses to hear arguments against a San Jose, California, ordinance that protesters claim interfered with their freedom of expression. The protesters had been arrested for picketing too close to an abortion doctor's home.

October 25. A federal jury in Dallas, Texas, awards an obstetrician-gynecologist $8.6 million from abortion opponents whom the doctor claimed had driven him from his practice, followed and harassed him continuously, and repeatedly threatened the lives of him and his wife. Those found liable for their actions against Dr. Norman Topkins include Operation Rescue, Dallas Pro-Life Action Network, Missionaries to the Pre-Born, and a number of individuals, including Operation Rescue head Flip Benham, who vowed to appeal the verdict.

October 26. In Portland, Oregon, lawyers for several abortion clinics and doctors file a $200 million class-action lawsuit against two extreme antiabortion groups, asserting that the groups are violating federal racketeering laws and the Freedom of Access to Clinic Entrances (FACE) Act by distributing a "hit list" of abortion doctors and "Wanted" posters identifying them. The suit seeks an injunction against distribution of the posters and the list, saying that, in an atmosphere in which clinics are being bombed and doctors shot, such literature should be treated not as constitutionally protected political speech but as genuine threats.

November 1. The House of Representatives votes to ban a rarely used late-term abortion procedure that the bill's sponsors call a "partial-birth abortion." In the method, technically referred to as "dilatation and extraction" or "intact extraction," the fetus is partially delivered feet first, then the base of the skull is punctured and the brain and spinal fluid suctioned out to collapse the skull so the head will fit through the vaginal canal. Only two doctors have publicly said that they use the procedure, which they claim is safer for the woman; one of the two, James McMahon, died October 28 in California. Opponents of the bill claim that it is so loosely worded that it would ban other late-term abortion techniques and that it is a step toward outlawing all abortions.

December 7. The Senate passes the House bill banning so-called "partial-birth abortions," with an amendment allowing an exception to save the woman's life. A second amendment providing a similar exception to preserve the woman's health was defeated. The bill must now be reconciled with the version passed by the House, which rejected both amendments. The White House has announced that President Clinton will probably veto the bill unless it includes both exceptions.

References

American Civil Liberties Union/Reproductive Freedom Project. April 1991; May 31, 1991; June 14, 1991; June 28, 1991; September 13, 1991; December 20, 1991; June 1995. *Reproductive Rights Update.*

Bates, Tom. 1994. "Terrorists Targeting Abortion" and "Militancy Splinters Abortion Foes." Two-part article distributed by Newhouse News Service (published in the *Rocky Mountain News*, November 27 and 28).

Benshoof, Janet. 1990. *Benshoof in Guam.* Washington, DC: ACLU Reproductive Freedom Project.

Committee on Government Operations, 101st Congress. 1989. *The Federal Role in Determining the Medical and Psychological Impact of Abortion on Women.* Washington, DC: U.S. Government Printing Office.

Drucker, Dan. 1990. *Abortion Decisions of the Supreme Court, 1973 through 1989.* Jefferson, NC: McFarland.

Faux, Marian. 1988. Roe v. Wade: *The Untold Story of the Landmark Supreme Court Decision That Made Abortion Legal.* New York: Macmillan.

———. 1990. *Crusaders: Voices from the Abortion Front.* New York: Birch Lane Press (published by Carol Publishing Group).

Francome, Colin. 1984. *Abortion Freedom: A Worldwide Movement.* London: George Allen & Unwin.

Frantz, Douglas. 1995. "The Rhetoric of Terror." *Time*, March 27.

Fryer, Peter. 1966. *The Birth Controllers*. New York: Stein and Day.

Glendon, Mary Ann. 1987. *Abortion and Divorce in Western Law*. Cambridge, MA: Harvard University Press.

Greenhouse, Linda. 1994. "High Court Backs Limits on Protest at Abortion Clinic." *New York Times*, July 1.

Hodgson, Jane, ed. 1981. *Abortion and Sterilization: Medical and Social Aspects*. London: Academic Press.

Hurst, Jane. 1989. *The History of Abortion in the Catholic Church: The Untold Story*. Washington, DC: Catholics for a Free Choice.

Jaffe, Frederick S., Barbara L. Lindheim, and Philip R. Lee. 1981. *Abortion Politics: Private Morality and Public Policy*. New York: McGraw-Hill.

Keller, Allan. 1981. *Scandalous Lady: The Life and Times of Madame Restell, New York's Most Notorious Abortionist*. New York: Atheneum.

Klitsch, Michael. 1989. *RU 486: The Science and the Politics*. New York: Alan Guttmacher Institute.

Lader, Lawrence. 1973. *Abortion II: Making the Revolution*. Boston: Beacon Press.

Luker, Kristin. 1984. *Abortion and the Politics of Motherhood*. Berkeley: University of California Press.

Merton, Andrew. 1981. *Enemies of Choice: The Right-to-Life Movement and Its Threat to Abortion*. Boston: Beacon Press.

Mohr, James. 1978. *Abortion in America: The Origins and Evolution of National Policy*. New York: Oxford University Press.

Nathanson, Bernard. 1979. *Aborting America*. New York: Doubleday.

National Abortion Federation. 1991. *Antiabortion Violence, 1977–1990*. Washington, DC: National Abortion Federation.

National Abortion Rights Action League. 1995. *Who Decides: A State-by-State Review of Abortion and Reproductive Rights*. 5th ed. Washington, DC: National Abortion Rights Action League.

Olasky, Marvin. 1988. *The Press and Abortion: 1838–1988*. Hillsdale, NJ: Lawrence Erlbaum Associates.

Packwood, Bob. 1986. "The Rise and Fall of the Right-to-Life Movement in Congress." In Butler, J. Douglas, et al., eds. *Abortion, Medicine and the Law*. 3d ed. New York: Facts on File.

Paige, Connie. 1983. *The Right-to-Lifers: Who They Are, How They Operate, Where They Get Their Money*. New York: Summit Books.

Petchesky, Rosalind. 1990. *Abortion and Woman's Choice: The State, Sexuality, and Reproductive Freedom*. Boston: Northeastern University Press.

Philips, Lynn. 1995. "The Breast Cancer and Abortion Question: What the Study's Author Thinks." *Glamour*, March, p. 103.

Roe v. Wade, 410 U.S. 113 (1973).

Tietze, Christopher, and Stanley K. Henshaw. 1986. *Induced Abortion: A World Review, 1986.* New York: Alan Guttmacher Institute.

Tribe, Laurence H. 1990. *Abortion: The Clash of Absolutes.* New York: W. W. Norton.

U.S. Commission on Civil Rights. 1975. *Constitutional Aspects of the Right To Limit Childbearing*, Washington, DC: U.S. Government Printing Office.

Biographical Sketches 2

To list all of the people who have figured significantly in the abortion debate would require a volume in itself, so selecting individuals to appear in a list such as this is indeed a daunting task. Following are brief portraits of some of the current movers and shakers on either side of the controversy.

Mary Cunningham Agee (1951–)

Mary Cunningham Agee is the founder and director of the Nurturing Network, a unique organization dedicated to offering alternatives to abortion for women who fear that their unintended pregnancies will do irreparable damage to their education or career. A graduate of Wellesley College and the Harvard Business School, Agee is herself a veteran of the "fast-track" to success, landing a high-level job at the former Bendix Corporation while still in her twenties. She regards the Nurturing Network as an extension of what she was trying to accomplish at Bendix in the early 1980s: help women gain options in their lives.

Before starting the network in 1986, Agee did an "industry analysis" and discovered that most abortion-alternative programs were geared to teenagers, while many of the women facing crisis pregnancies were in their twenties and already involved in college or careers. Such women, noted Agee, did not need referrals to homes for unwed mothers, which is what they were offered. Instead, the Nurturing Network provides women with such options as jobs in their own field in a different city or a transfer to a different but comparable school. The idea is to keep the woman's career on track while allowing her to complete the pregnancy and either work out a way to keep her child or find it a good adoptive home. In an interview with the *Wall Street Journal* (September 4, 1990), Agee stated that she started the network because she saw a signal "being sent in society, that women could either be mothers or working women. [This is] dangerous because its separates a lot of women from an integral part of themselves." By providing working women with different options for resolving problem pregnancies without compromising their own lives, she hopes to counter that message. Through Agee's efforts, the network has grown to include 22,000 individual volunteer members, corporations, and foundations all over the country, and has so far served more than 6,000 clients.

Although the Nurturing Network is inherently pro-life, Agee avoids getting involved in the political battles over abortion and, for the most part, tends to stay out of the public eye. Like other newer pro-life leaders such as Jeannie French, she is more concerned with solving the problems that cause women to choose abortion than with trying to take away their right to do so. As she wrote in the network's first brochure, "Those who support 'choice' can hardly dispute the value of creating another choice; those who support 'life' can hardly reject an alternative made real."

Luz Alvarez-Martinez (1943?–)

Luz Alvarez-Martinez is a cofounder and the director of the Oakland, California–based National Latina Health Organization/ Organización Nacional de La Salud de La Mujer Latina (NLHO), which is dedicated to achieving bilingual access to quality health care and the self-empowerment of Latinas through educational programs, outreach, and research. Reproductive choice has been a major focus of the NLHO since its inception, and Alvarez-Martinez is an outspoken advocate of reproductive rights, particularly for women of color.

The seventh of 11 children and a first-generation Mexican-American, Alvarez-Martinez grew up in the then mostly white city of San Leandro, near Oakland, California. The mother of four sons, she devoted most of her time to her family until 1977, when she returned to school with the intention of becoming a nurse-midwife. She became involved in school politics, the Women's Center, and the Berkeley Women's Health Collective (BWHC) and was part of a group that founded a satellite clinic of the BWHC, operated for and by women of color. In 1981, newly divorced and a single parent, Alvarez-Martinez enrolled in a Baccalaureate Nursing Program at Hayward State University, but she was forced to quit in 1983 due to financial and emotional stress.

A Roman Catholic by birth, Alvarez-Martinez left the church in 1964 when she was told she could not practice birth control and be within the laws of the church. In 1983, hospitalized for a tubal ligation, she found out by accident that women making decisions about birth control were shown two different films: the English-language version stressed alternative types of birth control, while the Spanish version emphasized sterilization. This and other experiences, as well as stories told to her by other Latinas, contributed to her growing awareness of reproductive abuses and inequities against Latinas, and to her determination to fight those abuses. In 1983, she attended the First National Conference of the National Black Women's Health Project (NBWHP), where "for the first time I saw how powerful a group of women of color could be." She stayed involved with the NBWHP, traveling to Kenya for the United Nations International Conference Ending the Decade of Women and participating in a number of local, national, and international conferences focusing on women's health issues.

On International Women's Day, 1986, Alvarez-Martinez and three other Latinas founded the NLHO, with which she has been involved ever since. In April 1989, she became a national board member of the National Abortion Rights Action League (NARAL), with the express intent of working toward expanding the abortion issue to one of full reproductive freedom and of involving more Latinas and women of color at the national level. In February 1990, Alvarez-Martinez joined with other Latinas in creating Latinas for Reproductive Choice, a special project of the NLHO. She continues to speak frequently at both the local and national level and has written several articles on Latinas and reproductive choice.

Byllye Avery (1936–)

Byllye Avery, founder and executive director of the National Black Women's Health Project (NBWHP), is one of a growing number of women of color who have become key participants in the reproductive rights movement, which until recently, consisted mostly of white middle- and upper-class women. A longtime health care activist, Avery has become a chief spokesperson for the new arm of the movement, which has been largely responsible for expanding the agenda beyond abortion rights to a demand for full reproductive freedom. This includes the right to have, as well as not to have, children, and calls for access to such services as prenatal care and affordable, quality day care as well as safe, effective contraceptives and legal, affordable abortion.

In the early 1970s, while living in Gainesville, Florida, Avery found herself identified as one of three "women who could help other women get abortions." She referred the women—who were mostly white and middle class—to a phone number in New York, where abortion was legal. She grew increasingly frustrated, however, at her inability to help black women, who didn't have the money to make the trip, much less pay for an abortion. When abortion became legal in 1973, Avery cofounded the Gainesville Women's Health Center, which provided abortion services as well as a well-woman gynecology clinic where "the educational work went on about getting in control of your body." Many of the clinic's clients were poor black women whose abortions were paid for by Medicaid until the Hyde amendment cut off Medicaid funding in 1977. Around that time Avery also became involved in the birthing movement, opening an alternative birthing center in Gainesville. She found that poor women faced the same kinds of barriers and the same lack of choice when it came to giving birth as they did in seeking abortions: "We have a medical system in which care is given in terms of money, so that poor women don't have options."

Avery has devoted her career to expanding those options. In 1981, she moved to Atlanta and founded the NBWHP, a self-help and advocacy organization committed to defining, promoting, and improving the physical, mental, and emotional well-being of women of African descent. While the NBWHP is involved in all aspects of black women's health, its Washington, D.C.–based Public Education and Policy Office focuses largely on reproductive health and rights issues. Through NBWHP's international program, SisteReach, Avery has taken her message abroad, working to facilitate exchange and mutual learning among women of African descent in the United States, Africa, and around the world. She is also a frequent and welcome speaker at reproductive rights events and conferences.

Among Avery's honors and awards are the coveted MacArthur Foundation Fellowship for social contribution and the 1989 Essence Award for community service. In October 1994, the Institute of Medicine awarded her the Gustav O. Lienhard Award for the advancement of health care, in recognition of her pioneering efforts to improve health care for black and underserved women in the United States. She is currently on the boards of the New World Foundation, the Global Fund for Women, the International Women's Health Coalition, the Boston Women's Health Book Collective, and the Advisory Committee for Kellogg International Fellowship Program.

Janet Benshoof (1947–)

Janet Benshoof is a lawyer who has devoted her career to the fields of health and women's rights, particularly in the area of reproductive rights. A native of Minnesota, Benshoof graduated summa cum laude from the University of Minnesota, received her law degree from Harvard Law School, and was admitted to the New York Bar in 1972. In 1977, she became the director of the American Civil Liberties Union's Reproductive Freedom Project (RFP), overseeing litigation and public education in the areas of abortion rights, contraception, public funding for reproductive health care, young women's reproductive rights, and international population policy. Under her direction, the RFP grew from a two-person project with a budget of $70,000 to the nation's leader of reproductive privacy litigation, with more than a dozen attorneys and an annual budget of over $2 million. During her tenure at the RFP, Benshoof argued several prominent abortion cases before the Supreme Court, including *City of Akron v. Akron Center for Reproductive Health, Harris v. McRae,* and *Hodgson v. Minnesota* [see chapter 3 for overviews of these cases], as well as a case challenging the constitutionality of the Adolescent Family Life Act. She was also actively involved in challenges to laws banning abortion in Utah and Guam.

In 1992, Benshoof left the RFP to found the Center for Reproductive Law and Policy (CRLP) with other reproductive rights attorneys and activists. As president of CRLP, she directs the development and implementation of the center's domestic and international programs, including litigation, advocacy, and public education, as well as serving as cocounsel in a number of CRLP cases involving challenges to laws that restrict abortion rights. Benshoof also speaks extensively on reproductive rights issues around the country, participating in media interviews, panel discussions and conferences, and lecturing at such law schools as Yale, Rutgers, and Columbia.

Benshoof has published articles on reproductive rights issues in such journals as the *Harvard Law Review,* the *Journal of the American Medical Association,* and the *New York University Journal of International Law and Policy.* She has also contributed chapters to several books that addressed issues of women's reproductive rights. Among her honors are the *Ms.* Foundation for Women's Gloria Steinem Award (1989), the National Abortion Foundation's Humanitarian Award (1988), and the Margaret Sanger Award for the Advancement of Family Planning (1986). In 1992, Benshoof received the prestigious MacArthur Foundation fellowship in recognition of her contributions to women's reproductive freedom. The *National Law Journal* cited her in its last two listings of the 100 most influential lawyers in the country, and she has received commendations from *Glamour, Working Woman,* and *Esquire* magazines.

Judie Brown (1944–)

Judie Brown is widely recognized as one of the foremost leaders of the pro-life movement. Indeed, her role is such that author Connie Paige wrote in her 1983 book *The Right-to-Lifers,* "If any single person is responsible for the growth of the right-to-life movement, that person is Judie Brown." Since the mid-1970s, Judie Brown and her husband, Paul, who have strong ties to such New Right leaders as Paul Weyrich and Richard Viguierie, have been major players in bringing abortion to the forefront as a political issue in the United States.

Brown first became involved in the abortion issue in Seattle in 1969, when she and her husband passed out literature on street corners as part of an unsuccessful campaign to defeat a referendum to liberalize Washington's abortion law. Paul's job required frequent transfers, and the couple moved next to Atlanta, where Judie became involved with Birthright, then to North Carolina and then to Ohio. With each move Judie's involvement in the movement deepened. In 1976, she was one of those chosen to represent Ohio Right-to-Life in the annual March for Life. She returned from the rally eager to move to Washington D.C.; serendipitously Paul was offered a transfer to the capital soon after. In Washington, Judie volunteered for the National Right to Life Committee (NRLC), and was soon offered a paid position as public relations director and right-hand woman to then-president Mildred Jefferson. During her tenure at NRLC, Judie showed a tremendous flair and skill for public relations. She began sending mailings to independent groups as well as NRLC state affiliates and developed several different kinds of mailings, including educational materials, legislative updates, medical developments, and media alerts. She made it a point to send people something every three months, keeping the committee in the front of everyone's minds. During the three years she was there, Judie helped to substantially increase not only NRLC's membership but its influence, both with its own affiliates and in the public arena.

In 1977, Paul quit his job in order to work full time combating abortion and other "antilife" issues, forming a political action committee to campaign for a human life amendment. Having worked her way almost to the top of the nation's largest pro-life organization, Judie became disillusioned with NRLC's "cumbersome structure" and internal squabbling. She was particularly unhappy with what she perceived as the movement's too-narrow educational and legislative initiatives, which she felt were not "addressing the root cause of the abortion holocaust: the ascension of the antilife ethic in America." Accordingly, in 1979 Judie left the NRLC and founded her own organization, the American Life League (ALL), to "attack the anti-life ethic at its roots rather than battle its symptoms." Within two years ALL claimed 68,000 newsletter subscribers and liaison with 4,000 groups; current membership numbers around 250,000. Through ALL, the devoutly Catholic Browns have worked to expand the abortion debate to include abortifacient contraceptives such as the IUD, as well as classroom sex education, euthanasia, and religious questions. Judie Brown has also played a key role in the debate over medical care for handicapped infants, particularly in the famous "Baby Doe" case. She appears frequently in the print and electronic media and has contributed editorial pieces to major newspapers and magazines.

Wanda Franz

Wanda Franz (birthdate not available) is the current president of the National Right to Life Committee (NRLC), the nation's largest pro-life organization. Franz is a developmental psychologist and a professor of child development in the division of Family Resources at West Virginia University in Morgantown. She has been involved in the pro-life movement since 1971, when she began speaking to student groups on fetal development.

Prior to taking over as the head of the NRLC, Franz served for 15 years as the president of West Virginians for Life. She has been a member of the NRLC Executive Committee since 1983, and was NRLC vice-president from 1984 until being elected president in June 1991. She is also president of the Association for Interdisciplinary Research in Values and Social Change, and trustee of the National Right to Life Educational Trust Fund.

As NRLC president, Franz has been profiled and quoted in a wide range of publications, including the *New York Times*, the *Washington Post*, *USA Today*, *U.S. News and World Report*, and the *Christian Science Monitor*. She has appeared on numerous television and radio programs, including *The MacNeil-Lehrer Newshour*, *CBS This Morning*, and NBC's *Today* show. She also hosts the NRLC's daily radio commentary, *Pro-Life Perspective*, which airs on more than 200 outlets nationwide.

Jeannie Wallace French (1961–)

Jeannie Wallace French is the founder and executive director of the National Women's Coalition for Life (NWCL), which was founded in 1992 and represents 14 national women's groups with a combined membership of over 1.2 million women. She is also the originator of Real Choices, NWCL's first major project. French's idea was to hold hearings across the country to allow women who had had abortions to talk about their experiences, in order to learn about the pressures and problems that led them to choose abortion over giving birth. The project also surveyed workers in crisis pregnancy centers to determine which situations they encountered most often and which problems were most difficult to solve. The project exemplifies a philosophy and approach that is becoming increasingly powerful among the newer pro-life leaders, most of whom are women: rather than protesting and trying to shut down clinics, they work to solve the problems of women with unintended pregnancies and thereby enable them to choose birth instead of abortion. "The answer to a crisis pregnancy," French says, "is not to get rid of the baby but to solve the crisis."

French is a second-generation pro-life activist. Her parents were involved in the fledgling movement that preceded *Roe v. Wade*; following the decision that legalized abortion, they took their 11 children to Washington, D.C., each January 22 to participate in the

March for Life. French herself has been active in the movement since college, when she founded the University of Pittsburgh Students for Life. In Chicago, she established the national office of the Professional Women's Network, a pro-life group, and has served as the director of the Respect Life Office for the Archdiocese of Chicago.

French's pro-life beliefs were put to a severe test when she learned, about halfway through her first pregnancy, that one of the twins she was carrying suffered from meningomylelocele, a rare birth defect that causes the spinal cord and brain membranes to grow outside the body. The baby, she was told, would not survive more than a few hours past birth. Doctors advised her to abort the defective fetus, but French refused, determined to give her child a chance at life. Because contractions were likely to kill the sick twin and possibly endanger the other, the babies were born by cesarean section at 37 weeks. One was a healthy boy, but the other, a girl, lived only six hours. Her parents chose to donate her organs, and two infants received heart valves, confirming French's view that "every life has a purpose."

French, who holds a masters degree in public health, is a member of the American College of Healthcare Executives and the Chicago Health Executives Forum. She currently works as a health care consultant in the Chicago area, reserving the majority of her time to raise her son, William, and coordinate the activities of the Women's Coalition.

David Grimes (1947–)

David Grimes is a physician and researcher who has spent much of his career developing better and safer abortion techniques. He first became interested in the abortion issue while still in medical school and during his residency at Chapel Hill, North Carolina. There he became involved in research on the use of prostaglandins for late-term abortions, following up on an interest in population biology that dated to his undergraduate days at Harvard. He spent his junior year in medical school working for the newly formed Abortion Surveillance division at the Centers for Disease Control (CDC). After serving two years as a resident at Chapel Hill, he interrupted his residency to join the military and served two years as a surgeon at CDC, where he returned again when his residency was complete.

Grimes served as assistant chief of the Abortion Surveillance division from 1979 until 1982 and as chief of the division from 1982 through 1983. At CDC, Grimes and his colleague Willard Cates produced numerous studies on abortion and did pioneering work in the field until they were both transferred to the Sexually Transmitted Diseases division in 1984. In 1986, citing political heat and censorship of his writing, Grimes left the CDC and moved to California, where he joined the faculty of the University of Southern California School of Medicine and began doing research at the Los Angeles County–University of Southern California Medical Center's Women's Hospital, the only institution in the nation involved in doing research on mifepristone, better known as RU 486, the French "abortion pill." He spent several years doing clinical trials of the drug in studies involving almost 400 women before Roussel-Uclaf, the drug's manufacturer, stopped supplying it in February 1990, citing antiabortion opinion in the United States.

Since 1993, Grimes has been chief of the department of obstetrics, gynecology, and reproductive sciences at San Francisco General Hospital. He also serves on the faculty of the University of California at San Francisco, in the department of obstetrics, gynecology, and reproductive sciences and the department of epidemiology and biostatistics. In May 1994, Roussel-Uclaf announced that it was donating its U.S. patent rights for mifepristone to the Population Council, a nonprofit organization. That same month, the University of California announced that Grimes would be directing a study of the drug's effectiveness as an emergency contraceptive. He believes that it will eventually be marketed in the United States: "It's safe, effective, and popular" in the countries where it is available.

Despite threats from antiabortion activists, Grimes spends much of his time lecturing internationally and in the United States on mifepristone and the worldwide tragedy of illegal abortion. He also continues both to teach abortion techniques and to provide abortions—he is one of the few doctors who will perform abortions on AIDS patients—as well as working on other research projects. He is currently the chair of the American College of Obstetricians and Gynecologists' Task Force on Violence, in addition to serving on a range of committees of various organizations involved in reproductive health issues.

Among Grimes's many honors and awards are the Christopher Tietze Humanitarian Award from the National Abortion Federation (1987), the Fundamental Right of Reproductive Freedom Award from the Southern California ACLU (1992), and the Alan Guttmacher Lectureship Award of the Association of Reproductive Health Professionals (1994). He has authored or coauthored numerous articles for professional journals and book chapters on abortion and other reproductive health-related topics.

Warren Hern (1938–)

Warren Hern is a physician, anthropologist, and epidemiologist who runs an abortion clinic in Boulder, Colorado. Hern literally wrote the book on abortion: his textbook *Abortion Practice,* first published in 1984, has been called the yardstick by which all other information on abortion should be measured. Republished in softcover in 1990, the book is used by practitioners and teaching institutions in several countries.

Hern's interest in abortion dates back to his days as a medical student at the University of Colorado School of Medicine. While working on the maternity ward, he was struck by the difference between women who planned to keep their babies and those giving infants up for adoption. The latter would stand at the nursery window and cry, he remembers; "they looked so sad." Later, as an intern in Panama and then as a Peace Corps physician in Brazil, he saw many women suffering from the effects of illegal abortions, a large percentage of whom died.

Hern originally planned a career in public health research, and he still sees abortion largely as a public health issue. In 1973, while working at the Office of Economic Opportunity in Washington, D.C., he spent time at the Preterm Clinic there and learned to perform abortions. He also became involved in several abortion rights groups, including the National Association for the Repeal of Abortion Laws (NARAL, now the National Abortion Rights Action League). He returned to Colorado in 1973, planning to finish his doctorate in epidemiology, but instead was recruited to help set up an abortion clinic in Boulder. He came under fire from abortion foes almost immediately, which only served to reinforce his growing conviction that doing abortions was "the most important thing I could do" in medicine. Two years later he opened his own clinic, where he has been ever since.

Hern's active and outspoken participation in the pro-choice movement and his performance of late-term abortions have made him a lightning rod for abortion opponents, who have targeted him and his clinic on multiple occasions. In 1995, his name appeared on a list of "dirty dozen" doctors put out by a group calling itself the American Coalition of Life Activists. Federal authorities interpreted the list as a death threat and placed Hern under 24-hour guard for several months. More painful, however, is the opposition he receives from others in the pro-choice movement who have fought his attempts to establish and enforce consistent standards for abortion clinics. In its efforts to play down the medical aspects of abortion, he believes, the movement has relegated physicians to second-class status, harmed women, and handed ammuntion to abortion opponents by allowing substandard care to go unchecked. This marginalization of doctors, along with anti-abortion violence, low reimbursement rates, and low status among other physicians, has helped create a shortage of abortion providers. "The right to a safe, legal abortion," he wrote in an essay published in the *New York Times,* "is meaningless if no one is able or willing to perform it."

In addition to his medical credentials, Hern holds a doctorate in Population Epidemiology from the University of North Carolina School of Public Health in 1988. He conducted his dissertation research in the Peruvian Amazon basin, where he has studied the effects of cultural change on the health and fertility of the Shipibo Indians since 1964. He is also an environmentalist who has led a 13-year movement to stop a water project that threatens to destroy a Colorado wilderness area. Despite his intense involvement in such issues, Hern does not regard himself as an activist. "I'm just doing my part as a physician and a citizen," he says. "The problem is that most people are inactive, so anyone who does what they are supposed to do is considered an activist."

A founding board member of the National Abortion Federation, Hern chaired its standards committee for two years. He is a Fellow of the American College of Preventive Medicine, a member of the American Association for the Advancement of Science and the Society for Applied Anthropology, and was the 1994–1995 chairman of the Population and Family Planning section of the American Public Health Association. A prolific writer, he has published numerous articles and op-ed pieces in newspapers, magazines, and professional journals, in addition to *Abortion Practice.* He has appeared on national and local television news and talk shows, including "60 Minutes," and been the subject of numerous media interviews. He is also a professional photographer whose work has been published in *Sierra* magazine, *Natural History,* Time-Life books, wildlife calendars, and elsewhere.

Jane Hodgson (1915–)

Jane Hodgson holds the distinction of being the first doctor convicted of performing an abortion in a hospital—a conviction that arose from her deliberate attempt to challenge Minnesota's restrictive abortion law. She is also one of the pioneers of and chief contributors to the abortion rights movement. A practicing obstetrician since 1947, a founding Fellow of the American College of Obstetrics and Gynecology, and a past president of the Minnesota Society of Obstetricians and Gynecologists, Hodgson had devoted most of her career to improving fertility and helping women deliver healthy babies. During the 1960s, however, she gradually realized that denying abortion to women who sought it was "lousy medicine." She became convinced that the only solution was total legalization, although she doubted it would happen in her lifetime.

Hodgson eventually became determined to challenge the law and started looking for a test case. She found it in April 1970 in Nancy Widmyer, a mother of three who had contracted rubella and who wanted an abortion. Backed by a lawyer provided by the Clergy Counseling Service (CCS), Hodgson began the legal motions to challenge the law in federal court. When the court refused to hear the case, she performed the abortion and was duly arrested, indicted, and convicted: "I really wanted to come to court—I thought that was the only way to educate the legislature. I expected the legislature would promptly pass a new law! But it didn't work out that way." Concerned about losing her license while her case was appealed, Hodgson continued to refer women through the CCS but did not perform abortions until 1972, when she went to Washington, D.C., to become the director of the recently opened Preterm Clinic, which became a model for the outpatient abortion clinics that sprang up around the country in the wake of *Roe v. Wade*.

Jubilant over the *Roe v. Wade* decision and the overturning of her Minnesota conviction, Hodgson returned to Minnesota, where, in addition to her private practice and teaching duties, she opened a fertility control clinic and worked on the development of safer techniques for second trimester abortions. She has spent much of her time training younger doctors in abortion techniques and still considers such training a major focus of her work. She has also worked to raise funds to help pay for abortions for low-income women who were denied funding under Minnesota law and has testified as an expert witness in numerous abortion cases. In 1981, Hodgson became the major plaintiff in a challenge to Minnesota's parental notification law. As the medical director of three clinics, she saw many teenage patients, some of whom had hitchhiked in the winter from rural areas seeking abortions. *Hodgson v. Minnesota* eventually reached the Supreme Court, which handed down a decision upholding the law in June 1990.

During the course of her long career, Hodgson devoted several years to Project Hope, spending time in Egypt, China, and Grenada as well serving three tours of duty on the hospital ship *Hope.* Her work on behalf of reproductive freedom and women's rights has taken her all over the world and garnered her numerous awards, including one named in her honor, the Jane Hodgson Reproductive Freedom Award. She was featured in a book by Peter Irons, *The Courage of Their Convictions: Sixteen Americans Who Fought Their Way to the Supreme Court* (New York: The Free Press, 1988). In 1995, she received the Margaret Sanger Award from the Planned Parenthood Federation of America.

Hodgson has published many articles on abortion and related topics, and she edited a book, *Abortion and Sterilization: Medical and Social Aspects* (London: Academic Press, 1981), which has been widely used in arguing court cases and as a medical textbook. Most recently, she contributed a chapter to *New Essays on Abortion and Bioethics,* edited by University of Tennessee philosophy professor Rem B. Edwards (Greenwich, CT: JAI Press, expected publication in spring 1996). At age 80, she continues to practice medicine and to speak out and work on behalf of abortion rights, periodically traveling 150 miles from her home in St. Paul to perform abortions at the Duluth Women's Health Center, a clinic she helped found in 1981. She also serves on the boards of directors of several pro-choice organizations, including the Center for Reproductive Law and Policy and Pro-Choice Resources, the educational arm of NARAL, which works to provide scholarships for medical students who are interested in becoming abortion providers.

Henry Hyde (1924–)

Henry Hyde was first elected to the United States Congress in 1974. A fervent opponent of abortion, the Republican Representative from Illinois is probably best known for the Hyde amendments that restrict federal funding for abortions for poor women. Born in Chicago, Hyde attended Catholic schools before winning admission to Georgetown University on a basketball scholarship. He interrupted his education to serve in the Navy from 1944 to 1946, then graduated from Georgetown and attended Loyola University Law School, receiving his law degree in 1949 and being admitted to the Illinois bar in 1950. Like his parents, Hyde was a Democrat until 1952, when he supported Eisenhower against Adlai Stevenson. Increasingly concerned by what he saw as the leftward drift of the Democratic party, Hyde changed his affiliation to Republican in 1958. In 1966, he ran for the state legislature, serving four terms before being elected to Congress in 1974.

A staunch conservative, throughout his legislative career Hyde has supported the death penalty and more stringent antidrug legislation and opposed the Equal Rights Amendment. In his first term in Congress, he was elected chairman of the 17-member freshman Republican class and won seats on the influential Judiciary and Banking and Currency Committees. It was as Congress's leading crusader against abortion, however, that he rose to fame. In 1976, Hyde and cosponsor Robert Bauman of Maryland introduced a hastily written amendment to the fiscal 1977 appropriations bill for the departments of Labor and Health, Education and Welfare that prohibited the use of federal funding for elective abortions under Medicaid. To his surprise, the amendment passed, and versions of it have passed every year since. The amendment permits abortion only to save the life of the pregnant woman, with the result that since 1977 federal funding for abortions has been virtually nonexistent. (In 1989, in the first serious challenge to the amendment, Congress passed legislation allowing funding in cases of rape or incest, but President Bush vetoed the measure.) In 1981, along with Senator Jesse Helms, Hyde introduced the Helms-Hyde Human Life Bill, which attempted to codify the belief that life begins at conception. The bill, however, was criticized not only by abortion rights activists but by pro-life groups who preferred a constitutional amendment over legislation that would be subject to judicial challenges. The bill eventually died in committee, but Hyde has continued to support efforts to pass either national legislation or a constitutional amendment that would ban abortion.

In recent years, Hyde has confounded liberal forces by joining them in advocating legislation that would promote better health care for women and reduce infant mortality. In 1989, he joined reproductive rights advocate Barbara Boxer, then a Democratic representative from California, in sponsoring a bill that would criminalize the practice of surrogate childbearing. He has also worked to encourage federal funding of adoptive services and other alternatives to abortion and called for an end to the welfare system, which he says encourages illegitimate births. In a move that surprised both friends and foes, Hyde also voted in favor of the 1990 Family Leave Act, which was later vetoed by President Bush. Most recently, Hyde has opposed welfare reforms that would cut off benefits to women who have additional children, fearing that it would increase the number of abortions.

Hyde's success in championing their cause in Congress, plus his willingness to travel around the country speaking in defense of the unborn, have endeared him to the pro-life community. A witty, dynamic speaker and skilled debater, he once introduced himself to a National Right to Life convention as a "626-month fetus." Although he denies that his opposition to abortion grows out of his Roman Catholic faith, he rejects the idea that religious values should not be part of political debate, and has challenged other Catholic politicians to join him in saving the unborn and in building a consensus against abortion.

Molly Kelly (ca. 1938–)

Molly Kelly is one of the most active and popular speakers on the pro-life circuit. The energetic and ebullient Kelly focused primarily on being a wife and mother to her six sons and two daughters until the death of her husband, Dr. James Kelly, in a sledding accident in 1975. A few years later, friends in the pro-life movement urged her to take over her husband's avocation of speaking on behalf of the unborn. She soon discovered that she had a gift for communicating to teenagers, who enthusiastically return her open admiration and affection for them. Kelly now speaks to some 100,000 teenagers a year, mostly in Catholic and public high schools throughout the United States and Canada; she has also spoken in Australia, England, Wales, and Italy. In 1993, she spoke to an audience of 7,000 young people at the National Catholic Youth Conference in Denver. She also occasionally speaks at colleges, medical schools, and theological schools, as well as at gatherings of Catholic clergy. In 1990, she was the only North American woman to speak to over 6,000 priests in Rome at the International Priests' Retreat, where she met Pope John Paul II and Mother Theresa. Kelly also appears frequently at local, state, and national pro-life conventions and youth rallies and gives training seminars on public speaking. She charges only expenses for her services, and is usually booked well over a year in advance.

Early in her speaking career, Kelly began adding a brief segment about abstinence to her talks about abortion. "I told teens that chastity is an option that is 100 percent effective, costs nothing, has no harmful side effects and puts teens in control of their own lives." Heartened by the response, she began focusing her talks on chastity and what she calls "saved sex," the idea that sex should be reserved for marriage. Decrying the mixed messages served up to teenagers by the media and the schools, Kelly aims to deliver a clear, direct, and ethically consistent message that invites her listeners to live on the "moral high ground" and to work together in influencing and supporting one another for their own good.

Kelly is the executive director of Pennsylvanians for Human Life and the founding president of the Pennsylvania Prolife Educational Foundation and the Delaware Valley Prolife Alliance, a network of groups that provides support to women with problem pregnancies. She participates regularly in two cable television shows, *Teen Video* and *Teen Catholic Apostolate*, and has appeared on national television, including *CBS This Morning* and *ABC Nightly News with Peter Jennings*. Among her honors are the Knights of Columbus Woman of the Year Award (1987), the Papal Medal, *Pro Ecclesia et Pontifice*, for outstanding service to the Catholic Church (1986), and the Pennsylvania Prolife Coalition–Dr. James D. Kelly Award (1985), plus several honorary doctorates.

Kelly has produced several videos for teenagers and adults, including one on abortion, and has written a book and several booklets, including *Abortion: Beyond Personal Choice*. She also writes articles for several pro-life and Catholic magazines.

Frances Kissling (1943–)

As president of Catholics for a Free Choice (CFFC), Frances Kissling is one of the most controversial voices in the Catholic Church, which would probably just as soon pretend she and her organization didn't exist. Dubbed a "philosopher of the pro-choice movement" by columnist Ellen Goodman, Kissling has been involved in reproductive rights for 25 years. A product of Catholic schools through the university level, she first became involved in social activism during the 1960s, protesting the war in Vietnam and joining the feminist movement. In 1970, she took a job running an abortion clinic in New York, which at that time was one of two states where abortion was legal. During 1974 and 1975, she worked as a consultant helping to establish abortion clinics in Italy, Austria, and Mexico. In 1976, she founded the National Abortion Federation, serving as its director until 1980. She became president of CFFC in 1982, and under her leadership it has steadily gained in both members and influence.

When Kissling returned to the Catholic Church, it was with the intent to act as a "social change agent" and to transform it into a church that is "more sensitive to all powerless people," including women. Accordingly, she talks to Catholics all over the world, promoting her message that the real issue in the struggle over abortion is not reproductive rights or the preservation of fetal life but control over women. If the church were really concerned about abortion, she asserts, they would be better off spending money to prevent unwanted pregnancy—a strategy that would conflict with the church's position on birth control. She sees the church's understanding of sexuality as "misconceived," one that "leaves no room for such values as love and companionship." The bishops are concerned by the fact that Catholic women have abortions at the same rate as other women, she says, because it indicates that they have not been able to control women through the church—and therefore they are attempting to use the state to enforce control over not just Catholics, but all women. Kissling, however, is determined to get the church to recognize women as free moral agents and to trust them to make good decisions.

With views such as these, it is not surprising that Kissling has many detractors, some of whom accuse her of not being a real Catholic. She insists, however, that the church can accommodate a pro-choice viewpoint and continues to call on everyone, not just Catholics, to focus on both rights and values. "It is time," she said during a 1988 address in Albuquerque, "for us to talk about the survival of this planet and about the kind of people we want to be—not the things we want to be allowed to do."

In addition to her work with CFFC, Kissling is a founder and treasurer of the Global Fund for Women, the founder and convener of the International Network of Feminists Interested in Reproductive Health and Ethics (IN/FIRE), and a founder and member of the advisory board of the Religious Consulation on Population, Reproductive Health, and Ethics. A former treasurer of the International Women's Health Coalition, she also serves on the executive board of the American Public Health Association and is active in Women-Church Convergence, a coalition of Catholic organizations committed to promoting women's rights within the church.

Kissling's contributions to women's reproductive health earned her a place on *Ms.* magazine's list of "Eighty Women To Watch in the '80s." A frequent public speaker both in the United States and abroad, she has appeared on network and public television, is frequently interviewed by national media, and has been profiled in numerous books and magazines. She coauthored *Rosie: The Investigation of a Wrongful Death* with Ellen Frankfort (New York: Dial Press, 1978), and she is a frequent contributor of articles and op-ed pieces to newspapers and religious magazines.

Kate Michelman (1942–)

Kate Michelman has headed the National Abortion Rights Action League (NARAL) since 1985. Under her tenure, NARAL has grown to more than 500,000 members and established its position as the political arm of the abortion rights movement, earning a nod from *Fortune* magazine as one of the top ten advocacy groups in the country.

Michelman's involvement with abortion rights grows out of both personal and professional experience. In 1970, she was a 28-year-old college student with three children, and pregnant with a fourth, when her husband left her for another woman. With no money, no car, and no credit, she was faced with deciding whether to "push my family into an unmanageable crisis or terminate the pregnancy and carry on with getting a job and nurturing my family back to health and stability." She went before a hospital review board, which required her to have her husband's written consent before she could obtain an abortion. She told them they would have to find him to get it. They did, and Michelman had the abortion and went on to finish her degree and begin work as a developmental psychologist. Much of her early career was spent working with abused children and their families, and "it was very clear to me that many of the problems originated because women didn't have many choices about reproduction." In 1978, Michelman developed and implemented a multidisciplinary diagnostic therapeutic treatment program for developmentally disabled preschool children and their families, a program that has been replicated by early childhood specialists in other parts of the country.

In 1980, Michelman became the director of the Harrisburg, Pennsylvania, Planned Parenthood, holding that position until 1985 when she became the executive director of NARAL. As head of NARAL, she led the successful 1987 campaign to block Senate confirmation of Supreme Court nominee Robert Bork and rallied 1,000 delegates to represent the abortion rights vote at the Democratic National Convention. Following the 1989 *Webster* ruling, Michelman was the chief architect of the slogan, "Who Decides?," which has become a unifying theme for the abortion rights movement and served to focus the debate around the issue of individual liberty—an issue that has hit home for many people previously unconcerned with the abortion controversy. In 1989, she was the primary force behind one of the largest demonstrations ever held in Washington, D.C., when an estimated 300,000 people filled the Mall in support of abortion rights.

In 1994, Michelman was selected to be a fellow at the John F. Kennedy School of Government's Institute of Politics at Harvard University. Named by *Washingtonian* magazine as 1 of the 100 most powerful women in Washington, Michelman is quoted frequently in leading newspapers and magazines. An articulate and thoughtful speaker, she spends much of her time traveling throughout the country promoting NARAL's message that the right to choose abortion is a fundamental one and that the government should not intrude into such private, personal decisions as whether or not to bear a child. She has appeared numerous times on network news and talk shows, including *Face the Nation, This Week with David Brinkley, Nightline,* and the *MacNeil-Lehrer Newshour,* and she regularly testifies before Congress on issues related to reproductive rights.

Bernard Nathanson (1926–)

Bernard Nathanson is perhaps the only person to have played a major role on both sides of the abortion debate. An alumnus of Cornell University and the McGill University Medical College, Nathanson has practiced obstetrics and gynecology since 1957, following in his father's footsteps. In New York in the late 1960s, he was a staunch and vocal advocate for abortion rights. In 1969, he helped to found the National Association to Repeal Abortion Rights (later the National Abortion Rights Action League), and from February 1971 through September 1972 he directed the Center for Reproductive and Sexual Health in New York City, then the largest abortion clinic in the world. He continued to play an important part in NARAL until 1975, when he resigned from his position on the board of directors and focused his attention on the growing science of fetology, which was causing him to have serious second thoughts about abortion.

In 1979, Nathanson published *Aborting America* (New York: Doubleday), the story of his gradual realization that abortion was not the simple, humane procedure he had thought it to be. "There are 75,000 abortions in my past medical career," he wrote, "those performed under my administration or that I supervised in a teaching capacity, and the 1,500 that I have performed myself. The vast majority of these fell short of my present standard that only a mother's life, interpreted with appropriate medical sophistication, can justify destroying the life of this being in inner space which is becoming better known to us with each passing year. I now regret this loss of life" (p. 248).

Nathanson is perhaps best known for his role in producing and narrating *The Silent Scream*, the most famous and controversial abortion film ever made. In 1983, he wrote *The Abortion Papers* (New York: Frederick Fell Publishers), a scathing indictment of the "abortion people" and what he and many others in the movement see as the pro-abortion bias of the media. In 1987, he produced another video, *Eclipse of Reason*, which graphically depicted a second trimester abortion. In his speeches, videos, and writing, Nathanson places heavy emphasis on the profits made by the abortion industry, a "billion dollar a year industry" that "invites skimming" and corruption. An avowed atheist who bases his opposition to abortion on nonreligious moral grounds, Nathanson is not opposed to contraception and in fact advocates better contraception as a way to prevent abortions. Though severely criticized by the abortion rights activists who were once his friends and colleagues, he is highly respected in the pro-life movement, for which he is a prominent and authoritative spokesperson. With his wife Adelle, he publishes a free bimonthly newsletter, *Bernadell Technical Bulletin*, which contains abstracts of medical literature on topics related to "life issues" with accompanying commentary by Nathanson, as well as other educational materials on bioethical issues.

Joseph Scheidler (1927–)

In the fight against abortion, Joseph Scheidler is a top commander and one of the leading strategists—Patrick Buchanan once called him the "Green Beret of the pro-life movement." A self-described "traditional Catholic" who once studied for the priesthood, Scheidler decided against ordination because he "didn't like the way the Church was going" in the years prior to Vatican II. As a seminary student, Scheidler studied abortion and delved into the concepts of ensoulment and hominization, concluding that abortion was not only homicide, but an "especially grievous sin [that] always caused one to lose membership in the Church." He recalls that he has always felt protective of children, a feeling he dates to his reaction to the Lindbergh kidnapping when he was quite young: "It frightened me to think that adults would use a child as a convenience to make money."

Scheidler's feelings did not translate into activism until 1973, when the *Roe v. Wade* Supreme Court decision so appalled him that he quit his job in public relations and founded the Chicago Office for Pro-Life Publicity, believing that if "Americans knew about the humanity of the unborn child and the dangers of abortion, they would resist this new ruling." Scheidler now heads the Pro-Life Action League, an activist organization whose work is based on the methodology outlined in his book, *Closed: 99 Ways To Stop Abortion*, first published in 1985 and recently updated. He believes that the movement has not yet done enough to educate the public about the realities of abortion, a gap he attempts to bridge as he travels throughout the United States and abroad promoting his view that abortion is never moral or permissible, because "when you come down to the issue of human life, you can't compromise."

In addition to speaking engagements, Scheidler appears frequently on television and radio and participates in "sidewalk counseling" and "rescues" at abortion clinics around the country, where he and his ever-present bullhorn are familiar figures. He also states that he has salvaged as many as 5,000 unborn children from clinic trash receptacles and given them proper funerals. An artist at generating publicity, Scheidler once hired private detectives to track down the address of an 11-year-old girl scheduled for an abortion and later attempted to remove her from her mother's custody. Scheidler was one of the main "stars" of *Holy Terror*, a video on the pro-life movement; he has also produced videos, including *The Abortion Providers*. He is a regular guest columnist in *USA Today* and has published articles in several national publications.

Patricia Schroeder (1940–)

Twelve-term congressional veteran Patricia Schroeder (D-CO) has long been a crusader for women's rights, including reproductive rights. The longest-serving woman in the House, she has also been one of its most outspoken and oft-quoted members. *The 1994 American Almanac of Politics* noted that Schroeder "sees herself less as a liberal than as part of the vibrant Old West history of skepticism about tradition and authority figures; in Washington, however, she is a symbol of feminism and liberalism—a kind of authority figure herself." As such, she arouses the ire and even the outright hatred of many conservatives, including abortion opponents.

Schroeder graduated magna cum laude from the University of Minnesota, where she was a member of the Phi Beta Kappa honor society, and received her law degree from Harvard Law School in 1964. She practiced law and lectured in Denver until making her first successful bid for Congress in 1972. During her congressional career, Schroeder has authored and/or sponsored numerous laws designed to benefit women and children. Among her recent successful efforts were the Violence against Women Act, which strengthened efforts by law enforcement agencies, prosecutors, and victim service organizations to combat violent crimes against women; the Economic Equity Act, which addressed a broad range of issues affecting women in the workplace; and the Child Support Responsibility Act. She cochaired the bipartisan Congressional Caucus for Women's Issues from 1979 until 1995, placing a major focus on the attempt to improve women's health policies, including investigating gender discrepancies in health research and services. In February of 1991, she was appointed to chair the House Select Committee on Children, Youth, and Families, which explored ways both the public and private sector could improve the condition of children and families in the United States. (The committee was abolished in 1995 by the Republican Congress.) Schroeder's campaign for families has extended beyond her work in Congress; in *Champion of the Great American Family* (Random House), published in 1989, she outlined a family policy agenda for the twenty-first century.

A fierce champion of abortion rights, Schroeder has fought congressional efforts to restrict access to abortion through such moves as outlawing late-term abortions and reinstituting the "gag rule" on providing information about abortion to clients of federally funded family planning clinics. She has been a key sponsor of the Freedom of Choice Act, which would codify the essential provisions of the 1973 *Roe v. Wade* decision into law. In 1995, she introduced two abortion-related bills into the 104th Congress. One, the Women's Right To Know Act, would amend the 1964 Civil Rights Act to prohibit any governmental restrictions on the right to provide or receive information on the availability of reproductive health care services, including family planning, prenatal care, adoption, and abortion services. The other, the Women's Choice and Reproductive Health Protection Act of 1995, would codify the right to abortion and put in place policies that would provide funding for abortion services for rape and incest victims; protect clinics from violent protests; implement breast cancer, cervical cancer, and chlamydia screening programs in each state; fully implement legislation to establish contraceptive and infertility research programs; authorize family planning programs; prohibit "gag rules" on information pertaining to reproductive medical services; assure fairness in the evaluation of mifepristone (RU 486) and other antiprogestins; prohibit governmental restrictions on insurance coverage for abortions; and guarantee the ability of military service personnel overseas to purchase abortion services at military facilities.

In December 1995, Schroeder surprised supporters and foes alike by announcing that she would not run for reelection in 1996. At the time of her announcement she had no definite plans for the future, though she has not ruled out running for another political office.

Eleanor Smeal (1939–)

Eleanor Smeal has been active and visible in women's rights issues for many years; her interest in abortion rights grew out of her wider concerns with women's rights in general. As president of the National Organization for Women (NOW) from 1977 through 1982 and again from 1985 through 1987, she helped build that organization from 35,000 to over 220,000 members. During her second term, she led the National March for Women's Lives in 1986, in addition to organizing seven other marches around the nation, working to defeat antiabortion referenda in four states, and developing an aggressive legal strategy against violence and harassment aimed at abortion clinics. She continues to serve NOW as the National Advisory Chair, and has gone on to form her own organization, the Feminist Majority, of which she is president. Reproductive rights issues are a major focus for the Feminist Majority, which has produced two videos on abortion, *Abortion: For Survival* and *Abortion Denied: Shattering Young Women's Lives*. Smeal is also on the National Abortion Rights Coalition's steering committee. In addition to being a frequent speaker at abortion rights rallies and events, she has appeared on many national television shows.

A Phi Beta Kappa graduate of Duke University, Smeal holds an M.A. from the University of Florida. She has won a number of honors, including being named by *The World Almanac* for 1983 as the fourth most influential woman in the United States and by *Time* magazine as one of the "50 Faces for America's Future" in its August 6, 1979, cover story; she was also featured as one of the six most influential Washington lobbyists in a story by *U.S. News and World Report*. President Jimmy Carter appointed her to presidential commissions concerned with the International Women's Year and the White House Conference on the Family. She also served on the executive committee of the Leadership Conference on Civil Rights; was a member of the Council of Presidents, an organization of major women's rights groups; and serves on the boards of many other civil rights and women's rights organizations.

Christopher Smith (1953–)

Representative Christopher Smith (R-NJ) is an eight-term congressman whose passionate hatred of abortion has made him the "point man" for the pro-life movement in Congress. Smith once compared the core group of House antiabortion legislators to a basketball team, with himself playing the role of "playmaking guard, sometimes taking the shot and other times passing, but stealing the ball as often as possible." Other members of his "team" include Representatives Henry Hyde (R-IL), the "slam dunker," Robert Dornan (R-CA), the "shooting guard," and William Dannemeyer (R-CA), a "forward."

Smith traces his interest in abortion back to 1972, when he was a student at Trenton State College. He read an Associated Press story about a fetus that survived an abortion, and that "got the wheels turning about where were those child's rights." After graduating in 1975, he worked in his family's sporting goods business and got involved in politics, managing the Senate campaign of Democrat Steve Foley. Foley lost, but Smith discovered an appetite for both hard work and the political arena. In 1976, he became the executive director of the New Jersey Right to Life Committee. He switched parties and ran for Congress in 1978 as the token opposition to Frank Thompson, then chairman of the House Administration Committee. In 1980, however, Thompson was convicted of bribery and conspiracy in the Abscam scandal and lost his seat to Smith. Critics said his election was a fluke and attributed it to luck, but Smith has since been reelected seven times, despite being targeted by abortion rights groups for defeat.

With respect to abortion, Smith is an absolutist, stating that all abortion is murder and anyone who performs an abortion is a murderer. He does not make exceptions for cases of rape, incest, or fetal defects. As cochairman and tactician of the Pro-Life Caucus in the House, he played a key role in maintaining congressional opposition to funding elective abortions through Medicaid and other government-financed health care programs. Most recently, he has been involved in efforts to reverse President Clinton's 1993 executive orders that loosened previously enacted restrictions on abortion. Affirming his commitment to life, he has also introduced legislation that promotes adoption and provides maternal health care vouchers to pregnant women.

Despite his hard-line stance on abortion, Smith sees himself as a moderate conservative with an intense commitment to human rights both in the United States and abroad. He repeatedly opposed the Reagan and Bush administrations on issues like health care and the environment, and votes frequently with Democrats on economic, foreign, and cultural issues. Prior to the collapse of the Soviet Union and other Communist governments in Eastern Europe, he was a leading critic of the widespread human rights abuses perpetrated by these regimes. In 1985, he introduced legislation that led to the revocation of Most Favored Nation trading status for Romania, due to the brutal policies of dictator Nicolae Ceaucescu. More recently, he has been a leader in efforts to revoke Most Favored Nation status for the People's Republic of China, in part because of the "one-child-per-couple" policy that has led to forced sterilizations and abortions. In 1989, he was appointed by President George Bush to serve as a congressional delegate to the United Nations. After the Republicans took control of the House in 1994, Speaker of the House Newt Gingrich picked Smith to serve as Chair of the Commission on Security and Cooperation, commonly known as the Helsinki Commission. He has received numerous awards for his work in the international arena, including the Leader for Peace Award from the Peace Corps in recognition of his legislative initiatives to increase the Corps' funding and volunteer base. Smith has also been widely credited with saving the Child Survival Fund, a federal program that provides immunizations, oral hydration therapy, and other health care services to children in Third World countries that had been slated for elimination.

Randall Terry (1959–)

In the late 1980s, Randall Terry skyrocketed to national fame as the founder and leader of Operation Rescue, the organization that has staged hundreds of demonstrations and clinic blockades around the country, leading to thousands of arrests. Terry himself has been arrested numerous times and has accumulated more than a year in jail. The intense, charismatic Terry, who makes no secret of his political ambitions, sees his battle against abortion as nothing less than a crusade to save the nation from God's judgment, which he believes will bring down immense suffering on Americans as punishment for their continued tolerance of abortion.

A New York native, Terry graduated from the Elim Bible Institute in Lima, New York, in 1981. While at Elim he learned about the work of Francis Schaeffer, an evangelical writer who advocated political action to attack the moral decay of western culture—decay that he attributed in large part to abortion. On January 22, 1984, Terry rode a bus to Washington, D.C., to participate in the annual March for Life. It was during that trip that Terry, whose preaching ability was already becoming known around Binghamton, says he first envisioned Operation Rescue. Later that year, he and his wife, Cindy, began Project Life, standing outside abortion clinics in Binghamton—she full time, he during lunch hours and days off— trying to persuade women not to enter. The two were soon joined by other members of their church. In October 1984, the Terrys opened a Crisis Pregnancy Center, followed three years later by a home for unwed mothers.

In January 1986, Terry and six others carried out their first rescue mission, locking themselves in one of the inner rooms of an abortion clinic before the clinic personnel were due to arrive. They were arrested, convicted, and fined $60. Terry refused to pay and was sentenced to jail for the first time. Nearly two years later, on November 28, 1987, he mounted his first large-scale "rescue." Three hundred people blocked the Cherry Hill Women's Clinic in Cherry Hill, New Jersey. Since Cherry Hill, Operation Rescue has conducted hundreds of "rescue" operations, generating huge amounts of publicity and incurring the wrath of abortion rights groups.

Terry has appeared on national television and been the subject of several news documentaries. He is the star of a video about Operation Rescue and the author of five books. Since February 1992, Terry has also had his own radio show, "Randall Terry Live." The show went into syndication in 1995, airing five days a week on about 40 stations, many of them in major markets. A singer and songwriter who plays saxophone and piano, Terry has also recorded record albums, including one of antiabortion songs called "When the Battle Raged." Despite numerous financial and legal setbacks, including lawsuits by abortion rights groups, jail sentences, and hefty fines, Terry continues undaunted, speaking frequently around the United States and rallying his loyal troops in the ongoing fight against abortion, infanticide, and euthanasia. He has also started a Christian leadership school in Windsor, New York, where his radio show is based.

Sarah Weddington (1945–)

In 1967, as a young attorney fresh out of the University of Texas School of Law, Sarah Weddington was looking to make her mark on the world. By 1973, she had done so, as the lawyer who argued for the winning side in one of the most famous (or infamous) cases ever to be decided by the Supreme Court, *Roe v. Wade.*

Born in Abilene, Texas, Weddington grew up in small, rural Texas towns, the daughter of a Methodist preacher and a college business teacher. After graduating from law school, she found the opportunities for women attorneys in Texas rather limited. For the next two years she worked as Assistant Reporter for the American Bar Foundation Special Committee on the Reevaluation of Ethical Standards. In 1969, Weddington met with a group of women who wanted to know if they would be breaking the law by referring women to places where they could get safe abortions in Mexico. In the process of researching their question, Weddington decided to challenge the constitutionality of Texas's restrictive abortion laws. She enlisted the help of Linda Coffee, who had been in her law school class, and by December of that year the two women had succeeded in locating a plaintiff for their case—Norma McCorvey, who would be known to the world as Jane Roe. As they had hoped, the case eventually ended up in the Supreme Court, where Weddington became, as far as is known, the youngest woman ever to win a case.

In the meantime, Weddington had gone into private practice in Austin as a family law specialist and become the first woman from Austin to be elected to the Texas House of Representatives. She served three terms before going to Washington, D.C., as general counsel for the U.S. Department of Agriculture. From 1978 to 1981, she served as an assistant to President Jimmy Carter on women's issues and appointments. After a year spent as a law professor at the University of New Mexico, she returned to Washington and became the top lobbyist for the state of Texas as director of the Office of State-Federal Relations.

Although currently in practice in Austin, Weddington spends a great deal of her time traveling and lecturing on the *Roe v. Wade* decision and other law topics related to abortion and reproductive rights. She is in constant demand as a speaker, giving as many as three speeches a week at campuses, state bar conventions, law schools, and attorneys' organizations and appearing on radio and national television. She also teaches part-time at the University of Texas at Austin in the Departments of Government and American Studies. A past president of the National Abortion Rights Action League (NARAL), she currently serves on the boards of several nonprofit foundations. She has written columns and articles for national magazines, and in 1992 she published *A Question of Choice*, an autobiographical account of the events leading up to and following *Roe v. Wade* [see chapter 5]. Weddington has received numerous honors and awards, including being named an "Outstanding Young Leader" by *Time* magazine, one of the ten "Outstanding Women in America" in 1979, and an "American under 40 Making Things Happen" by *Esquire* in 1984, and receiving the "Woman of the Future Award" from *Ladies Home Journal*. She has received several honorary doctorates and was named by the National Association for Campus Activities as 1990 Lecturer of the Year.

John C. Willke (1925–)

John C. Willke is one of the most powerful and best-known leaders in the pro-life movement. He is the founder and president of both the International Right to Life Federation and Life Issues Institute, a pro-life educational foundation. He was a founding board member of the National Right to Life Committee, the country's largest pro-life organization, which he served as president from 1981 through 1991. In addition, Willke hosts a daily radio program, "Life Issues," which is broadcast on almost 300 stations, and serves as a principal pro-life contact for members of Congress.

A native of Ohio, Willke attended Catholic schools before graduating from Oberlin College and the University of Cincinnati medical school. He went into private practice as a physician in Cincinnati in the early 1950s, not long after marrying Barbara, a nurse. Devout Catholics, the Willkes have been fighting abortion since 1970, when they began incorporating abortion into their sex education lectures. They had begun giving talks on sex in 1953, first to Bible study classes, then in churches and at church-related functions. Soon they were doing premarriage counseling and talking to parents about how to teach their children about sex. In 1964, the Willkes published *How To Teach Children the Wonders of Sex*, the first of ten books the couple has written in the field of abortion and sexuality. The popular book was recently revised, after 16 printings in 20 years.

Soon after they began talking about abortion, the Willkes began collecting pictures of aborted fetuses to use in their presentations. In 1971, they incorporated the pictures into the *Handbook on Abortion*, which has been called the "bible of the pro-life movement" [see chapter 5]. It has since been supplanted by *Abortion: Questions and Answers*, a pocket-sized book that contains over 1,000 questions and answers and that is meant to be carried in a purse or wallet. Willke's most recent book is *Abortion and Slavery: History Repeats* (Cincinnati: Hayes Publishing, 1970). In addition to their own books, the Willkes have contributed to several other books, published articles in more than 70 publications, and had their works translated into 28 languages. They have also appeared in five educational movies and numerous videos. Through their own publishing company, Hayes Publishing, the Willkes produce and market a wide array of materials on abortion and related issues, including books, slide presentations, videos, posters, flyers, and brochures. A frequent guest on radio and national television, Willke has been featured in *People* magazine and, with his wife, has lectured in 63 countries during the last decade.

Facts and Statistics 3

This chapter provides general facts and statistics relating to abortion in several areas, so that readers can construct a basis for evaluating what they read, see, and hear about abortion in other books, in the media, and from individuals and organizations. The information given is as factual as possible; of course, interpretations of the meaning or significance of a given fact or statistic will vary greatly with respect to individual positions and feelings on the issues involved. Of necessity, the information contained here is relatively brief. Therefore, suggestions for further reading are included where appropriate.

The chapter includes the following sections:

- **Abortion Laws and Policies.** An overview of abortion laws and policies in the United States and around the world.
- **Landmark Court Cases.** Brief summaries of significant Supreme Court cases regarding abortion.
- **Abortion Statistics.** An overview of abortion statistics, with emphasis on abortions in the United States. Included are statistics on the number,

rate, and frequency of abortions; characteristics of women having abortions; weeks of gestation; types of techniques used; why women have abortions; reasons for having late abortions; and abortion-related deaths.

- **Abortion Access.** A statistical overview of the availability of abortion services in the United States.
- **Harassment of Abortion Providers and Antiabortion Violence.** A statistical overview of violence and illegal or harassing acts directed at abortion providers since the legalizing of abortion in 1973, plus a description of the Freedom of Access to Clinic Entrances (FACE) Act.
- **Public Opinion and Abortion.** A brief statistical overview of opinion polls about abortion, including a discussion of the issues involved in measuring public opinion about controversial issues such as abortion.
- **Abortion Techniques.** Brief descriptions of the medical techniques used for abortions, including instrumental techniques such as vacuum aspiration, medical techniques such as intra amniotic instillation, major surgical techniques, and folk methods. Also included in this section is a discussion of mifepristone (RU 486), the so-called French "abortion pill."
- **Abortion Complications and Long-Term Impact.** An overview of the possible medical complications and long-term medical and psychological impact of abortion.
- **Overview of Embryonic and Fetal Development.** A descriptive overview of the stages of human development from fertilization through birth.

Abortion Laws and Policies

Worldwide

Worldwide, the laws and policies governing induced abortion range from complete prohibition to abortion on request, at least in the early stages of pregnancy. In a number of countries, particularly in Europe and the United States [see below], abortion laws have been in a state of flux in recent years. The most recent comprehensive study of abortion laws worldwide is still Stanley Henshaw's "Induced Abortion: A World Review, 1990," originally published in *Family Planning Perspectives*. According to Henshaw, as of January 1, 1990:

- 53 countries (including dependent territories) with populations of 1 million or more prohibited abortions except to save the life of the pregnant woman; these countries comprise 25 percent of the world's population.

- 42 countries, comprising 12 percent of the world's population, permitted abortion on broad medical grounds, including threats to the woman's general health. In some countries, the woman's physical health must be threatened; others explicitly or by interpretation include threats to mental health as well. Some of these countries also permit abortion for genetic or juridical indications, as in the case of rape.
- 14 countries, comprising 23 percent of the world's population, allowed abortions for social or social-medical indications, including "adverse social conditions." Practically speaking, abortion is available virtually on request in many of these countries, including Australia, Finland, Great Britain, Japan, and Taiwan.
- 23 countries, comprising about 40 percent of the world's population, permitted abortion on the request of the pregnant woman. These include China, the Soviet Union, the United States, and about half of Europe. Sweden and Yugoslavia were among several countries that explicitly define abortion as the right of a pregnant woman.

Table 1 [see page 102] shows a detailed breakdown of countries in each category.

Further Reading

For further reading on abortion laws in other countries [see chapter 5 for complete listings]:

Francome, Colin. *Abortion Freedom: A Worldwide Movement.* London: George Allen & Unwin, 1984.

Glendon, Mary Ann. *Abortion and Divorce in Western Law.* Cambridge, MA: Harvard University Press, 1987.

Henshaw, Stanley K. "Induced Abortion: A World Review, 1990." In *Abortion Factbook, 1992 Edition: Readings, Trends, and State and Local Data to 1988,* edited by Stanley Henshaw and Jennifer Van Vort. New York: Alan Guttmacher Institute, 1992.

Jacobson, Jodi. *The Global Politics of Abortion: Worldwatch Paper 97.* Washington, DC: Worldwatch Institute, 1990.

Rolston, Bill, and Anna Eggert, eds. *Abortion in the New Europe: A Comparative Handbook.* Westport, CT: Greenwood Press, 1994.

Sachdev, Paul, ed. *International Handbook on Abortion.* Westport, CT: Greenwood Press, 1988.

Tietze, Christopher, and Stanley K. Henshaw. *Induced Abortion: A World Review, 1986.* New York: Alan Guttmacher Institute, 1986.

Table 1. Countries, by restrictiveness of abortion law, according to region, January 1, 1990

Law	Africa	Asia & Oceania	Europe	North America	South America
To save a woman's life	Angola Benin Botswana Burkina Faso Central Afr. Rep. Chad Côte d'Ivoire Gabon Libya Madagascar Malawi Mali Mauritania Mauritius Mozambique Niger Nigeria Senegal Somalia Sudan Zaire	Afghanistan Bangladesh Burma Indonesia Iran Iraq Laos Lebanon Oman Pakistan Philippines Sri Lanka Syria United Arab Emirates Yemen Arab Rep. Yemen, Peoples' Democratic Rep.	Belgium Ireland	Dominican Rep. El Salvador*,† Guatemala Haiti Honduras Mexico* Nicaragua Panama	Brazil* Chile Colombia Ecuador* Paraguay Venezuela
Other maternal health reasons	Algeria Cameroon* Congo Egypt† Ethiopia Ghana*,† Guinea Kenya Lesotho Liberia*,† Morocco Namibia*,† Rwanda Sierra Leone South Africa*,† Tanzania Uganda Zimbabwe*,†	Hong Kong*,† Israel*,† Jordan* Korea, Rep. of*,† Kuwait† Malaysia*,† Mongolia Nepal New Zealand*,† Papua New Guinea Saudi Arabia Thailand*	Albania Northern Ireland Portugal*,† Spain*,† Switzerland	Costa Rica Jamaica Trinidad & Tobago	Argentina* Bolivia* Guyana Peru
Social and social-medical reasons	Burundi Zambia†	Australia† India**,†† Japan*,†,§§ Korea, Dem. Rep.*,† Taiwan*,†	Bulgaria*,†,‡ Finland*,†,‡,‡‡ German Fed. Rep.*,†,‡‡,*† Great Britain† Hungary*,†,‡,‡‡ Poland*,§§,‡‡		Uruguay*,§
On request	Togo Tunisia‡‡	China Singapore Turkey§§ Vietnam	Austria‡‡,*† Czechoslovakia‡‡ Denmark‡‡ France§§ German Dem. Rep.‡‡ Greece‡‡ Italy‡‡ Netherlands Norway‡‡ Romania‡‡ Soviet Union‡‡ Sweden*‡ Yugoslavia††	Canada Cuba†† Puerto Rico United States	

[Notes appear on facing page]

United States

Prior to the 1973 *Roe v. Wade* Supreme Court decision, state laws on abortion were a patchwork ranging from complete prohibition to abortion essentially on request; during the late 1960s and early 1970s there was a slow but recognizable trend toward liberalization of abortion laws. In one stroke, however, *Roe v. Wade* invalidated the laws of nearly all 50 states and established the trimester system of regulating abortion. Under this system, the Court ruled that:

- The state does not have any compelling interest in regulating abortions during the first trimester (12 weeks) of pregnancy, except to require that an abortion be performed by a licensed physician in a medical setting.
- The state's only interest in regulating abortions during the second trimester (12 through 24 weeks) is to protect maternal health.
- When the fetus becomes viable (capable of independent survival outside the womb, with or without artificial life support) the state may choose to limit abortions to women for whom continued pregnancy would be life-threatening. The determination as to viability, however, is a medical and not a legal or judicial matter. Although *Roe* made abortion technically legal throughout pregnancy, it specifically permitted states to restrict abortions following viability, which most medical experts consider to be around the twenty-fourth week of gestation.

States began to test the limits of the ruling almost immediately, passing such restrictions as parental and spousal consent requirements and refusing to use Medicaid funds to pay for abortions.

Table 1 Notes

*Includes juridical grounds, such as rape and incest.   †Incudes abortion for genetic defects.

‡Approval is automatic for women who meet certain age, marital and/or parity requirements.

§Not permitted for health reasons but may be permitted for serious economic difficulty.

**During the first 20 weeks.   ††During the first 10 weeks.

‡‡During the first three months or 12 weeks.

§§No formal authorization is required, and abortion is permitted in doctor's office; thus, abortion is de facto available on request.

*†Gestational limit is for interval since implantation.   *‡During the first 18 weeks.

Notes: Table does not include countries with fewer than one million inhabitants or those for which information on the legal status of abortion could not be located (e.g., Bhutan and Kampuchea). All abortions are permitted only prior to fetal viability unless otherwise indicated in footnotes.

Source: Stanley K. Henshaw, "Induced Abortion: A World Review, 1990." *Family Planning Perspectives*, Vol. 22, No. 2 (March/April 1990), p. 77.

Throughout the 1970s, the Supreme Court overruled most attempts to restrict abortion. During the 1980s, however, the Court began to shift in the opposite direction. In *Harris v. McRae* (1980), by a slim majority, the Court upheld the constitutionality of the Hyde amendment, a law originally passed in 1976 that barred the use of federal Medicaid funds to pay for abortion except to save the mother's life. During the rest of the decade, as liberal justices began to retire and were replaced by more conservative Reagan and Bush appointees, the Court became increasingly willing to uphold laws restricting abortion.

The 1989 *Webster v. Reproductive Health Services* decision marked a major turning point in the debate. In *Webster*, the Court upheld nearly all of the provisions of Missouri's abortion law, including a parental consent requirement, a prohibition on the use of public facilities or public employees for performing abortions, and a requirement that physicians test for fetal viability in pregnancies of 20 weeks or more. In doing so, the Court explicitly rejected the trimester framework of *Roe v. Wade* and emphasized the state's compelling interest in protecting life throughout pregnancy. In their opinions, four of the justices clearly indicated their desire to overturn the fundamental privacy right to choose abortion found in *Roe*.

In the wake of *Webster*, states continued to pass more restrictive laws, which the Court for the most part upheld, along with the Reagan and Bush administrations' "gag rule" prohibiting federally funded planning clinics from even mentioning abortion to their clients. Many people expected that it was only a matter of time before the Court struck down *Roe v. Wade* altogether. In 1992, however, in *Planned Parenthood v. Casey*, the Supreme Court issued a fragmented, no-majority decision that reaffirmed the essential holding of *Roe*—that women have a constitutional right to abortion—while simultaneously affirming the state's "profound interest" in protecting potential life. The decision meant that although states cannot prohibit abortion, they may enact regulations to make sure that women are informed, to encourage them to bear children rather than choose abortion, and to further the health or safety of women seeking abortions. Essentially, the justices said, restrictions on abortion were allowable as long as they did not impose a "substantial obstacle" or "undue burden" on a woman seeking an abortion.

The combined effect of *Webster*, *Casey*, and the other decisions was to put abortion regulation largely back in the hands of the states. With the addition of Clinton appointees Ruth Bader Ginsburg and Stephen Breyer, plus the apparent moderate stance of Reagan and Bush appointees Anthony Kennedy, Sandra Day

O'Connor, and David Souter, the Supreme Court has shifted more toward the center and is unlikely either to vanquish *Roe* or revitalize it any time soon. As a result, the focus has shifted largely away from the courts and into state legislatures.

On a national level, abortion continues to be a hotly debated topic in Congress. Since 1973, antiabortion lawmakers have tried repeatedly to pass legislation or a constitutional amendment banning abortion. They have not succeeded, but neither have their opponents succeeded in enacting the provisions of *Roe* into federal law. As of 1995, abortion opponents hold a solid majority of seats in the House and a slim majority in the Senate, but probably cannot muster the strength to override an almost-certain presidential veto of any law prohibiting or seriously restricting abortion. Abortion is certain to be an issue in the 1996 presidential and congressional races, and the tug-of-war is likely to continue into the foreseeable future and beyond.

A Snapshot of State Abortion Laws

The following is an overview of state abortion laws as of January 1995:*

Abortion Bans

- After *Webster*, two states (Louisiana and Utah) and the territory of Guam enacted laws banning virtually all abortions. In *Planned Parenthood v. Casey*, the Supreme Court indicated that a total ban on abortion would be unconstitutional. In 1992 and 1993, respectively, the Court turned down requests to review lower court rulings that found the Guam and Louisiana laws unconstitutional. In 1994, Utah abandoned its challenge to a 1991 ruling striking down its law.
- Unenforceable pre-*Roe* laws prohibiting abortion in most cases are on the books in 16 states and the District of Columbia.

Counseling Bans

Three states (Louisiana, Missouri, and North Dakota) have "gag rules" that prohibit health care providers who are employed by the state or by entities receiving state funding from counseling women about abortion or referring them to abortion services.

---

* Source: *Who Decides: A State-by-State Review of Abortion and Reproductive Rights.*
 5th ed. Washington, DC: National Abortion Rights Action League, 1995.

Spousal Consent Requirements

Eleven states have laws requiring notice or consent of the husband before a woman may obtain an abortion. The laws are currently unenforceable because, in *Planned Parenthood v. Casey*, the Supreme Court held that mandatory spousal notification or consent provisions are unconstitutional.

Restrictions on Minors' Access to Abortion

- Thirty-five states have laws on the books that require parental notification or consent before a minor can obtain an abortion; these laws are enforced in 24 states. In 20 of the states, minors can appear before a judge and request to have the requirement waived.
- In three states (Maryland, Tennessee, and West Virginia), a physician can waive the notice requirement.
- Two states (Connecticut and Maine) do not require that parents be notified, but do require a minor to receive counseling that includes discussing the possibility of involving her parents.

Informed Consent/Waiting Periods

- Thirty-one states have laws that require a woman to give "informed consent" before having an abortion. In many of the states, the woman must receive a lecture and state-prepared materials on fetal development, prenatal care, and adoption. Such informed consent provisions were upheld by the Supreme Court in *Planned Parenthood v. Casey*.
- Fifteen states with informed consent laws also have mandatory waiting periods ranging from 1 to 72 hours (most are 24 hours); these are enforced in seven states (Kansas, Mississippi, Nebraska, North Dakota, Ohio, Pennsylvania, and Utah).

Legislative Declarations

- Four states (Illinois, Kentucky, Louisiana, and South Dakota) have passed laws declaring the intent of the legislature to prohibit abortions if and when *Roe v. Wade* is overturned.
- Four states (Connecticut, Maine, Maryland, and Washington) have laws affirming a woman's right to choose abortion before viability, and at any time to preserve her life or health.

- One state (Nevada) has a law that protects a woman's right to choose abortion during the first 24 weeks of pregnancy; the law cannot be changed without a referendum vote.

Public Funding for Abortions

- Nine states refuse to use medical assistance (Medicaid) funds to pay for abortion except when the woman's life is endangered, in defiance of a federal law that requires states that participate in Medicaid to fund abortion in cases of rape, incest, or life endangerment.
- Twenty-two states fund abortion in cases of rape, incest, or where the woman's life is in danger.
- Two states fund abortion in cases of rape, incest, life endangerment, and some health circumstances.
- Seventeen states and the District of Columbia fund abortion in almost or all circumstances.

Other Restrictions

- In 43 states, abortions must be performed by a licensed physician.
- Five states (Kentucky, Louisiana, Missouri, North Dakota, and Pennsylvania) prohibit the use of public facilities for abortion services.
- Three states (Alabama, Louisiana, and Missouri) require physicians to test for viability in certain circumstances; the Louisiana law has been ruled unconstitutional.

Further Reading

Sources of further information or discussion on abortion laws and policies include [see chapter 5 for detailed listings]:

Abortion in the United States: A Compilation of State Legislation. Buffalo, NY: William S. Hein, 1991.

Butler, J. Douglas, and David F. Walbert, eds. *Abortion, Medicine, and the Law.* 4th ed. New York: Facts on File, 1992.

Glendon, Mary Ann. *Abortion and Divorce in Western Law.* Cambridge, MA: Harvard University Press, 1987.

Henshaw, Stanley K. "Induced Abortion: A World Review, 1990." In *Abortion Factbook, 1992 Edition: Readings, Trends, and State and Local Data to 1988*, edited by Stanley Henshaw and Jennifer Van Vort. New York: Alan Guttmacher Institute, 1992.

National Abortion Rights Action League (NARAL). *Who Decides: A State-by-State Review of Abortion and Reproductive Rights.* 5th ed. Washington, DC: National Abortion Rights Action League, 1995.
Tietze, Christopher, and Stanley K. Henshaw. *Induced Abortion: A World Review, 1986.* New York: Alan Guttmacher Institute, 1986.

Several organizations [see chapter 4] have legislative hotlines and/or publish periodic updates and/or analyses of current and pending legislation and court decisions, including:

- American Civil Liberties Union Reproductive Freedom Project
- Americans United for Life Legal Defense Fund
- National Abortion Rights Action League
- National Organization for Women
- National Right to Life Committee
- Religious Coalition for Reproductive Choice

Landmark Court Cases

Griswold v. Connecticut, 381 U.S. 479 (1965)

In 1961, two Connecticut Planned Parenthood officials, Estelle Griswold and Dr. C. Lee Buxton, were arrested for dispensing contraceptives and information regarding their use to married couples—an arrest they had deliberately sought in order to challenge the state's 1879 law banning the use of contraceptives by married couples. They were convicted in state court and fined $100. The state appeals court upheld the convictions, and the defendants appealed to the Supreme Court, seeking to have the law declared unconstitutional on the grounds that it violated married persons' right to privacy.

The Court announced its decision on June 7, 1965. By a seven-to-two vote, the justices declared the Connecticut law invalid because it violated a right to privacy that was implicit in the First, Third, Fourth, Fifth, and Ninth Amendments to the Constitution. Writing for the majority, Justice William O. Douglas cited the "zone of privacy created by several fundamental constitutional guarantees."

The *Griswold v. Connecticut* decision was the first time the Court specifically stated that a right to privacy is inherent in the Constitution. As such, the case served as a critical precedent for a number of later controversial cases, including the 1973 *Roe v. Wade* decision.

Baird v. Eisenstadt, 405 U.S. 438 (1970)

In 1967, during a lecture at Boston University, activist Bill Baird publicly challenged the Massachusetts "crimes against chastity" statute, under which only married couples could receive birth control information or materials, and then only from physicians. Before an audience of 1,500, Baird offered to distribute packages of contraceptive foam and read the names of Tokyo clinics specializing in abortion. Twelve women came forward to receive the foam, and Baird was arrested and later convicted. He appealed, and the case eventually reached the Supreme Court.

In its 1970 ruling, the Court overturned the Massachusetts law and extended to single people the right to privacy granted to married persons in *Griswold v. Connecticut*. The *Baird* decision provided another strong precedent for the *Roe v. Wade* decision three years later.

United States v. Vuitch, 402 U.S. 62 (1971)

In May 1968, Dr. Milan Vuitch, a Washington, D.C., surgeon, was arrested for performing nontherapeutic abortions in violation of the District's law prohibiting induced abortions except "as necessary for the preservation of the mother's life or health." Dr. Vuitch claimed that the abortions were performed to preserve the women's mental well-being and were therefore permitted under the "health" provision of the statute. Before the case could go to trial, the district court judge dismissed the charges on the ground that the statute was unconstitutionally vague, because the word "health" was ambiguous, and because a doctor who had performed an abortion was presumed guilty and therefore bore the burden of proving to a jury that the abortion was medically necessary.

The government appealed the judgment directly to the Supreme Court. On April 21, 1971, the Court issued its decision upholding the constitutionality of the law by a vote of five to two, with two justices not voting. In effect, however, the decision actually strengthened abortion rights in the District of Columbia, by broadening two existing rights. Ruling that the phrase "preservation of life or health" was not unconstitutionally vague, the Court nonetheless expanded the definition of health to include "psychological as well as physical well-being." Further, the Court placed the burden of proof as to whether or not an abortion was necessary on the prosecution rather than on the physician, stating, "We are unable to believe that Congress intended that a physician be required to prove his innocence." The case was remanded to federal district court, but the Justice Department elected not to pursue the charges against Vuitch.

Roe v. Wade and Doe v. Bolton

Roe v. Wade, 410 U.S. 113 (1973)

Late in 1969, two young Texas attorneys, Sarah Weddington and Linda Coffee, set out to overturn the state's restrictive abortion law. The statutes, passed in 1857, made performing abortion a crime except to save the life of the mother, with no exceptions for rape or incest. It took the lawyers several weeks to find an appropriate plaintiff in the person of Norma McCorvey, a 21-year-old high school dropout and waitress who was pregnant with her third child. Barely able to support herself, much less a child (the first lived with McCorvey's mother, the second with the child's father), she wanted to terminate the pregnancy. However, she did not want to risk an illegal abortion, and she could not afford to travel to another state to obtain a legal one. Although doing so was unlikely to help her win an abortion for herself (she later had the child and gave it up for adoption), McCorvey agreed to serve as the plaintiff for the challenge to the Texas laws under the pseudonym of Jane Roe. Except for signing a brief affidavit stating her situation, "Roe" had no further actual involvement in the case, which the lawyers were handling pro bono.

On behalf of Jane Roe, a married couple, John and Mary Doe, and Dr. James Hubert Hallford, a physician who had been charged under the Texas law, Weddington and Coffee filed lawsuits against Henry Wade, the Dallas County district attorney, to prevent him from enforcing the Texas statutes. The attorneys asked for a three-judge court, consisting of a member of the federal circuit court of appeals and two district court judges, to make the decision. On June 17, 1970, the three-judge panel handed down its decision declaring the Texas law unconstitutional because it deprived married couples and single women of their privacy right, as secured by the Ninth Amendment, not to have children. However, the court refused to order the district attorney not to prosecute doctors for performing abortions, and Wade soon announced that he would continue to prosecute. This decision allowed Weddington and Coffee to immediately appeal their case to the Supreme Court, bypassing the Fifth Circuit Court of Appeals.

Doe v. Bolton, *410 U.S. 179 (1973)*

Doe v. Bolton, the lesser-known companion case to *Roe v. Wade,* arose from a challenge to Georgia's abortion laws. The Georgia statute, enacted in 1968, prohibited abortions except in cases where, in the best judgment of the physician, continuing the pregnancy would endanger the woman's life or "seriously and permanently injure her health"; where the fetus would "very likely be born with grave, permanent, and irreparable mental or physical defect"; or where the pregnancy was the result of rape or incest. The law also required that abortions be performed in hospitals accredited by the Joint Commission on Accreditation of Hospitals (JCAH); that the abortion be approved by a majority vote of a three-doctor hospital committee, as well as by two physicians in addition to the woman's personal physician; and that a woman receiving an abortion must be a Georgia resident.

In March 1970, Mary Doe, an indigent 22-year-old Georgia woman, requested a therapeutic abortion. She had already had three children, two of whom had been placed in foster care and the other put up for adoption because she was unable to care for them. Marital and financial problems had increased the stress in her life to the point where she had become a patient at a state mental hospital. For these reasons, she claimed that continuing her pregnancy would present a grave risk to her mental and physical well-being. She was denied the abortion, and in April a lawsuit was filed in the District Court of Northern Georgia on behalf of Doe and 23 other plaintiffs, including physicians, clergy, nurses, and social workers. The suit asked the court to strike down the Georgia law and issue an injunction against its enforcement.

The district court invalidated some of the law's restrictions, including the provisions that limited legal abortions to pregnancies that resulted from rape or incest, in which there was a risk of fetal defect, or where the woman's life or health was threatened. The case was then appealed to the Supreme Court.

The Decisions

The Court heard arguments in both cases in December 1971 and again in October 1972. Roe's lawyers argued that the Texas law violated fundamental personal rights secured by the First, Fourth, Ninth, and Fourteenth Amendments. They also cited evidence showing that the government did not treat fetuses as persons in any other instance and that fetuses were therefore not protected under the Fourteenth Amendment. The arguments by the state of

Texas centered on the state's right to make its own decisions regarding the regulation of abortion and on its compelling interest in protecting the mother's health during pregnancy and protecting the "potential life" of the unborn child, whose right to life outweighed a woman's right to privacy. In the Georgia case, Doe's lawyers also argued that the client's inability to obtain a legal abortion deprived her of her constitutional rights to privacy and abridged her rights under the Fourth, Ninth, and Fourteenth Amendments.

On January 22, 1973, the Court handed down decisions in both cases. By seven-to-two votes, the Court struck down both laws as unconstitutional. Voting with the majority on both cases were Chief Justice Warren Burger and Justices Harry Blackmun, William Brennan, Lewis Powell, Potter Stewart, Thurgood Marshall, and William O. Douglas. Justices William Rehnquist and Byron White dissented.

The rulings were largely based on the precedent of a constitutional right to privacy established in the *Griswold v. Connecticut* contraception ruling of 1965. The Court interpreted the First, Fifth, Ninth, and Fourteenth Amendments to the Constitution to support a woman's right to an abortion, particularly the liberty clause in the Fourteenth Amendment, which forbids any state to "deprive any person of life, liberty, or property, without due process of law." Writing for the majority in *Roe*, Justice Harry Blackmun stated that "This right of privacy, whether it be founded in the Fourteenth Amendment's concept of personal liberty and restrictions upon state action, as we feel it is, or as the district court determined, in the Ninth Amendment's reservation of rights to the people, is broad enough to encompass a woman's decision whether or not to terminate her pregnancy."

However, Blackmun continued, this right was not absolute and must be weighed against other factors. "Although the right to privacy cannot be overruled by the state, the state does retain an interest in the protection of the health of the pregnant woman and the potential life she carries." Therefore, the state is entitled to regulate abortion in some degree, and that degree increases as the pregnancy progresses. Blackmun then went on to apply the concepts of pregnancy trimesters and viability, stating in essence that:

- The state does not have any compelling interest in regulating abortions during the first trimester (12 weeks) of pregnancy, except to require that an abortion be performed by a licensed physician in a medical setting.

- The state's only interest in regulating abortions during the second trimester (12 through 24 weeks) is to protect maternal health.
- When the fetus becomes viable (capable of independent survival outside the womb, with or without artificial life support) the state may choose to limit abortions to women for whom continued pregnancy would be life-threatening. The determination as to viability, however, is a medical and not a legal or judicial matter.

In *Doe v. Bolton*, the Court upheld the provision that the decision of whether to perform an abortion should be made by a physician based on "his best clinical judgment." It struck down the provisions requiring abortions to be performed in accredited hospitals and approved by medical committees, as well as the residency requirement.

The justices specifically refused to deal with the question of "when life begins," but stated that, although the Constitution never defines what the word "person" includes, the word "person" as used in the Fourteenth Amendment does not include the unborn. These distinctions became important in later rulings regarding various state and federal restrictions on abortions and public funding for abortions.

Planned Parenthood of Central Missouri v. Danforth, 428 U.S. 52 (1976)

Two Missouri physicians who performed abortions filed a class-action suit challenging the state's restrictive abortion law on behalf of themselves and other physicians performing or desiring to perform abortions and pregnant women seeking to terminate their pregnancies. Among the provisions of the 1974 law were requirements that:

- The woman certify in writing her informed, noncoerced consent to the abortion.
- The woman obtain the written consent of her spouse, if she were married, or of a parent or guardian if she were a minor.
- Abortions done after the twelfth week be performed in a hospital.
- The attending physician certify that the fetus was not viable.

- The physician exercise professional care to preserve the life and health of the fetus, under penalty of a manslaughter charge.

The law also prohibited saline infusion abortions after the twelfth week and imposed strict reporting and record-keeping requirements on abortion providers.

The plaintiffs argued that the law deprived them and their patients of several constitutional rights, including the right to practice medicine as they saw fit and the right of female patients to decide for themselves whether to bear children. The federal district court upheld most of the provisions of the law, and the plaintiffs appealed to the Supreme Court.

The Court heard arguments in the case on March 23, 1976, and issued its decision on July 1 of that year. By a vote of six to three, the Court struck down the spousal and parental consent provisions, as well as the prohibition of saline infusion abortions after the first trimester and the requirement that physicians exercise professional care to preserve the fetus's life and health. It rejected the statute's attempt to define viability, stating that determining the point of viability is a medical, rather than a legislative or judiciary, decision. The Court upheld the provisions requiring a woman's written consent for abortion and the reporting and record-keeping requirements, noting that the records were required to remain confidential. Justices Blackmun, Brennan, Stewart, Marshall, Stevens, and Powell agreed with the majority. Chief Justice Burger and Justices White and Rehnquist dissented.

Bellotti v. Baird, 428 U.S. 132 (1974), 443 U.S. 623 (1977)

In 1974, Massachusetts passed a set of abortion laws that included a clause requiring unmarried women under the age of 18 to obtain the consent of both parents before having an abortion. The law included a provision allowing the parents' veto to be overridden by a judge; however, in such cases the parents had to be notified and allowed to present their side of the dispute in court.

A lawsuit challenging the law was filed by Bill Baird and four pregnant minors. Baird was president and director of the Parents' Aid Society, a nonprofit corporation that provided abortion services and counseling. The minors claimed to represent all others in their situation who were capable of giving mature, informed consent to an abortion without the consent or knowledge of their parents. The suit asked for injunctive and declarative relief on the basis that the statute violated the plaintiffs' Fourteenth Amendment rights. The defendants in the suit included the state attorney general and the district attorneys of all Massachusetts counties, plus Jane Hunerwadel, who, as a state resident and the parent of an unmarried teenager, was allowed to represent all other parents in similar situations.

A three-judge district court panel ruled the statute unconstitutional, declaring that it added another "tier" to the abortion decision by allowing a parental veto of a decision already reached by a physician and patient. The defendants appealed the decision to the Supreme Court, and arguments were heard on March 23, 1976.

On July 1, 1976, in a unanimous decision, the Supreme Court overturned the ruling of the lower court and reinstated the statute on the basis that the law did provide options for minors wishing to terminate their pregnancies. However, the Court remanded the case to federal district court for certification to the Supreme Judicial Court of Massachusetts, citing unresolved questions about the state legislature's intent and the meaning of several provisions.

On February 27, 1979, new arguments on the Massachusetts statute were heard before the Court. The plaintiffs this time were Bill Baird, Dr. Gerald Zupnick, who performed abortions at the Parents' Aid Clinic, and "Mary Moe," an unmarried pregnant teenager who lived with her parents and had been denied an abortion because she did not want to inform them about her decision. Moe represented all teenagers in similar situations. The defendants were the same as in the earlier case.

On July 2, 1979, the Supreme Court ruled that the parental consent provision was constitutionally defective in that it permitted courts to deny an abortion to a "mature and fully competent minor" and required parental notification and consultation, regardless of the minor's maturity, without giving her the opportunity to obtain an "independent judicial remedy." Voting with the majority were Justices Burger, Stewart, Rehnquist, Stevens, Marshall, Brennan, and Blackmun, with Justice White dissenting.

Maher v. Roe and *Beal v. Doe*

Maher v. Roe, 432 U.S. 464 (1977)

In 1975, the Connecticut Department of Social Services enacted a regulation saying that the department would make Medicaid payments for abortion only when a doctor had certified that the abortion was medically necessary (medical necessity included psychiatric reasons). The abortion had to be performed in an accredited hospital during the first trimester of pregnancy. Prior to receiving the abortion, the patient (or her parent or guardian, if she was a minor) had to submit a written request for the abortion and have it authorized by the Chief of Medical Services in the department's Division of Health Services.

A 16-year-old woman, "Mary Poe," had an abortion in a Connecticut hospital but could not pay for it. The Department of Social Services refused to reimburse the hospital on the grounds that the abortion was not medically necessary. Another woman, "Susan Roe," was not able to get an abortion because her doctor would not certify that it was medically necessary. The two women filed a lawsuit claiming that the regulation was unconstitutional and violated their Fourteenth Amendment rights. A three-judge district court panel agreed with the plaintiffs, and the case was appealed to the Supreme Court.

Beal v. Doe, 432 U.S. 438 (1977)

Pennsylvania also refused to provide Medicaid funds for abortions unless a doctor had certified that the procedure was medically necessary. When the state refused to pay for her elective abortion, "Ann Doe" sued, saying that since the state paid Medicaid funds for childbirth services, its refusal to pay for abortions contravened Title XIX (the portion of the Social Security Act that created Medicaid) and violated her Fourteenth Amendment rights. The district court rejected the suit, stating that nothing in the Constitution or the Social Security Act obligated states to pay for elective abortions. The plaintiffs appealed the decision to the Supreme Court.

The Decisions

The Supreme Court announced its decisions in both cases on June 20, 1977. The Court sided with the states and affirmed the lower courts' rulings, saying that "the Constitution does not provide judicial remedies for every social and economic ill." Chief Justice Burger and Justices Powell, Stewart, White, Rehnquist, and Stevens voted with the majority; Justices Brennan and Blackmun dissented.

Colauti v. Franklin, 439 U.S. 379 (1979)

In 1974, the Pennsylvania legislature overcame a gubernatorial veto to pass a law that required a physician to determine that a fetus was not viable prior to performing an abortion. If a doctor had reason to believe that the fetus might be viable, he or she was required to exercise "professional skill, care, and diligence" to preserve its life. Further, the abortion technique used must be one that "would provide the best opportunity for the fetus to be born alive so long as a different technique would not be necessary to preserve the life and health of the mother."

Before the law could go into effect, a suit was filed by John Franklin, an obstetrician and gynecologist who was director of Planned Parenthood of Southern Pennsylvania, and Concern for Health Options, Information, Care, and Education (CHOICE), a nonprofit clergy consultation service (CHOICE was later dismissed as a plaintiff). The suit, which named Pennsylvania Welfare Secretary Aldo Colautti as the defendant, charged that the language in the law was unconstitutionally vague. A three-judge district court panel agreed with the plaintiffs, and the state appealed the case to the Supreme Court.

The Court heard arguments in the case in October 1978 and announced its decision on January 9, 1979. By a six-to-three vote, the Court agreed with the district court that the Pennsylvania law was unconstitutional on two grounds; first, that it was "impermissibly vague" and, second, that the abortion technique restriction interfered with a physician's ability to choose the technique that was in the patient's, rather than the fetus's, best interest. Justices Blackmun, Brennan, Stewart, Marshall, Powell, and Stevens voted with the majority. Chief Justice Burger and Justices White and Rehnquist dissented.

Harris v. McRae, 448 U.S. 297 (1980)

In 1976, Congress passed an appropriations bill that contained an amendment barring the use of federal Medicaid funds to pay for abortions except to save the mother's life. The amendment was named for its sponsor, Representative Henry Hyde, an Illinois Republican. Following Congress's lead, many states soon passed their own restrictions on Medicaid funding for abortions (Medicaid funding is paid in part by the federal government and in part by states).

Following the first passage of the amendment in 1976, a New York woman, Cora McRae, filed a suit in federal district court on behalf of herself and other low-income women who could not obtain abortions because of the funding restrictions. On January 15, 1977, U.S. District Court Judge John Dooling ruled that the Hyde amendment, by excluding most medically necessary abortions from covered services, violated the First Amendment guarantees of the free exercise of religion or conscience and the Fifth Amendment rights of privacy, due process, and equal protection of the laws for poor women eligible under the program. He issued an injunction to keep the law from being enforced. The federal government appealed the case to the Supreme Court, which refused to stay Judge Dooling's order. Pending a final decision, the Department of Health, Education, and Welfare resumed Medicaid payments for medically necessary abortions and notified states that they were required to pay their share.

In June 1977, the Supreme Court announced its decisions in the *Maher v. Roe* and *Beal v. Doe* cases [see above], upholding states' rights to restrict Medicaid funding for abortions. In July, the Court remanded the *McRae* case to Judge Dooling for reconsideration in light of those rulings. In January 1980, Judge Dooling again ruled that the Hyde amendment was invalid because it violated women's liberty interests under the First and Fifth Amendments. Health and Human Services Secretary Patricia Harris appealed the ruling to the Supreme Court on behalf of the federal government.

During the interim, Congress re-passed the amendment each year. In 1977, the Senate modified the amendment to extend Medicaid funding for abortions in cases of rape or incest or where the woman could suffer lasting health damage as a result of the pregnancy. By 1979, however, funding was again restricted to cases where the pregnancy threatened the woman's life or where it was a result of rape or incest.

On June 30, 1980, by a five-to-four vote, the Supreme Court upheld the constitutionality of the Hyde amendment in its most restrictive version. The ruling effectively shut off any further litigation of the amendment and eliminated virtually all federal funding for abortion. The justices also ruled that the Medicaid law did not require participating states to fund medically necessary abortions if there were no federal reimbursement. Affirming its earlier *Maher v. Roe* ruling, the Court declared that a state or the federal government had a legitimate interest in promoting childbirth while refusing to pay for abortion, even in cases where denying an abortion could endanger the health of the mother or of the child that would eventually be born. In their dissenting opinion, Justices Brennan, Marshall, and Blackmun charged that the Hyde amendment unconstitutionally coerced poor women to have babies they did not want and denied them medically necessary treatment simply because that treatment involved an abortion. In a separate minority opinion, Justice Stevens charged the majority with placing protection of the potential life of the fetus before protection of the pregnant woman's health, thus going against the duty imposed on them by *Roe v. Wade*.

Williams v. Zbaraz, 448 U.S. 358 (1980)

In a companion decision to *Harris v. McRae*, the Court held that Title XIX of the Social Security Act did not require Illinois to pay for abortions for which federal funds were unavailable under the Hyde amendment, and that Illinois funding restrictions did not violate the Equal Protection Clause of the Constitution.

H.L. v. Matheson, 450 U.S. 398 (1981)

Utah's abortion law required a physician to notify a woman's husband, if she were married, or her parents or guardian, if she were a minor, before performing an abortion. The doctor was also required to obtain the woman's written consent after informing her about adoption services available in Utah, the "development of unborn children," and abortion procedures, including foreseeable risks and complications.

In 1978, a pregnant 15-year-old girl, "H.L." sought an abortion. H.L. lived with her parents but did not want them to know about her decision. Her doctor agreed that the abortion was medically in her best interest, but refused to perform it without informing her parents. H.L. filed a court action against the governor of Utah, asking that the law be declared unconstitutional and an injunction be issued to prevent its enforcement. When the district court ruled against her and dismissed her complaint, she appealed to the Utah Supreme Court. When the state court also determined the law was constitutionally valid and rejected her appeal, she appealed to the Supreme Court. On March 23, 1981, the Court announced its decision upholding the law, stating that, since the law did not give parents "veto power" over the abortion, it was not unconstitutional. Voting with the majority were Chief Justice Burger and Justices Stewart, White, Powell, Stevens, and Rehnquist. Dissenting were Justices Marshall, Brennan, and Blackmun.

City of Akron v. Akron Center for Reproductive Health, 462 U.S. 416 (1983)

In 1978, the city of Akron, Ohio, passed a list of ordinances restricting abortion within the city. Among the restrictions were:

- A requirement that abortions after the first trimester be performed in a hospital.
- A parental notification requirement for minors, with an additional consent requirement for minors under 15.
- A requirement that the woman be told that "the unborn child is a human life from the moment of conception," given detailed descriptions of fetal development and information on particular physical and psychological risks associated with abortion, and reminded that assistance was available from the father or social services should she choose to have the baby.
- A 24-hour waiting period.
- A requirement that "the remains of the unborn child be disposed of in a humane and sanitary manner."

In April, before the ordinances could go into effect, a class-action suit was filed in district court by three Akron abortion clinics and a doctor who performed abortions at one of the clinics. In August 1979, the district court ruled several sections of the ordinances unconstitutional, including the parental notification and consent clause and the disposal of fetal remains clause. The court declared the rest of the ordinances to be constitutional. Both sides appealed the decision to the Sixth Circuit Court of Appeals, which agreed with the lower court, but also found the informed consent and waiting period clauses to be unconstitutional.

After numerous appeals, the case reached the Supreme Court, which heard arguments in November 1982. On June 15, 1983, the Court handed down its decision agreeing with the Sixth Circuit Court of Appeals. In addition, it declared the requirement that second trimester abortions be performed in a hospital to be unconstitutional as well. Chief Justice Burger and Justices Powell, Brennan, Marshall, Blackmun, and Stevens voted with the majority. Justices O'Connor, White, and Rehnquist dissented.

Planned Parenthood of Kansas City v. Ashcroft, 462 U.S. 476 (1983)

Like Akron, the city of Kansas City, Missouri, passed a set of ordinances restricting abortion, including a parental or judicial consent provision for minors, a requirement that a pathologist's report be filed with the state following each abortion, a requirement that all abortions after the first 12 weeks be performed in an accredited hospital, and a requirement that, if the fetus was viable, a second physician must be present to "take control of and provide immediate medical care for a child born as the result of an abortion." (A Missouri state law prohibited abortions after viability except when necessary to save the life of the mother.)

Planned Parenthood of Kansas City and two Missouri doctors who performed abortions filed a complaint in federal district court against the laws, claiming the ordinances were unconstitutional. In 1981, the district court invalidated all but one of the laws. This decision was partially upheld and partially reversed by the court of appeals.

The case was appealed to the Supreme Court, which held hearings in November 1982 and announced its decision on July 15, 1983. In a mixed decision, the Court ruled that all of the laws were constitutional, with the exception of the requirement that second trimester abortions be performed in a hospital.

Simonopoulos v. State of Virginia, 462 U.S. 506 (1983)

Virginia's abortion law required abortions done after the first trimester to be done in a state-licensed hospital. As defined by the state health department, the word *hospital* was defined as a facility that performed surgical operations on outpatients. A violation of the statute was a class 4 felony and carried a penalty of a mandatory license revocation and an automatic prison term of two to ten years.

An obstetrician-gynecologist was convicted under the law for performing a second trimester saline abortion on a minor at his private office, which was not licensed as a hospital by the state. Following the saline infusion, the girl had gone to a motel, where she aborted the 22-week fetus about 48 hours later. Police later discovered the fetus in the motel room wastebasket, along with a prescription for a painkiller and instructions written by the doctor. The doctor's conviction was upheld by the state supreme court and his case was appealed to the U.S. Supreme Court.

On June 15, 1983, the Court announced its decision upholding the statute on the grounds that the definition of hospital included outpatient clinics and that the requirement that abortions be performed in licensed hospitals was a reasonable means of furthering the state's interest in protecting women's health. Justices Powell,

Brennan, Marshall, Blackmun, O'Connor, White, and Rehnquist and Chief Justice Burger agreed with the majority. Justice Stevens dissented on mostly technical grounds.

Thornburgh v. American College of Obstetricians and Gynecologists, 106 U.S. 2169 (1986)

In 1982, the state of Pennsylvania passed the Abortion Control Act, a set of laws that imposed a number of restrictions, including:

- An "informed consent" clause that required doctors to counsel women on fetal development and the risks of abortion and childbirth, as well as provide information on medical assistance available for prenatal and neonatal care and childbirth, adoption services, and the legal obligations of the father.
- A requirement that all abortion facilities register with the state.
- A requirement that materials be printed and distributed providing information on adoption and other alternative services and on gestational development.
- A requirement that abortions after the first trimester be performed in a hospital.
- A requirement that a doctor certify nonviability before performing a second trimester abortion.
- A prohibition on abortions after viability except to preserve the life or health of the mother.
- Requirements that any abortions performed after viability use a technique that would "provide the best opportunity for the child to be born alive" and that a second doctor be present during such abortions to care for the child.
- Complex reporting requirements that would make available publicly such information as the woman's age, race, marital status, residence, and number of prior pregnancies, as well as "the length and weight of the aborted unborn child when measurable."
- A requirement for pathological examinations of removed tissue, including, if the doctor had certified nonviability, that the fetus be analyzed for possible viability.

Following passage of the law a class-action suit was filed in district court by a group of plaintiffs that included individual physicians, the American College of Obstetricians and Gynecologists, Pennsylvania abortion clinics, and clergy members. The district court granted part of the request for a preliminary injunction, and the case was appealed to the Third Circuit Court of Appeals. In May 1984, the circuit court invalidated a number of the statutes, including the counseling requirement, the materials distribution requirement, the postviability technique and second physician requirements, and the detailed reporting requirements.

The state appealed to the Supreme Court, which heard arguments on November 5, 1985, in what many believed was a test case on the possibility of overturning *Roe v. Wade*. On June 11, 1986, the Court affirmed the ruling of the lower court, striking down the reporting requirements and the "informed consent" requirements. The Court also held that a physician was not required to try to preserve the life of a "viable" fetus if doing so would pose any additional risk to the health of the pregnant woman. Justices Blackmun, Brennan, Marshall, Powell, and Stevens voted with the majority; Chief Justice Burger and Justices White, O'Connor, and Rehnquist dissented. Justice White and Justice O'Connor each filed dissenting opinions, in which Justice Rehnquist concurred, harshly criticizing the "opposition" and the Court itself, not only for this ruling but for nearly all its abortion rulings since *Roe v. Wade*.

Webster v. Reproductive Health Services, 492 U.S. 490 (1989)

In 1986, Missouri amended its 1974 abortion laws with the intent of "[granting] the right to life of all humans, born and unborn, and [regulating] abortion to the full extent permitted" by the Constitution, Supreme Court decisions, and federal statutes. Among other things, the laws:

- Defined "unborn child" as the "offspring of human beings from the moment of conception until birth and at every stage of its biological development."
- Required parental consent for minors seeking abortions, with a judicial bypass provision.
- Prohibited the use of public facilities (including private facilities built on land leased from the state) for performing abortions.
- Prohibited public employees from performing abortions or encouraging or counseling women to have abortions.

- Required physicians to test for fetal viability in pregnancies of 20 weeks or more.
- Banned the use of state funding for "encouraging and counseling women on the abortion procedure."
- Prohibited abortions for the purpose of "providing fetal organs or tissue for medical transplantation."
- Required that women be given information on fetal development, the risks and possible complications of abortion, and alternatives to abortion.
- Imposed strict record-keeping and reporting requirements.

A federal district court and the Eight Circuit Court of Appeals found a number of the statutes to be unconstitutional, including the prohibition on the performance of abortions in public facilities, the ban on abortion counseling by public employees, the prohibition on the use of public funds for abortion counseling, the requirement that a physician determine viability, and the requirement that abortions after 16 weeks be performed in a hospital. The statute's preamble, granting the right of life to "all human beings, born and unborn" was also ruled unconstitutional.

When the Supreme Court agreed to hear the case on January 10, 1989, many activists and legal experts predicted that the Court would seize the opportunity to overturn *Roe v. Wade*. On July 3, 1989, in a five-to-four decision, the Court reversed most of the lower court rulings and upheld the majority of the statutes, but declined to explicitly overturn *Roe v. Wade*. In their opinions, however, four justices indicated their desire to overturn the fundamental privacy right to choose abortion established in *Roe v. Wade*. In upholding the provision requiring tests for fetal viability, the justices explicitly rejected the trimester framework established in *Roe v. Wade* and emphasized the state's "compelling interest" in protecting potential human life throughout pregnancy. The Court declined to rule on the constitutionality of the preamble, on the basis that the preamble merely expressed the state's value judgment favoring childbirth over abortion and was not used to restrict individuals' actions.

Hodgson v. Minnesota and Ohio v. Akron Center for Reproductive Health

Hodgson v. Minnesota, 497 U.S. 417 (1990)

In 1981, Minnesota passed one of the strictest abortion laws in the nation. One of its provisions required a physician to notify *both* parents of a minor 48 hours before performing an abortion, with no exception for divorce or situations in which one parent had not been involved in the girl's life. However, the statute included a judicial bypass option as well as contingencies in the event that (1) one parent was dead or "[could] not be located through diligent effort"; (2) emergency treatment was "necessary to prevent the woman's death"; or (3) the minor was a victim of sexual abuse or physical abuse that had been reported to the proper authorities.

Before the law could go into effect, a lawsuit was filed in federal district court by two Minnesota obstetrician-gynecologists, four clinics that provided abortion and contraceptive services, six pregnant minors representing a class of pregnant minors, and the mother of a pregnant minor. The plaintiffs charged that the statute violated the due process and equal protection clauses of the Fourteenth Amendment, as well as several provisions of the Minnesota constitution. The district court issued a temporary injunction against enforcement of the law. A trial was not held until 1986, when the district court ruled that both the two-parent notification requirement and the 48-hour waiting period were invalid and that the law was unconstitutional. The case was appealed to the Eighth Circuit Court of Appeals, which reversed the lower court ruling and upheld the law. The plaintiffs appealed to the Supreme Court.

Ohio v. Akron Center for Reproductive Health, 497 U.S. 502 (1990)

Ohio's 1985 abortion law required an abortion provider to notify one parent at least 24 hours before performing an abortion on a minor. The law included a judicial bypass option that permitted the physician to notify another adult relative if the minor feared she would be abused as a result of telling a parent, or allowed the minor to consent to the abortion herself if she could prove she was mature and informed enough to do so. A doctor could also proceed with an abortion if he could not give the notice after a "reasonable effort" and had provided at least 48 hours "constructive notice" by both ordinary and certified mail.

In 1986, just before the law was due to go into effect, a lawsuit was filed in federal district court on behalf of the Akron Center for Reproductive Health, an abortion clinic; a doctor who performed abortions at the center; and "Rachel Roe," an unmarried pregnant minor. The district court invalidated the law and issued a permanent injunction against its enforcement. The decision was affirmed by the Sixth Circuit Court of Appeals, and the state of Ohio appealed to the Supreme Court.

The Decisions

The Court announced its decisions in both cases on June 25, 1990. In the Minnesota case, five justices (Rehnquist, White, O'Connor, Scalia, and Kennedy) voted to uphold the two-parent notification requirement, but struck down an alternative portion of the law that would have eliminated the judicial bypass option and required "absolute notice" of both parents except in the contingencies cited in the statute. Six (the above plus Stevens) voted to uphold the 48-hour waiting period, stating that it was reasonable and did not pose a great obstacle to obtaining an abortion. By a six-to-three vote, the Court also upheld the Ohio law. In writing their opinions, the majority held that a woman's interest in obtaining an abortion was a "liberty interest." This was a significant departure from the "fundamental right" wording of earlier decisions. In effect, the new wording meant that, in order to regulate abortion, states had to show only that there was a "rational basis" for their restrictions, as opposed to a "compelling interest," which is much more difficult to prove.

Rust v. Sullivan, 500 U.S. 173 (1991)

Title X of the 1970 Public Health Service Act forbade the use of federal funds for programs where "abortion is a method of family planning." In 1987, the Reagan administration proposed cutting federal funds to any clinic that included abortion as an alternative for pregnant women. In 1988, Health and Human Services Secretary Louis Sullivan issued a regulation that prohibited family planning clinics that received federal funding under Title X from performing abortions or providing any information about abortion to pregnant women. Under the "gag rule," as it became known, a woman who requested information about abortion was to be told that abortion was not considered an appropriate method of family planning. The regulation, which affected more than 3,900 clinics around the country, was continued under the Bush administration.

Planned Parenthood of New York City, along with the New York City and New York State governments, challenged the regulations, claiming that they violated both Title X and the First Amendment guarantee of freedom of speech. Several lower courts issued injunctions prohibiting the regulations from taking effect, though with conflicting conclusions on their constitutionality. The Bush administration, while defending the regulations, asked the Supreme Court to resolve the issue in light of the conflicting rulings.

On May 23, 1991, in a five-to-four decision, the Court ruled that the regulation was legal and that Secretary Sullivan had interpreted Title X reasonably when issuing it. In its opinion, the Court stated that just because abortion was a constitutional right did not mean that the government was obligated to support it. Further, the regulation did not interfere with free speech, since doctors were not being asked to lie, just not to talk about abortion. Chief Justice Rehnquist and Justices White, Scalia, Kennedy, and Souter voted with the majority. Justices Marshall, Blackmun, Stevens, and O'Connor dissented. The ruling became moot when Bill Clinton revoked the gag rule upon becoming president in 1993. (In 1995, the House of Representatives attached an amendment to an appropriations bill reinstating the gag rule; at the end of 1995, the amendment had not yet been acted on by the Senate.)

Planned Parenthood of Southeastern Pa. v. Casey, 112 S. Ct. 2791 (1992)

In 1988 and 1989, Pennsylvania amended its 1982 Abortion Control Act to include a 24-hour waiting period, a parental consent requirement for minors, and a spousal notification requirement. The spousal notification clause required a married woman to certify, under penalty of a one-year jail sentence, that she had told her husband of her intent to have an abortion, unless she had reported to police that the pregnancy resulted from a rape by the husband or unless she feared physical abuse by him, could not locate him, or said that he was not the father. Women could be exempted from these requirements only in the event of a "medical emergency." The law also included reporting requirements for abortion providers and revived the 1982 act's "informed consent" clause [see *Thornburgh v. American College of Obstetricians and Gynecologists,* above].

Before the new provisions could take effect, a suit was filed in federal district court by five abortion clinics and a physician representing both himself and a class of physicians who performed abortions. The suit challenged each provision as being unconstitutional on its face. The district court ruled the waiting period and the parental and spousal notification requirements unconstitutional and issued an injunction against their enforcement. The case was appealed to the Third Circuit Court of Appeals. The appeals court partially affirmed and partially rejected the lower court ruling, upholding the waiting period and parental notification but declaring the spousal notification requirement unconstitutional. The case was then appealed to the Supreme Court, which heard arguments on April 22, 1992.

On June 29, 1992, the Court issued a fragmented, no-majority decision upholding the findings of the appeals court. In their joint opinion, Justices O'Connor, Kennedy, and Souter reaffirmed the essential holding of *Roe v. Wade*—that it is a "constitutional liberty of the woman to have some freedom to terminate her pregnancy"—while rejecting *Roe*'s "rigid trimester framework." A woman's right to abortion ends at viability, when the state's "profound interest" in protecting potential life takes precedence. Further, because of the state's interest in protecting potential life throughout pregnancy, "not all regulations must be deemed unwarranted." The state may take measures to make sure that a woman is informed and to encourage her to bear her child rather than choose abortion. As with any medical procedure, the state may also enact regulations to further the health or safety of women seeking abortions. Therefore, neither the 24-hour waiting period nor the parental notification requirement imposed an "undue burden" on a woman's constitutional right to seek an abortion. However, the Court noted, millions of women suffer physical or sexual abuse at the hands of their husbands, and these women might have very good reasons for not wanting to inform their husbands of their decision to seek an abortion. Further, these women might be justifiably afraid not only of suffering physical abuse but of the consequences of reporting prior abuse to the authorities as required under the abortion law. The spousal notification requirement imposed a "substantial obstacle" and an undue burden on such women, and was therefore invalid.

The three justices were joined in part by Justices Stevens and Blackmun, who supported the reaffirmation of *Roe* while disagreeing with the constitutionality of the Pennsylvania laws. In their dissenting opinion, Chief Justice Rehnquist and Justices White, Scalia, and Thomas expressed their belief in the constitutionality of all the Pennsylvania provisions, along with their extreme disappointment in the Court's failure to take this opportunity to reverse

Roe v. Wade, which they asserted was wrongly decided and deserved to be overturned.

Like the *Roe v. Wade* decision nearly 20 years earlier, *Casey* created a significant dividing line in the history of abortion. While upholding a woman's basic constitutional right to an abortion, the Court simultaneously gave the states great latitude in determining how that right would be exercised. The result was to move the battle over abortion mostly out of the courts and into state legislatures.

Bray v. Alexandria Women's Health Clinic, 113 S. Ct. 753 (1993)

The Civil Rights Act of 1871, also known as the Ku Klux Klan Act, made it illegal to deprive a class of people of equal protection or equal privileges and immunities under the law. The Alexandria Women's Health Clinic sued to keep Operation Rescue from conducting demonstrations at abortion clinics in the Washington, D.C., metropolitan area, claiming that the demonstrators had violated the Ku Klux Klan Act by conspiring to deprive women seeking abortions of their right to obtain abortions and their right to interstate travel (by keeping women from other states from entering the clinics). The clinic also claimed that Operation Rescue violated state laws by trespassing on clinic property and creating a public nuisance. The district court ruled in favor of the clinics, as did the Fourth Circuit Court of Appeals. Operation Rescue appealed to the Supreme Court, which heard arguments in the case in October 1991 and again in October 1992.

The Court announced its decision on January 13, 1993. By a six-to-three vote, the Court overturned the lower court ruling, stating that women seeking abortions did not constitute a protected class under the Ku Klux Klan Act. Operation Rescue's actions were not directed at women as a class, but instead sought to provide physical intervention between "abortionists and their innocent victims." Further, Operation Rescue was not restricting women's rights to interstate travel, but only restricted movement in the immediate vicinity of the clinics. The Court also rejected the clinic's claim that Operation Rescue's violation of state trespassing laws should be redressed in federal court simply because its intent was to prevent abortions. Voting with the majority were Chief Justice Rehnquist and Justices White, Scalia, Kennedy, Souter, and Thomas. Justices Blackmun, Stevens, and O'Connor dissented.

Madsen v. Women's Health Center, 114 S. Ct. 2516, 129 L. Ed. 2d 593 (1994)

In September 1992, a Florida state court issued an injunction to prevent protestors from blocking or interfering with public access to a Melbourne, Florida, abortion clinic and from physically abusing persons entering or leaving the clinic. Six months later, the state court broadened the injunction in response to complaints from the clinic operators. The court found that, despite the initial injunction, protesters were continuing to impede access to the clinic by congregating on the paved portions of the street leading up to the clinic and by marching in front of the clinic's driveways. As cars heading toward the clinic slowed to allow protesters to move out of the way, they were approached by "sidewalk counselors" who attempted to give antiabortion literature to their occupants. The number of protesters ranged from a few to as many as 400; their singing, chanting, and shouting could be heard inside the clinic, causing stress to patients and staff. Doctors and clinic workers were also harassed away from the clinic. Protesters picketed their homes, shouted at passersby, rang the doorbells of neighbors and gave them literature identifying the employees as "baby killers," and even confronted minor children of employees who were home alone.

Because of these actions, the court extended the injunction, creating 300-foot buffer zones around the clinic within which protesters could not make uninvited approaches to patients of employees. The court also imposed 300-foot buffer zones around the homes of clinic doctors and employees.

The injunction was challenged before the Florida supreme court and the Eleventh Circuit Court of Appeals. The state supreme court upheld the injunction, but the appeals court struck it down, calling the dispute a clash "between an actual prohibition of speech and a potential hindrance to the free exercise of abortion rights." The Supreme Court agreed to resolve the conflict between the decisions.

On June 31, 1994, the Court issued its ruling partially upholding the amended injunction. By a six-to-three vote, the Court upheld the use of a 36-foot buffer zone around the clinic to protect unfettered access to the clinic parking lot and entrance and to ensure that protesters did not block traffic on the public street. Chief Justice Rehnquist, writing for the majority, stated that such a zone burdened speech "no more than necessary to accomplish the government's interest" in protecting the right of patients and employees to have unimpeded access to clinics and promoting the free flow of traffic on public streets and sidewalks. The ruling struck down the 300-foot buffer zones around the clinic and around doctors' and employees' houses as being too broad. It indicated, however, that smaller zones or restrictions on the size and duration of demonstrations at the houses would be constitutional.

Chief Justice Rehnquist was joined in the majority opinion by Justices Blackmun, O'Connor, Souter, and Ginsburg, and in part by Justice Stevens. Justices Scalia, Kennedy, and Thomas dissented.

Further Reading

The complete texts of Supreme Court decisions are contained in the *United States Reports*, which is available in law school and bar association libraries as well as some public libraries. The method of citation used to refer to decisions includes the volume of the *Reports* in which the text appears, the page number on which the case begins, and the year when it was decided. For example, the citation for *Roe v. Wade* is 410 U.S. 113 (1973), meaning the case is found in volume 410, beginning on page 113, and it was decided in 1973.

Texts of Supreme Court decisions can also be accessed through the Internet: telnet to federal.bbs.gpo.gov, or dial up by modem direct to (202) 512-1387. All issues are online; files are in Wordperfect 5.1 (DOS) format. Issue names are by year: 1992–1993 session is SC92; 1993–1994 session is SC93, and so on.

The following books give more information on the legal history of abortion and on important court cases [see chapter 5 for complete listings]:

Drucker, Dan. *Abortion Decisions of the Supreme Court, 1973 through 1989*. Jefferson, NC: McFarland & Company, 1990.

Friedman, Leon, ed. *The Supreme Court Confronts Abortion: The Briefs, Arguments, and Decision in* Planned Parenthood v. Casey. New York: Farrar, Straus and Giroux, 1993.

Harrison, Maureen, and Steve Gilbert. *Abortion Decisions of the Supreme Court: The 1990s*. Beverly Hills, CA: Excellent Books, 1993.

Rubin, Eva. *The Abortion Controversy: A Documentary History*. Rev. ed. Westport, CT: Greenwood Press, 1987.

Roe v. Wade: *The Complete Text of the Official U.S. Supreme Court Decision*. Annotated by Bo Schambelan. Philadelphia: Running Press, 1992.

Abortion Statistics

Sources of Abortion Statistics

The CDC Abortion Surveillance

In 1969, the Centers for Disease Control (CDC), a division of the United States Department of Health and Human Services, began an annual abortion surveillance to "document the number and characteristics of women obtaining abortions and to assist efforts to identify and reduce preventable causes of morbidity and mortality associated with abortion" (CDC 1995). The CDC figures are collected from 52 reporting areas: all 50 states, the District of Columbia, and New York City. For most reporting areas, data are obtained from the central health agency (that is, state health departments and the health departments of New York City and the District of Columbia). Data for the remaining areas are provided by hospitals and other medical facilities.

The CDC data are broken down by state, age (in five-year groups), race, marital status, number of previous live births, type of procedure, and weeks of gestation at the time of the abortion.

Alan Guttmacher Institute (AGI) Survey Data

While CDC figures provide a fairly reliable general picture of abortion in the United States, the number of abortions actually performed is certainly greater than the number reported to the CDC, which receives its information on abortions from central health agencies with widely varying requirements for reporting. Therefore, a frequently used source of abortion statistics is the Alan Guttmacher Institute (AGI), a private, nonprofit research organization that conducts periodic surveys of all identified providers of abortion services, including hospitals, freestanding clinics, and private physicians.

AGI attempts to locate all facilities that provide abortion services through a variety of sources, including Planned Parenthood affiliates, National Abortion Rights Action League (NARAL) state coordinators, state health departments, metropolitan area yellow pages directories, a newspaper clipping service, and mailing lists from companies and other organizations. Information is then obtained from the providers through a combination of mailed questionnaires, health department reports, and telephone interviews. Through this methodology AGI obtains a more complete picture of abortion statistics than the CDC. In 1991, for example, the CDC reported approximately 12 percent fewer total abortions than AGI.

AGI routinely asks providers for more detailed information than what is reported to the CDC. For example, in the 1989 survey, providers were asked to report the number of abortions performed, the number or proportion past 12 weeks' gestation, and the maximum gestation at which abortions are generally provided. Nonhospital providers were asked to provide additional information, including information about harassment, fees charged for abortions with and without general anesthesia, services for nonabortion patients, distances patients traveled to their facility, charges for other services for abortion patients, services for HIV-positive abortion patients, decision counseling, and facility licensing.

AGI surveys were conducted annually from 1974 to 1979, with each survey collecting data for the previous year (1973 to 1978). Subsequent surveys have been conducted biannually, in 1981, 1983, 1986, 1989, and 1993, with each survey gathering data for the previous two years (1979–1980, 1981–1982, 1984–1985, 1987–1988, and 1991–1992, respectively). No data were collected for 1983 and 1986.

Number and Frequency of Abortions

The number and frequency of abortions are measured in three ways:

- Absolute *numbers* of abortions.
- Abortion *ratio:* the number of abortions per 1,000 live births.
- Abortion *rate:* the number of abortions for every 1,000 females of childbearing age.

Prior to Legalization

There is no way to know exactly how many abortions were performed prior to the start of legalization in 1970, other than the relatively low number of legal, "therapeutic" abortions performed each year. Estimates have, however, remained remarkably consistent since the middle of the last century, when the ratio of abortions to live births was appraised at anywhere from one-fifth to one-third. Estimates of the number of illegal abortions performed in the United States prior to 1973 range from 500,000 to 1 million or more annually, though some antiabortion groups dispute these figures.

Following Legalization

CDC Data

According to the CDC [see Table 2 and Figure 1]:

- The reported *number* of abortions increased every year from 1970 through 1982, with the largest percentage increase occurring during the period from 1970 to 1972. From 1976 through 1982, the annual increase declined continuously, reaching a low of 0.2 percent from 1980 to 1981. From 1980 through 1990, the number of abortions remained relatively stable, with year-to-year fluctuations of 5 percent or less. From 1990 to 1992, the last year for which figures are available, the number of abortions declined, though not substantially. In 1992, 1,359,145 abortions were reported to the CDC, a decrease of 2.1 percent from 1991.
- The *ratio* of abortions to live births increased from 1970 into the 1980s, reaching a high of 364 per 1,000 live births in 1984. The ratio remained fairly stable until 1987, after which it declined steadily, to 339 in 1991, and 335 in 1992.

Figure 1. Number, ratio,* and rate† of legal abortions performed annually—United States, 1970–1991

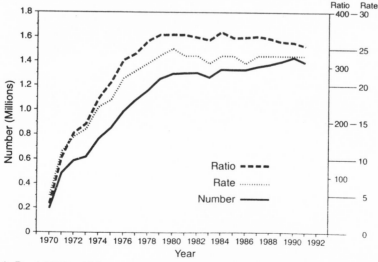

* Per 1,000 live births.
† Per 1,000 women 15–44 years of age.

Source: Centers for Disease Control. *Morbidity and Mortality Weekly Report: CDC Surveillance Summaries.* Vol. 44, No. SS-2 (May 5, 1995), p. 26.

- The *rate* of abortions increased from 17 abortions per 1,000 women aged 15 to 44 in 1974 to 25 per 1,000 in 1980. It has since remained stable at 23–24 per 1,000.

AGI Data

AGI data corroborate the CDC findings that the number of legal abortions increased until the early 1980s, when it stabilized at just under 1.6 million per year [see Table 3]. The most recent AGI data show a 5 percent decline in the number of abortions from 1988 to 1992 [see Table 4]. As Table 4 shows, the percentage decrease varied considerably by state and geographic region.

Table 2. Number, ratio,* and rate† of legal abortions and source of reporting—United States, 1970–1991

Year	Total no. of abortions	Ratio	Rate	No. of areas reporting Central health agency§	Hospitals/ Facilities¶
1970	193,491	52	5	18	7
1971	585,816	137	11	19	7
1972	586,760	180	13	21	8
1973	615,831	196	14	26	26
1974	763,476	242	17	37	15
1975	854,853	272	18	39	13
1976	988,267	312	21	41	11
1977	1,079,430	325	22	46	6
1978	1,157,776	347	23	48	4
1979	1,251,921	358	24	47	5
1980	1,297,606	359	25	47	5
1981	1,300,760	358	24	46	6
1982	1,303,980	354	24	46	6
1983	1,268,987	349	23	46	6
1984	1,333,521	364	24	44	8
1985	1,328,570	354	24	44	8
1986	1,328,112	354	23	43	9
1987	1,353,671	356	24	45	7
1988	1,371,285	352	24	45	7
1989	1,396,658	346	24	45	7
1990	1,429,577	345	24	46	6
1991	1,388,937	339	24	47	5

* Number of abortions per 1,000 live births.
† Number of abortions per 1,000 women 15–44 years of age.
§ Abortion data reported from central health agency.
¶ Abortion data reported from hospitals and/or other medical facilities in state.

Source: Centers for Disease Control. *Morbidity and Mortality Weekly Report: CDC Surveillance Summaries.* Vol. 44, No. SS-2 (May 5, 1995), p. 27.

Table 3. Number and percentage distribution of legal abortions, abortion rate per 1,000 women, and percentage of pregnancies terminated by abortion, by age, United States, 1973–1988

	1973	1975	1975	1976	1977	1978	1979	1980
Number of abortions								
Total	744,610	898,570	1,034,170	1,179,300	1,316,700	1,409,600	1,497,670	1,553,890
<15	11,630	13,420	15,260	15,820	15,650	15,110	16,220	15,340
15–19	232,440	278,280	324,930	362,680	396,630	418,790	444,600	444,780
15–17	u	u	u	(152,700)	(165,610)	(169,270)	(178,570)	(183,350)
18–19	u	u	u	(209,980)	(231,020)	(249,520)	(266,030)	(261,430)
20–24	240,610	286,600	331,640	392,280	449,660	489,410	525,710	549,410
25–29	129,600	162,690	188,900	220,500	246,680	265,990	284,200	303,820
30–34	72,550	89,810	100,170	110,050	124,380	134,280	141,970	153,060
35–39	40,960	48,770	52,740	56,720	61,700	65,350	65,070	66,580
≥ 40	16,820	19,000	20,530	21,250	22,000	20,670	19,900	20,900
Percental distribution of abortions								
Total	100.0	100.0	100.0	100.0	100.0	100.0	100.0	100.0
<15	1.6	1.5	1.5	1.3	1.2	1.1	1.1	1.0
15–19	31.2	31.0	31.4	30.8	30.1	29.7	29.7	28.6
15–17	u	u	u	(13.0)	(12.6)	(12.0)	(11.9)	(11.8)
18–19	u	u	u	(17.8)	(17.5)	(17.7)	(17.8)	(16.8)
20–24	32.3	31.9	32.1	33.3	34.2	34.7	35.1	35.4
25–29	17.4	18.1	18.2	18.7	18.7	18.9	19.0	19.6
30–34	9.7	10.0	9.7	9.3	9.4	9.5	9.5	9.8
35–39	5.5	5.4	5.1	4.8	4.7	4.6	4.3	4.3
≥ 40	2.3	2.1	2.0	1.8	1.7	1.5	1.3	1.3
Abortion rate*								
Total	16.3	19.3	21.7	24.2	26.4	27.7	28.8	29.3
<20 †	23.9	28.2	32.5	35.8	39.0	41.1	43.9	44.4
<15 ‡	5.6	6.4	7.2	7.6	7.6	7.5	8.3	8.4
15–19	22.8	26.9	31.0	34.3	37.5	39.7	42.4	42.9
15–17	u	u	u	(24.2)	(26.2)	(26.9)	(28.8)	(30.2)
18–19	u	u	u	(49.3)	(54.1)	(58.4)	(61.9)	(61.0)
20–24	26.2	30.4	34.3	39.6	44.3	47.2	49.9	51.4
25–29	16.4	19.6	21.8	24.1	26.9	28.4	29.6	30.8
30–34	10.9	13.0	14.0	15.0	15.7	16.4	16.5	17.1
35–39	7.1	8.4	8.9	9.3	9.8	9.8	9.4	9.3
≥ 40 §	2.9	3.3	3.6	3.7	3.9	3.6	3.4	3.5
Percentage of pregnancies terminated by abortion**								
Total	19.3	22.0	24.9	26.5	28.6	29.2	29.6	30.0
<20	25.6	29.0	33.4	25.8	28.4	39.6	40.7	41.2
<15	u	u	u	u	41.1	40.9	43.0	42.7
15–19	u	u	u	u	38.3	39.5	40.6	41.1
15–17	u	u	u	u	(38.7)	(39.7)	(41.3)	(42.4)
18–19	u	u	u	u	(37.9)	(39.3)	(40.1)	(40.1)
20–24	17.6	20.0	22.8	25.0	27.6	28.7	29.4	30.1
25–29	13.2	15.4	17.2	18.6	20.2	20.8	21.1	21.8
30–34	18.7	21.7	23.5	23.1	23.7	23.5	23.0	23.3
35–39	28.3	32.8	35.4	36.6	38.5	38.6	37.3	37.2
≥ 40	39.7	44.4	46.6	50.2	52.5	51.6	50.4	51.7

u = unavailable.

Source: Stanley K. Henshaw and Jennifer Van Vort. *Abortion Factbook, 1992 Edition: Readings, Trends, and State and Local Data to 1988.* New York: Alan Guttmacher Institute, 1992.

Table 3 (continued)

	1981	1982	1983	1984	1985	1986	1987	1988
Number of abortions								
Total	1,577,340	1,573,920	1,575,000	1,577,180	1,588,550	1,574,000	1,559,110	1,590,750
<15	15,240	14,590	16,350	16,920	16,970	15,690	14,270	13,650
15–19	433,330	418,740	411,330	398,870	399,200	389,240	381,640	392,720
15–17	(175,930)	(168,410)	(166,440)	(160,900)	(165,630)	(165,240)	(161,120)	(158,330)
18–19	(257,400)	(250,330)	(244,890)	(237,970)	(233,570)	(224,000)	(220,520)	(234,390)
20–24	554,940	551,680	548,130	551,110	548,020	531,380	518,290	519,600
25–29	316,260	326,380	328,280	332,280	336,280	339,450	337,450	347,250
30–34	167,240	168,020	171,560	175,780	180,560	185,830	191,540	197,210
35–39	69,510	73,250	78,090	81,840	86,540	91,730	93,030	95,870
≥ 40	20,820	21,260	21,260	20,380	20,980	20,680	22,890	24,450
Percental distribution of abortions								
Total	100.0	100.0	100.0	100.0	100.0	100.0	100.0	100.0
<15	1.0	0.9	1.0	1.1	1.1	1.0	0.9	0.9
15–19	27.5	26.6	26.1	25.3	25.1	24.7	24.5	24.7
15–17	(11.2)	(10.7)	(10.6)	(10.2)	(10.4)	(10.5)	(10.3)	(10.0)
18–19	(16.3)	(15.9)	(15.5)	(15.1)	(14.7)	(14.2)	(14.2)	(14.7)
20–24	35.2	35.0	34.8	34.9	34.5	33.8	33.2	32.7
25–29	20.0	20.7	20.8	21.1	21.2	21.6	21.6	21.8
30–34	10.6	10.7	10.9	11.1	11.4	11.8	12.3	12.4
35–39	4.4	4.7	5.0	5.2	5.4	5.8	6.0	6.0
≥ 40	1.3	1.4	1.4	1.3	1.3	1.3	1.5	1.5
Abortion rate*								
Total	29.3	28.8	28.5	28.1	28.0	27.4	26.9	27.3
<20 †	44.8	44.4	45.2	45.0	45.7	44.4	43.8	45.5
<15 ‡	8.6	8.3	9.2	9.3	9.2	9.2	8.8	8.6
15–19	43.3	42.9	43.5	43.2	43.8	42.6	42.2	44.0
15–17	(30.1)	(30.1)	(30.8)	(30.0)	(30.7)	(30.0)	(29.7)	(30.3)
18–19	(61.8)	(60.0)	(60.4)	(61.5)	(63.0)	(61.9)	(61.0)	(63.5)
20–24	51.1	51.2	51.1	51.8	52.3	52.2	52.5	54.2
25–29	31.4	31.5	31.1	30.9	30.9	30.9	30.8	31.8
30–34	17.7	17.7	17.8	17.8	17.8	17.9	17.9	18.1
35–39	9.5	9.3	9.6	9.5	9.7	9.7	9.8	9.9
≥ 40 §	3.4	3.3	3.1	2.9	2.9	2.8	2.9	3.0
Percentage of pregnancies terminated by abortion**								
Total	30.1	30.0	30.4	29.7	29.7	29.4	28.8	28.8
<20	41.3	41.2	42.3	41.2	42.1	41.8	41.0	40.7
<15	43.7	42.9	46.0	45.9	45.7	43.8	41.0	39.1
15–19	41.2	41.2	42.2	41.6	42.0	41.7	41.0	40.7
15–17	(42.2)	(42.0)	(43.2)	(42.5)	(43.2)	(42.9)	(42.0)	(40.9)
18–19	(40.3)	(40.5)	(41.4)	(40.9)	(41.0)	(40.7)	(40.2)	(40.6)
20–24	30.4	30.6	31.4	31.3	31.5	31.5	31.3	31.3
25–29	22.0	22.3	22.5	22.0	22.0	22.0	21.6	21.7
30–34	23.9	23.2	23.0	22.1	21.8	21.5	21.1	20.6
35–39	35.7	34.2	34.2	32.8	32.2	31.9	30.4	29.1
≥ 40	51.3	51.4	51.4	49.4	49.4	46.2	45.3	43.9

* Denominator is women aged 15–44
† Denominator is women aged 15–19
‡ Numerator is abortions obtained by girls younger than 15; denominator is number of 14-year-old females.
§ Numerator is abortions obtained by women 40 and over; denominator is women aged 40–44.
** Denominator is live births six months later (to match time of conception with abortions) and abortions. Preganancies exclude miscarriages and stillbirths. Births and abortions are adjusted to age of woman at time of conception

Table 4. Number of reported abortions, rate per 1,000 women aged 15–44 and percentage change in rate, by state of occurrence, 1988, 1991, and 1992

State	Number			Rate			% change, 1988–1992
	1988	1991	1992	1988	1991	1992	
Total	1,590,750	1,556,510	1,528,930	27.3	26.3	25.9	−5
New England	87,450	83,760	78,360	27.9	26.5	25.2	−10
Connecticut	23,630	20,530	19,720	31.2	26.7	26.2	−16
Maine	4,620	4,210	4,200	16.2	14.7	14.7	−9
Massachusetts	43,720	44,150	40,660	30.2	30.2	28.4	−6
New Hampshire	4,710	4,260	3,890	17.5	15.7	14.6	−17
Rhode Island	7,190	7,500	6,990	30.6	31.5	30.0	−2
Vermont	3,580	3,110	2,900	25.8	22.7	21.2	−18
Middle Atlantic	299,710	297,990	300,450	34.0	33.9	34.6	2
New Jersey	63,900	55,800	55,320	35.1	30.9	31.0	−12
New York	183,980	190,410	195,390	43.3	44.5	46.2	7
Pennsylvania	51,830	51,780	49,740	18.9	19.2	18.6	−2
East North Central	223,180	204,270	204,810	22.4	20.6	20.7	−8
Illinois	72,570	64,990	68,420	26.4	24.1	25.4	−4
Indiana	15,760	15,940	15,840	11.9	12.1	12.0	1
Michigan	63,410	55,800	55,580	28.5	25.1	25.2	−11
Ohio	53,400	52,030	49,520	21.0	20.4	19.5	−7
Wisconsin	18,040	15,510	15,450	16.0	13.6	13.6	−15
West North Central	68,550	61,430	57,340	16.7	15.3	14.3	−15
Iowa	9,420	7,200	6,970	14.6	11.7	11.4	−22
Kansas	11,440	12,770	12,570	20.1	22.9	22.4	11
Minnesota	18,580	16,880	16,180	18.2	16.3	15.6	−14
Missouri	19,490	15,770	13,510	16.4	13.5	11.6	−29
Nebraska	6,490	6,230	5,580	17.7	17.5	15.7	−11
North Dakota	2,230	1,600	1,490	14.9	11.4	10.7	−28
South Dakota	900	980	1,040	5.7	6.4	6.8	19
South Atlantic	276,640	273,010	269,200	27.7	26.2	25.9	−7
Delaware	5,710	5,720	5,730	35.7	34.9	35.2	−1
District of Columbia	26,120	21,510	21,320	163.3	136.1	138.4	−15
Florida	82,850	84,570	84,680	31.5	29.9	30.0	−5
Georgia	36,720	39,720	39,680	23.5	24.2	24.0	2
Maryland	32,670	33,000	31,260	28.6	27.5	26.4	−8
North Carolina	39,720	37,210	36,180	25.4	23.2	22.4	−12
South Carolina	14,160	13,520	12,190	16.7	15.8	14.2	−15
Virginia	35,420	35,170	35,020	23.7	22.8	22.7	−5
West Virginia	3,270	2,590	3,140	7.5	6.3	7.7	2
East South Central	56,950	53,670	54,060	15.6	14.9	14.9	−4
Alabama	18,220	17,400	17,450	18.7	18.2	18.2	−3
Kentucky	11,520	8,270	10,000	13.0	9.5	11.4	−12
Mississippi	5,120	8,160	7,550	8.4	13.5	12.4	48
Tennessee	22,090	19,840	19,060	18.9	16.9	16.2	−14
West South Central	136,400	126,140	127,070	21.3	19.6	19.6	−8
Arkansas	6,250	7,150	7,130	11.6	13.6	13.5	16
Louisiana	17,340	13,930	13,600	16.3	13.7	13.4	−18
Oklahoma	12,120	9,130	8,940	16.2	12.8	12.5	−23
Texas	100,690	95,930	97,400	24.8	23.0	23.1	−7
Mountain	69,410	71,530	69,600	21.9	21.9	21.0	−4
Arizona	23,070	19,690	20,600	28.8	23.2	24.1	−16
Colorado	18,740	21,010	19,880	22.4	25.3	23.6	6
Idaho	1,920	1,740	1,710	8.2	7.5	7.2	−12
Montana	3,050	3,680	3,300	16.5	20.6	18.2	11
Nevada	10,190	14,450	13,300	40.3	49.0	44.2	10
New Mexico	6,810	6,190	6,410	19.1	17.2	17.7	−7
Utah	5,030	4,250	3,940	12.8	10.4	9.3	−27
Wyoming	600	520	460	5.1	4.9	4.3	−16
Pacific	372,460	384,710	368,040	41.5	40.6	38.7	−7
Alaska	2,390	2,400	2,370	18.2	16.9	16.5	−10
California	311,720	320,960	304,230	45.9	44.4	42.1	−8
Hawaii	11,170	12,130	12,190	43.0	45.9	46.0	7
Oregon	15,960	16,580	16,060	23.9	24.9	23.9	0
Washington	31,220	32,640	33,190	27.6	27.6	27.7	0

Note: In this and subsequent tables, numbers of abortions are rounded to the nearest 10. *Sources:* 1988—see reference 4, 1991–1992—see sources to Table 1.

Source: Stanley K. Henshaw and Jennifer Van Vort. "Abortion Services in the United States, 1991 and 1992." *Family Planning Perspectives*, Vol. 26 (1994), pp. 100–106, 112.

Accounting for the Decrease in Abortions

Possible reasons for the decrease in abortions since 1991 include:

- Increased birthrates for women of all reproductive ages.
- Reduced access to abortion services due to changes in laws (such as parental consent or notification requirements and mandatory waiting periods) and a decrease in the number of abortion providers.
- Changes in contraceptive practices.
- Attitudinal changes concerning abortion and/or carrying unplanned pregnancies to term.
- The possibility that the number of unintended pregnancies has decreased (CDC 1995).

Geographic Distribution of Abortions

As Table 4 shows, the number of abortions varies considerably by state and region. The states with the highest populations reported the highest numbers of abortions: California, New York, and Texas. This is corroborated by the CDC, which reported that in 1991 the largest numbers of abortions were performed in California, New York City, and Texas. The states reporting the smallest numbers of abortions were North Dakota, South Dakota, West Virginia, and Wyoming. This is consistent with previous years (CDC 1995).

Henshaw and Van Vort (1994) caution about interpreting abortion rates by state of occurrence because they do not always reflect the number of abortions obtained by residents, who may travel to other states for abortion services. For example, in 1987 the number of Wyoming residents who had abortions in other states was greater than the number of residents who had abortions in Wyoming. Similarly, the rates in some states are inflated by the number of abortions provided to out-of-state women.

According to the CDC, in 1991 about 92 percent of women obtained abortions in their home states. That year, the percentage of abortions obtained by out-of-state residents ranged from about 51 percent in the District of Columbia to less than 1 percent in Hawaii (CDC 1995).

Comparing U.S. Abortion Statistics with Those of Other Countries

During the 1980s, the abortion rate in other countries ranged from more than 100 per 1,000 women of reproductive age in the Soviet

140 Facts and Statistics

Table 5. Number of abortions, abortion rate per 1,000 women aged 15–44, abortion ratio per 100 known pregnancies, and total abortion rate, by completeness and reliability of data and country

Type of data and country	N‡	Rate	Ratio	Total rate
Statistics believed to be complete				
Australia (1988)	63,200	16.6	20.4	484
Belgium				
In Belgium§ (1985)	10,800	5.1	8.7	u
All** (1985)	15,900	7.5	12.2	u
Bulgaria (1987)	119,900	64.7	50.7	u
Canada				
In Canada (1987)	63,600	10.2	14.7	299
All†† (1985)	74,800	12.1	16.6	u
China (1987)	10,394,500	38.8	31.4	u
Cuba (1988)	155,300	58.0	45.3	u
Czechoslovakia (1987)	156,600	46.7	42.2	1,400
Denmark (1987)	20,800	18.3	27.0	548
England and Wales‡‡ (1987)	156,200	14.2	18.6	413
Finland (1987)	13,000	11.7	18.0	356
German Democratic Republic (1984)	96,200	26.6	29.7	u
Hungary (1987)	84,500	38.2	40.2	1,137
Iceland (1987)	700	12.0	14.0	336
Netherlands ‡‡ (1986)	18,300	5.3	9.0	155
New Zealand (1987)	8,800	11.4	13.6	323
Norway (1987)	15,400	16.8	22.2	493
Scotland §§ (1987)	10,100	9.0	13.2	255
Singapore (1987)	21,200	30.1	32.7	840
Sweden (1987)	34,700	19.8	24.9	600
Tunisia (1988)	23,300	13.6	9.8	u
United States (1985)	1,588,600	28.0	29.7	797
Vietnam (1980)	170,600	14.6	8.2	u
Yugoslavia (1984)	358,300	70.5	48.8	u
Statistics that are incomplete				
Bangladesh (FY 1969)	77,800	3.4	1.6	u
France*† (1987)	161,000	13.3	17.3	406*‡
German Federal Republic				
In country (1987)	88,500	6.7	12.1	197
All** (1986)	92,200	7.0	12.8	u
Hong Kong (1987)	17,600	12.7	20.1	u
India (FY 1987)	588,400	3.0	2.2	u
Ireland*§ (1987)	3,700	4.8	5.9	139
Israel (1987)	15,500	16.2	13.5	u
Italy (1987)	191,500	15.3	25.7	460
Japan (1987)	497,800	18.6	27.0	564
Poland (1987)	122,600	14.9	16.8	u
Romania†* (1983)	421,400	90.9	56.7	u
Soviet Union (1987)	6,818,000	111.9	54.9	u
Estimates based on surveys or other data				
Bangladesh (FY 1986)	241,400	12	5	u
Japan (1975)	2,250,000	84	55	u
South Korea (1984)	528,000	53	43	u
Soviet Union (1982)	11,000,000	181	68	u
Spain (1987)	63,900	8	u	u
Switzerland (1984)	13,500	9	15	u
Turkey (1987)	531,400	46	26	u

[Notes appear on facing page]

Union to 5 per 1,000 women in the Netherlands. The rate of induced abortion in the United States was higher than in Australia, Canada, Japan, and Western European countries, and lower than in Cuba, China, and Eastern European countries (Henshaw 1990).

Table 5 shows how the number, rate, and ratio of abortions in the United States compares with abortions in other countries for which data are available. Note that most of these figures are for legal abortions; according to Hartmann (1987), half of abortions worldwide (30 to 50 million a year) are estimated to be illegal.

Characteristics of Women Having Abortions

Both AGI and the CDC have collected considerable data on the characteristics of women having abortions, including age, race, marital status, and parity (number of prior live births). AGI has also collected data on such characteristics as religion, living arrangements, employment, and income.

Table 6 is based on data reported to the CDC. It is important to note that, although the *absolute numbers* of abortions reported by the CDC are lower than those reported by the Alan Guttmacher Institute, the *percentages* of women meeting various criteria are very close to those found by AGI. For example, in 1982 AGI reported that 57.3 percent of women having abortions were experiencing their first pregnancy; the CDC figure for the same year was 57.8 percent.

Table 5 Notes

*Known pregnancies are defined as legal abortions plus live births. Births have not been lagged by six months because the necessary birth data are unavailable for most countries.

†The number of abortions that would be experienced by 1,000 women during their reproductive lifetimes, given present age-specific abortion rates.

‡Rounded to the nearest 100 abortions.

§Abortions performed in 17 hospitals and 20 nonhospital facilities, usually illegally.

**Including abortions obtained in the Netherlands and England.

††Including abortions obtained in Canadian clinics and in the United States.

‡‡Residents only.

§§Including abortions obtained in England.

*†Provisional data.

*‡1986 data.

*§Based on Irish residents who obtained abortions in England.

†*Combining counts of illegal abortions with treated complications and of legal abortions.

Note: Sources of country data for this table . . . available from author; u=unavailable.

Source: Stanley K. Henshaw, "Induced Abortion: A World Review, 1990."
Family Planning Perspectives, Vol. 22, No. 2 (March/April 1990), p. 78.
© 1990 The Alan Guttmacher Institute.

Table 6. Characteristics of women obtaining legal abortions— United States, selected years, 1972–1991

Characteristic	1972	1973	1976	1980	1985
Reported no. of legal abortions	586,760	615,831	988,267	1,297,606	1,328,570
Residence					
In-state	56.2	74.8	90.0	92.6	92.4
Out-of-state	43.8	25.2	10.0	7.4	7.6
Age (yrs)					
≤19	32.6	32.7	32.1	29.2	26.3
20–24	32.5	32.0	33.3	35.5	34.7
≥25	34.9	35.3	34.6	35.3	39.0
Race					
White	77.0	72.5	66.6	69.9	66.6
Black	23.0[†]	27.5[†]	33.4[†]	30.1[†]	29.8
Other[§]	—	—	—	—	3.5
Hispanic origin					
Hispanic	—	—	—	—	—
Non-Hispanic	—	—	—	—	—
Marital status					
Married	29.7	27.4	24.6	23.1	19.3
Unmarried	70.3	72.6	75.4	76.9	80.7
No. of live births[¶]					
0	49.4	48.6	47.7	58.4	56.3
1	18.2	18.8	20.7	19.4	21.6
2	13.3	14.2	15.4	13.7	14.5
3	8.7	8.7	8.3	5.3	5.1
≥4	10.4	9.7	7.9	3.2	2.5
Type of procedure					
Curettage	88.6	88.4	92.8	95.5	97.5
Suction curettage	65.2	74.9	82.6	89.8	94.6
Sharp curettage	23.4	13.5	10.2	5.7	2.9
Intrauterine instillation	10.4	10.4	6.0	3.1	1.7
Other**	1.0	1.2	1.2	1.4	0.8
Weeks of gestation					
≤8	34.0	36.1	47.0	51.7	50.3
9–10	30.7	29.4	28.1	26.2	26.6
11–12	17.5	17.9	14.4	12.2	12.5
13–15	8.4	6.9	4.5	5.1	5.9
16–20	8.2	8.0	5.1	3.9	3.9
≥21	1.2	1.7	0.9	0.9	0.8

* Because the number of states that reported each characteristic varies from year to year, temporal comparisons should be made cautiously. Percentage distributions are based on data from all areas reporting a given characteristic and exclude unknown values.
† Reported as black and other races.
§ Includes all other races.
¶ For 1972–1976, data indicate number of living children.
** Includes hysterotomy and hysterectomy
— Not available.

1986	1987	1988	1989	1990	1991
1,328,112	1,353,671	1,371,285	1,396,658	1,429,577	1,388,937
92.4	91.7	91.4	91.0	91.8	91.6
7.6	8.3	8.6	9.0	8.2	8.4
25.3	25.8	25.3	24.2	22.4	21.0
34.0	33.4	32.8	32.6	33.2	34.4
40.7	40.8	41.9	43.2	44.4	44.6
67.0	66.4	64.4	64.2	64.8	63.8
28.7	29.3	31.1	31.2	31.8	32.5
4.3	4.3	4.5	4.6	3.4	3.7
—	—	—	—	9.8	13.5
—	—	—	—	90.2	86.5
20.2	20.8	20.3	20.1	21.7	21.4
79.8	79.2	79.7	79.9	78.3	78.6
55.1	53.6	52.4	52.2	49.2	47.8
22.1	22.8	23.4	23.6	24.4	25.3
14.9	15.5	16.0	15.9	16.9	17.5
5.3	5.5	5.6	5.7	6.1	6.4
2.6	2.6	2.6	2.6	3.4	3.0
97.0	97.2	98.6	98.8	98.8	98.9
94.5	93.4	95.1	97.1	96.0	97.3
2.5	3.8	3.5	1.7	2.8	1.6
1.4	1.3	1.1	0.9	0.8	0.7
1.6	1.5	0.3	0.3	0.4	0.4
51.0	50.4	48.7	49.8	51.6	52.3
25.8	26.0	26.4	25.8	25.3	25.1
12.2	12.4	12.7	12.6	11.7	11.5
6.1	6.2	6.6	6.6	6.4	6.1
4.1	4.2	4.5	4.2	4.0	3.9
0.8	0.8	1.1	1.0	1.0	1.1

Source: Centers for Disease Control. *Morbidity and Mortality Weekly Report: CDC Surveillance Summaries.* Vol. 44, No. SS-2 (May 5, 1995).

Table 7. Percentage distribution of women having abortions in 1987 and of all women aged 15–44, index of abortion incidence, and age-standardized index, all by selected characteristics

Charac- teristic	Abortion patients	All women	Index	Index (adj.*)	Charac- teristic	Abortion patients	All women	Index	Index (adj.*)
Age					**Marital status**				
<15	0.9	u	na	na	Married	18.5	52.1	0.36	0.52
15–17	10.8	9.4	1.15	na	Separated	6.4	3.3	1.94	2.62
18–19	13.8	6.2	2.23	na	Divorced	11.2	8.2	1.37	2.05
20–24	33.1	17.0	1.95	na	Widow	0.6	0.7	0.81	2.01**
25–29	22.3	18.9	1.18	na	Never-married	63.3	35.7	1.77	1.35
30–34	11.7	18.4	0.64	na					
35–39	5.7	16.3	0.35	na	**Living arrangements**				
≥40	1.7	13.7†	0.12	na	Cohabiting††	17.4	3.4	5.12	4.65
					Not cohabiting	82.6	96.6	0.86	0.86
Ethnicity									
Hispanic	12.8	8.4	1.52	1.44	**Employment status**				
Non-Hisp.	87.2	91.6	0.95	0.96	Employed	68.1	64.2	1.06	1.09§
					Not employed	31.9	35.8	0.89	0.81§
Race									
White	68.6	83.3	0.82	0.83	**Family income**				
Nonwhite	31.4	16.7	1.88	1.80	<$11,000	33.1	14.9	2.22	1.99
					$11,000–				
Religion					$24,999	33.8	29.2	1.16	1.10
Protestant	41.9	57.9	0.72	0.74	≥$25,000	33.1	55.9	0.59	0.62
Catholic	31.5	32.1	0.98	0.95					
Jewish	1.4	2.5	0.56	0.69	**Medicaid status**				
Other	2.9	2.0	1.45	2.04	Covered	23.8	9.0	2.64	2.44
None	22.2	5.5	4.04	3.68	Not covered	76.2	91.0	0.84	0.85
Born again/					**Childbearing intention**				
Evangelical‡	15.8	32.0	0.49	0.51	More children	69.7	61.6	1.13	0.90
Not born again	84.2	68.0	1.24	1.23	No more	30.3	38.4	0.79	1.32
School enrollment					**Residence status**				
Enrolled	31.1	20.5	1.52	1.51§	Metro	85.7	77.1	1.11	1.11
Not enrolled	68.9	79.5	0.87	0.94§	Nonmetro	14.3	22.9	0.62	0.62
Total	100.0	100.0	1.00	1.00	Total	100.0	100.0	1.00	1.00

*Age-standardized.   †Women 40–44 only.   ‡Based on women 18–44.
§Standardized on women 25–44.   ††Among women not currently married.
**Standardized on women 20–44.   Notes: na = not applicable; u = unavailable.
Sources: **Hispanic origin**—U.S. Bureau of the Census, "The Hispanic Population in the United States: March 1986 and 1987 (Advance Report)," *Current Population Reports*, Series P–20, No. 416, 1987, Table 3; ——, "The Hispanic Population in the United States: March 1985," *Current Population Reports*, Series P–20, No. 422, 1988, Table 6. **Race**—U.S. Bureau of the Census, "United States Population Estimates, by Age, Sex, and Race: 1980 to 1987," *Current Population Reports*, Series P–25, No. 1022, 1988, Table 2. **Religion**—Special tabulation of the National Survey of Family Growth (NSFG), Cycle III, 1988. **Born again**—Special tabulations (six Gallup Polls), The Roper Center for Public Opinion Research, Storrs, Conn., 1988. **Marital status and cohabitation**—U.S. Bureau of the Census, "Marital Status and Living Arrangements: March 1987," *Current Population Reports*, Series P–20, No. 423, 1988, Tables 1 and 7. **School enrollment**—R. Bruno, unpublished data, Current Population Survey, Oct. 1986, U.S. Bureau of the Census, May 31, 1988. **Employment status**—U.S. Department of Labor, Bureau of Labor Statistics, "Employment and Unemployment: A Report on 1987," Jan. 1988, Table 3. **Family income**—U.S. Bureau of the Census, unpublished data from Current Population Survey, Table PF1; ——, "Money Income of Households, Families and Persons in the United States: 1985," *Current Population Reports*, Series P–60, No. 156, 1987, Table 18. **Medicaid coverage**—AGI, *The Financing of Maternity Care in the United States*, New York, 1987, Table 105. **Future childbearing intentions**—Special tabulation, NSFG, Cycle III, 1988. **Metropolitan area**—Distributions of the female population by age according to metro status, U.S. Bureau of the Census, 1980 Census, General Population Characteristics PC80–1–B1, U.S. summary, Table 43: updated to 1986 using U.S. Bureau of the Census, *Statistical Abstract of the United States 1988*, U.S. Government Printing Office, Washington, D.C., 1988, Table 30.

Source: Henshaw, Stanley K., and Jane Silverman. "The Characteristics and Prior Contraceptive Use of U.S. Abortion Patients." *Family Planning Perspectives*, Vol. 20, No. 4 (July/August 1988).

Table 7, which is based on data reported to AGI, provides a more detailed breakdown, comparing the proportion of women who obtained abortions in 1987 with the proportion of all women of childbearing age by such characteristics as age, ethnicity, marital status, religion, school enrollment, and employment status.

As these tables show, women having abortions range across all sociodemographic categories and all socioeconomic and cultural backgrounds, as well as across all age groups within the childbearing years. There are, however, distinct differences among groups.

Age Group Differences

In 1991, 41 states, the District of Columbia, and New York City reported legal abortions to the CDC by age. According to the CDC:

- Women aged 20–24 obtained 34 percent of all abortions. Women under 15 accounted for less than 1 percent of

Figure 2. Abortion ratios,* by age group† of women who obtained a legal abortion—United States, 1974–1991

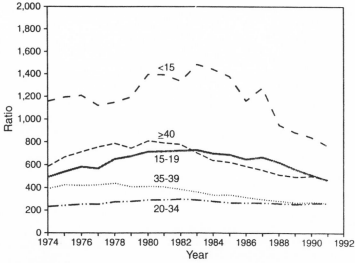

*Per 1,000 live births.
†In years.

Source: Centers for Disease Control. *Morbidity and Mortality Weekly Report: CDC Surveillance Summaries*. Vol. 44, No. SS-2 (May 5, 1995), p. 36.

abortions. More than half of women obtaining abortions (55 percent) were under age 25; 21 percent were teenagers. Twenty-two percent were 30 or older, with less than 2 percent being 40 or older.

- Women aged 20 to 24 had the highest abortion rate: 42 per 1,000 women.
- For most age groups, the ratio of abortions to live births rose between 1974 and the early to mid-1980s and declined thereafter, particularly for the youngest and oldest women of reproductive age [see Figure 2].
- Teenagers aged 15 and younger and women aged 40 and older have the highest frequency of abortions to live births, even though the numbers and rates of abortions in these age ranges are small [see Figure 2].
- The percentage of legal abortions obtained by women 19 years old and younger has decreased steadily since the mid-1980s, from 26 percent in 1984 to 24 percent in 1989 and 21 percent in 1991. In 1991, the abortion ratio for women aged 15 to 19 was the lowest ever recorded for that age group.

Racial, Socioeconomic, Marital Status, and Religious Differences

- White women obtained almost two-thirds of all abortions reported to the CDC in 1991. However, the abortion ratio for black women (502 per 1,000 live births) was more than twice the ratio for white women (246 per 1,000 live births). The abortion rate for black women was 41 per 1,000 women of reproductive age, 2.6 times that of white women (16 per 1,000 women).
- For Hispanic women, the ratio was 300 abortions per 1,000 live births, slightly lower than for non-Hispanics in the same areas (332 per 1,000 births). The rate for Hispanic women was 28 per 1,000 women of reproductive age, compared to 22 per 1,000 non-Hispanic women.
- Seventy-six percent of women who obtained abortions were unmarried. The percentage varied by state, from 59 percent in Utah to 82 percent in Kansas. The abortion ratio was more than nine times greater for unmarried women than for married women (815 versus 89 abortions per 1,000 live births).

- Poor women (those with family incomes under $11,000) are proportionately more likely to have abortions than those in the middle class.
- The percentage of Catholic women obtaining abortions is comparable to the percentage of Catholics in the general population, while the percentage of Protestant women having abortions is somewhat lower than the percentage of Protestants in the general population, and the percentage of Evangelical Christians having abortions is considerably lower than the percentage of Evangelicals overall.

Previous Abortions and/or Live Births

- As Table 6 shows, in 1991 approximately 45 percent of women whose abortions were reported to the CDC had had at least one previous abortion. Ten percent had had two previous abortions, and 6 percent had had three or more.
- Fifty-three percent of the women obtaining abortions had had at least one previous birth.

These figures are comparable to those reported to AGI.

Weeks of Gestation

As Table 6 shows, most abortions (89 percent) are performed within the first 12 weeks of pregnancy; at least half are performed within the first 8 weeks. Approximately 6 percent are performed between 13 and 15 weeks, and 4 percent between 16 and 20 weeks. Around 1 percent of abortions are performed after 20 weeks.

The number of abortions performed in the third trimester (after 24 weeks) is a matter of some controversy. Estimates range from 100 to 200 (AGI 1994) to as many as 4,000 (former Surgeon General C. Everett Koop, quoted by Gianelli 1993) annually. Only three or four doctors in the country perform legal, late-term abortions; virtually all of these are done because of fetal death, severe fetal defects, and/or conditions that threaten the life of the mother.

Type of Abortion Technique Used

As Table 6 shows, the overwhelming majority (almost 99 percent) of abortions reported to the CDC for 1991 were performed by curettage, with most of these being done by suction curettage, or vacuum aspiration. This includes abortions performed by dilatation and evacuation (D & E). Fewer than 1 percent of abortions were performed using medical induction (saline or prostaglandin instillation), and about 0.4 percent by "other," including hysterotomy and hysterectomy.

Why Women Have Abortions

In 1987, the Alan Guttmacher Institute conducted a survey of 1,900 abortion patients to determine why they were having abortions. The majority of respondents (93 percent) said that they had more than one reason for deciding to have an abortion; the mean number of reasons was just under four. The most commonly cited

Table 8. Percentage of abortion patients reporting that a specific reason contributed to their decision to have an abortion, by age, and percentage saying that each reason was the most important

Reason	Total	Age <18	18–19	20–24	25–29	≥30	% most important
Woman is concerned about how having a baby could change her life	76	92	82	75	72	69	16
Woman can't afford baby now	68	73	73	70	64	58	21
Woman has problems with relationship or wants to avoid single parenthood	51	37	46	56	55	50	12
Woman is unready for responsibility	31	33	40	36	25	18	21
Woman doesn't want others to know she has had sex or is pregnant	31	42	41	35	21	22	1
Woman is not mature enough, or is too young to have a child	30	81	57	28	7	4	11
Woman has all the children she wanted, or has all grown-up children	26	8	12	23	31	51	8
Husband or partner wants woman to have an abortion	23	23	29	25	18	20	1
Fetus has possible health problem	13	9	13	12	14	17	3
Woman has health problem	7	3	4	7	8	15	3
Woman's parents want her to have abortion	7	28	12	4	3	2	‡
Woman was victim of rape or incest	1	1	1	1	1	‡	1
Other	6	2	5	8	5	8	3

‡ Less than 0.5 percent.

Source: Torres, Aida, and Jacqueline Darroch Forrest. "Why Do Women Have Abortions?" *Family Planning Perspectives*, Vol. 20, No. 4 (July/August 1988), p. 170.

Table 9. Percentage of respondents offering various additional details for each of the three leading reasons women gave for having an abortion

Reason	% citing main reason
Unready for how having a baby could change her life (N=1,339)	
A baby would interfere with job, employment or career	67
A baby would interfere with school attendance	49
Children or other people depend on her for care	28
Can't afford baby now (N=856)	
Woman is student or is planning to study	41
Woman is unmarried	22
Woman is unemployed	19
Woman has low-paying job	14
Woman can't leave job	9
Woman is on welfare	7
Woman's husband or partner is unemployed	6
Woman can't afford basic needs	5
Woman receives no support from her husband or partner	4
Problems with relationship or with single parenthood (N=790)	
Woman doesn't want to marry partner	49
Couple may break up soon	32
Partner doesn't want to or can't marry	29
Woman is not in a relationship	25
Woman's husband or partner mistreats respondent or children	6
Woman is unready to commit herself to a relationship	5

Source: Torres, Aida, and Jacqueline Darroch Forrest. "Why Do Women Have Abortions?" *Family Planning Perspectives*, Vol. 20, No. 4 (July/August 1988), p. 172. © 1988 The Alan Guttmacher Institute.

reason was that having a baby would interfere with work, school, or other responsibilities, followed by not being able to afford a child. About one-half of the women said that they either were having relationship problems or did not want to become single parents. Table 8 shows the percentages of respondents citing each reason, broken down by age, as well as the percentage of respondents stating that a given reason was the most important.

A number of respondents offered additional details for their reasons for deciding to have abortions; those for the three leading reasons are summarized in Table 9.

Reasons for Having Late Abortions

The AGI survey included several facilities that provided late-term abortions; women having abortions at 16 weeks since their last menstrual period or later were also asked their reasons for delaying the abortion. Most of these women reported that more than two factors were involved in the delay. Nearly three-quarters (71 percent) said that they either had not realized they were pregnant or did not know soon enough how long they had been pregnant. Almost half said that the delay was caused by problems in arranging the abortion, usually because they needed time to raise the money. Tables 10 and 11 show the reasons cited for having late abortions and the percentages of women citing each reason, including detailed breakdowns of the three most cited reasons.

Table 10. Among women who provided information relating to three specific reasons for having abortions at 16 or more weeks gestation, percentage who gave various detailed reasons for delay

Reason	%
Woman failed to recognize pregnancy or misjudged gestation (N=277)	
She didn't feel physical changes	50
She hoped she was not pregnant	50
She had irregular periods	33
She thought she had had her period	32
Her MD underestimated gestation	20
She was practicing contraception	20
Her pregnancy test was negative	9
She didn't know where or how to get a pregnancy test	7
Woman found it hard to make arrangements for an abortion (N=185)	
She needed time to raise money	60
She tried to get an abortion from a different clinic or MD	32
She had to arrange transportation because there was no nearby provider	26
She didn't know where to get an abortion	20
She couldn't get an earlier appointment	16
She took time to notify her parents or get their consent	11
She needed child care or a Medicaid card	9
She need time to obtain court permission	0
Woman took time to decide to have an abortion (N=74)	
She found having an abortion to be a difficult decision	78
She had religious or moral reasons for waiting	19
She talked with her parents/husband/partner	11

Source: Torres, Aida, and Jacqueline Darroch Forrest. "Why Do Women Have Abortions?" *Family Planning Perspectives*, Vol. 20, No. 4 (July/August 1988), p. 175. © 1988 The Alan Guttmacher Institute.

Table 11. Percentage of women who reported that various reasons contributed to their having a late abortion and who cited specific reasons as accounting for the longest delay

Reasons	All (N=399)	Longest Delay (N=311)
Woman did not recognize that she was pregnant or misjudged gestation	71	31
Woman found it hard to make arrangements for abortion	48	27
Woman was afraid to tell her partner or parents	33	14
Woman took time to decide to have abortion	24	9
Woman waited for her relationship to change	8	4
Someone pressured woman not to have abortion	8	2
Something changed after woman became pregnant	6	1
Woman didn't know timing is important	6	*
Woman didn't know she could get an abortion	5	2
A fetal problem was diagnosed late in pregnancy	2	1
Other	11	9

*Less than 0.05 percent

Source: Torres, Aida, and Jacqueline Darroch Forrest. "Why Do Women Have Abortions?" in *Family Planning Perspectives*, Vol. 20, No. 4 (July/August 1988), p. 175. © 1988 The Alan Guttmacher Institute.

Abortion-Related Deaths

Deaths from Illegal Abortions

Illegal abortions are a leading cause of death for women in many parts of the world. This is true not only in countries where abortion is illegal, but in countries where legal abortions are too expensive or difficult for poor women to obtain, so that they resort to illegal abortions. Worldwide, about 500,000 maternal deaths occur each year. According to Henshaw (1990), the World Health Organization (WHO) has estimated that 115,000 to 204,000 of these deaths are brought about by complications of illegal abortions performed by unqualified practitioners. A more conservative estimate, derived from hospital studies suggesting that, on average, 20 to 25 percent of maternal mortality is attributable to abortion, is 100,000 to 125,000 deaths annually.

The WHO estimates that more than one-half of the deaths from illegal abortion occur in South and Southeast Asia, with the next largest proportion occurring in sub-Saharan Africa (Henshaw 1990). According to Hartmann (1987), in Latin America, where abortion is mostly illegal, one-fifth to one-half of maternal deaths are due to illegal abortion. And in Bolivia, complications from illegal abortions account for over 60 percent of the country's obstetrical and gynecological expenses.

In the United States, the number of abortion-related deaths has declined dramatically since abortion became legal in 1973. The number of deaths from illegal abortions prior to 1973 is impossible to ascertain, and estimates vary. Although abortion rights groups tend to talk in terms of "thousands" of deaths, a few hundred per year is probably more accurate. Seaman and Seaman, from *Women and the Crisis in Sex Hormones* (cited in Hartmann 1987), state that before 1973, deaths in the United States from induced abortion averaged 292 a year. Table 12, which is based on CDC figures, shows a decline from an average of 364 deaths per year from 1958 to 1962 to 11 in 1981 and 18 in 1982.

Table 12. Number of deaths associated with abortion, by type of abortion, United States, 1958–1982

Year or Average	All abortions	Legally induced[1]	Other than legal total	Illegally induced[2]		Spontaneous
1958–62[3,4]	364	5	359	na		na
1963–67	276	4	272	na		na
1968–69	164	4	160	111		49
1970	168	36	132	109		23
1971	143	54	89	65		24
1972[5]	90	24	66	41	(2)	25
1973	57	25	32	22	(3)	10
1974	54	26	28	7	(1)	21
1975	48	29	19	5	(1)	14
1976	27	11	16	3	(1)	13
1977	37	17	20	4		16
1978	25	9	16	7		9
1979	26	18	8	0		8
1980	17	9	8	2	(1)	6
1981	11	7	4	1		3
1982	18	11	7	1		6

Note: na = data not available.
1. Excludes 10 deaths during 1973–79 that occurred shortly after legal abortion was attempted and that are attributed to ectopic pregnancy.
2. Numbers in parentheses are deaths classified as unknown by the CDC.
3. Figures for 1958–69 are annual averages.
4. Estimates for 1958–71 are based on deaths attributed to abortion inflated to comparability with data for later years.
5. For 1972–82 figures represent deaths reported by the CDC (excluding ectopic-related deaths). The number of deaths has been updated and may be more than previously reported.

Source: Tietze, Christopher, and Stanley K. Henshaw. *Induced Abortion: A World Review, 1986.* New York: Alan Guttmacher Institute, 1986, p. 131.
© 1986 The Alan Guttmacher Institute.

Deaths from Legal Abortions

In countries where abortion is both legal and relatively available, abortion mortality is very low, averaging less than one death per 100,000 abortions (Henshaw 1990). This is true in the United States. However, complication and death-to-case rates vary according to gestational age of the fetus and the method used, with the risks rising with each additional week of gestation. Estimates of the increase in the mortality rate for abortion range from 30 to 50 percent with each additional week of gestation after the twelfth week.*

In the United States, from 1981 to 1985, the number of deaths per 100,000 legal abortions was 0.2 at 8 or fewer weeks LMP, 0.3 at 9 to 10 weeks, 0.6 at 11 to 12 weeks, 3.7 at 16 to 20 weeks, and 12.7 at 21 weeks or more (Henshaw 1990). As noted above, however, most abortions in the United States are performed within the first 12 weeks, and the vast majority of these are performed by instrumental evacuation, including vacuum aspiration and curettage. The death-to-case rate for these is about 1 per million (0.1 per 100,000) (Hern 1984).

According to Hern (1984), most deaths related to legal abortion result from anesthesia complications. A CDC review of death-to-case rates for general versus local anesthesia for first trimester abortions from 1972 to 1977 found a two to four times greater risk of death for general anesthesia. Another study found that general anesthesia was twice as likely to be associated with uterine perforation and cervical injury, while the relative risk of blood transfusion, cervical suture, and major surgery was 3.9, 2.1, and 7.6, respectively, for general as compared with local anesthesia (ibid.).

Risk of Death from Abortion versus Term Pregnancy and Contraceptive Use

From 1981 to 1985, the maternal mortality rate, excluding deaths from abortion and ectopic pregnancies, was 6.6 deaths per 100,000 live births—a rate more than 30 times as high as for abortions up to 8 weeks LMP, and twice as high as for abortions performed between 16 and 20 weeks. After 20 weeks the death rate

---

* Measured as weeks since the start of the last menstrual period (LMP). Since fertilization generally takes place midway through the menstrual cycle, gestational age is about two weeks less than the number of weeks LMP.

for abortion is higher. In studying comparative mortality risks of term pregnancy, contraception, and induced abortion, Tietze and associates (1986) concluded that "reliance on barrier methods, with early abortion as a backup, is the safest reversible regimen of fertility regulation at any age" (p. 115).

Ory (1983) lists the risks in ascending order:

- Barrier methods backed by abortion.
- Barrier methods alone.
- Abortion alone.
- IUD only.
- Oral contraceptives only in women who do not smoke.

The highest risk is for women aged 35 and over who smoke and use oral contraceptives.

Abortion Access

In 1992, the Alan Guttmacher Institute (AGI) identified 2,380 facilities that provided abortion services. This included hospitals, abortion clinics, other nonhospital clinics, and doctor's offices. Most abortions (69 percent in 1992) are performed in the nation's 441 abortion clinics, defined as nonhospital clinics in which half or more of patient visits are for abortion services. Hospitals accounted for only about 7 percent of the total abortions in 1992. The remainder were performed in doctors' offices or in other clinics (group practices with clinic names, surgical centers, health maintenance organizations, and other facilities with clinic names).

Table 13 shows the numbers of each type of provider and the approximate abortion caseload for each type, as well as the numbers of abortions and the types of facilities where they were obtained.

The Decline in Abortion Services

Since the late 1980s, there has been a steady decrease in the number of physicians qualified and willing to perform abortions, and a corresponding decrease in the number of facilities that provide abortion services. This is shown graphically in Figure 3. Additionally, many areas have only small providers who do not want a large abortion caseload and who do not advertise abortion services,

Table 13. Number and percentage distribution of abortion providers and abortions, by type of facility, according to caseload, 1992

Caseload*	Total		Hospitals		Abortion clinics		Other clinics		Physicians' offices†	
	N	%	N	%	N	%	N	%	N	%
Providers	**2,380**	**100**	**855**	**36**	**441**	**19**	**448**	**19**	**636**	**27**
<30	699	29	439	18	0	0	45	2	215	9
30–390	926	39	351	15	13	1	141	6	421	18
400–990	282	12	45	2	68	3	169	7	na	na
1,000–4,990	428	18	18	1	318	13	92	4	na	na
≥5,000	45	2	2	‡	42	2	1	‡	na	na
Abortions	**1,528,930**	**100**	**109,950**	**7**	**1,057,500**	**69**	**307,020**	**20**	**54,460**	**4**
<30	6,480	‡	3,390	‡	0	0	510	‡	2,580	‡
30–390	111,970	7	35,170	2	2,740	‡	22,180	1	51,880	3
400–990	183,970	12	26,640	2	49,610	3	107,720	7	na	na
1,000–4,990	877,430	57	30,840	2	679,980	44	166,610	11	na	na
≥5,000	349,080	23	13,910	1	325,170	21	10,000	1	na	na

*In this table and Table 6, caseloads are rounded to nearest 10. † In this table and Table 6, physicians' offices reporting 400 or more abortions a year are classified as clinics (either abortion clinics or "other clinics"). ‡Fewer than 0.5%. *Note:* na = not applicable. Percentages may not add to 100 because of rounding.

Source: Henshaw, Stanley K., and Jennifer Van Vort. "Abortion Services in the United States, 1991 and 1992." *Family Planning Perspectives,* Vol. 26 (1994), p. 104.

which means that women may have difficulty finding out about and obtaining such services. According to AGI, in 1992:

- 84 percent of all counties in the United States lacked any abortion providers.
- Among nonmetropolitan counties, 94 percent had no abortion services.
- Among metropolitan counties, 51 percent had no abortion services.
- Of the country's 320 metropolitan areas, 91 had no identified abortion provider in 1992. Another 14 had providers who performed fewer than 50 abortions in 1992.

Figure 3. Number of providers, by type of provider and metropolitan status, 1977–1982, 1984–1985, 1987–1988, and 1991–1992

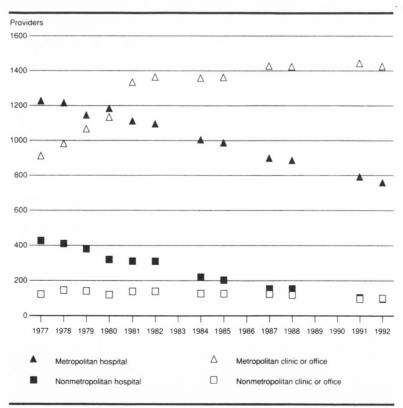

Source: Henshaw, Stanley K., and Jennifer Van Vort. "Abortion Services in the United States, 1991 and 1992." *Family Planning Perspectives*, Vol. 26 (1994), p. 106.

- In 22 states, no more than five counties had a facility that reported performing at least 1 abortion in 1992.
- In 8 states, fewer than one-third of women lived in a county with a provider.
- All states except North Dakota and South Dakota had at least 5 providers, but several states lost providers between 1988 and 1992. North and South Dakota each had only 1 facility that provided abortion services.
- Nationally, in 1992 there were 4 providers for each 100,000 women aged 15 to 44 in the population. Ten states, however, had fewer than 1.5 providers per 100,000 women. These states had a correspondingly low abortion rate compared to other states (7 to 14 abortions per 1,000 women of reproductive age versus a median rate of 18 for all states).

Harassment of Abortion Providers and Antiabortion Violence

Harassment and violence directed toward abortion providers continues to be a visible and troubling issue in the United States. Large-scale clinic blockades, demonstrations, and incidents such as arsons, bombings, chemical attacks, and invasions have decreased since 1993, probably due to a combination of mobilization of abortion rights supporters, the enactment of the Freedom of Access to Clinic Entrances (FACE) Act of 1994 [see below], and the Supreme Court's 1994 decision in *Madsen v. Women's Health Center,* which upheld the validity of buffer zones around clinics. During the same period, however, death threats and actual attacks against doctors and clinic personnel have increased. In one 1994 survey of 314 clinics, 24.8 percent of the clinics reported that members of their staff had received death threats during the previous year (Schmidt and Jackman 1995).

The vast majority of abortion opponents also oppose violence against abortion providers; however, a small number of activists actively promote the use of deadly force to stop abortion. In March 1993, Michael Griffin shot and killed Dr. David Gunn outside the abortion clinic in Pensacola, Florida, where Gunn worked. Since then, four more people have died in antiabortion violence, and several others have been wounded. Many others have received death threats against themselves and their families, and have had

Table 14. Incidents of violence and disruption against abortion providers, 1995[1]

VIOLENCE (# Incidents)	1977–1983	1984	1985	1986	1987	1988	1989	1990	1991[2]	1992	1993	1994	1995	TOTAL
Murder	0	0	0	0	0	0	0	0	0	0	1	4	0	5
Attempted Murder	0	0	0	0	0	0	0	0	2	0	1	8	0	11
Bombing	8	18	4	2	0	0	2	0	1	1	1	3	0	40
Arson	13	6	8	7	4	4	6	4	10	16	9	5	10	102
Attempted Bomb/Arson	5	6	10	5	8	3	2	4	1	13	7	4	1	69
Invasion	68	34	47	53	29	6	25	19	29	26	24	2	1	348
Vandalism	35	35	49	43	29	29	24	26	44	116	113	42	17	602
Assault & Battery	11	7	7	11	5	5	12	6	6	9	9	7	1	96
Death Threats	4	23	22	7	5	4	5	7	3	8	78	59	24	249
Kidnapping	2	0	0	0	0	0	0	0	0	0	0	0	0	2
Burglary	3	2	2	5	7	1	0	2	1	5	3	3	3	37
Stalking[3]	0	0	0	0	0	0	0	0	0	0	188	22	16	226
TOTAL	149	131	149	133	72	52	76	68	97	194	434	159	73	1,787

DISRUPTION

Hate Mail & Phone Calls	9	17	32	53	32	19	30	21	142	469	628	381	113	1,946
Bomb Threats	9	32	75	51	28	21	21	11	15	12	22	14	28	339
Picketing	107	160	139	141	77	151	72	45	292	2,898	2,279	1,407	315	8,083
TOTAL	125	209	246	245	137	191	123	77	449	3,379	2,929	1,802	456	10,368

CLINIC BLOCKADES

No. Incidents	0	0	0	0	2	182	201	34	41	83	66	25	4	638
No. Arrests[4]	0	0	0	0	290	11,732	12,358	1,363	3,885	2,580	1,236	217	52	33,713

1. Numbers represent incidents reported to NAF as of 8/29/95; actual incidents are most likely higher.
2. The sharp increase in incidents for 1991 may be partially attributable to the computerization of NAF's tracking system in mid-1991.
3. Stalking is defined as the persistent following, threatening, and harassing of an abortion provider, staff member, or patient *away from the* clinic. Especially severe stalking incidents are noted on NAF's Incidents of Extreme Violence fact sheet. Tabulation of stalking incidents began in 1993.
4. The "number of arrests" represents the total number of arrests, not the total number of *persons* arrested. Many blockaders are arrested multiple times.

Source: National Abortion Federation

their homes picketed or been followed and otherwise harassed. As a result of such intimidation, many doctors have ceased performing abortions at all. Many of those who continue to do so wear bullet-proof vests as a matter of course; some have hired full-time bodyguards.

The National Abortion Federation has tracked successful and attempted bombings, arsons, and other acts of violence at abortion facilities since 1977. Table 14 shows the different types of incidents that occurred during the years 1977 through 1983, during each year from 1984 through 1994, and through August 1995.

The Freedom of Access to Clinic Entrances (FACE) Act of 1994

On May 26, 1994, President Clinton signed into law the Freedom of Access to Clinic Entrances (FACE) Act. FACE is a federal statute aimed at strengthening protection for abortion clinics and their patients in the wake of increased antiabortion violence. Introduced in 1993, the bill eventually passed by wide margins in both houses of Congress. Among its supporters were many abortion opponents who felt compelled to act against clinic violence and who were convinced of the bill's constitutionality.

FACE prohibits the use of force, threats of force, physical obstruction, and property damage intended to interfere with those obtaining or providing reproductive health services. It does not apply to peaceful praying, picketing, or communication by protestors as long as these activities do not obstruct physical access to clinics. The maximum penalty for a first conviction of a prohibited act of violence is a $100,000 fine and one year in prison. This may be increased to ten years if the violation results in bodily injury, or to life imprisonment if it results in death. The maximum first-time penalty for nonviolent physical obstruction is $10,000 and six months imprisonment.

Under FACE, a civil lawsuit may be brought by the attorney general of the United States, a state attorney general, or anyone who is impeded in obtaining or providing reproductive health services. Those harmed by a violation of the law may sue for injunctive relief and compensatory and/or punitive damages. Civil penalties may also be assessed—up to $15,000 for the first violent offense or up to $10,000 for first-time nonviolent physical obstruction.

FACE was immediately challenged by abortion opponents. A number of groups and individuals filed lawsuits to block its enforcement, claiming that it went beyond its stated goals of stopping violence and intimidation and restricted their right to peaceful protest as well. As of June 1995, seven federal district courts and one federal circuit court of appeals had issued decisions upholding the law's constitutionality. One case, from Virginia, had reached the Supreme Court as of this writing; on June 20, without comment, the Court left intact the lower court ruling stating that the law does not infringe on anyone's freedom of expression. As of late 1995, only one federal district court had invalidated FACE, based not on the First Amendment but on an interpretation of the Commerce Clause (*Reproductive Rights Update* June 1995).

The first person to be prosecuted under the law was Paul Hill, a 40-year-old former minister. On July 29, 1994, Hill shot and killed Dr. John Bayard Britton and his volunteer bodyguard, retired Air Force Lt. Col. James Barrett, outside the Pensacola, Florida, abortion clinic where Britton worked. Barrett's wife, June, was wounded in the attack. Under FACE, Hill was convicted and sentenced to two life sentences, plus ten years for wounding June Barrett and five years for a weapons violation. Hill was also tried under Florida state law; he was convicted of first-degree murder and sentenced to die in the electric chair.

Public Opinion and Abortion

Measuring public opinion about abortion is a difficult task, not only because of the intense emotionalism associated with the issue but also because of the problems in shaping questions so as to get objective results. Further, many so-called polls, such as "reader surveys" published by popular magazines or television call-in surveys, are methodologically flawed—the respondents are self-selected, rather than random, and there are no safeguards against individuals submitting multiple responses, to mention just two problems.

Despite these difficulties, numerous attempts have been made to determine what Americans think and feel about abortion, with surprisingly consistent results. At their most basic, most polls indicate that a minority of people subscribe to either extreme viewpoint. About 12 to 15 percent think that abortion should be legal in all circumstances, and a similar number believe that it should be illegal in all circumstances. The rest are somewhere in the middle. In fact, it seems apparent that for the vast majority of Americans—70 to 80 percent—neither of the polarized positions describes their beliefs or feelings adequately.

When people are asked whether they believe abortion is acceptable under specific circumstances or for specific reasons, they express diminishing support. Although the exact numbers vary, in multiple surveys large majorities (over 90 percent) have said abortion should be allowed in cases where the woman's health or life is in jeopardy. Slightly fewer (85 to 88 percent) support allowing abortion in cases of rape or incest. Fewer people support it in instances where the fetus is deformed, and so on, down to interference with school or career or a desire for a child of a specific sex, both of which most respondents reject as acceptable reasons for abortion.

Despite their disapproval of abortion for what they believe to be trivial or frivolous reasons, most people (70 to 75 percent) oppose government bans on abortion. A majority do, however, support some restrictions, such as parental consent requirements for minors and limits on late-term abortions.

Beyond these simplistic answers are many shades of subtlety and a host of surrounding issues, many related to basic values and outlooks. Dealing with such complexities is well beyond the scope of this book. Readers who wish to pursue this path further would do well to consult the following [see the listings in chapter 5 for more information on both of these books]:

- *Between Two Absolutes: Public Opinion and the Politics of Abortion*, by Elizabeth Adell Cook, Ted G. Jelen, and Clyde Wilcox (Boulder, CO: Westview Press, 1992) addresses the subject specifically and in depth.
- *Abortion and American Politics*, by Barbara Hinkson Craig and David M. O'Brien (Chatham, NJ: Chatham House Publishers, 1993) contains an excellent chapter on public opinion and abortion that includes an analysis of the problems inherent in opinion polls in general and polls on abortion in particular.

Another good source of information is polling organizations themselves. Both Gallup and Louis Harris and Associates have conducted opinion polls at various times regarding abortion. The National Opinion Research Center (NORC) at the University of Chicago has asked questions on abortion as part of its General Social Survey (GSS) since 1972.

Gallup Organization
P.O. Box 628
Princeton, NJ 08542
(609) 924-9600

Louis Harris and Associates
630 Fifth Avenue
New York, NY 10020
(212) 975-1600

NORC
University of Chicago
1155 E. 60th Street
Chicago, IL 60637
(312) 702-1213; (312) 702-1014; (312) 702-1200

Abortion Techniques

In the following descriptions, length of pregnancy is measured by the number of weeks since the last menstrual period, referred to as weeks LMP. Since fertilization generally takes place midway through the menstrual cycle, gestational age is about two weeks *less* than the number of weeks LMP. Weeks LMP is the method of measurement used by most medical professionals.

Instrumental Techniques

Menstrual Extraction

Menstrual extraction is the extraction of uterine contents before confirmation of pregnancy. It is defined by Edelman and Berger (in Hodgson 1981) as "any procedure used to terminate a suspected pregnancy no later than 14 days after the expected onset of a menstrual period" (6 weeks LMP). Menstrual extraction has been promoted as a "do-it-yourself" abortion method, requiring only a small, flexible cannula and a hand suction device such as a syringe, with no need for dilatation or anesthesia. According to Hern (1984), it is a controversial and dangerous practice for several reasons:

- There is a higher incidence of continued pregnancy—in other words, the embryo may be too small and may be missed.
- Some studies have shown a higher incidence of complications for abortions performed at less than 7 weeks LMP.
- A high proportion of menstrual extraction patients turn out not to be pregnant, and thus have exposed themselves to unnecessary risks.
- Menstrual extraction has a higher retained tissue rate than procedures performed later.
- Statistical studies and clinical experience indicate very early abortion may be more difficult and hazardous than those performed after the sixth week of pregnancy.
- It allows denial of pregnancy, which "may not assist the patient in dealing positively with the need for contraception to prevent future unplanned pregnancy or in dealing realistically with the sense of loss and grief that many women experience at the time of pregnancy termination" (pp. 121–122).

Vacuum Aspiration (Suction Curettage)

The vast majority of legal abortions performed in the United States (97 percent) use the vacuum aspiration technique, which may be used up to about 14 weeks LMP. Vacuum aspiration is also used in later dilatation and evacuation (D & E) abortions to supplement the use of forceps and sharp curettage [see Dilatation and Evacuation, below].

The use of vacuum aspiration was reported in Communist China as early as 1958, but was not recognized in this country until 1967, when *Obstetrics and Gynecology* published two articles on the technique. Following the legalization of abortion in New York in 1970 and the development of more sophisticated suction equipment, the technique rapidly gained popularity, largely replacing the traditional D & C (dilatation and sharp curettage) procedure.

Vacuum aspiration may be performed under either local or general anesthetic, though local is usually preferred for several reasons:

- It is safer. Hern (1984) notes that most abortion deaths result from anesthesia complications. A Centers for Disease Control review of death-to-case rates for general versus local anesthesia for first trimester abortions from 1972 to 1977 found a two to four times greater risk of death for general anesthesia. Another study found that general anesthesia was twice as likely to be associated with uterine perforation and cervical injury, while the relative risk of blood transfusion, cervical suture, and major surgery was 3.9, 2.1, and 7.6, respectively, for general as compared with local anesthesia.

- The risks of perforating the uterus are lower. With general anesthetic, the uterus is softer and thus more easily perforated (Hodgson 1981).
- A conscious, alert patient can report unusual pain or other symptoms, increasing the likelihood of quick diagnosis and correction of any problems. Also, notes Hern (1984), "the use of general anesthesia eliminates physician-patient interaction during the abortion and insulates the physician from the patient's emotional experience. This is a serious loss for physicians and may make it extremely difficult for them to relate to the emotional problems encountered by abortion patients. It does nothing to enhance the physician's empathy for the abortion patient's dilemma or the physician's understanding of the importance of this experience for the patient's life."

The vacuum aspiration technique consists of two steps. First, the cervix is dilated, which is usually done one of two ways:

- With tapered metal rods called dilators, which are progressively larger in diameter. These are inserted in the cervix one at a time, each time using a slightly larger size, until the cervix is dilated enough to insert the vacuum cannula.
- With laminaria tents. These are sticks made from the stems of a kind of seaweed. As the sticks absorb moisture, they swell from two to three times their original size. The tents are inserted into the cervix and left from a few hours to overnight. As the tent swells, the cervix is gradually dilated. Laminaria tents are commonly used for later (D & E) abortions, but some practitioners prefer them over forcible dilatation even for early abortions, since the gradual dilatation decreases the need for local anesthetic.

Other methods of dilatation include plastic dilators; plastic foam sponges that, like laminaria, swell when wet; and prostaglandin suppositories, which cause the cervix to soften and make dilatation easier.

When the cervix is adequately dilated, the operator inserts a hollow tube, or cannula, into the uterine cavity. The cannula, which may be either metal or plastic, is attached to a suction device, which is usually electrical but may be hand-operated. The vacuum pump is then started and the cannula is gently rotated to empty the uterus. In many cases, the operator then uses a small, sharp curette, or spoon-shaped instrument, to check for any residual tissue. The average time for the procedure is less than five minutes. In the earlier stages of pregnancy (up to about 12 weeks) the cannula is about the diameter of a drinking straw.

Dilatation and Curettage   *anesth.*

Until the mid-1970s, dilatation and sharp curettage, or D & C, was the most common method for performing early abortions. In this procedure the cervix is dilated using manual dilators and a sharp curette is used to scrape out the uterine contents. The procedure is usually performed under general anesthetic. According to Hodgson (1981), the advantages of vacuum aspiration over D & C are:

- Less time required.
- More complete removal of tissue.
- Less blood loss.
- Fewer major complications.
- More adaptable to local anesthesia.

Dilatation and Evacuation

Since the late 1970s, dilatation and evacuation, or D & E, has been the preferred method for abortions performed from about 13 to 20 weeks of pregnancy, rather than the more hazardous and traumatic saline or prostaglandin induction methods [see below]. In most cases, D & E is a two-stage process, because the cervix must be dilated more than in early abortions. The procedure varies according to the clinic and operator, but usually laminaria are used to dilate the cervix. These are inserted and left anywhere from several hours to overnight, depending on the length of pregnancy. Sometimes manual dilators are also used.

Once the cervix is dilated, the physician removes the fetus and placenta using a combination of vacuum suction, forceps, and sharp curettage. This may be done either under general anesthesia, spinal or epidural anesthesia, or a paracervical block. For pregnancies up to about 16 weeks, it is possible to use large cannula that will remove all of the uterine contents with suction. For later pregnancies and in cases where large cannula are not available, forceps are used to crush and dismember the fetus and withdraw it through the cervix.

Possible complications include perforation of the uterus, cervical laceration, hemorrhage, incomplete abortion, and infection. Dilatation and evacuation is generally agreed to be safer and more effective than instillation methods, and it is less traumatic for the patient. However, it is more upsetting for the physician and assistants, particularly in later pregnancies where the fetus must be crushed and dismembered before it can be removed.

In a little-used variation of the procedure, called dilatation and extraction (D & X) or intact dilation and evacuation, the fetus is removed intact. This may require inserting a tube into the neck to suction out the spinal fluid and collapse the skull so the head will fit through the vaginal canal. According to Hern (1995), this procedure carries greater risk to the woman, although its advocates claim it is safer. As of late 1995, the House and Senate had passed different versions of bills outlawing this procedure. The versions are expected to be reconciled and sent to President Clinton, who has promised to veto the bill.

Medical Induction Techniques

Intraamniotic Instillations

Until recently, amnioinfusion with a saline solution was the most common method for abortions performed at 16 weeks or later LMP. It has been largely replaced by dilatation and evacuation for pregnancies of 20 weeks or less. Saline abortions usually require hospitalization. Under local anesthetic, a large needle is inserted into the uterus and used to withdraw 100 to 200 milliliters of amniotic fluid. A similar amount of 20 percent hypertonic saline solution is then infused into the uterine cavity. In most cases, the fetal heartbeat stops within about one and one-half hours, and the woman goes into labor and delivers the dead fetus within 24 to 72 hours. The time between the injection and the abortion may be reduced by the insertion of laminaria at least six hours prior to the infusion; this also reduces the risk of cervical injury. Oxytocin is also often used to stimulate uterine contractions and shorten the injection to abortion time.

Saline abortions carry a higher risk of complications than dilatation and evacuation abortions. Occasionally, though rarely, the fetus is born alive. Other possible complications include accidental injection of saline solution into a vein, hypernatremia (an increase in blood sodium levels), blood coagulation disorders, water intoxication, cervical injuries, infection, hemorrhage, and incomplete abortion. Instillation abortions can also be traumatic for the woman, who must endure a long and painful labor and the delivery of a dead, immature fetus.

Prostaglandins

Prostaglandins are naturally occurring hormones or hormonelike substances that have proved effective in causing uterine contractions and expulsion of the fetus. They may be administered intravenously, intramuscularly, vaginally (through suppositories), or into the uterus itself, either extraamniotically, between the fetal membranes and the uterine wall, or intraamniotically, directly into the amniotic sac. Laminaria may be used to facilitate cervical dilatation and decrease the number of contractions needed to expel the fetus, as well as to shorten the instillation to abortion time. In some cases oxytocin is also used. Sometimes saline and prostaglandins may be used together.

Prostaglandins compare favorably in safety with saline for inducing second trimester abortions. Blood clotting is considerably less likely and there is no risk of hypernatremia. Also, the instillation to abortion time is generally shorter. Because prostaglandins act on the musculature of the gastrointestinal tract as well as the uterus, they can cause severe gastrointestinal side effects. Other possible complications include a higher incidence of retained placenta, as well as cervical trauma, infection, hemorrhage, and sudden death. Also, up to 7 percent of fetuses will show brief signs of life (Hern 1984; Tietze and Henshaw 1986).

According to Hern (1984), a comparison of complication rates for saline instillation versus prostaglandin abortions from 1972 to 1978 showed higher risks for prostaglandin. The actual number of deaths, however, was low—a total of 136 during the period. Of these, the highest number, 47, was for abortions done from the sixteenth to the twentieth week. The lowest complications were for D & E abortions performed from 13 through 16 weeks.

Prostaglandins may also be combined with mifepristone [see below] to induce abortions up to 9 weeks LMP.

Mifepristone (RU 486): The French "Abortion Pill"

How It Works

Mifepristone is a progesterone antagonist, or an "antiprogesterone." Progesterone is a hormone that is produced by a woman's body midway through her menstrual cycle, signaling the uterus to develop the endometrium, the inner lining of the uterus, in preparation for receiving a fertilized egg, or ovum. If fertilization does not take place, progesterone production ceases and the ovum, along with the uterine lining, is shed during menstruation. If the ovum is fertilized, it begins to divide, eventually forming a tiny hollow sphere called a blastocyst. About 22 days after fertilization, the blastocyst attaches itself to the uterine wall and begins to release chorionic gonadotropin, or hCG, a hormone that stimulates the ovaries to keep producing progesterone. (Pregnancy tests work by detecting hCG in the woman's blood or urine.) The progesterone keeps the uterus from shedding the lining, as well as blocking ovulation and the beginning of a new cycle. It relaxes contraction of the uterine muscle and tightens the cervix, thus helping to keep the blastocyst from being expelled. Progesterone also aids in the development of the placenta and inhibits the production of natural prostaglandins, hormones that cause uterine contractions and make the cervix softer and more pliable.

Mifepristone works by neutralizing the effects of progesterone. It does this by binding to progesterone receptors in the uterus, in effect blocking the progesterone from delivering its hormonal "message." As a result, the uterus sloughs off its lining as if fertilization had not taken place. At the same time, the absence of progesterone causes production of prostaglandins to increase. This causes the cervix to soften and the uterus to contract, thereby facilitating the dislodging and expulsion of the blastocyst or embryo.

Taken alone, mifepristone is about 90 percent effective during very early pregnancy. If the dose of mifepristone is followed one or two days later with a prostaglandin administered orally or vaginally, the effectiveness is increased to at least 96 percent through the ninth week following the last menstrual period (LMP). (During the ninth and tenth weeks, the placenta begins producing progesterone in larger amounts, and mifepristone is no longer effective.) The use of a prostaglandin also speeds up the process. With mifepristone alone, it takes seven to ten days, and in some cases longer, for the abortion to be complete. With the combination of mifepristone and prostaglandin, the time is reduced to a few hours after the administration of the prostaglandin.

The original prostaglandin used with mifepristone was sulprostone, which had to be administered by intramuscular injection. During 1990 and 1991, three French women suffered cardiovascular complications associated with sulprostone, and one of them died. Sulprostone has since been replaced with misoprostol, a different form of prostaglandin that has been used for more than a decade in the prevention and treatment of gastric ulcers. Misoprostol is preferable to sulprostone for several reasons: it is less expensive; it can be administered orally or in vaginal suppositories rather than injected; and it is not associated with any serious cardiovascular side effects. Unlike sulprostone, it is also readily available in the United States under the brand name Cytotec.

Current Status

Since 1981, mifepristone has been used in dozens of clinical trials in more than 20 countries, including the United States, France, Britain, Spain, Germany, the Netherlands, Switzerland, Scandinavia, and the former Soviet Union (Hodgson 1996). As of October 1994, government regulatory agencies in France, Great Britain, China, and Sweden had approved the drug for marketing. In Europe, more than 150,000 women have used mifepristone as a medical abortifacient in conjunction with an oral, injectable, or vaginal suppository prostaglandin. In France, mifepristone is currently used in combination with an oral dose of misoprostol; this combination has been used successfully by more than 52,000 women. Women in Great Britain and Sweden currently use a suppository form of prostaglandin.

In May 1994, Roussel Uclaf, mifepristone's manufacturer, donated its U.S. patent rights to the Population Council, a New York–based nonprofit organization. In October 1994, the Population Council announced that clinical trials of the drug were under way at more than a dozen clinics around the country. The trials ran through September 1995 and involved 2,100 volunteers over the age of 18; their purpose was to test the safety, efficacy, acceptability, and feasibility of using mifepristone in combination with an oral dose of misoprostol to induce abortion in women at 49, 56, and 63 days LMP. The council planned to publish the results of the trials in 1996, followed by selection of a manufacturer and a distributor and application for FDA approval, with the goal of bringing mifepristone to market sometime in 1996.

Once approved for marketing, mifepristone would be available to any physician qualified to determine the age of a pregnancy and diagnose the possibility of an ectopic pregnancy. The physician must also be trained and licensed to provide abortions and have access to backup facilities for surgical abortion or medical emergency, such as transfusions (Population Council 1994). The cost is expected to be about the same as for a surgical abortion.

The campaign to introduce mifepristone in the United States may be boosted by the fact that the drug has a number of other promising applications, including treatment for such diseases as breast and prostrate cancer, brain tumors, glaucoma, and Cushing's syndrome, as well as easing difficult labor and aiding in term deliveries that might otherwise require cesarean sections. It may also provide a safe, effective means of birth control when taken, for example, on a weekly basis to prevent ovulation or once a month to induce menstruation.

The Process

Although it is noninvasive and potentially more private than a surgical abortion, a medical abortion is not a "do-it-yourself" option. It requires a minimum of two visits to a doctor's office or clinic, one to take the dose of mifepristone and a second about two days later to take the misoprostol. In most countries a third visit is required to ensure that the abortion is complete and there are no complications. Some countries and/or clinics also require an initial counseling session followed by a waiting period before the woman receives the mifepristone.

The trial regimen in the United States required at least three visits. Presumably, the process will be similar if the drug is approved for marketing. In order to be eligible, a woman must have her pregnancy confirmed and be no more than 63 days past the last menstrual period. The first visit includes counseling on the woman's options, a complete obstetrical and medical history, a physical examination, and determination of the length of pregnancy using vaginal ultrasound. If there are no contraindications, the woman swallows three 200-microgram (mg.) tablets of mifepristone in the doctor's presence and stays at the clinic under observation for half an hour. She returns to the clinic 36 to 48 hours later and takes two 200-mg. tablets of misoprostol under supervision and remains at the clinic under observation for four hours. About two-thirds of women abort during this period; the rest abort after they leave the clinic.

Twelve days after taking the misoprostol, the woman returns to the clinic to ensure that the abortion is complete; if it is not, vacuum curettage is used to complete the procedure.

Advantages and Disadvantages

The advantages of using the mifepristone/misoprostol combination are that:

- It can be used as soon as a woman suspects she is pregnant (vacuum abortions are not performed before 7 weeks LMP).
- It is noninvasive and does not require surgery.
- It does not require anesthesia.
- Side effects are usually moderate.
- There is no risk of uterine perforation or cervical injury.
- It is potentially more private.
- Many women report a feeling of greater control over their own bodies as compared to undergoing a surgical procedure.

By contrast, medical abortions also have some disadvantages:

- They require multiple office visits, compared to a single visit for a surgical abortion.
- They have a lower effectiveness rate (about 96 percent versus more than 99 percent for vacuum curettage).
- The woman is more aware of blood loss and of the actual passing of the product of conception.

Other Drugs

Research is currently being conducted in the United States and other countries on using other drugs and drug combinations to induce abortions early in pregnancy. One possibility is methratraxate, a tissue growth inhibitor currently approved in the United States for treating cancer, arthritis, psoriasis, and ectopic pregnancies. When used in combination with misopristol, methratraxate has been reported to be 96 percent effective in inducing abortions up to 8 weeks LMP. As of this writing (late 1995), clinical trials using methratraxate and misopristol to induce abortions are being conducted in the United States and Britain.

Additionally, at least 400 other antiprogestins have been created since Dr. Etienne-Emile Baulieu and his research team first produced mifepristone in 1981. However, the bitter controversy over abortion has stifled much of the research into the effectiveness of other antiprogestins as abortifacients, particularly in the United States (Klitsch 1989).

Major Surgery Techniques

Hysterotomy and Hysterectomy

Hysterotomy resembles a cesarean section. An incision is made in the abdomen and the uterus, and the fetus is removed through the incision. If done early in the second trimester, a hysterotomy may be done vaginally. Because it carries high risks compared to other techniques, hysterotomy is rarely used unless other abortion techniques have failed, usually repeatedly, or if the patient's medical condition makes other procedures unusable. Sometimes hysterotomy is performed in conjunction with sterilization. Even more rarely, a hysterectomy (removal of the uterus) is performed—almost always only in cases where a hysterectomy is already indicated, as in the case of a malignant tumor. Both hysterotomy and hysterectomy are performed under general anesthesia.

Folk Methods

For thousands of years women have tried various methods to induce abortion. These range from the innocuous—and ineffective—such as taking very hot baths, to the dangerous, such as swallowing poison or having someone jump on one's abdomen. Although folk methods have declined in countries where abortion is legal and generally available, they are still used in many places around the world. Historically and in many areas today, the most common method is inserting some kind of foreign object into the uterus, such as a twig, a catheter, or the infamous coat hanger. Sometimes the root of a plant, such as cassava, is used. Intense abdominal massage is the most common technique in rural Indonesia and Thailand. Another common technique is the injection of soapy water or household disinfectants into the uterus. These methods often kill the woman as well as the fetus; at the least they can lead to serious infection and often sterility. Some women drink gasoline or detergent, or take large doses of aspirin or chloroquine to bring on violent contractions (Jacobson 1990). Over the ages, a number of herbs, such as pennyroyal and tansy, have been touted as abortifacients, but most of them are at best ineffective and at worst fatal to the woman.

Abortion Complications and Long-Term Impact

Surgical Abortion

Most women experience some cramping and/or soreness following a surgical abortion; these effects are usually transient and rarely last more than a day or two. Beyond this, complications that may result from surgical abortion include:

- **Incomplete abortion.** This occurs when the uterus is not completely emptied during the procedure. It may result in bleeding and/or infection and is usually treated by follow-up suction or manual curettage.
- **Infection.** This may occur as a result of bacteria from the vagina or cervix entering the uterus. It can be prevented or treated with antibiotics.
- **Bleeding.** Many women experience some light bleeding for up to two weeks following an abortion. In rare cases the bleeding may be severe enough to require a blood transfusion.
- **Damage to the uterus.** This usually is a result of an instrument perforating the uterine wall or tearing the cervix. It may result in injury to other organs such as the bowel or bladder, requiring surgery to repair the injury. The risk of perforation or cervical tears is about 1 in 1,000 abortions; this risk increases with the length of gestation.
- **Complications from anesthesia.** In the United States, the vast majority of abortions are done under local anesthesia, which poses small risk of complications. General anesthesia carries much greater risks, including a higher risk of perforating the uterus, because it is softer.
- **Death.** For suction curettage abortions, the risk of death is less than 1 in 100,000. The risk is slightly higher for later procedures. Overall, compared to other surgical procedures, legal abortion has a very low death-to-case rate,

carrying approximately half the risk of death of a routine tonsillectomy.

The risks associated with abortion increase with the length of gestation. According to Cates and Grimes (in Hodgson 1981), the lowest risk of complications is at seven to eight weeks of pregnancy. After eight weeks gestation, the risk of major complications appears to rise 15 to 30 percent for each week of delay. The risk of complications also varies with the type of procedure used, as noted in the procedure descriptions above. Other variables affecting complications include the patient's age, race, gravidity, parity, and socioeconomic status, as well as preexisting conditions such as sickle cell anemia or heart conditions.

The use of prophylactic antibiotics, development of safer techniques such as vacuum aspiration, and increased experience among physicians performing abortions has greatly reduced the incidence of complications. Also, where abortion is legal, women tend to get abortions earlier, when the procedure is less risky, and any complications that do develop are more likely to receive prompt treatment.

Medical Abortions

Medical abortions, such as those induced by mifepristone (RU 486), carry a smaller risk of complications than surgical abortions. No anesthesia is required, and, because there is no instrumental intervention, there is no risk of cervical injury or uterine perforation. There is also less chance of tissue remaining in the uterus. Nevertheless, it is important that the drug be taken under close medical supervision.

Following the oral dose of mifepristone, some women experience light uterine bleeding. Other reported side effects include nausea, headache, weakness, and fatigue, similar to the "morning sickness" of a normal pregnancy; these may in fact be effects of the pregnancy itself.

After taking the prostaglandin, about 80 percent of women experience cramps and abdominal pain, similar to those associated with a very heavy menstrual period. About one-third of women may experience nausea, with smaller numbers having vomiting and/or diarrhea, which may be severe enough to require medication (these effects are reduced when the prostaglandin is administered vaginally rather than orally). Most women also experience vaginal bleeding and spotting that can last anywhere from one day to over a month; the average is about nine days to two weeks. The total amount of blood loss is comparable to that of a surgical abortion. In about 1 percent of women, vacuum aspiration or dilatation and curettage may be needed to control bleeding. In rare cases (fewer than 1 in 1,000 in France), bleeding may be severe enough to require a transfusion.

In about 4 out of 100 cases, the abortion is unsuccessful. These include both incomplete abortions (3 out of 100) and continuing pregnancy (1 in 100). In these cases the abortion must be completed surgically by vacuum aspiration or curettage (Population Council 1994).

Cardiovascular Complications

Sulprostone, the injectable prostaglandin originally used in France in conjunction with mifepristone, has been associated with three cases of serious cardiovascular complications. In 1990, two French women, both smokers, experienced cardiac problems after receiving injections of sulprostone. In 1991, a 31-year-old woman, a heavy smoker in her thirteenth pregnancy, suffered a fatal heart attack soon after receiving the prostaglandin injection. After these incidents, at the request of the French health ministry, abortion centers stopped providing nonsurgical abortions to women who were at increased risk of cardiovascular complications associated with prostaglandins, including women who were over 35 and/or were regular smokers (Klitsch 1989).

In 1992, France replaced sulprostone with a different class of prostaglandin, misoprostol. Misoprostol can be administered either orally or in the form of vaginal suppositories. It is less expensive than sulprostone and, in its oral form, has a decade-long history of satisfactory use in the prevention and treatment of peptic ulcer disease. As of October 1994, 52,000 French women had used the mifepristone/oral misoprostol combination. None experienced serious heart conditions. There is no evidence that misoprostol is associated with any cardiovascular side effects such as those associated with sulprostone (Population Council 1994).

Birth Defects

There is no evidence that mifepristone is teratogenic (causes fetal abnormalities) in humans. In early animal studies, newborn rabbits that had been exposed to mifepristone were prone to skull abnormalities, but no similar effects appeared in studies using monkeys. Three infants born to British women who had taken the mifepristone but not the follow-up prostaglandin early in pregnancy were born healthy.

Subsequent Pregnancies

Mifepristone has not been shown to have any effect on subsequent pregnancies.

The Long-Term Impact of Abortion

Problems in Determining Long-Term Risks of Abortion

The subject of long-term risks of abortion is a matter of considerable controversy. Although abortion opponents claim that abortions may lead to subsequent fertility problems, including sterility, premature birth, low birth weight, and miscarriages, researchers attempting to study such effects run into serious methodological problems. Among these are the following:

- Abortion techniques used now are safer than those used 20 years ago. This fact confounds statistics on morbidity, mortality, and risks to subsequent pregnancies, since statistics on repeat abortions often include abortions by older methods that are no longer used.
- Many studies also do not indicate at what gestational age the abortions were performed, and later abortions carry much higher risks for both short-term complications and long-term effects.
- Many women are reluctant to admit to prior abortions, so data on "first abortions" are not reliable.
- Many earlier studies failed to control for background factors, such as age, parity, ethnicity, socioeconomic status, and smoking habits, that might cause such pregnancy problems as low birth weight, premature birth, or miscarriage.

Effects on Subsequent Pregnancies

According to Tietze and Henshaw (1986), based on the best available data, "there can be no doubt that any adverse effects of terminating the first pregnancy by suction curettage must be quite small. . . . The few available evaluations of secondary sterility or reduced ability to conceive lead to the same conclusion. . . . This is also true for complications of labor and delivery." They go on to state, "The absolute risk attributable to the termination of the first pregnancy by suction curettage abortion . . . was negative for subsequent spontaneous midtrimester abortion, virtually zero for premature delivery and less than one per 100 live births for low birth weight" (p. 99).

Studies following the long-term effect of abortions done by surgical curettage seem to indicate a somewhat higher risk of adverse effects on subsequent pregnancies, but "it is not clear to what extent these higher risks reflect greater traumatization by the method or the manner in which it was used, inadequate correction for confounding variables or other biological or social factors associated with geography. No consistent pattern was found in the few sites where both methods of abortion were used and studied" (ibid.).

Little is known about the risks for women having more than one abortion, although some doctors believe that more than one abortion may increase the risk for low birth weight or preterm birth in subsequent pregnancies (American College of Obstetricians and Gynecologists 1994).

Increased Risk of Breast Cancer

In October 1994, Dr. Janet Daling, a scientist at the Fred Hutchinson Cancer Research Center in Seattle, Washington, announced the results of a ten-year study on abortion and breast cancer. The researchers found that women who had had an induced abortion had a 50 percent greater risk of developing breast cancer before the age of 45. It should be noted that breast cancer in younger women is relatively rare; the average increase in risk is from slightly more than one case per 100 women to almost two cases per 100 women. Women who had an abortion before 18 or after 30 appear to be at highest risk. The increased risk did not appear in women who had miscarriages.

The researchers theorized that the increased risk is somehow related to the way breast tissue responds to hormonal changes during the first trimester of pregnancy. The data also indicated that the risk could be reduced by obtaining the abortion as early as possible in the pregnancy, before major hormonal changes can occur.

Psychological Effects of Abortion

The question of whether abortion has negative psychological consequences for women is a controversial one. Advocates of legal abortion claim that the negative effects of abortion, if any, are transient, and that most women experience relief following an abortion. Abortion opponents, however, claim that most, if not all, women who have abortions will suffer to some extent from "post-abortion syndrome" (PAS), a collection of symptoms ranging from guilt and depression to alcoholism, drug abuse, and suicidal tendencies.

The problems in determining the psychological effects of abortion are similar to the problems encountered in determining long-term medical effects. A report presented to the Surgeon General by the American Psychological Association (APA) in 1987 cited some of these problems: inadequate methodology, researcher bias, lack of consensus in defining psychological sequelae and on selecting comparison groups, lack of standardization in data collection methods, lack of preabortion comparison data, small sample size, and the fact that "studies of women's response to abortion do not all examine the same event or medical procedure." Given these limitations, however, the APA goes on to state that the majority of studies indicate that although "at some level, abortion is a stressful experience for all women. . . psychological sequelae are usually mild and tend to diminish rapidly over time without adversely affecting general functioning" (American Psychological Association 1987).

These findings are supported by a team of psychologists headed by Nancy Adler, which conducted an in-depth review of 19 studies on the psychological impact of abortion. Their report, published in 1990, cites weaknesses and gaps such as problems of representativeness, lack of baseline data, lack of long-term studies, and the need for studies that separate the experience of abortion from the characteristics of women seeking abortions and from the context of resolving an unwanted pregnancy. Overall, however, the studies consistently found that negative responses following abortion were relatively rare and that in most instances psychological distress decreased after abortion.

By contrast, in their review of 76 articles on the psychological impact of abortion published between 1966 and 1988, James Rogers, George Stoms, and James Phifer noted that outcome incidence and methodological profiles varied substantially across the studies. The authors concluded: "Both advocates and opponents of abortion can prove their points by judiciously referencing only articles supporting their political agenda" (Rogers et al. 1989).

Characteristics of Women Suffering Psychological Distress after Abortions

Regardless of their overall conclusions, studies consistently indicate similarities among women who experience negative psychological effects after abortions:

- The review by Adler et al. in 1990 found evidence that women who are terminating wanted, personally meaningful pregnancies, who lack support from their parents or partners for the abortion, who have abortions in the second trimester, or who feel more conflict or uncertainty about the abortion decision are more likely to experience emotional stress following the abortion.
- Paul Sachdev, in a study of 70 Canadian women who had undergone legal abortions in major hospitals, found that adverse psychological reactions were influenced by the following factors: emotional conflicts or dilemmas stemming from the woman's commitment to the pregnancy and her attitude toward abortion, the ease with which she is able to negotiate with the medical system to obtain the abortion and the attitudes of the service providers, and the woman's relationship with the man involved in the pregnancy and her attitude toward sex (Sachdev 1993).
- Most of the women who responded to a survey conducted by Women Exploited by Abortion (WEBA) reported that they had been pressured into having abortions by male partners or parents. Additionally, many of the women felt that the treatment they received in abortion clinics was cold, uncaring, and coercive (Reardon 1987).

For more information about the risks and the long-term impact of abortion, see the listings under "Medical and Legal Aspects of Abortion" and "Psychological and Health Aspects of Abortion" in chapter 5.

Overview of Embryonic and Fetal Development

Fertilization (2 Weeks LMP)

This is the union of sperm and egg, which takes place around the middle of the menstrual cycle—about 2 weeks since the last menstrual period, or 2 weeks LMP—within one of the woman's fallopian tubes. About 20 hours after a single sperm (out of several hundred million released during ejaculation) succeeds in penetrating the fertile ovum, the nuclei of the sperm and egg fuse to form a single cell called a zygote, which contains the full human complement of 46 chromosomes. About 12 hours later, the zygote begins to divide. As cell division continues, the zygote begins to travel down the tube toward the uterus. If it fails to reach the uterus and implants in the fallopian tube, an ectopic pregnancy results.

Implantation (3 to 4 Weeks LMP)

About four or five days after fertilization, the still-dividing cells have formed a hollow, fluid-filled sphere called a blastocyst, which is about one-hundredth of an inch in diameter. The blastocyst floats around the uterine cavity for several days before attaching itself to the inner lining of the uterus. There it begins producing a hormone that signals the ovaries to make progesterone, which in turn signals the woman's pituitary gland that she is pregnant and stops the uterine lining from being shed through menstruation. By the twelfth day after fertilization, the dividing cells have begun to specialize: some of them will begin to form the embryo, while the rest will become the placenta. It is important to note that as many as four out of ten fertilized eggs never make it to this stage, and of those that do, many more will not survive much longer. When a fertilized egg fails to implant, it is simply expelled from the body, and the woman never realizes that she was pregnant. For reasons not yet fully understood, it is estimated that at least 50 percent of fertilized eggs never fully develop into babies (this is not counting induced abortions).

Embryonic Development (5 to 8 Weeks LMP)

At the start of the fifth week, the embryo is about one millimeter, or seventy-eight–thousandths of an inch, long. It floats in the embryonic sac, which is about two-thirds of an inch in diameter. Its cells have begun to differentiate and to form the rudiments of organs, bones, muscles, and blood vessels—a process known as organogenesis. The primitive streak, which will become the spine, forms.

By the end of the fifth week, the vertebrae, spinal cord, and nervous system are beginning to form, as is the brain. The tubular, S-shaped primitive heart has begun to beat, allowing the growing organism to circulate nutrients and waste products and exchange them through the placenta. Rudiments of eyes have formed. The embryo is now about one-quarter of an inch long. It has a separate blood system from its mother, to whom it is connected through the placenta.

During the sixth week, the head begins to form. The beating heart is still located outside the body. The intestinal tract starts to form from the mouth cavity downward. At this stage the embryo, which has a rudimentary tail, is visually indistinguishable from the embryos of many other species, including mice, chickens, pigs, and elephants.

By the end of the sixth week, the backbone is formed and the spinal cord has closed over. The brain is growing rapidly, but its neurons have not yet begun to form synapses, or connections, with one another. Tiny buds indicate the beginning of arms and legs, and depressions show where eyes and ears will form. Germ cells that will develop into either ovaries or testes have formed. The embryo is about one-half of an inch long.

By the end of the seventh week, the chest and abdomen have formed and the heart is now contained in the chest cavity. External ears are perceptible, and the face is starting to flatten. Big toes have appeared on the paddlelike feet. The tail is nearly gone. Lung buds have started to form, and the mouth opens. The embryo is about five-eighths of an inch long and weighs one-hundredth of an ounce; its heart beats about 150 times a minute.

During the eighth week, the face and features begin to form, along with the teeth and facial muscles. Rudimentary fingers and toes appear, and in male embryos the penis begins to appear as well. The cartilage and bone of the skeleton are beginning to form, and neurons are beginning to establish connections with one another through synapses. The fetus is now about three-quarters of an inch long and weighs three-hundredths of an ounce.

If even a small defect occurs during this stage of development, a spontaneous abortion, or miscarriage, is likely to result. Spontaneous abortions occur in 15 to 20 percent of diagnosed pregnancies.

Fetal Development (9 to 40 Weeks LMP)

The growing organism is now referred to as a fetus. By the end of the ninth week its face is completely formed, and the arms, legs, hands, and feet are partially formed, with stubby toes and fingers. The eyes have developed lenses, corneas, and irises. If female, the fetus begins to develop a clitoris. The fetus is now recognizably human, looking much like a tiny infant. It is, however, structurally immature and functionally quite limited. It is a little over one inch long and weighs about one-tenth of an ounce.

During the tenth week, the eyes begin to move from the sides of the head to the front, and the face begins to look human. The heart is beginning to form four chambers, and major blood vessels are developed. The heart beats about 120 to 160 times per minute. The head is very large in proportion to the body. The number of synapses in the neural system increases rapidly, and the fetus begins to display reflexive movements such as hiccuping and moving its arms and legs. It is about one and six-tenths inches long.

At thirteen-and-one-half weeks, the arms, legs, hands, feet, fingers, toes, and ears are completely formed. Fingernails and toenails appear. External genital organs begin to differentiate. The fetus kicks, curls its toes, bends its arms, forms fists, squints closed eyes, and opens its mouth. It may swallow amniotic fluid and urinate. All of these movements, however, are reflexive; the brain is not yet well-enough organized to control movements or form even the most basic perceptions. The fetus is now about three inches long and weighs one ounce.

At 18 weeks, the sex of the fetus is clearly distinguishable. The fetus's movements can be felt by the mother ("quickening") and the heartbeat can be heard with a stethoscope. The skin is covered with fine, downy hair, and eyebrows and eyelashes have begun to appear. The fetus is about eight and one-half inches long and weighs six ounces.

At 20 to 22 weeks, the first synapses begin to form among neurons in the cortex, the part of the brain that deals with thought and perception. By 23 weeks, hair has begun to appear on the head. The fetus is about 12 inches long and weighs as much as a pound. A fetus born at this stage may live very briefly, but will almost certainly not survive, even with intensive care.

At 27 weeks, the skin is wrinkled and covered with a cheese-like secretion called vernix caseosa. The eyes are open. The neurons of the cortex begin to synapse with neurons in the thalamus and to develop the branchy structure characteristic of the adult brain. The brain wave patterns become more regular. Over the next few weeks they will begin to resemble the waking and sleeping states of the adult brain. The fetus is now about 14 inches long and weighs about two pounds. If born at this stage, it has a two out of three chance of survival with expert care, although it may suffer moderate to severe abnormalities.

By the end of 32 weeks, the fetus is well-enough developed that, if born, it has an 85 percent chance of survival. It is about 16 inches long and weighs well over three pounds. Thereafter, the chances of survival increase with each day of development.

At about 40 weeks, the fetus is ready to be born. Although it can now survive outside its mother with proper care, it will take months before the newborn's nervous system and brain have developed enough for it to sit up, several months to more than a year before it can stand and walk, and years before it can function and survive on its own.

Suggestions for Further Reading

Grobstein, Clifford. *Science and the Unborn: Choosing Human Futures.* New York: Basic Books, 1988 [see listing in chapter 5].

Guttmacher, Alan. *Pregnancy, Birth and Family Planning.* Rev. ed. Revisions by Irwin H. Kaiser. New York: New American Library, 1987.

Nilsson, Lennart. *A Child Is Born.* New York: Delacorte Press, 1990. Excerpted in "The First Days of Creation." *Life* 13:10 (August 1990), pp. 26–46

References

Adler, Nancy E., Henry P. David, Brenda N. Major, Susan H. Roth, Nancy F. Russo, and Gail E. Wyatt. 1990. *Psychological Responses After Abortion.* American Psychological Association.

Alan Guttmacher Institute. 1994. *Facts in Brief: Abortion in the United States.* Fact sheet. New York: Alan Guttmacher Institute.

American Civil Liberties Union Reproductive Freedom Project. 1995. "The Freedom of Access to Clinic Entrances Act of 1994 (FACE)." *Reproductive Rights Update*, June, pp. 2–3.

American College of Obstetricians and Gynecologists. 1994. *Induced Abortion: Important Medical Facts* (brochure). Washington, DC: American College of Obstetricians and Gynecologists.

American Psychological Association. 1987. *Testimony on the Psychological Sequelae of Abortion.* Paper presented to the Office of the U.S. Surgeon General, December 2.

Centers for Disease Control. 1990. *Morbidity and Mortality Weekly Report: CDC Surveillance Summaries.* Vol. 39, No. SS-2 (June).

Cook, Elizabeth Adell, Ted G. Jelen, and Clyde Wilcox. 1992. *Between Two Absolutes: Public Opinion and the Politics of Abortion.* Boulder, CO: Westview Press.

Gianelli, Diane. 1993. "Shock-Tactic Ads Target Late-Term Abortion Procedure." *American Medical News*, July 5.

Greenhouse, Linda. 1994. "High Court Backs Limits on Protest at Abortion Clinic." *New York Times*, July 1.

Grobstein, Clifford. *Science and the Unborn: Choosing Human Futures.* New York: Basic Books, 1988.

Guttmacher, Alan. *Pregnancy, Birth and Family Planning.* Rev. ed. Revisions by Irwin H. Kaiser. New York: New American Library, 1987.

Hartmann, Betsy. 1987. *Reproductive Rights and Wrongs: The Global Politics of Population Control and Contraceptive Choice.* New York: Harper and Row.

Henshaw, Stanley K. 1990. "Induced Abortion: A World Review, 1990." *Family Planning Perspectives*, Vol. 22, No. 2 (March/April), pp. 76–89.

Hern, Warren. 1984. *Abortion Practice.* Philadelphia: J. B. Lippincott.

———. 1995. Personal interview with author. September 1.

Hodgson, Jane. 1996. "Abortion Procedures and Abortifacients." In *New Essays on Abortion and Bioethics*, edited by Rem B. Edwards. Greenwich, CT: JAI Press.

———, ed. 1981. *Abortion and Sterilization: Medical and Social Aspects.* London: Academic Press.

Jacobson, Jodi. 1990. *The Global Politics of Abortion: Worldwatch Paper 97.* Washington, DC: Worldwatch Institute.

Klitsch, Michael. 1989. *RU 486: The Science and the Politics.* New York: Alan Guttmacher Institute.

Lake, Alice. 1990. "The New French Pill." *McCalls*, March, pp. 58–63.

Nilsson, Lennart. *A Child Is Born.* New York: Delacorte Press, 1990. Excerpted in "The First Days of Creation." *Life* 13:10 (August 1990), pp. 26–46

Ory, H.W. 1983. "Mortality Associated with Fertility and Fertility Control." *Family Planning Perspectives*, Vol. 15, p. 57.

Philips, Lynn. 1995. "The Breast Cancer and Abortion Question: What the Study's Author Thinks." *Glamour*, March, p. 103.

Planned Parenthood, Denver, Colorado. 1995. Telephone conversation with representative, March.

Population Council. 1994. "The Population Council Announces Mifepristone (RU 486) Clinical Trials Are Under Way in the U.S." News release, October 27.

———. Undated. "General Information about Medical Abortion and the Clinical Trials." Paper.

Reardon, David C. 1987. *Aborted Women: Silent No More.* Chicago: Loyola University Press.

Rogers, James L., George B. Stoms, and James L. Phifer. 1989. "Psychological Impact of Abortion: Methodological and Outcomes Summary of Empirical Research between 1966 and 1988." *Health Care for Women International*, Vol. 10, pp. 347–376.

Sachdev, Paul. 1993. *Sex, Abortion and Unmarried Women*. Westport, CT: Greenwood Press.

Schmidt, Kimberly, and Jennifer Jackman. 1995. "Clinic Violence Survey Shows Rise in Death Threats." *The Feminist Majority Report*, Winter.

Tietze, Christopher, and Stanley K. Henshaw. 1986. *Induced Abortion: A World Review, 1986*. New York: Alan Guttmacher Institute.

Tribe, Laurence H. 1990. *Abortion: The Clash of Absolutes*. New York: W. W. Norton.

Ulmann, Andre, Georges Teutsch, and Daniel Philibert. 1990. "RU 486." *Scientific American*, Vol. 262, No. 6 (June), pp. 42–48.

Directory of Organizations

Alan Guttmacher Institute
120 Wall Street, 21st floor
New York, NY 10005
(212) 248-1111
(212) 246-1951 (FAX)

The Alan Guttmacher Institute (AGI) is an independent, nonprofit corporation that performs research, public policy analysis, and public education related to reproductive health issues. AGI's underlying goal is to "enhance and defend the reproductive rights of all women and men, with particular attention to and concern for those who may be disadvantaged because of age, race, poverty, education or geographical location." To this end, the institute seeks to provide information and influence public policies and attitudes in order to:

- Prevent unintended pregnancies.
- Guarantee the freedom to terminate unwanted pregnancies.
- Protect the ability to have children and to achieve wanted pregnancies.
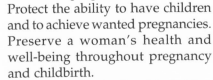
- Preserve a woman's health and well-being throughout pregnancy and childbirth.
- Promote the birth of healthy babies.

AGI conducts research and disseminates information both in the United States and abroad. Although decidedly pro-choice, AGI is known for its objectivity in collecting and analyzing information; it is probably the most-used source for statistical and factual information on reproductive health issues, including abortion.

PUBLICATIONS: *Family Planning Perspectives*, a bimonthly journal; *International Family Planning Perspectives*, a quarterly journal that includes Spanish and French-language summaries of each article; *Washington Memo*, a biweekly newsletter analyzing federal policy developments; and *State Reproductive Health Monitor*, a quarterly compilation of state legislation related to reproductive health. Books and materials on reproductive health issues include *Abortion Factbook, 1992 Edition*, which contains national, state, and local statistics on women who have abortions, abortion providers, and barriers to service, plus reprints of articles from *Family Planning Perspectives* on key topics related to abortion; *Abortion and Women's Health: A Turning Point for America?*, a look at the effects of current and potential state restrictions on abortion; *Abortion Services in the United States, 1991 and 1992*, which includes information on government funding, availability of services, abortion rates, and patient characteristics; *Induced Abortion, A World Review: 1986* and *Induced Abortion, A World Review: 1990 Supplement*, the "single most authoritative source of information on worldwide abortion services, laws and policies"; *The Politics of Blame: Family Planning, Abortion, and the Poor*; plus fact sheets and public policy analyses.

American Association of Pro Life Obstetricians and Gynecologists
4701 N. Federal Highway, Suite B4
Ft. Lauderdale, FL 33308-4663
(305) 771-9242

The American Association of Pro Life Obstetricians and Gynecologists was founded in 1973 by Dr. Matthew J. Bulfin to "meet the needs of women who were pregnant and who did not want to have their babies delivered by doctors who performed or arranged abortions." The organization also works to educate the public about abortion and to "persuade our pro-abortion colleagues to return with us to the traditional role of the obstetrician, protecting both the mother and her unborn, perfect or imperfect." Membership is open to all physicians who are either members of the American

College of Obstetricians and Gynecologists (ACOG) or Board Certified or Board Eligible by the American Board of Obstetricians and Gynecologists. Once elected, members agree not to perform abortions or to promote abortions either directly or indirectly. The association meets once each year, usually in conjunction with the annual ACOG meeting. Dues are $75 per year; retired members pay $10 per year and residents pay $5 per year.

PUBLICATION: *Lifeline,* a quarterly newsletter.

American Civil Liberties Union Reproductive Freedom Project
132 W. 43rd Street
New York, NY 10036
(212) 944-9800 ext. 515
(212) 730-4652 (FAX)

The Reproductive Freedom Project was started in 1973 as a special project of the American Civil Liberties Union, with its own staff of attorneys, paralegals, and support personnel. Its goal is to protect the constitutional right of privacy, particularly with regard to issues of reproductive choice, including "the right to choose between childbirth and abortion; the right to obtain and use contraceptives regardless of age; and the right to choose between sterilization and fertility." The project pursues its goals through:

- Public education, including sponsorship of and participation in conferences, meetings, and rallies; media campaigns; public speeches, articles and media interviews by staff attorneys; research projects; and pro bono training programs.
- Legislative advocacy at the state and federal level, including technical assistance and development of model briefing papers, analyses, and strategies for countering antiabortion arguments.
- Litigation, including blocking the implementation of federal, state, and local laws and federal administrative actions designed to restrict access to reproductive rights; providing legal and technical assistance for attorneys and organizations litigating reproductive rights cases; filing of and coordination of amicus curiae briefs; and presentation of arguments in state and federal appellate cases.

An important focus of the Reproductive Freedom Project is building coalitions with organizations and individuals who are building the reproductive rights movement among women of color.

PUBLICATIONS: *Reproductive Rights Update,* a quarterly newsletter; *The Rights of Women,* a handbook that includes several chapters related to reproductive freedom; *Reproductive Freedom: The Rights of Minors,* a briefing paper; *Shattering the Dreams of Young Women: The Tragic Consequences of Parental Involvement Laws,* a pamphlet; *No Way Out: Young, Pregnant, and Trapped by the Law;* and various fact sheets.

American College of Obstetricians and Gynecologists
409 12th Street, SW
Washington, DC 20024
(202) 638-5577

With more than 35,000 members—approximately 90 percent of American obstetricians and gynecologists—the American College of Obstetricians and Gynecologists (ACOG) is the leading organization for medical professionals involved in women's health care. ACOG concentrates its efforts in four major areas: (1) serving as an advocate for quality health care for women; (2) maintaining high standards of clinical practice and continuing education for its members; (3) promoting patient education and stimulating patient understanding of, and involvement in, medical care; and (4) increasing awareness among its members and the public of the changing issues facing women's health care. ACOG supports legal, safe, readily available, publicly funded abortion services for all women who desire them and works actively toward this end, including working to educate legislators and other government officials and filing amicus curiae briefs. To qualify for ACOG membership, physicians must be certified by the American Board of Obstetrics and Gynecology, have limited their practice to obstetrics and gynecology for at least five years, and demonstrate high moral and ethical standards.

PUBLICATIONS: *Public Health Policy Implications of Abortion: A Government Relations Handbook for Health Professionals* (1990), a "resource document designed to assist the health professional in responding to new legislative and public policy initiatives on abortion"; "Induced Abortion: Important Medical Facts," a patient education brochure.

American Life League, Inc.
P.O. Box 1350
Stafford, VA 22555
(703) 659-4171; (703) 659-2586 (FAX)
(703) 690-2049 (Metro DC); (703) 659-7111 (electronic bulletin board)

The American Life League, Inc. (ALL) was founded in the late 1970s by Judie Brown, who felt that most pro-life organizations had failed to "attack the anti-life ethic at its roots rather than battle its symptoms." ALL has grown into an umbrella organization that includes a full range of educational, research, and political activities. ALL's primary focus is on educating the public on life issues, including abortion, contraception, euthanasia, school-based clinics, and medical ethics, including the treatment of handicapped newborns. To promote its "no-compromise" message, ALL produces and distributes a wide variety of publications, conducts training seminars, and is involved in a variety of other activities, including nonviolent protests at abortion clinics, sidewalk counseling, crisis pregnancy counseling, post-abortion counseling, and adoption referrals. ALL also produces *Celebrate Life,* a series of nationally syndicated television and radio programs. Affiliate groups include:

- The American Life League Advocates, a legal research and advisory group.
- American Life League Affiliates, which consists of local and state groups involved in various pro-life activities.
- Athletes for Life, an organization of professional athletes.
- Castello Institute of Stafford, a research and educational group that has published numerous studies and "refutations of pro-death literature."
- Executives for Life, a group of pro-life business leaders.
- Teen American Life League (TALL), a peer-support group for 11- to 18-year-olds "who wish to say 'NO' to promiscuity, abortion, and other life-threatening temptations facing young Americans today."
- American Life Lobby, ALL's political arm, which with its internal political action committee, ALLPAC, works actively to lobby for a human life amendment and to promote total prohibition of abortion, as well as campaigning against euthanasia, sex education, school-based clinics, and taxpayer funding of "anti-life" programs from organizations such as Planned Parenthood and the American Civil Liberties Union.

PUBLICATIONS: *All About Issues,* a magazine published nine times/year; *communique,* a biweekly news report; plus a wide variety of books, manuals, booklets, flyers, and pamphlets.

American Rights Coalition
P.O. Box 487
Chattanooga, TN 37401
(615) 698-7960
(615) 698-7893 (FAX)
(800) 634-2224 (hotline)

American Rights Coalition (ARC) is a Christian pro-life organization ministering to women who have been hurt physically and/or emotionally by abortion. This assistance includes helping women pursue legal options where malpractice, misrepresentation, and fraud are indicated. Women who contact ARC are referred to local volunteer "support teams" who will assist them in finding medical help if necessary, act as liaisons with ARC in determining whether legal action is indicated and channeling them to the appropriate resources if it is, and provide sympathetic support. Women are also encouraged to join Christian postabortion healing groups and to attend church. Wherever possible, support team participants are persons who have had personal experience with abortion. ARC also seeks to fight abortion through legislative action, working with local regulatory boards, and exposing abuses by abortion providers. People with information about abortion-related injuries are urged to fax it in, call, or write.

PUBLICATION: *The Abortion Injury Report,* a monthly bulletin featuring reprints of news stories about women who have been injured by abortions, abortion-related lawsuits and convictions, clinic closings, and other events.

Americans United for Life Legal Defense Fund
343 S. Dearborn Street, Suite 1804
Chicago, IL 60604
(312) 786-9494

Americans United for Life Legal Defense Fund (AUL) is a nonprofit, nonsectarian public interest law firm serving as the legal arm of the pro-life movement. Founded in 1971, AUL was the first national pro-life organization. It is committed to "defending human life through vigorous judicial, legislative and educational efforts." Funded by 7,500 private contributors, AUL has a 24-member board whose members include Congressmen Henry Hyde and Christopher Smith, Northwestern University Law Professor Victor Rosenblum, and Harvard University's Arthur Dyck. Its staff of 30 includes 7 attorneys. AUL has participated in more than 20 Supreme Court cases, including *Roe v. Wade* and all subsequent abortion-related cases, as well as "right-to-die" cases. AUL was also involved in passing the Adolescent Family Life Act, which set up programs encouraging sexual abstinence by teenagers and the promotion of adoption over abortion. AUL's activities include:

- Drafting model legislation to be used at the state level.
- Writing and filing amicus curiae briefs before the Supreme Court and lower courts.
- Providing legal counsel to parties defending pro-life laws.
- Representing key parties in the federal courts.
- Providing legal counsel to state legislators and lobbyists.
- Providing expert testimony during hearings in support of pro-life legislation.
- Conducting quantitative research and publishing law review articles, books, and periodicals.
- Sponsoring education activities, including periodic forums, conferences, and workshops.
- Conducting media relations campaigns, including appearances by spokespersons on network and local television and radio broadcasts.

PUBLICATIONS: *Life Docket*, a monthly pro-life legal news summary sent to reporters and "public policy influencers"; *Lex Vitae*, a quarterly report on key pro-life litigation and legislation around the country; *AUL Studies in Law, Medicine and Society*, a monograph series of law review and other scholarly articles relating to abortion and euthanasia; *AUL Forum*, a quarterly newsletter for AUL friends and supporters; *AUL Insights*, periodic in-depth analyses of pertinent court cases and legislation.

Care Net
109 Carpenter Drive, Suite 100
Sterling, VA 20164
(703) 478-5661
(703) 478-5668 (FAX)

Care Net, a special ministry of the Christian Action Council, was founded in 1975 to "defend the sanctity of human life, to resist abortion and related practices that kill innocent people, and to provide biblical alternatives to abortion, infanticide and euthanasia." In an "ambitious effort to create the most accessible and effective abortion alternatives ministry ever known in North America," more than 450 affiliated pregnancy care centers provide women in crisis pregnancies with such practical services as free pregnancy tests; birth, abstinence, and post-abortion counseling; housing and referrals; and financial, medical, and material assistance. Local affiliate churches and centers receive extensive support and assistance from the national council, including training and educational materials, newsletters, and legislative alerts, as well as national conferences, regional planning meetings, and on-site leadership training.

PUBLICATIONS: wide selection of books, manuals for churches and pregnancy care centers, educational brochures, booklets, bulletin inserts and handouts, fact sheets, and videotapes.

Catholics for a Free Choice
1436 U Street, NW, Suite 301
Washington, DC 20009-3997
(202) 986-6093
(202) 332-7995 (FAX)

Established in 1973, Catholics for a Free Choice (CFFC) is an international educational organization that supports the right to legal reproductive health care, especially in family planning and abortion. CFFC also works to reduce the incidence of abortion and to increase women's choices in childbearing and child-rearing through advocacy of social and economic programs for women, children, and families. In the United States, CFFC works to counter the efforts of the Roman Catholic hierarchy to overturn *Roe v. Wade* and implement a ban on all abortions. A Latin American affiliate, Católicas por el Derecho a Decider (CDD), is working to shape the emerging debate about legal abortion in "a way that is both pro-choice and sensitive to the Catholic traditions of the region." CFFC is especially concerned with working with the "middle ground"— the more than 75 percent of the public that holds uncertain or seemingly contradictory views about the legality and morality of various reproductive issues, including abortion. CFFC's goal is to further dialogue on these issues in order to assist the policy process and work toward national consensus. Its activities include:

- Maintaining an education and communications program, including electronic and print media exposure, public speaking, seminars, and conferences.
- Researching, producing and disseminating publications and educational materials.
- Conducting a national public affairs program for policy-makers.
- Stimulating grassroots education in targeted states and regions.
- Networking with Catholic and secular women and groups in Latin America and the Caribbean in support of reproductive rights and U.S. international family planning assistance (in conjunction with CDD).
- Working with pro-choice and Catholic organizations to "increase the level of concern and responsiveness to the moral and ethical dimensions of pro-choice issues."

Associate dues of $25.00/year include a subscription to *Conscience*.

PUBLICATIONS: *Conscience*, a bimonthly news journal; *Abortion: A Guide to Making Ethical Choices; Bishop's Watch Reports*, a series of monographs including an in-depth analysis of surveys on Catholics' opinions and practices in the areas of family planning, abortion, and teenage sexuality; *Currents*, an occasional series on ethics and public policy that includes original articles and reprints; *Abortion in Good Faith Series*, a series of monographs including one on the history of abortion in the Catholic Church; *Guide for Pro-Choice Catholics: The Church, the State, and Abortion Politics*, a report on church-sponsored sanctions or directives limiting the participation of pro-choice policymakers in religious life; plus several Spanish-language publications, brochures, booklets, and stickers.

The Center for Reproductive Law and Policy
120 Wall Street
New York, NY 10005
(212) 514-5534
(212) 514-5538 (FAX)

The Center for Reproductive Law and Policy was formed in 1992 by a group of nationally recognized reproductive rights attorneys and activists. It is an independent organization dedicated to ensuring that all women, including young, low-income, and rural women and women of color, have access to freely chosen reproductive health care. Through litigation and public education, the center's mission is to:

- Protect a woman's right and ability to choose a full range of reproductive health services, including abortion, contraception, and new reproductive technologies.
- Ensure that reproductive health providers are able to provide services without harassment and to counsel their patients privately about the various options available to them.
- Defend the rights of pregnant women by countering punitive measures taken against them in the name of "fetal rights."
- Support the rights of young people to obtain age-appropriate sex education and reproductive health care.
- Promote the advancement of women's reproductive freedom as an international human right.

Through its Domestic Program, the center represents women, reproductive and other health professionals, religious leaders, and scientists in lawsuits that seek to guarantee access to abortion, contraception, and reproductive technologies. It also provides legal analyses and strategic assistance to a wide range of organizations in the battle for reproductive freedom throughout the United States. The State Program provides technical assistance on legislative proposals and strategies to legislators, state and local coalitions, and policymakers around the country. The center's International Program includes a range of activities, from monitoring legal developments and policies concerning reproductive issues to participating in key international meetings on population, family planning, and women's health issues.

PUBLICATION: *Reproductive Freedom News*, a newsletter.

Common Ground Network for Life and Choice
1601 Connecticut Avenue, NW, Suite 200
Washington, DC 20009
(202) 265-4300
(202) 232-6718 (FAX)

Search for Common Ground is an international organization dedicated to helping resolve conflict between groups that most people perceive as being hopelessly polarized. The Common Ground Network for Life and Choice, the organization's first domestic project, is aimed at opening new channels of communication and promoting cooperative efforts between pro-life and pro-choice supporters. The network began as a grassroots movement in Buffalo, New York, where in 1992 the Buffalo Council of Churches began a community initiative aimed at bridging the city's deep divisions, particularly over the abortion conflict. Similar efforts have sprung up in communities around the country, including the Baltimore-Washington area; Denver; Pensacola, Florida; and St. Louis, Missouri. The working groups focus primarily on two issues of joint concern: making adoption more available and acceptable, and addressing the underlying factors related to unintended pregnancy in young women. For such groups, the network provides support and assistance in the form of dialogue and problem-solving workshops, facilitation training, and meeting planning, as well as resource materials and ongoing advice. Specific activities include:

- Producing and providing information and models for interaction and community organizing to pro-choice and pro-life individuals.
- Working directly with local organizers to develop and implement pro-life/pro-choice dialogues and joint actions.
- Training local common ground activists in facilitation, conflict management, and coalition-building skills.
- Working with community-based efforts to develop media programs presenting the common ground approach to the abortion conflict, including locally produced television programs.
- Acting as a clearinghouse and resource center for information about common ground efforts and approaches.
- Identifying and developing, on the national level, common ground initiatives where joint action by pro-choice and pro-life advocates can make a positive impact on issues of mutual concern.

A national conference was in the planning stages at the time of this writing. A basic individual membership in the network is $25, which includes a subscription to the quarterly newsletter.

PUBLICATIONS: A quarterly newsletter; *Finding Common Ground in the Abortion Conflict*, a resource manual; plus the videos *What's the Common Ground on Abortion?* and *What's the Common Ground on Abortion in Buffalo?*

Doctors for Life
39 Tealwood Drive
St. Louis, MO 63141
(314) 567-3446

Doctors for Life is an organization of physicians who believe that human life begins at fertilization and who have vowed to uphold the portion of the Hippocratic oath specifying that a doctor will not participate in, assist, or condone either euthanasia or abortion. The organization, founded in 1978, seeks to complement other pro-life groups by providing educational materials and assistance in developing programs, as well as working to form a Pro-Life Caucus within the American Medical Association. Members of the Doctors for Life Advisory Board include such well-known pro-life physicians as Matthew Bulfin, Thomas Hilgiers, Mildred Jefferson, Carolyn Gerster, Bernard Nathanson, Joseph Stanton, and John Willke. Doctors for Life is an affiliate to the World Federation of Doctors Who Respect Human Life.

EMILY's List
805 15th Street, NW, Suite 400
Washington, DC 20005
(202) 326-1400
(202) 326-1415 (FAX)

EMILY's List is a political donor network for pro-choice, pro-ERA Democratic women who are campaigning for gubernatorial or congressional office. Founded in 1985, EMILY's List (the acronym stands for "Early Money Is Like Yeast") targets races; recruits, recommends, and trains candidates; and raises money early in the election cycle in order to fund initial campaign efforts, including staffing, fund-raising, research, and other components "essential to establishing a candidate as credible and capable of winning." Donor members receive profiles of each recommended candidate. They then decide which candidates they wish to support and write checks directly to those candidates. EMILY's List also conducts research and analysis on topics that concern women candidates, such as the problems women may encounter when running for public office and the impact of the pro-choice issue on Democratic candidates. Membership requires a minimum donation of $100, plus a promise to consider donations of at least $100 each to two or more of the recommended candidates.

PUBLICATIONS: *Notes from EMILY,* a quarterly newsletter; candidate profiles; and various white papers and reports.

The Feminist Majority
1600 Wilson Boulevard, Suite 801
Arlington, VA 22209
(703) 522-2214
(703) 522-2219 (FAX)

8105 West 3rd Street, Suite 1
Los Angeles, CA 90048
(213) 651-0495
(213) 653-2689 (FAX)

The Feminist Majority was founded by former National Organization for Women president Eleanor Smeal with the goal of involving more women in "areas of power," i.e., politics, business, and government. The organization consists of two separate groups, the Feminist Majority and the Feminist Majority Foundation. The Feminist Majority is a lobbying and political advocacy group whose current activities are aimed at ending parental notification/consent laws; repealing the Hyde amendment, which prohibits federal funding for abortions; and increasing abortion access, regardless of income level. The foundation spearheads the National Clinic Defense Project, which aims to counter antiabortion activities such as clinic blockades by mobilizing supporters to keep the clinics open. The foundation is the organization's research and education arm; in addition to developing educational materials and activities, it pursues projects on the use of initiatives and referenda for women's rights and contraceptive research and development. Activities include collecting election rules for states that allow the initiative process and analyzing former campaigns waged for ballot measures on abortion rights, the Equal Rights Amendment, and pay equity in order to develop model language, strategies, and implementation plans for future referenda and initiatives on these and other issues of importance to women. The foundation was the main organization that pressured Roussel-Uclaf and Hoescht AG to release the license for mifepristone (RU 486) to the Population Council so that the drug could be tested and eventually distributed in the United States. Other activities include programs for increasing awareness of and opportunities for women and girls in sports and working to promote women's rights internationally.

PUBLICATIONS: *Feminist Majority Report,* a quarterly newsletter; and two videos, *Abortion: For Survival* and *Abortion Denied: Shattering Young Women's Lives,* each with an optional viewer guide.

Feminists for Life of America
733 15th Street, NW, Suite 1100
Washington, DC 20005
(202) 737-3352

Established in 1972, Feminists for Life of America (FFLA) is a nonsectarian, grassroots volunteer organization that "seeks true equality for all human beings, particularly women, [and opposes] all forms of violence, including abortion, euthanasia, and capital punishment [as being] inconsistent with core feminist principles of justice, non-violence, and non-discrimination." FFLA focuses its efforts on education, outreach, and advocacy, as well as helping to facilitate resources and support for women in need. Areas of focus include enforcement of child support orders, opposition to welfare reform that would hurt children, as well as efforts to stop abortion. Beginning in the spring of 1996, FFLA plans to hold annual national assemblies in Washington, D.C., where state leaders can gather to exchange ideas and experiences.

Membership is $25 per year ($15 for students) and includes a subscription to the quarterly newsletter, an FFLA bumper sticker, and membership in the state chapter.

PUBLICATIONS: *The American Feminist,* a quarterly newsletter; plus several brochures; some local chapters have their own newsletters.

First Way Life Center
686 N. Broad Street
Woodbury, NJ 08096
(609) 848-1818 or (609) 848-1819
(609) 848-2380 (FAX)
(800) 848-LOVE (clients)

First Way is a nonprofit, interdenominational volunteer organization that operates a network of crisis pregnancy centers throughout the United States and Canada. First Way operates on the belief that women are driven to abortion by such problems as financial crisis, physical or emotional illness, or "social quandaries" created by extramarital or premarital conception, and that "there is no reason why a woman who is guided and assisted through a difficult pregnancy cannot love and accept her child." It therefore attempts to offer women sympathy and friendship as well as the resources to cope with their problems so that they will not have to resort to abortion. Accordingly, the centers offer a full array of services to women with unplanned pregnancies, including pregnancy testing, counseling, housing, medical care, legal assistance, adoption referral, maternity and baby clothing, and job placement. To receive help, pregnant women may call a toll-free number that operates from 8:00 A.M. to 12:00 midnight (Eastern time) every day, or they may call local centers, which are listed in telephone directories under the heading "Abortion Alternatives."

Heartbeat International
1213½ S. James Road
Columbus, OH 43227-1801
(614) 239-9433

Heartbeat (formerly Alternatives to Abortion International) is a nonprofit, Christian federation of service providers and individuals dedicated to offering alternatives to abortion through "education, action and creative services." Affiliates include pregnancy service centers, residential centers, hotlines, and support services, including postabortion support and counseling services. Heartbeat offers its affiliates and members the following:

- An annual conference featuring a variety of speakers and workshops on topics of interest to service providers.
- Specialized regional training seminars in areas such as grant writing, postabortion support, and board development.
- Networking opportunities.
- An information clearinghouse, with a continuously updated list of brochures, educational handouts, manuals, posters, etc.
- Consulting and personalized training services.
- Adopt-a-Center program for helping struggling centers in the United States and abroad.
- An annual worldwide directory of organizations offering pro-life pregnancy services.

Heartbeat also responds to requests from the public for educational material on abortion alternatives. Membership is $35 per year.

PUBLICATION: *Heartbeat,* a quarterly newsletter (included with membership).

International Life Services, Inc.
2606½ W. 8th Street
Los Angeles, CA 90057
(213) 382-2156
(213) 382-4203 (FAX)

International Life Services, Inc. (ILSI) is a nonprofit, nonsectarian organization that works to promote the right to life for human beings from the moment of conception to natural death. Its education division sponsors a variety of activities, including:

- The Annual Learning Center, a week-long program providing instructions on everything from fund-raising and handling the media to crisis pregnancy and postabortion counseling.
- Workshops held throughout the United States and abroad.
- A series of training videotapes for counselors.
- Production of various publications.

ILSI also has a counseling division that consists of 20 Pregnancy Help Centers located throughout southern California. The centers provide information, counseling, assistance, and referrals at no cost to pregnant women; they also provide postabortion counseling.

PUBLICATIONS: *Pro-Life Resource Directory,* listing more than 3,000 pregnancy service centers and more than 2,000 pro-life education and social action groups throughout the United States; *Living World,* a quarterly magazine covering topics such as abortion, teenage sexuality, medical ethics, and family life; plus a variety of brochures and pamphlets. ILSI also offers *Pro-Life Counseling Educational Tapes,* consisting of three series: Series I is a five-tape training course for beginners in crisis pregnancy counseling; Series II is a four-tape series designed for experienced counselors that gives advice on specialized counseling problems; and Series III is a five-tape series providing training in postabortion counseling. A six-tape series on public speaking called *Speak Out for Life* includes a manual and speaker's notes in camera-ready format for copying.

Medical Students for Choice
2484 Shattuck Avenue, Suite 250
Berkeley, CA 94704
(510) 540-1195

Medical Students for Choice was founded in 1995 to encourage medical students to become abortion providers and to support their colleagues who perform abortions. Its primary goal is to achieve its purpose through changes in medical education curricula. As of mid-1995, the organization had groups at more than 100 medical schools around the country. Activities include distributing pro-choice information to students, sponsoring events and seminars, and organizing speaker panels. Membership is open to any medical student.

PUBLICATION: *The Abortion Action* (booklet), a guide for student activists on how to organize and educate around reproductive health issues on campus.

National Abortion Federation
1436 U Street, NW, Suite 103
Washington, DC 20009
(202) 667-5881
(202) 667-5890 (FAX)
(800) 772-9100 (consumer hotline)

Founded in 1977, the National Abortion Federation (NAF) is an association of abortion service providers and supporters dedicated to making safe, legal abortions accessible to all women. Institutional members include proprietary clinics, nonprofit clinics, feminist clinics, Planned Parenthood affiliates, doctors' offices, and services affiliated with hospitals, as well as other health care providers and national organizations such as the National Abortion Rights Action League, the Planned Parenthood Federation of America, the Alan Guttmacher Institute, and other foundations and research organizations. Individual memberships are also available. A major function of NAF is to provide standards, guidelines, training, and education to help providers offer the best possible care and services to patients. This includes reviewing membership applications; conducting on-site evaluations; investigating consumer complaints; and providing assistance and professional training on a variety of topics, including nursing, counseling, public affairs, political education, public relations, management, medical and legal issues, and prevention and management of complications. Other key activities include:

- Providing information on the variety and quality of services available in abortion facilities to legislative bodies, public policy organizations, medical groups, concerned citizens, and women with unwanted pregnancies.
- Monitoring and participating in public policy developments affecting reproductive health care.
- Public education, including publications, workshops, and a toll-free consumer education hotline.

In response to attacks on abortion clinics, NAF also has a Clinic Defense Project that keeps track of harassment and acts of violence around the country; works with providers and local and federal law enforcement officials; and provides technical assistance and training regarding clinic security, protection of staff and patients, and organizing community resources to stop the violence.

PUBLICATIONS: A monthly membership newsletter; *The Truth about Abortion,* a series that includes fact sheets on violence against abortion clinics and public support for abortion; *Consumer's Guide to Abortion Services/Guia sobre servicios de aborto,* with information in both English and Spanish; and *Standards for Abortion Care,* covering obligatory and recommended standards for NAF member facilities, including ethical aspects, counseling and informed consent, nursing care, administrative procedures, advertising, reporting, and referral.

National Abortion Rights Action League
1156 15th Street, NW, Suite 700
Washington, DC 20005
(202) 828-9300
(202) 973-3096 (FAX)

With more than 500,000 current members, the National Abortion Rights Action League (NARAL) is the largest organization in the country working expressly to defend abortion rights. It is also one of the most politically active and visible pro-choice organizations. Founded in 1969 as the National Association to Repeal Abortion Laws, the organization changed its name to the National Abortion

Rights Action League following the 1973 *Roe v. Wade* Supreme Court decision. NARAL and its network of affiliate state organizations work on a variety of fronts to "counteract the new and continued threats to reproductive freedom through political and grassroots organizing." The NARAL Foundation, established in 1977, supports a variety of legal, research, public education, and training programs, including:

- Providing national, regional, and local training for affiliate directors, board members, and volunteers in such areas as organizational skills, phone banking, fund-raising, and strategic planning.
- Providing information on abortion-related cases and legislation on both the state and federal levels to elected officials, members of the press, affiliates, and field activists.
- Conducting public opinion research and analysis.
- Providing educational materials to pro-choice student groups on college campuses.
- Sponsoring petition drives.
- Lobbying activities.
- Conducting media campaigns, rallies, and other public education efforts.
- Providing legal assistance and filing amicus curiae briefs in abortion-related court cases.

Affiliate activities include sponsoring counterdemonstrations at pro-life protests, escorting women into abortion clinics, fund-raising, and responding to media inquiries.

PUBLICATIONS: *Who Decides? A State-by-State Review of Abortion Rights in America,* an analysis of abortion laws, recent legislative action, recent litigation, and the political climate in each state, updated periodically; *Reproductive Rights: A Status Report* (1989); *The Voices of Women: Abortion: In Their Own Words,* letters from women who had illegal abortions prior to 1973; *Choice: Legal Abortion: Arguments Pro and Con; Who Decides: A Reproductive Rights Issues Manual; NARAL News,* a quarterly newsletter; *NARAL Campus Newsletter,* a quarterly newsletter; plus two videos, *Voices,* featuring women who had illegal abortions, a doctor whose hospital cared for women who had had illegal abortions, and various elected and NARAL officials, and *One Year Later,* a response to the *Webster* decision.

National Black Women's Health Project
Public Education and Policy Office
1211 Connecticut Avenue, NW, Suite 310
Washington, DC 20036
(202) 334-2383

The National Black Women's Health Project (NBWHP) is an Atlanta-based self-help and health advocacy organization dedicated to improving the overall health of black women. Begun in 1981 as a pilot program of the National Women's Health Project, the NBWHP was incorporated as a nonprofit organization in 1984. NBWHP seeks to empower women of African descent to reach and maintain full health through informal support groups that enable them to share their concerns and problems and learn how to cope effectively with health issues. Currently the organization has members in 42 states.

In 1990, the NBWHP established its Public Education and Policy Office in Washington, D.C., to increase black women's awareness of critical women's health issues, encourage their participation in national and state health policy debates, and promote a more expansive reproductive health agenda that is sensitive to issues confronting black women. This is being accomplished through:

- Legislative representation to ensure that black women's health is addressed in federal policy debate.
- Providing technical assistance and support to state activists working to promote health and reproductive rights.
- Speaking and media activities to improve public understanding of health and reproductive technology issues and their impact on black women.
- Serving as a clearinghouse for information exchange on black women's health issues, including reproductive choice.

National Latina Health Organization
P.O. Box 7567
1900 Fruitvale Avenue
Oakland, CA 94601
(510) 534-1362
(510) 534-1364 (FAX)

The Organización Nacional de La Salud de La Mujer Latina, or National Latina Health Organization (NLHO), was founded in March

1986 to "raise Latina consciousness about our health and health problems, so that we can begin to take control of our health and our lives."
NLHO is committed to working toward the goal of bilingual access
to quality health care and the self-empowerment of Latinas through
education, health advocacy, and work aimed at affecting public policy.
In the area of abortion and reproductive rights, NLHO engages in a
number of activities intended to:

- Break the silence on reproductive rights within the Latino
  community and provide a platform for open discussion.
- Ensure that Latina voices are heard in the debate over abortion and other reproductive health issues by promoting
  Latinas on the boards of mainstream reproductive rights
  groups.
- Mobilize Latinas in the struggle for full reproductive freedom, including access to culturally relevant quality health
  care and information, prenatal care, freedom from sterilization and other reproductive abuses, education about
  sexuality and contraception for young Latina women, and
  access to alternative forms of birth control.
- Debunk the myths surrounding Latinas through public
  education.
- Advocate and pressure elected officials, organizations, and
  individuals to support reproductive choice for Latinas.

In 1988, NLHO held the First National Conference on Latina
Health Issues with over 350 women attending, including several
from Puerto Rico and Mexico. Since 1988, the organization has also
conducted a workshop series, "Latina Health Issues . . . Better
Health through Self-Empowerment," covering such topics as mental health, patients' rights, teen pregnancy, and AIDS.

National Organization for Women
P.O. Box 7813
Washington, DC 20044
(202) 331-0066

NOW Legal Defense and Education Fund
99 Hudson Street
New York, NY 10013
(212) 925-6635
(212) 226-1066 (FAX)

The National Organization for Women was founded in 1966 to further "true equality for all women in America [and] a fully equal

partnership of the sexes, as part of the world-wide revolution of human rights now taking place within and beyond our national borders." Support for reproductive freedom, including access to safe, legal abortion, has been a major focus of NOW since its inception. Since the 1989 *Webster* Supreme Court decision, NOW has stepped up its activity in support of abortion rights and has experienced a dramatic increase in membership, with approximately 280,000 members and approximately 800 chapters nationwide. During 1990, NOW sponsored the Freedom Caravan for Women's Lives, a state-by-state campaign to recruit volunteers and promote pro-choice candidates for the 1990 elections. Other activities include letter-writing campaigns and demonstrations. Affiliated groups include the NOW Political Action Committee (NOWPAC) and the NOW Legal Defense and Education Fund.

PUBLICATIONS: *NOW Times,* a bimonthly newspaper. A number of materials related to abortion and reproductive rights are also available through the NOW Legal Defense and Education Fund (NOWLDEF). These include *Legal Resource Kit—Reproductive Rights,* which includes an annotated bibliography and resource list and an analysis of public opinion polls on reproductive rights issues; *Attorney Referral Services List,* with addresses and telephone numbers of organizations that make attorney referrals; *Facts on Reproductive Rights,* a manual on the medical, legal, and social issues involved; *Protecting Young Women's Right to Abortion: A Guide to Parental Notification and Consent Laws,* an analysis of reproductive rights in light of recent Supreme Court decisions; and copies of briefs and complaints filed by NOWLDEF in various related court cases.

National Right to Life Committee
419 7th Street, NW, Suite 500
Washington, DC 20004-2293
(202) 626-8800
(202) 737-9189 (FAX)
(202) 393-LIFE (legislative update line)

The National Right to Life Committee (NRLC) is the largest and best-known pro-life organization in the country, with over 3,000 local chapters. The NRLC has a representative structure, with local chapters represented at the state level and each state and the District of Columbia electing a director to the national board. In addition, three at-large directors are elected by the membership. The NRLC was founded in June 1973 in response to the *Roe v. Wade* Supreme Court decision legalizing abortion. NRLC is a nonsectarian organization with members from across the religious and political spectrum. In conjunction with the National Right to Life Trust Fund, the NRLC is involved in a broad range of education, outreach, citizen action, and lobbying efforts aimed at stopping abortion, infanticide, and euthanasia. Affiliate groups include:

- National Right to Life Political Action Committee, formed in 1980 to support pro-life candidates of either party running for federal office, through volunteers, endorsements, advertisements, and campaign contributions.
- American Victims of Abortion.
- Black Americans for Life, founded in 1985 to reach out to black communities.
- National Teens for Life, founded in 1985 for junior high and high school youth, offering conventions, seminars, fund-raisers, services for unwed teenage mothers, and opportunities for political involvement.

NRLC's many projects include a voter identification project, a religious outreach program, and a nationally syndicated five-minute radio program, *Pro-Life Perspective,* aired daily on some 300 stations.

PUBLICATIONS: *National Right to Life News,* a semimonthly newspaper; a set of booklets containing key abortion-related votes in Congress, updated regularly; fact sheets on various topics, including legislative updates and abortion statistics; plus a wide variety of books, pamphlets, videos, audiovisual programs, reprints, brochures, and booklets.

National Women's Coalition for Life
P.O. Box 1553
Oak Park, IL 60304
(708) 848-5351

The National Women's Coalition for Life (NWCL) was founded in 1992 as an educational, nonsectarian coalition of national pro-life women's organizations. Its purpose is to unite the organizations and facilitate joint educational, research, and service efforts aimed at regaining respect for unborn children and their mothers, as well as to publicize both support services for women and children and the existence of national pro-life women's organizations. Currently the coalition represents 14 organizations with a combined membership of over 1.2 million. The groups represent diverse philosophies, ranging from Feminists for Life of America to the National Council of Catholic Women. Membership is open to any national women's organization that takes a pro-life position with regard to unborn children and that provides free services to women and their families during and after pregnancy or after abortion. NWCL's first major project was providing staffing and support for the Real Choices research project, which examined core issues of support and prevention in reducing the number of abortions. The project resulted in the publication of the book *Real Choices: Offering Practical Life-Affirming Alternatives to Abortion* by project director Frederica Mathewes-Green [see chapter 5].

The Nurturing Network
910 Main Street, Suite 360
P.O. Box 2050
Boise, ID 83701
(208) 344-7200
(208) 344-4447 (FAX)
(800) 866-4666 (TNN-4MOM)

The Nurturing Network is a nonsectarian, nonprofit organization dedicated to making sure that the "freedom to choose" includes the choice to carry an unplanned pregnancy to term. The Nurturing Network takes no position on the legality or morality of abortion; instead it seeks to "discover the vast common ground that can nurture the seeds of mutual understanding." Its primary concern is meeting the needs of women facing unplanned and unwanted pregnancies, with particular emphasis on those who are most often overlooked—young middle-class college-educated and career-oriented women who tend to feel that they have too much to lose by continuing their pregnancies and who lack the resources and support for choosing to give birth rather than to have an abortion. The network consists of more than 22,000 volunteers who are active in all 50 states. Services are aimed at providing counseling and practical support services so that "the birth alternative may become more attractive, feasible and available to more women" and include:

- A counselor network made up of degreed and licensed professional nurses, counselors, and social workers.
- Nurturing Homes, private families who open their homes to prospective mothers.
- A medical network of doctors and nurses who provide prenatal and obstetrical care and nutritional guidance.
- An education network through which women can arrange temporary transfers from one college to another of comparable academic standing so that they can continue their education during pregnancy without violating confidentiality.
- An employer network that assists clients in designing a work plan and provides a woman with the option of relocating and working "in a challenging professional environment for an employer who understands her needs at this particular time."
- Adoption referrals and assistance.
- Financial assistance.
- Classes and workshops in parenting and child care.

All services are provided without charge to client women. Funding is provided through individual, corporate, and foundation donations. Strict confidentiality is also maintained for all clients, and services are provided without regard to race, religion, or creed.

PUBLICATIONS: A twice-yearly newsletter (Mother's Day and Thanksgiving) and descriptive brochures.

Operation Rescue National
P.O. Box 740066
Dallas TX 75374
(214) 907-2280
(214) 907-0277 (FAX)
(214) 907-0585 (24-hour recorded information line)

Operation Rescue's declared mission is to "bring the church of Jesus Christ to the abortion mill [in order to] present moms with an informed choice and provide a defense for children." Growing out of a frustration with the slowness of political approaches to stopping abortion, Operation Rescue started as a grassroots organization based on the principles of civil disobedience and a belief that "when man's laws conflict with God's laws, God's laws must be obeyed." It soon became famous for "rescue missions," in which singing and praying protesters attempted to temporarily shut down abortion clinics by creating human blockades. The missions are usually carried out in conjunction with pro-life counselors who take advantage of the blocked access to attempt to persuade women not to have abortions. Since 1988, rescue missions have resulted in thousands of arrests and a number of convictions leading to stiff fines and/or jail sentences, often under the federal Racketeer Influenced and Corrupt Organizations (RICO) law. These activities have generated massive publicity for the pro-life movement, as well as for Operation Rescue's charismatic founder, Randall Terry.

Operation Rescue National does not itself have any members, but acts as a sort of central clearinghouse for "people who want to stop abortion." Operation Rescue operates a 24-hour information line for those wishing to learn about national events, pending legislation, and other abortion-related information. The organization also has its own publishing affiliate, Rescue Education and Publishing (REAP).

PUBLICATIONS: *Operation Rescue, Accessory to Murder,* and *Why Does a Nice Guy Like Me Keep Ending Up in Jail,* books by Randy Terry; *To Rescue the Children,* a "nuts and bolts, practical manual on starting a Christ-centered, pro-life activist ministry"; *Rescue Report,* a monthly newsletter; plus various brochures, books, manuals, tracts, videos, and audiocassettes.

Planned Parenthood Federation of America
810 Seventh Avenue
New York, NY 10019
(212) 541-7800
(212) 765-4711 (FAX)

Planned Parenthood Federation of America (PPFA) is the largest and best-known organization dedicated to "[assuring] access to family planning information and services for all who want and need them." This includes both direct provision of services and educational and other activities aimed at increasing support and access to reproductive health services, including legal, safe, affordable abortion. On the local level, PPFA affiliates provide a range of reproductive health services, including contraceptive instruction and materials, infertility screening and counseling, voluntary sterilization, testing for sexually transmitted diseases, parenthood decision-making counseling, pregnancy testing and counseling, abortion, and adoption referrals. Local affiliates also offer educational programs that are aided by national leadership and programming support. These include:

- Presentations on reproductive health issues for schools, churches, and community groups.
- Programs for teenagers and parents "designed to enhance sexuality learning within the family."
- Workshops and training seminars for teachers, physicians, nurses, social workers, and other health professionals.

Additionally, PPFA is involved in a wide range of programs at the local, state, and national levels aimed at increasing access to reproductive health services; reducing pregnancy and birthrates among American teenagers; increasing the American public's understanding of and comfort with sexuality; and ensuring the widest possible choice of safe and effective fertility management for American women and men, including access to reliable contraception and medically safe, affordable abortion. Activities include:

- Building networks with other community and national groups.
- Advertising, media, and public education campaigns, including the "Keep Abortion Safe and Legal" campaign, implemented in the wake of the 1989 *Webster* decision.
- Organizing and participating in public rallies and demonstrations.
- Engaging in litigation to "protect individuals from restrictive legislation"; as well as providing amicus curiae briefs in relevant Supreme Court cases.
- Providing technical assistance and background information to other organizations, the medical community, the media, religious and community leaders, health and civil rights groups, and concerned individuals on such topics as contraceptive options and mifepristone (RU 486), the French "abortion pill."
- Providing educational information to the public and elected officials and policymakers.
- Monitoring affiliate research projects in areas such as high-risk sexual behavior, sterilization, and other topics.

- Working with affiliates to expand the scope and volume of medical services, particularly to underserved low-income, adolescent, and minority populations.

Through its international division, Family Planning International Assistance, PPFA also provides family planning services abroad. PPFA is a founding member of the International Planned Parenthood Federation, which comprises family planning associations in 125 countries.

PUBLICATIONS: *Current Literature in Family Planning*, a monthly collection of abstracts of books and journal articles; *LINKLine*, a bimonthly newsletter on sexuality, reproductive health, and family planning; *Echoes from the Past* and *70 Years of Family Planning in America*, books on the history of Planned Parenthood; *Nine Reasons Why Abortions Are Legal* and *Five Ways To Prevent Abortion (and One Way That Won't)*, booklets; plus books, curriculum guides, booklets, pamphlets, posters, videos, gifts, novelties, and other items on reproductive health, sexuality, and related topics.

The Population Council
One Dag Hammarskjöld Plaza
New York, NY 10017
(212) 339-0500
(212) 755-6052 (FAX)

Established in 1952, the Population Council is an international nonprofit organization that seeks to "improve the well being and reproductive health of current and future generations around the world and to help achieve a humane, equitable, and sustainable balance between people and resources." To this end, the council pursues social and health science programs and research relevant to developing countries and conducts biomedical research aimed at developing and improving contraceptive technology. A particular emphasis is on research into male reproductive physiology, with the goal of developing safe and effective contraceptives for use by men. An important focus for the council is the reduction and treatment of unsafe abortion. Current programs include:

- A research program for the prevention of unsafe induced abortion and its adverse consequences in Latin America and the Caribbean.

- Projects designed to analyze and document the magnitude of social and health problems associated with incomplete and septic abortions in sub-Saharan Africa, including programs in Kenya and Zaire.

The council also provides advice and technical assistance to governments, international agencies, and nongovernmental organizations and disseminates information on population issues through publications, conferences, seminars, and workshops.

In May 1994, the French drug manufacturer Roussel-Uclaf donated its U.S. patent rights for mifepristone, better known as RU 486, to the Population Council. In October of that year, the council announced that it would be conducting clinical trials of the drug at over a dozen clinics around the country, with the goal of gaining FDA approval and bringing mifepristone to market in the United States some time in 1996.

PUBLICATIONS: *Population and Development Review,* a quarterly journal; *Studies in Family Planning,* a bimonthly journal; plus books, working papers, pamphlet series, newsletters, and software.

Pro-Life Action League
6160 N. Cicero Avenue
Chicago, IL 60646
(312) 777-2900
(312) 777-3061 (FAX)
(312) 777-2525 (24-hour action line)

The Pro-Life Action League (PLAL) is one of the country's most visible and confrontational activist groups. Working to "[save] babies' lives through non-violent direct action," PLAL volunteers participate in such activities as sidewalk counseling, picketing, and rescue missions at abortion clinics, as well as directly confronting politicians and organizations that support legal abortion. Putting into practice the methods described by founder and director Joseph Scheidler in his book, *Closed: 99 Ways To Stop Abortion,* PLAL has directed its efforts toward closing abortion clinics in Chicago and around the country. Other activities include conducting seminars, workshops, and conferences, lecturing to student groups, and helping pro-life activists develop effective local programs. PLAL also operates a 24-hour hotline to keep pro-life activists informed about abortion-related events and to suggest concrete actions they can take to stop abortion.

PUBLICATIONS: *Pro-Life Action News,* a quarterly newsletter; *Closed: 99 Ways To Stop Abortion,* handbook by Joseph Scheidler (updated in 1994); and *Meet the Abortion Providers,* a video and audiocassettes featuring testimony of former abortion assistants, clinic owners, and doctors.

Prolife Nonviolent Action Project

P.O. Box 2193
Gaithersburg, MD 20879
(301) 774-4043

The Prolife Nonviolent Action Project (PNAP) was founded in 1977 "to promote direct action to protect our brothers and sisters from abortion, to unleash a dynamic of peace and reconciliation within families, [and] to challenge and invigorate the moribund right to life establishment" through nonviolent demonstrations aimed at preventing women from having abortions. Since 1988, PNAP has conducted an annual "Rachel's Rescue" on January 22, the anniversary of the *Roe v. Wade* Supreme Court decision, at abortion clinics in the Washington, D.C., area. Rachel's Rescue was the "first national rescue led by women who have suffered abortion"; since 1990, men affected by abortion have also participated. These and other "parents of aborted children" also serve as spokespersons for the group. PNAP also serves as an information and referral group.

PUBLICATIONS: *Nonviolence Is an Adverb* and *No Cheap Solutions,* booklets by John Cavanaugh O'Keefe; *She Trespasses Too?,* the transcript of a trial of nine pro-lifers in Baltimore; *In Need of Defense,* a trial transcript in which the three defendants spoke on behalf of the "victims of abortion" rather than themselves; plus videos of sit-ins and rescues.

Religious Coalition for Reproductive Choice

1025 Vermont Avenue, NW, Suite 1130
Washington, DC 20005
(202) 628-7700
(202) 628-7716 (FAX)

The Religious Coalition for Reproductive Choice (formerly the Religious Coalition for Abortion Rights) was formed in 1973 by 10 denominations and faith groups as a response to efforts to overturn the *Roe v. Wade* Supreme Court decision legalizing abortion. As of 1995, the coalition included 38 Protestant, Jewish, and other faith groups that support all reproductive options and oppose antiabortion violence. Through its member faith groups and more than 50 state and local affiliates, the Religious Coalition mobilizes pro-choice religious people to:

- Make clear that abortion can be a moral, ethical, and religiously responsible decision.
- Create a public opinion climate that is conducive to pro-choice policymaking by educating elected officials, religious people, and the media.
- Develop broad-based participation and leadership, recognizing that restrictions on reproductive choice disproportionately affect women of color, young women, and the poor.

Religious Coalition affiliate staff and volunteers provide all-options counseling to women who seek spiritual guidance in their decision making, educate state legislators and the public about policy affecting reproductive choice, and organize "peaceful presence" at besieged clinics. The coalition also sponsors a nationwide Clergy for Choice network that includes more than 7,000 clergy members representing every state and virtually every denomination. Additionally, the coalition's Women of Color Partnership program seeks to inform and motivate religious people to work together to:

- Counter the racism and misperceptions that contribute to punitive policies and practices.
- Address the needs and circumstances of low-income women.
- Build and nurture a diverse movement with full participation and leadership from women of many traditions and cultures.

Ongoing efforts include multicultural and antiracism training, the formation of caucuses throughout the denominations, the creation of culturally relevant materials, and development of media exposure for religious people of color.

PUBLICATIONS: *Religious Coalition News,* a periodic newsletter; *Abortion: Finding Your Own Truth,* by Corrintha Rebecca Bennett, a brochure; plus fact sheets on various topics.

Seamless Garment Network
109 Pickwick Drive
Rochester, NY 14618
(716) 442-8497

The Seamless Garment Network (SGN) is an informal network of about 150 organizations and a number of individuals devoted to promoting a consistent ethic of reverence for life. The consistent ethic links issues perceived as life-threatening—including war, poverty, the arms race, the death penalty, and euthanasia, as well as abortion—and challenges groups and individuals working on some or all of these issues to "maintain a cooperative spirit of peace, reconciliation and respect in protecting the unprotected." SGN also supports social justice, pro-life feminism, human rights, and disabled rights.

PUBLICATIONS: *Harmony*, a bimonthly, nondenominational journal with coverage of consistent ethic news and events plus writings on peace, justice, and life issues; and *Consistent Ethic Resource Directory*, which includes organizations, speakers, books, and periodicals.

Victims of Choice
P.O. Box 815
Naperville, IL 60566
(708) 378-1680

Victims of Choice (VOC) is a Christian organization that provides assistance and training for counselors working with women suffering from postabortion syndrome (PAS). In addition to training PAS counselors and providing materials for churches, crisis pregnancy centers, and other pro-life organizations, VOC has a national referral system for PAS counselors. The organization also works to educate the public on the negative effects of abortion, through press conferences and speeches at rallies and church meetings as well as testimony before local, state, and national legislatures. VOC also sponsors an annual National Memorial of Mourning, in which "aborted women" take part in a march and funeral.

PUBLICATIONS: *Post Abortion Syndrome: A Therapy Model for Crisis Intervention*, a manual for counselors; "Post Abortion Counselor Training," a video; audiocassette series on abortion recovery training; PAS Information Packet; plus various brochures, bumper stickers, and buttons.

Women Exploited by Abortion
National Headquarters
P.O. Box 278
Dawson, TX 76639
(817) 578-1681

Women Exploited by Abortion (WEBA), founded in 1982, is a non-profit, nondenominational Christian organization for "women who have had an abortion and now realize it was the wrong decision." In addition to ministering to women who have had abortions through individual counseling and support groups, WEBA works to prevent abortions by educating women on the trauma of abortion and provides a forum for "aborted women" to share their experiences through counseling other women who have had the same experience. WEBA currently has chapters in most of the 50 states and some foreign countries. Membership is $10 per year; associate memberships are also available for those who have not personally experienced abortion but who "want to help."

PUBLICATIONS: *Before You Make the Decision, Joy Comes in the Mourning,* and *Surviving Abortion: Help for the Aborted Woman,* brochures.

Selected Print Resources 5

Bibliographies

Abortion Bibliography. New York: Whitson Publishing Company, 1970–1986. LC 72-78877.

Appearing serially each fall for more than 15 years, *Abortion Bibliography* sought to provide a comprehensive world bibliography on abortion and related subjects. The 1984 edition, for example, includes article citations from over 600 English and non-English-language journals, as well as dissertations, gleaned from more than 50 indexes and collections of abstracts. Articles are listed both by title and according to subject; the more than 120 subject headings include such topics as abortion in specific countries, abortion statistics, abortion techniques, abortion and economics, birth control attitudes, family planning research, and sterilization. A separate section lists books, government publications, and monographs. An author index is also included.

Centers for Disease Control. **Division of Reproductive Health Publications Related to Abortion: 1980–Present.** Atlanta, GA:

Division of Reproductive Health Center for Health Promotion and Education, Centers for Disease Control, 1988.

This is a nonannotated listing of abortion-related papers, articles, and book chapters produced by researchers at the CDC since 1980. Each listing includes the author, title, and publication (book or journal issue) where the paper or article appeared. Available on request from the Centers for Disease Control, Atlanta, GA 30333.

Fitzpatrick, Diane E., comp. **The History of Abortion in the United States: A Working Bibliography of Journal Articles.** Monticello, IL: Vance Bibliographies, 1991. Public Administration Series: Bibliography #P 3041. 13 pp. ISSN 0193-970X. ISBN 0-7920-0761-1.

This brief but wide-ranging bibliography deals with the history of abortion in the United States from 1880 to 1990, with emphasis on the 1960s through the 1980s. The articles address social, religious, legal, and political aspects of abortion and represent a wide range of viewpoints and publications, from the *Human Life Review* to *U.S. News and World Report* to *International Socialist Review*.

Fitzsimmons, Richard, and Joan P. Diana, comps. **Pro-Choice/Pro-Life: An Annotated, Selected Bibliography (1972–1989).** New York: Greenwood Press, 1991. 251 pp. Index. ISBN 0-313-27579-3.

The purpose of this lengthy, annotated bibliography is to "provide access to the literature published on the pro-choice/pro-life issue, interrelating abortion, birth control, contraception, and family planning." The citations include periodical articles and monographs published in both print and nonprint formats (including videos) between January 1972 and December 1989. The focus is on items that deal with the ethical, legal, moral/religious, social, and medical aspects of the pro-choice/pro-life controversy itself; items dealing with other areas of concern on the subject, such as contraceptive devices, solely medical issues such as the relationship between strokes and "the pill," or articles that peripherally discuss abortion in the context of other issues, were excluded. Each item was personally examined and annotated by the compilers; the annotations consist of brief (one-to-three sentence), objective descriptions of the article's or book's content. The compilers note that all of the listed items are accessible through public, academic, and school libraries. The items are listed alphabetically by author. A subject index provides access by topic, with all citations assigned at least one subject heading.

National Right to Life Committee. **Selected Bibliography.** Updated periodically.

This nonannotated bibliography lists more than 70 books, most of them recent publications, although a few date back to the early 1970s. The majority are about abortion and/or the pro-life movement, although a number of selections are included under the headings of medical ethics, euthanasia, infanticide, population, and postabortion healing. The books are written primarily from an antiabortion perspective, with the exception of some selections that have been included because they are "so revealing of how pro-abortionists think and operate that [they are] very much worth reading." Available from National Right to Life Committee, 419 7th Street, NW, Suite 500, Washington, DC 20004-2293; telephone: (202) 626-8800.

Nordquist, Joan, comp. **Reproductive Rights.** Contemporary Social Issues: A Bibliographic Series: No. 9. Santa Cruz, CA: Reference and Research Services (511 Lincoln Street, Santa Cruz, CA 95060), 1988. ISSN 0887-3569. ISBN 0-937855-17-0.

This slender bibliography contains nonannotated listings of books and articles on a variety of issues related to reproductive rights. The section on abortion is divided into three subcategories: Legal and Ethical Concerns, Minors and Abortion, and the Pro-life and Pro-choice Movements. Relevant entries may also be found under the sections on fetal rights and paternal rights. Nearly all of the listings were published in 1981 or later, with the majority bearing copyright dates of 1984 or later. Other than that, there is no clear criteria for selection, and there is no commentary by the compiler other than an occasional notation as to whether a particular book or article is "pro-life" or "pro-choice." A listing of organizations is included in the back of the book.

Winter, Eugenia B., comp. **Psychological and Medical Aspects of Induced Abortion: A Selective, Annotated Bibliography, 1970–1986.** Bibliographies and Indexes in Women's Studies: No. 7. New York: Greenwood Press, 1988. Indexes. ISSN 0742-6941.

This useful volume contains 500 listings, primarily of books and articles, although a few audiovisual items are also included. The items selected are "either classics in the field or representational of the kinds of writing being published on the subjects of interest." Most of the materials were originally published in English, although some translated works were deemed "too significant in terms of their influence on the field to leave out." The bibliography is divided into ten broad subject areas: Abortion (General), Abortion Clinics, Abortion Decision, Abortion Techniques (General), Abortion Techniques (Specific), Counseling, Morbidity and Mortality, Abortion Effects on Subsequent Pregnancy, Psychological Effects, and Psychosocial Aspects. Also included are author, title, and subject indexes and a review of the literature. The brief, mostly nonevaluative annotations are essentially content summaries.

Anthologies

Baird, Robert M., and Stuart E. Rosenbaum, eds. **The Ethics of Abortion.** Buffalo, NY: Prometheus Books, 1989. 172 pp. ISBN 0-87975-521-0.

The essays in this collection were chosen to represent the most prominent and influential positions around the issue of whether "the current practice of allowing women to choose for themselves how to deal with unwanted pregnancies [is] a fundamental violation of the core of Western moral, religious, social or intellectual traditions . . . [or falls] comfortably and justifiably within the Western custom of respecting individual autonomy." The book opens with an excerpt from the majority opinion by Justice Blackmun in the 1973 *Roe v. Wade* decision, followed by a section from Justice White's dissent in that decision, and closes with portions of written opinions from the fragmented *Webster* decision more than 16 years later. In between are 11 essays, most of them by philosophers who have written extensively on abortion and related issues. Included is the 1972 Judith Jarvis Thompson essay, "In Defense of Abortion," along with writings by Michael Tooley, Mary Anne Warren, Jane English, Charles Hartshorne, Joan Callahan, Richard Selzer, Paul Ramsey, Harry Gensler, and Sidney Callahan, and the text of a 1987 sermon by Baptist minister Roger Paynter.

————. **The Ethics of Abortion, Revised Edition.** Buffalo, NY: Prometheus Books, 1993. 270 pp. Bibliography. ISBN 0-87975-805-8.

In this revised and expanded version of their earlier work, the editors have retained 9 of the original selections and added 13 new ones. For this edition, the essays have been divided into five "clus-ters." The first consists of three brief essays that focus alternately on the horrors of "the killing in abortions" and "of life without safe, legal abortion." The second deals with abortion as a constitu-tional issue and includes excerpts from three Supreme Court deci-sions—*Roe v. Wade*, *Webster v. Reproductive Health Services*, and *Planned Parenthood v. Casey*, plus a *New York Times* op-ed article by Robert Bork, a response by Melvin Wulf, and an essay by Ronald Dworkin. The third cluster of essays deals with abortion and femi-nism and includes Sidney Callahan's essay from the earlier vol-ume and a feminist defense of abortion by Sally Markowitz. The fourth cluster spotlights Christianity and abortion and features essays by theologians Gary Leber, Daniel Maguire, Stanley Hauerwas, Paul Simmons, and Roger Paynter. The final cluster consists of philosophical treatments of abortion and includes Judith Jarvis Thompson's, Mary Anne Warren's, and Joan Callahan's es-says from the first edition, plus essays by John Wilcox, Harry Gensler, and Charles Gardner. As a group, the selections provide a succinct yet comprehensive overview of the issues involved in the abortion debate.

Bonavoglia, Angela, ed. **The Choices We Made: 25 Women and Men Speak Out about Abortion.** New York: Random House, 1991. 201 pp. ISBN 0-394-58463-5.

This is a collection of personal stories by well-known people who had or were in some way involved with abortions before they be-came legal. Contributors include authors such as Grace Paley, Ursula LeGuin, and Linda Ellerbee; performers such as Polly Bergen, Whoopi Goldberg, Margot Kidder, and Anne Archer; and activists such as Byllye Avery. Also included are accounts by Norma McCorvey, the "Jane Roe" of *Roe v. Wade*, an anonymous woman who was the first minor to ask for a judicial bypass of Alabama's parental consent law, and a male journalist whose daughter be-came pregnant as a result of a brutal gang rape. The foreword is by Gloria Steinem.

Burtchaell, James Tunstead, ed. **Abortion Parley.** New York: Andrews and McMeel, 1980. 352 pp. ISBN 0-8362-3600-9.

In October 1979, the University of Notre Dame convened a Na-tional Conference on Abortion in the hopes of having an "open and honorable discussion" that would "clarify the issue, . . . establish the facts, and . . . elevate the discussion from inflammatory rhetoric on both sides to more sober and reasoned positions." About 75 persons attended the conference, including representatives from pro-life and pro-choice organizations, abortion providers, clergy, law professors, executives, and "ordinary citizens." This anthology consists of 12 papers presented at the conference, covering such diverse topics as a statistical profile of individuals likely to take a position at one or the other extreme of the debate; the myths and realities of adoption as an alternative; public policy aspects of abortion, including public funding; psychological characteristics of women at risk for unplanned pregnancy; and a critique of Christian arguments against abortion. Well written and free of polemic, the papers provide a valuable contribution toward clarifying issues involved in the debate.

Butler, J. Douglas, and David F. Walbert, ed. **Abortion, Medicine, and the Law.** 4th ed. New York: Facts on File, 1992. 890 pp. Indexes. ISBN 0-8160-2535-5.

This is the fourth edition of the reference volume that began as a special issue of Case Western Reserve University's *Law Review* in 1966. The special issue contained a series of essays specially commissioned by the editors, which were published in book form in 1967 under the title *Abortion and the Law.* A second volume appeared in 1973 under the title *Abortion, Society, and the Law,* and yet a third edition was published in 1986 as *Abortion, Medicine, and the Law.* The current edition retains the title and several essays from the third edition. The 30 articles are divided into three parts: law, medicine, and ethics. Within these broad categories, the articles cover a wide range of topics. In the part on law, for example, the reader will find essays on state abortion legislation in the 1990s, minors' right to confidential abortion, comparisons of abortion law in other countries, the concept of wrongful life/wrongful birth, and Stanley Henshaw's 1990 world review of induced abortion. The section on medicine includes an essay on RU 486 by Dr. Etienne-Emile Baulieu, an overview of abortion services in the United States during 1987 and 1988, medical and research uses of human fetal tissue, and psychological effects of unwanted pregnancy. A sampling of the ethics-related articles includes Senator Robert Packwood's essay on the right-to-life movement in Congress from 1973 to 1983, Daniel Callahan's essay on the ethical issues of abortion, a historical perspective on the right to privacy, and an essay on religious approaches to abortion. Each essay is preceded by a brief abstract. The volume also includes five appendices: the text of former U.S. Surgeon General C. Everett Koop's report on the health effects of abortion, the report of the Human Fetal Tissue Transplantation Research Panel, excerpts from the Supreme Court's decisions in *Webster v. Reproductive Health Services* and *Planned Parenthood v. Casey*, and the text of the Freedom of Choice Act. The book also contains subject and case indexes. Overall, *Abortion, Medicine, and the Law* provides a useful and comprehensive overview of the legal, medical, and ethical aspects of the increasingly complex issues surrounding abortion.

Callahan, Sidney, and Daniel Callahan, eds. **Abortion: Understanding Differences.** New York: Plenum Press, 1984. 338 pp. Index. ISBN 0-306-41640-9.

Daniel Callahan, a philosopher with a special interest in biomedical ethics, and his wife Sidney, a psychology professor, have studied, talked, and written about abortion for nearly 30 years—from opposing sides. In creating the project that resulted in this volume, they sought to "illuminate, enrich, and deepen the dialogue on abortion" by exploring the linkages between people's feelings about abortion and their "broader, more encompassing world views and life commitments." The 12 contributors—all women with the exception of Daniel Callahan—represent such diverse fields as sociology, psychiatry, theology, political science, and philosophy, and are about equally divided between viewpoints in favor of and opposing abortion rights. In the opening chapter, Mary Ann Lammana discusses the "middle course" steered by most Americans with respect to abortion. This is followed by Kristin Luker's discussion of her research on the worldviews of activists on either side of the issue. In the remaining papers, contributors explore their views on abortion within the context of their values and views on such fundamental issues as the role of the family, children and child-rearing, women and feminism, and social and cultural life. Each essay is followed by a commentary written by a participant representing the opposite point of view, thus establishing a "dialogue." Throughout, the writers display empathy and respect for each other's positions, while providing thoughtful and articulate defenses of their own views.

Ebersole, Lucinda, and Richard Peabody, eds. **Coming to Terms: A Literary Response to Abortion.** New York: The New Press, 1994. 183 pp. ISBN 1-56584-187-5.

This brief yet powerful collection of short stories and excerpts from novels focuses on women's and men's personal experiences of abortion. Most of the stories are by well-known writers, including Alice Walker, Langston Hughes, Joan Didion, Ellen Gilchrist, William Faulkner, and Richard Brautigan. The tales span almost a century of writing; most take place in the United States, though the periods, settings, characters, and tone vary widely. The book does not attempt to promote any political agenda; it simply lets the writers speak, which they do eloquently. As the editors note: "This collection does not attempt to offer answers or solutions. . . . [It] is not a book about the passion of politics. It is not about politics at all. It is about passion. The passion of women and men who have written about their feelings on abortion."

Eggebroten, Anne, ed. **Abortion: My Choice, God's Grace.** Pasadena, CA: New Paradigm Books, 1994. 238 pp. ISBN 0-932727-79-0 (cloth); 0-932727-69-7 (paper).

This book, which was several years in the making, consists of personal accounts by Christian women about their experiences with abortion and why they support the right to choose abortion. The stories are divided into two groups. The first section, "My Abortion," contains narratives by women who have had abortions, including a pastor's wife, a woman who experienced both her own illegal abortion and her daughter's legal one, and a woman who was forced to have an abortion by her publicly antiabortion husband. The second section, "Other Perspectives," includes several different essays, including one by a woman who was the only Christian to serve as an escort at a clinic in Ft. Wayne, Indiana; a woman who participated in the March for Women's Lives in Washington, D.C., in 1992; and a pastoral counselor who works with young women who have suffered sexual abuse by pastors and in church youth groups. This section also includes an essay by the editor about an unplanned—and unwanted—pregnancy that she chose to carry to term. Eggebroten concludes the book with an essay on "The Bible and Choice." Also included are a brief bibliography and a list of organizations, including several pro-choice Christian groups and a group that is struggling to find the "common ground" between activists on both sides, the Common Ground Network for Life and Choice [see chapter 4].

Henshaw, Stanley K., and Jennifer Van Vort, eds. **Abortion Factbook, 1992 Edition: Readings, Trends, and State and Local Data to 1988.** New York: Alan Guttmacher Institute, 1992. 212 pp. ISBN 0-939253-07-0.

This useful compilation contains reprints of articles that appeared in *Family Planning Perspectives* between 1988 and 1992, along with cumulative statistics based on information gathered by the Alan Guttmacher Institute (AGI) since 1973. The readings are divided into six sections: an overview; abortion services; politics and public opinion; state laws: public funding; state laws: parental involvement; and legal developments. Among the reprints are Stanley Henshaw's *Induced Abortion: A World Review, 1990*, a copy of AGI's abortion fact sheet, Henshaw and Jacqueline Forrest's 1988 article, "Why Do Women Have Abortions?," and the letter written by former U.S. Surgeon General C. Everett Koop to then-President Reagan regarding the 1987–1988 abortion study commissioned by Reagan. The statistics section includes an overview of the methodology used in the 1987–1988 abortion provider survey, copies of the questionnaires used in the survey, and 17 tables summarizing abortion-related statistical data from 1973 through 1988.

Hilgiers, Thomas W., M.D., Dennis J. Horan, and David Mall, eds. **New Perspectives on Human Abortion.** Frederick, MD: University Publications of America, 1981. 504 pp. Index. ISBN 0-89093-379-0.

Contributors to this anthology include professionals representing a range of fields and specialties, including pediatrics, nuclear medicine, obstetrics and gynecology, psychology, philosophy, theology, and ethics. Part I addresses medical aspects of abortion, including characteristics of the fetus and fetal development; mongoloidism (Down's syndrome), abortion-related mortality; short- and long-term complications of abortion; psychiatric effects of abortion; a model for estimating the number of criminal abortions; and sexual assault and pregnancy. Part II concerns legal aspects of abortion, including abortion and midwifery; the experience of pain by the unborn; the Supreme Court and abortion funding; religion and abortion; the West German abortion decision and the European Commission on Human Rights; and abortion and the law. Part III contains essays addressing various social and philosophical aspects of abortion. The majority, though not all, of the selections argue against abortion. The articles and essays are uniformly well written, carefully thought out, and thoroughly documented, and present ample food for thought.

Hodgson, Jane E., ed. **Abortion and Sterilization: Medical and Social Aspects.** London: Academic Press and Orlando, FL: Grune & Stratton, 1981. 594 pp. Index. ISBN 0-12-792030-7 (Academic Press); 0-8089-1344-1 (Grune & Stratton).

Originally developed as a textbook, this anthology has been widely used by legal and medical professionals, as well as students, instructors, and researchers. In addition to providing teaching material on the growing and controversial field of fertility control, the book was intended to "legitimate abortion and sterilization for the sake of those who need and seek the service" and to "present the best techniques, in the proper medical perspective, as well as the social and political history, epidemiology and public health aspects." Accordingly, contributions were sought from leaders in the field from around the world. The American contributors include Henry P. David, Christopher Tietze, Roy Lucas, Willard Cates, David Grimes, Malcolm Potts, and Jane Hodgson, who also edited the volume. The 23 papers cover a variety of topics, including abortion policies, the epidemiology of induced abortion, abortion law, abortions for teenagers, abortion morbidity and mortality, abortion and mental health, delayed complications of induced abortion, abortion and contraception in relation to family planning services, the provision and organization of abortion and sterilization services in the United States, and detailed, illustrated discussions of abortion and sterilization techniques. Though currently out of print, this volume is still available through legal and medical libraries.

Jung, Patricia Beattie, and Thomas A. Shannon, eds. **Abortion and Catholicism: The American Debate.** New York: Crossroad, 1988. 331 pp. ISBN 0-8245-0884-X.

This anthology was collected with the view that "only open, honest, and respectful dialogue" will help to resolve the abortion debate within the Catholic community. The editors sought to avoid articles that represented radical perspectives or "purely ideological or authoritarian pronouncements," instead focusing on "the middle ground—where the arguments are both more responsible, more complex, and often not that far apart." As a result, the articles are refreshingly free of the polemic that often characterizes arguments about abortion; rather, they are thoughtful—often painfully so—and thought-provoking. The book is divided into three parts, each focusing on one aspect of the debate: moral, political, and ecclesiastical. Part I includes defenses of the prohibition of abortion and discussions on the moral status of the fetus, as well as different feminist approaches to the issue. Part II contains articles addressing religion, morality, and public policy, and Part III addresses two aspects of the ecclesiastical debate: the implications of moral consistency and dissent within the church. The contributors include several archbishops; a number of professors of theology, philosophy, ethics, and religion; a magazine editor; an author and lecturer; a law student; and former New York governor Mario Cuomo.

Melton, Gary B., ed. **Adolescent Abortion: Psychological and Legal Issues.** Lincoln, Nebraska: University of Nebraska Press, 1986. 152 pp. Indexes. ISBN 0-8032-3094-X.

This volume was produced by a committee that was sponsored by several divisions of the American Psychological Association and that was formed to review psychological issues involved in the Supreme Court's analysis of adolescent abortion policy and to provide guidelines for researchers and for psychologists who counsel minors regarding abortion. It provides a psycholegal analysis of adolescent abortion, supported by four background papers that examine the epidemiological context of adolescent abortion, the psychological issues involved in abortion for adolescents, the consequences of adolescent abortion and childbearing, and legal and ethical issues involved in counseling pregnant adolescents. The authors suggest that many assumptions about psychological issues in adolescent abortion policy are not supported by available research, nor does the research justify special provisions for minors' consent to abortion.

Pojman, Louis P., and Francis J. Beckwith, eds. **The Abortion Controversy: A Reader.** Boston: Jones and Bartlett Publishers, 1994. 461 pp. ISBN 0-86720-956-9.

Louis Pojman and Francis Beckwith are philosophers and friends who respectfully disagree about abortion. They compiled this reader out of a mutual conviction that Americans must "move beyond the irrationality, stereotyping, and political posturing that tends to predominate the abortion debate as it is depicted in the popular media" and raise the debate to a higher level. To facilitate this goal, they have gathered 29 articles intended to provide readers with the "best arguments of those on all sides of the debate." The book has eight parts, each dealing with a different aspect of the debate. Part I, Breaking Through the Stereotypes, contains an essay coauthored by Daniel and Sidney Callahan on how people on either side tend to stereotype their opponents and disregard the many values and beliefs they hold in common. Part II examines the three major Supreme Court decisions on abortion, *Roe v. Wade, Webster v. Reproductive Health Services,* and *Planned Parenthood v. Casey.* Part III contains evaluations of the Supreme Court's reasoning in *Roe v. Wade* and features essays by Dennis Horan and Thomas Balch, Catherine McKinnon, and Supreme Court Justice Ruth Bader Ginsburg. Parts IV, V, and VI present the contemporary philosophical arguments for and against abortion rights. Among the articles in these chapters are Judith Jarvis Thompson's classic essay and essays by John Noonan, Michael Tooley, and each of the editors, among others. Part VII offers varying views on the link between feminism and abortion rights. The final section addresses the volatile issue of abortion politics and militancy by both pro-life and pro-choice activists. Each major section opens with a brief introduction and concludes with a list of materials for further reading. Within the sections, each article is preceded by a brief introduction and followed by a list of study questions designed to stimulate thought and discussion.

Rolston, Bill, and Anna Eggert, eds. **Abortion in the New Europe: A Comparative Handbook.** Westport, CT: Greenwood Press, 1994. 312 pp. Bibliography, index. ISBN 0-313-28723-6.

Authors from 19 European countries contributed to this collection, which provides a comprehensive overview of abortion laws, practice, and politics in mid-1990s Europe. The editors, both of whom have worked on behalf of abortion rights in their native Ireland, sought out authors who could "tell us succinctly and clearly about the current legal, medical, and social situation regarding abortion in each of their countries; the history of how that situation came about; and the political forces mobilized for and against a woman's right to choose, historically and currently." To this end, they supplied the contributors with a detailed blueprint of questions to be answered and topics to be considered in relation to their countries. The result is a fascinating look at abortion as it affects and is affected by a range of cultures, histories, and social and political climates. Although the authors are uniformly in favor of abortion rights, anyone interested in a comparative analysis of abortion law, practice, and politics, both within Europe and between Europe and the United States, will find this book an invaluable tool.

Rubin, Eva, ed. **The Abortion Controversy: A Documentary History.** Westport, CT: Greenwood Press, 1994. 312 pp. Index. ISBN 0-313-28476-8.

This useful volume is part of a series designed to provide high school and college students with easy access to the "key primary documents on a given historical event or contemporary issue." The purpose of the series is to provide both substantive and background material and to trace the controversial aspects of the event or issue through documents such as speeches and letters, congressional testimony, Supreme Court and lower court decisions, government reports, biographical accounts, position papers, statutes, and news stories. The 92 documents in this volume are grouped into five parts, each with its own introduction. Part I provides historical material on abortion prior to 1960. Part II covers the abortion reform movement from 1960 through 1972. Part III focuses on the 1973 abortion cases, *Roe v. Wade* and *Doe v. Bolton*. Part IV reviews the growth of abortion as a political issue during the period from 1973 to 1980. Part V looks at events during the Reagan-Bush era and beyond. Each document is preceded by a brief explanation. At the end of each part is a list of suggestions for further reading. Also included are two appendices: a list of major Supreme Court decisions on abortion from 1973 to 1993 and a chronology.

Sachdev, Paul, ed. **International Handbook on Abortion.** Westport, CT: Greenwood Press, 1988. 520 pp. ISBN 0-313-23463-9.

This is a one-volume compendium on abortion policies and practices in 33 countries. An introduction surveying international trends is followed by 33 chapters on individual countries, grouped according to region: Africa, Asia, Eastern and Western Europe, the

Nordic countries, Latin America and the Caribbean, North and South America, and the Middle East. Each chapter was written by a public health specialist and includes detailed information on:

- The historical development of abortion policy.
- The roles of the medical profession, news media, religious and women's organizations, and other pressure groups in legislative enactments.
- Attitudes over time of the medical community and the public toward abortion practices.
- Demographic data on women seeking abortions, including incidence, age, parity, marital status, gestation period, pre- and postabortion contraceptive use, and repeat abortions.
- Abortions among special groups such as teenagers and minorities.
- The impact of abortion on fertility behavior and on family planning policy and programs.
- Data on illegal abortion, including incidence, complications, and morbidity.
- Abortion research.

Many chapters contain supplementary statistical tables and references. This rigorously objective book contains a wealth of useful data for comparing national policies and trends on abortion throughout the world.

————, ed. **Perspectives on Abortion.** Metuchen, NJ: The Scarecrow Press, 1985. 281 pp. Indexes. ISBN 0-8108-1708-X.

This collection of 19 original essays is meant as a sourcebook for researchers; service providers in the health care, social work, and related fields; and teachers. The contributors represent such areas as sociology, obstetrics and gynecology, family planning, social work, health, social medicine, population studies, philosophy, and theology; among them are James Mohr, Malcolm Potts, and Christopher Tietze. The scholarly, carefully documented, and generally objective essays are based on empirical research and address abortion primarily as a political and social issue rather than a moral one. The book is divided into four thematic sections. Part I deals with the bases of the conflict over abortion in American society, discussing it in terms of its historical origins, religious and sociopolitical contexts, and moral perspectives, and suggesting possibilities for a compromise solution acceptable to most Americans. Part II concerns women who seek abortions—who they are, how they make their decisions, and the consequences of those decisions, including psychological and emotional effects, morbidity and mortality, trends in repeat abortions, and effects on future family goals. Part III examines how attitudes toward abortion are shaped over time and how they affect both the provision and the use of abortion services. Part IV addresses problem-pregnancy counseling, particularly the lack of empirically based information on such counseling services, the importance of both pre- and post-abortion counseling, and the difficulty of conducting research on problem-pregnancy counseling.

Segers, Mary C., and Timothy A. Byrnes, eds. **Abortion Politics in American States.** Armonk, NY: M. E. Sharpe, 1995. 279 pp. Index. ISBN 1-56324-449-7.

As the Supreme Court has redefined and largely eroded the tenets of *Roe v. Wade*, the battle over abortion has shifted largely back to the states. The result is a complex and multifaceted process that both reflects and defies the diverse political climates around the country. This interesting book was written in response to these ongoing changes as a collaborative effort to "capture the vitality and diversity of state-level abortion politics in the United States." Ten of the chapters are "case studies," each focusing on a representative state. The case-study method was chosen to allow an exploration of "both the particularities of individual states and the significant patterns that emerge across the country." The contributors, most of whom are professors of political science, endeavored to place abortion politics within the context of each state's broader cultural life, examining such factors as the diversity of organized interests within the state, the role played by religion and religious institutions in state politics, and the influence of public opinion on state abortion policies. Also included are essays on the pro-life and pro-choice movements in the wake of *Planned Parenthood v. Casey*, plus a brief historical overview and a concluding analysis of the results.

Stotland, Nada L., ed. **Psychiatric Aspects of Abortion.** Washington, DC: American Psychiatric Press, 1991. 210 pp. Index. ISBN 0-88048-451-9.

This avowedly pro-choice book is intended as a "guide for psychiatrists and counselors who must grapple with the effects of judicial, legislative, and cultural change on the psychiatric health of their patients." The contributors, who include both practicing clinical psychiatrists and psychologists as well as academics, explore a number of psychotherapeutic issues related to abortion. These include, among others, an overview of research findings on the psychiatric consequences of abortion, an examination of contraceptive use and failure, issues in decision making by women confronted with problem pregnancies, issues for staff who are involved with abortion, male experience of elective abortion, racial and ethnic issues in abortion, and ethical issues for clinicians. "Abortion and the recent added constraints on choice have profound implications for psychiatrists," writes the editor. Whether they are serving as a source of clinical and scientific information for policymakers, colleagues, or the press or working directly with patients, psychiatrists must be knowledgeable about the mental health issues surrounding abortion and "examine and manage the values, beliefs, and feelings about abortion that they bring to the public and clinical setting."

Szumski, Bonnie, ed. **Abortion: Opposing Viewpoints.** St. Paul, MN: Greenhaven Press, 1986. 214 pp. Bibliographies, index. ISBN 0-89908-380-3 (cloth); 0-89908-355-2 (paper).

This book is one of the Opposing Viewpoints series, the purpose of which is to encourage critical thinking by helping readers learn to evaluate sources of information, separate fact from opinion, identify stereotypes, and recognize ethnocentrism. This volume contains more than 30 articles, essays, and excerpts representing conflicting points of view on several questions: When does life begin? Should abortion remain a personal choice? Is abortion immoral? Can abortion be justified? Should abortion remain legal? Are extremist tactics justified in the abortion debate? A number of prominent voices from both sides of the abortion debate (and a few from the middle) are represented, including Kristin Luker, Joseph Scheidler, Kathleen McDonnell, Cardinal John O'Connor, Daniel Maguire, and James Burtchaell, as well as more general thinkers such as columnist Ellen Goodman and essayist Barbara Ehrenreich. Each selection is preceded by questions to consider while reading the article, and each chapter concludes with a related activity aimed at helping the development of critical thinking skills, as well as a periodical bibliography. Included are a list of abortion rights and antiabortion organizations and a brief annotated book bibliography. This is an excellent tool for encouraging thought and discussion, especially among young people, and for gaining an overview of the diversity of thought on abortion.

Trager, Oliver, ed. **Abortion: Choice and Conflict.** New York: Facts on File, 1993. 208 pp. Index. ISBN 0-8160-2872-9.

This is a collection of newspaper editorials and cartoons written in response to judicial, legislative, and political events related to abortion from 1988 through mid-1992. The editorials are organized into four sections, each with a summary introduction: Abortion and the Courts; Politics and Abortion; Pro-Life and Pro-Choice; and Health, Youth, and Abortion. Within each section the editorials are grouped according to the specific event, such as a court ruling or demonstration, or issue, such as the French "abortion pill" (mifepristone), that they address. The editorials, which are reprinted in full, were selected from more than 150 newspapers in all 50 states, the District of Columbia, and eight Canadian provinces, and represent a cross-section of viewpoints.

Walsh, Mary Roth, ed. **Psychology of Women: Ongoing Debates.** New Haven, CT: Yale University Press, 1987. 484 pp. Indexes. ISBN 0-300-03965-4 (cloth); 0-300-03966 (paper).

This anthology includes two previously published articles on the psychological effects of abortion: "Psychological Reaction to Legalized Abortion" (Osofsky and Osofsky 1972), and "Women's Responses to Abortion" (Lodl, McGettigan, and Bucy 1985). Although the editor introduces the articles as representing opposing viewpoints, both actually reach a similar conclusion, specifically that the reaction experienced by the majority of women is relief, and that only a small percentage of women experience lasting negative effects. The second article does, however, discuss factors related to negative responses and emphasizes the need for effective postabortion counseling to help those women who do experience psychological problems. The volume also includes Carol Gilligan's article "In a Different Voice" (1977), which includes an analysis of the thought processes of women deciding whether to have abortions.

Books and Monographs

Abortion — General

Beckwith, Francis. **Politically Correct Death: Answering the Arguments for Abortion Rights.** Grand Rapids, MI: Baker Books, 1993. 256 pp. Bibliography, index. ISBN 0-8010-1050-0.

This book is intended to provide abortion opponents with morally reasoned responses to the arguments most commonly offered in favor of legal abortion. Beckwith, a philosophy lecturer at the University of Nevada, sets out to use logical arguments to "present a clear defense of the pro-life position on abortion, [which] can be defined in the following way: since the unborn entity is fully human from the *moment of conception*, and abortion typically results in the unborn entity's death, therefore abortion ordinarily entails the unjustified killing of a human being who has a full right to life." He divides the arguments in favor of abortion into six groups: Prenatal Development, Abortion Methods, and Fetal Pain; Arguments from Pity; Arguments from Tolerance and Ad Hominem; Arguments from Decisive Moments and Gradualism; Arguments from Bodily Rights; and Arguments from Theology and the Bible. However, his rebuttals all seem to come down to one thing—that if the fetus is fully human from the moment of conception, the argument in question is morally indefensible. This sounds suspiciously like the kind of reasoning Beckwith says he is trying to refute: "One begs the question when one assumes what one is trying to prove." As a result, his reasoning is unlikely to convince anyone who does not already agree with it. The book has several appendices, including a summary list of arguments for abortion rights; a selection of "choice quotes" of "bizarre statements made by abortion-rights activists," an imaginary dialogue between Socrates and former presidential candidate Michael Dukakis, and an abridged version of the Supreme Court decision in *Planned Parenthood v. Casey.*

Benderly, Beryl Lieff. **Thinking about Abortion: An Essential Handbook for the Woman Who Wants To Come to Terms with What Abortion Means in Her Life.** Garden City, NY: Doubleday, 1984. 204 pp. Bibliography, index. ISBN 0-385-27757-1.

Meticulously researched and clearly written, this compact book addresses the social, medical, emotional, and moral aspects of unwanted pregnancy and the alternatives for dealing with it. The author does not pull any punches—her descriptions of abortion techniques and the experience itself are blunt and explicit, and her essay on the moral questions raised by abortion is both succinct and powerful. Without giving any answers, and without claiming the process is anything but difficult, Benderly explores the implications of what it means to choose whether to have an abortion and to take full responsibility for that choice.

Dworkin, Ronald. **Life's Dominion: An Argument about Abortion, Euthanasia, and Personal Freedom.** New York: Alfred A. Knopf, 1993. 273 pp. Index. ISBN 0-394-58941-6

In this extended essay, law professor and legal scholar Dworkin claims that the moral arguments over abortion cannot be understood if we focus on what many consider to be the key question in the debate—whether or not a fetus is a person with its own rights and interests. Instead, he focuses on a different view that he believes nearly everyone shares—that human life, in and of itself, is sacred. "Almost everyone shares, explicitly or intuitively, the idea that human life has objective, intrinsic value that is quite independent of its personal value for anyone, and disagreement about the right interpretation of that shared idea is the actual nerve of the great debate about abortion. For that reason, the debate is even more important to most people than an argument about whether a fetus is a person would be, for it goes deeper—into different conceptions of the value and point of human life and of the meaning and character of human death." Looked at in this way, it is understandable that many people can believe that abortion is morally wrong while also insisting that it should be legal. In his exploration of this view and its implications for a free society, Dworkin delves into religion, philosophy, law, and the broader issues of the meaning and interpretation of the Constitution. The result is an eloquent and passionate argument for the freedom to make our own moral choices based on our understandings of the sacred nature of our own individual lives. "We care intensely what other people do about abortion and euthanasia, and with good reason, because these decisions express a view about the intrinsic value of all life and therefore bear on our own dignity as well. . . . But though we may feel our own dignity at stake in what others do about death, and may sometimes wish to make others act as we think right, a true appreciation of dignity argues decisively in the opposite direction—for individual freedom, not coercion, for a regime of law and attitude that encourages each of us to make moral decisions for himself."

Frohock, Fred M. **Abortion: A Case Study in Law and Morals.** Westport, CT: Greenwood Press, 1983. 226 pp. Bibliography, index. ISBN 0-313-23953-3.

This well-written and often engaging book attempts to step outside of the emotional atmosphere surrounding abortion and to engage in rational discourse in order to discover "how morals and the law can be fitted together to represent a rational abortion practice." Frohock, a professor of political science, begins by examining the various justifications for state enforcement of morals as they relate to abortion, the moral arguments for and against abortion, the legal issues related to abortion, and the realities of abortion practice since *Roe v. Wade*. He then explores possible resolutions of the conflict, arriving at what he sees as the most agreeable moral, legal, and practical resolution for all involved. As part of his research, Frohock interviewed activists on both sides of the debate, and he quotes liberally from the interviews to weave a "dialogue" of arguments for and against abortion throughout the book. Each chapter includes suggestions for further reading. Also included is a bibliography divided into subject areas, including general studies, ethical issues, statistical studies, the politics of abortion, attitudes toward abortion, law and morals, legal issues, and case law on abortion and other moral issues.

Gardner, Joy. **A Difficult Decision: A Compassionate Book about Abortion.** Trumansburg, NY: Crossing Press, 1986. 115 pp. Bibliography.

Joy Gardner is a counselor and holistic healer who specializes in loss and death issues. After finding that many of her clients bore emotional scars from abortions, some of which had occurred decades earlier, she developed a workshop called "Abortion—Healing the Wounds." This book, which might be described as a New Age handbook on abortion, discusses methods Gardner uses to help women and couples overcome problems associated with abortions, including emotional release exercises, in-depth counseling, stress control, nutrition, herbs, visualization, and color therapy. While supporting the right to legal, safe abortion, Gardner also addresses the problems of women who would prefer to give birth but lack the resources to do so. She offers guidelines for making clear decisions about whether to have an abortion or to have the child and either raise it or give it up for adoption, offering full support for whatever decision is made. A special section addresses the feelings and experience of men involved in an unexpected pregnancy; another describes fetal development up to 25 weeks LMP. While some might be put off by the New Age approach, many readers will find this book supportive and helpful, whether they are dealing with a current pregnancy or a past abortion.

Guernsey, JoAnn Bren. **Abortion: Understanding the Controversy.** Minneapolis, MN: Lerner Publications, 1993. 111 pp. Bibliography, index. ISBN 0-8225-2605-0.

This slim volume is part of the Pro/Con series of books, which are designed to help young people understand different points of view on contemporary issues in order to form their own opinions and make "honest, informed decisions." As such, it succeeds quite well, presenting a succinct and comprehensive overview of the major issues involved in the controversy, including statistics on public opinion and characteristics of women who have abortions, fetal development and the debate over fetal personhood and rights, changing roles of women and motherhood, activists for and against legal abortion, the morality of abortion, the *Roe v. Wade* decision and its repercussions, current abortion laws in the states and other countries, methods of abortion, and alternatives to abortion. Also included are a list of organizations, a bibliography, and a glossary.

Hertz, Sue. **Caught in the Crossfire: A Year on Abortion's Front Line.** New York: Prentice-Hall, 1991. 242 pp. Index. ISBN 0-13-381914-0.

The "front line" of the title is the Preterm Clinic in Brookline, Massachusetts, the largest and busiest abortion clinic in New England. Journalist Hertz spent a year—from March 1989 to March 1990—observing and talking with clinic staff, doctors, patients, police, and activists to develop her account of the abortion war as it is lived on a daily basis by those caught up in it through conviction or fate. Hertz is not ambivalent about where her sympathies lie—with the clinic staffers and the women of all types who brave angry protesters, sidewalk counselors, and their own conflicts to enter the clinic and endure the often grueling process that is the only way they see to resolve an impossible problem. Nonetheless, she does not flinch from exploring the clinic's disturbing aspects, from a vivid portrayal of a second trimester abortion and the dilemma of counselors faced with women who return to the clinic two, three, or more times to the anguish of women there because someone else—a boyfriend, a husband, parents—insisted they have an abortion, not a baby. The result is an intimate, sometimes humorous, and often painful portrait of people dealing with the day-to-day realities of, rather than abstract arguments about, abortion. A grim footnote: Hertz's title became all too appropriate on December 30, 1994, when a gunman entered the Preterm Clinic and opened fire, killing a receptionist and wounding three other people. He had already shot two people, killing one, at the Planned Parenthood clinic one and one-half miles away.

Howe, Louise Kapp. **Moments on Maple Avenue: The Reality of Abortion.** New York: Macmillan, 1984. 209 pp. Bibliography. ISBN 0-002-555170-1.

This is a sensitively written, "you-are-there" account of an "ordinary day" in an abortion clinic in White Plains, New York. Through her observations of and conversations with the clinic's staff and patients, as well as the boyfriends, husbands, parents, and women friends who accompanied some of the patients, the author brings the abortion debate down to an intensely personal level that leaves little room for polemic or absolute answers on either side. She concludes by suggesting some societal changes that must take place if the number of abortions is to be reduced and women are to have real choices as to when and with whom they will bear children.

Hunter, James Davison. **Before the Shooting Begins: Searching for Democracy in America's Culture War.** New York: The Free Press/Macmillan, 1994. 310 pp. Bibliography, index. ISBN 0-02-915501-0.

This provocative and disturbing book uses the abortion controversy as a focus for examining what the author sees as the broader "culture war" currently being fought in the United States—a war that has already engendered violence and could provoke much more. Debates over abortion and other culturally loaded topics such as sexual harassment and homosexual rights have been dominated by power politics played out by the media, special-interest groups, and civil institutions. At the same time, ordinary citizens are dismayingly ignorant about and unable to articulate clear views concerning volatile issues such as abortion. As a result, Hunter says, discussions on these topics are influenced far more by feelings than by serious reflection and debate. Our cultural conflicts cannot be resolved through political solutions. Instead, Hunter calls for a renewal of substantive democracy at its most basic level, in the form of serious public argument and persuasion that recognizes and honestly attempts to deal with the very real differences among Americans. "In the end, it is only in the context of the moral and sociological communities we inhabit over the course of our lives, and not the public environment defined by direct mail, electronic sound bites, or paid political advertisements, that public debate will have integrity with various but shared biographies. It is only in the context of revitalized communities, where obligations and rights are balanced against each other, that persuasive arguments can have lasting effects."

LaFleur, William R. **Liquid Life: Abortion and Buddhism in Japan.** Princeton, NJ: Princeton University Press, 1992. 257 pp. Bibliography, index. ISBN 0-691-07405-4.

The first precept of Buddhism states, "I will not willingly take the life of a living thing." Yet abortion is today a legal and generally accepted practice in Buddhist Japan. In this intriguing book, William LaFleur examines the history and practice of *mizuko kuyo* rites, in which parents of aborted fetuses honor, and apologize to, the children they have prevented from coming into the world. In doing so, he explores a culture and a set of religious traditions that are strikingly different from our own in hopes not only of revealing something about a country that seems mysterious and foreign to most Americans but of offering "a heuristic tool for looking at—and trying to solve—our own abortion dilemma." LaFleur argues that the Japanese acceptance of abortion stems in large part from a deeply felt belief in the value of children and the family: "[O]ne of the reasons the Japanese legalized abortion is that it promotes their goal of making sure that the children who are born are also *maximally wanted*. Achieving this has meant the rejection of fecundism and a societal switch to thinking about children in terms of the quality of their lives. The 'having' of a child is never merely equivalent to giving birth to it." In an increasingly crowded world, he asserts, we could all benefit from resisting our biological impulse to grow in numbers, which in many cultures has been enhanced with religious ideas that "in essence, turned reproductivity into a mode of being godly." Although there is little we can do to offset the biological urge to multiply, "we should be able to have more success in dealing with those religious ideas and motifs that have, in fact, become inimical and even hazardous to our human future."

Maloy, Kate, and Maggie Jones Patterson. **Birth or Abortion? Private Struggles in a Political World.** New York: Plenum Press, 1992. 344 pp. Bibliography, index. ISBN 0-306-44327-9.

This unusually balanced and compassionate book steps away from the political controversy surrounding abortion to examine the intensely personal stories of 50 women and couples who found themselves dealing with problem pregnancies. The stories cover a period from the early 1950s through the present, and they are woven into a social and historical context that gives them expanded meaning and poignancy. About half of the women interviewed decided to continue their pregnancies to term; the others chose to abort. Whatever the problems surrounding a pregnancy, the authors found, the factors underlying the choice between birth and abortion are practical and emotional ones—the relationship between the woman and her partner, the relationship between the woman and her parents, the financial and logistical resources available, the current course of her life, the health of the fetus. The decisions take place within a complicated web of relationships and responsibilities, far from the abstract language of justice and "rights" that dominates the public controversy. Drawing on the work of Carol Gilligan, Mary Belensky, and others, the authors suggest that we move away from confrontation and toward a new caretaking standard in which "[o]ur concepts of both justice and care would broaden until each encompassed the other, and we would keep the human faces of a profound moral dilemma plainly in view."

Mathewes-Green, Frederica. **Real Choices: Offering Practical Life-Affirming Alternatives to Abortion.** Sisters, OR: Multnomah Books, 1994. 257 pp. Index. ISBN 0-88070-678-3.

Real Choices is the result of a research project conceived by Jeannie French, founder of the National Women's Coalition for Life (NWCL) [see chapter 4]. French's idea was to hold hearings across the country to allow women who had had abortions to talk about their experiences, in order to learn about the pressures and problems that led them to choose abortion over giving birth. By identifying the real reasons women have abortions, pro-lifers could explore ways to solve those problems and provide "real choices" to women faced with unintended pregnancies. Mathewes-Green, NWCL's communication director, spearheaded the project, which began with distributing a detailed survey to pregnancy care centers around the country. Building on a 1988 study by the Alan Guttmacher Institute that asked women why they had had abortions, the survey asked center workers which situations they encountered most often and which problems were most difficult to solve. Centers were also asked to provide information about the resources they offered and about client demographics. The second part of the study involved locating women who had chosen abortion and were willing to talk about it. Mathewes-Green met with small groups of such women in seven cities around the country. The results were surprising—rather than the practical problems cited by the care centers, the women "uniformly talked about pressures in relationships; the abortion was done, each told us, either to please someone or protect someone." Mathewes-Green interweaves accounts of the listening sessions with chapters exploring the problems that lead women to have abortions and their possible solutions. The pregnancy care center survey and its results, along with the results of several other surveys, are detailed in appendices. Also included are a summary of the listening session results, a directory of NWCL member groups, and copies of letters sent to pro-choice leaders inviting their participation in the project—an invitation that unfortunately went unanswered. Intelligent, compassionate, and well written, *Real Choices* should be useful to anyone who works with women facing unintended pregnancies or psychological repercussions from abortion. It should also be required reading for anyone involved in the political war over abortion, regardless of the position they are defending.

McDonnell, Kathleen. **Not an Easy Choice.** Boston: South End Press, 1984. 157 pp. Bibliography, index. ISBN 0-89608-265-5 (cloth); 0-89608-264-4 (paper).

Kathleen McDonnell is a Canadian feminist who was moved to reevaluate the feminist position on abortion by the birth of her daughter, which "gave the idea of the fetus in the womb a new concreteness." The result is this thoughtful and provocative book, which dares to risk "splitting the women's movement and giving ammunition to our enemies" by discussing aspects of abortion that many feminists have been too fearful to address: the grief, sense of loss, and ambivalence experienced by many, if not most, women who undergo abortions, and abortion's moral dimension, which continues to trouble the "great middle ground of people" who nonetheless support the right to choose. McDonnell acknowledges that the pro-life movement, to its benefit, openly discusses these and other bioethical issues: "Their solutions are for the most part wrong-headed and simplistic, but they are asking what is to many minds the right question: is life of value in itself? For it is not much of a leap from that abstract question to: 'is *my* life of any value?'" Through her exploration, McDonnell comes full circle to a renewed conviction that women must have access to legal, safe, and affordable abortion, as part of "reclaiming our reproduction [by] embracing it, celebrating it as the joyous miracle that it is, while at the same time affirming that it is not the totality of our existence, that we have needs, visions and potentials as broad and varied as the rest of humanity."

Morowitz, Harold J., and James S. Trefil. **The Facts of Life: Science and the Abortion Controversy.** New York: Oxford University Press, 1992. 179 pp. Bibliography, index. ISBN 0-19-507927-2.

The authors of this book have endeavored to bring a different perspective—that of the biological sciences—to the abortion controversy. Such questions as when life begins and whether the fetus is a person are, they say, the wrong questions. Instead we should ask, "When does a fetus (or embryo or zygote) acquire humanness?" In order to address this question, they set out first to identify the properties that distinguish human beings from other living things, then examine the development of a human being from the fertilized egg to birth to determine when those properties are acquired. They conclude that "humanness" derives from the frontal lobe of the cerebral cortex, that part of the brain that allows humans to perform functions no other animal can, from participating in simple social interactions to using language to writing a symphony. They then go on to demonstrate that, although nerve cells begin accumulating and differentiating early in pregnancy, the brain does not begin to form the synaptic connections that enable it to function until about the twenty-fourth week of pregnancy—a process that continues well into childhood. "Just as a pile of microchips isn't a computer . . . a pile of nerve cells is not a functioning cortex. It is only when the system is 'wired up' by synaptic connections that the fetus, in our terms, has acquired humanness." In conclusion, the authors propose guidelines for regulating abortion based on their findings. "By tying the question of abortion rights to the onset of humanness, we feel that we have formulated a policy that is profoundly in tune with biological reality. The onset of humanness provides a fundamental . . . marker in the development of the individual, one that is different from either conception or birth. It should be accorded the importance it deserves."

Rodman, Hyman, Betty Sarvis, and Joy Bonar. **The Abortion Question.** New York: Columbia University Press, 1987. 223 pp. Bibliography, index. ISBN 0-231-05332-0.

The Abortion Question is a dispassionate, balanced, and thorough examination of the moral, medical, emotional, social, and legal issues surrounding abortion. An earlier book by Rodman and Sarvis, *The Abortion Controversy,* published shortly after the 1973 *Roe v. Wade* Supreme Court decision, was widely praised for its even-handed analysis of the complex issues surrounding the debate. This work retains that balance and also manages to say a great deal within a short space. Though meticulously researched, it is not cloaked in scholarly language; instead it is straightforward, clear, and highly readable. Beginning with a succinct historical overview, the authors explore the rise of the abortion controversy; the social and cultural dynamics of fertility control; the central issues in the moral debate; the medical, pyschosocial and emotional aspects of abortion; the developments leading up to *Roe v. Wade;* the legal controversy since 1973; and attitudes about abortion. They note that arguments about abortion "may be framed in rational and objective terms, but the conclusions are typically linked to subjective beliefs and values." In a final chapter, "Where Do We Go from Here?" the authors examine possible solutions to the controversy, finally predicting the adoption of an approach that, while it may not please either of the polar groups, will eventually "be accepted as reasonable and relatively noncontroversial public policy."

Rosenblatt, Roger. **Life Itself: Abortion in the American Mind.** New York: Random House, 1992. 194 pp. Bibliography. ISBN 0-394-58244-6.

In this brief, thoughtful book, essayist, columnist, and editor Roger Rosenblatt adds his voice to those who are attempting to propose a solution, however imperfect, to the conflict over abortion in American society. "For the past twenty years," he writes, "abortion has existed mainly as a shouting match that has been overheard by ordinary people. I believe we need a discussion in which ordinary people can recognize their own thoughts and feelings and in which we can also recognize one another." Rosenblatt first explores the history of social attitudes toward abortion by looking at how different individuals and cultures have addressed "three fundamental concerns: 1) When is a fetus a person? 2) What circumstances justify an abortion? 3) Who decides?" He then recounts his conversations with a number of people in Iowa, a state he feels represents "middle America." Based on these, as well as on opinion polls showing that a majority of Americans think of abortion as a form of murder *and* at the same time believe that it should be legal, Rosenblatt concludes that a policy of "permit but discourage" would best reflect the feelings of most Americans.

Terkel, Susan Neiburg. **Abortion: Facing the Issues.** New York: Franklin Watts, 1988. 160 pp. Bibliography, index. ISBN 0-531-10565-2.

This is a remarkably balanced and succinct summary of what abortion involves and the issues surrounding it. Susan Terkel has a degree in child development and family relationships from Cornell University and has written several books for children, including one on sexual abuse (with Janice Rench). In her preface, she states that she has tried to write an "objective, *passionate* book about abortion." Because her work has garnered criticisms from both camps, with each insisting that she favors the other, she feels she has succeeded—as indeed she has. Within this short volume, Terkel surveys the history of abortion laws in the United States, explains the *Roe v. Wade* decision and its impact, describes how abortions are performed, looks at the abortion industry, discusses who has abortions and why, explores public opinion regarding abortion, and examines the politics of abortion and the public controversy that surrounds it, including the moral issues involved—all the while displaying sympathy and compassion for different points of view and the lives and emotions involved. Clearly written and carefully researched, this book serves as an excellent overview of the abortion issue. Particularly recommended for young people.

Tietze, Christopher, and Stanley K. Henshaw. **Induced Abortion: A World Review, 1986.** New York: Alan Guttmacher Institute, 1986. 143 pp. ISBN 0-939253-05-4.

This is the sixth edition of the "abortion fact book" that Christopher Tietze created in 1973. Since Tietze's death, the work he pioneered has been carried on by coauthor Stanley Henshaw [see *Abortion Factbook, 1992 Edition*, under Anthologies, above]. This book contains a wealth of carefully documented statistical and factual information on abortion laws, policies, and practices, as well as its social and medical aspects, throughout the world, and is one of the most cited sources in the field. Included is information on abortion laws and policies in different regions; the incidence of abortion; demographic and social characteristics of women obtaining abortions; periods of gestation; descriptions of and statistics on various abortion procedures; sterilization; abortion complications and sequelae; abortion mortality; abortion and contraception; repeat abortions; abortion service delivery; and the effects of abortion policy on mortality, morbidity, legal and illegal abortion, fertility, and children. Much of the information is presented in useful tabular and graphic form. An important resource.

Tribe, Laurence H. **Abortion: The Clash of Absolutes.** New York: W. W. Norton, 1990. 270 pp. Index. ISBN 0-393-02845-3.

Laurence Tribe is a respected authority on constitutional law and a Harvard law professor who has presented 19 cases to the Supreme Court, at least 13 of them successfully. In this far-ranging and provocative book, Tribe explores the complicated historical, social, cultural, political, and legal issues surrounding the abortion debate and lays the framework for a "negotiated peace" that can end the bitter conflict between "pro-choice" and "pro-life," or, as Tribe puts it, between "liberty" and "life." Writing with crystal clarity, logic, and respect for the truth that exists on both sides of the debate, Tribe addresses the arguments for and against legal abortion, especially those that pit the rights of fetuses against the rights of pregnant women. He discusses the constitutional "rightness" of *Roe v. Wade*, examines in detail the potential implications of overturning that landmark decision, and outlines the repercussions of possible compromises. Finally, he asks readers to look at the deeper values underlying their feelings and opinions about abortion and to recognize that "what is at stake is not really the absolute in whose name the battle has been fought." Such honesty, he says, may enable us finally to "get beyond our once intractable dispute about the question of abortion."

Whitney, Catherine. **Whose Life? A Balanced, Comprehensive View of Abortion from Its Historical Context to the Current Debate.** New York: William Morrow, 1991. 272 pp. Bibliography, index. ISBN 0-688-09622-0.

Despite its subtitle, this book tilts heavily in favor of abortion rights. The author endeavors to place abortion in a historical and social context by portraying its "human story." The story ranges from prehistoric times through 1990, but focuses primarily on the Reagan-Bush era and the gradual dismantling of abortion rights that took place during that time. Interwoven with the accounts of events are personal stories and anecdotes about activists, politicians, policymakers, and women who have had abortions, both legal and illegal. The book also includes a brief "scorecard" of Supreme Court decisions on abortion from *Roe v. Wade* through *Hodgson v. Minnesota* and an overview of state regulations on abortion as of 1990. Although it is well-written and passionate, the book breaks no new ground, and its extreme editorializing counteracts the author's stated intention.

Willke, Dr., and Mrs. J. C. Willke. **The Handbook on Abortion.** Cincinnati, OH: Hiltz Publishing, 1971. 169p.

This compact book has been called the "bible" of the pro-life movement. In a question-and-answer format, it addresses the issues of when life begins, fetal development, abortion techniques, and arguments for abortion such as rape, incest, a woman's right to control her body, and the population explosion. It then offers advice and information on alternatives to abortion, "the words we use," and resources for working against abortion. *The Handbook on Abortion* is perhaps most famous for being the first publication to use dramatic color pictures of aborted fetuses—pictures that have since proliferated on posters, pamphlets, and protest signs and that have come to symbolize the antiabortion movement. Also included is a short story dramatizing a society that enforces euthanasia for those over 50 years old who are no longer "useful"—a scenario that the Willkes and others claim will be one result of continued tolerance of abortion. Since the handbook's publication, the Willkes have become two of the movement's most visible and active spokespersons.

Wilt, Judith. **Abortion, Choice, and Contemporary Fiction: The Armageddon of the Maternal Instinct.** Chicago: University of Chicago Press, 1990. 183 pp. Index. ISBN 0-226-90158-0.

The built-in drama of abortion makes it a powerful plot device for exploring complex issues of psyche and relationships. In this book, Boston College English professor Judith Wilt examines the role of abortion in a number of contemporary novels by such writers as John Barth, Margaret Atwood, Joan Didion, Marge Piercy, William Faulkner, Alice Walker, Mary Gordon, John Irving, Ernest Hemingway, Toni Morrison, and others. Underlying the literary analyses is Wilt's exploration of the "profound psychocultural shock" created as maternity, once regarded as instinctual, becomes a matter of conscious choice. In an opening chapter, Wilt discusses the ways in which stories, both real and fictional, shape perceptions and emotions about abortion: "Debate about abortion may begin with reasons, proceed to statistics, but it always comes down, really, to stories." After discussing several "true stories" about abortion, Wilt proceeds to explore her theme in relationship to various novelists' treatment of abortion and the issues that surround it— issues of gender inequality, racial and sexual oppression, fears of change and abandonment, empowerment and disempowerment, and the choice of whether to allow "potentiality" to become real. Though extremely academic, this is an unusual and interesting book that has the additional advantage of pointing the way to a rich and varied reading list of abortion-related fiction.

Abortion Activists and Activist Movements

Alcorn, Randy. **Pro Life Answers to Pro Choice Arguments.** Sisters, OR: Multnomah Books, 1992. 294 pp. Index. ISBN 0-88070-472-1.

This book was written to fill what the author sees as a serious information gap among even well-educated Americans—a lack of knowledge and understanding of the pro-life position on abortion. Due largely to media bias, most people, writes Alcorn, have heard not the pro-life position but what pro-choice advocates say is the pro-life position. The result is "like having a Ford dealer tell you about the difference between Ford and Toyota trucks, and then saying you know all about Toyota trucks." The book presents 39 common arguments in favor of abortion rights or against abortion opponents; for example, "Every woman should have control over her own body. Reproductive freedom is a basic right." Each argument is followed by several pro-life responses and a detailed explanation of each one. Alcorn concludes with "Final Appeals" to women considering abortion, abortion and family planning clinics, physicians, the media, and other participants in the debate. Also included are several appendices: "Finding Forgiveness after an Abortion," "Abortion in the Bible and Church History," "Fifty Ways To Help Unborn Babies and Their Mothers," and a list of pro-life resources.

Blanchard, Dallas A. **The Anti-Abortion Movement and the Rise of the Religious Right: From Polite to Fiery Protest.** New York: Twayne Publishers, 1994. 177 pp. Index.

This is a sociological analysis of the antiabortion movement in the United States from the 1960s to the present. Blanchard argues that many participants in the movement, particularly in its more radical and violent aspects, are driven by religious and cultural fundamentalism that manifests itself in such traits as authoritarianism, self-righteousness, prejudice against minorities, moral absolutism, and antianalytical, anticritical thinking. Such fundamentalists reject what they see as a liberal, corrupt society and advocate a return to a religion-centered, "traditional" lifestyle in which men wield authority both in society and within their families. They also have a moralistic view that condemns homosexuality and sex outside of marriage and divorced from procreation. Blanchard draws three primary conclusions: that the New Right helped to influence the movement for its own political purposes, primarily to put Ronald Reagan and George Bush into office; that men dominate the leadership of the movement, especially among the more radical groups, while women are used as foot soldiers filling traditionally female roles; and that evangelicals in the movement are primarily fundamentalists who act out of defense of their conceptions of male and female roles and their desire to reinstitute the medieval hegemony of religion over other social institutions, particularly the law.

Faux, Marian. **Crusaders: Voices from the Abortion Front.** New York: Birch Lane Press, published by Carol Publishing Group, 1990. 289 pp. Index. ISBN 1-55972-020-4.

In her second book about abortion, freelance writer Marian Faux profiles six individuals who are deeply embroiled in the controversy: Frank Sussman, the St. Louis, Missouri, lawyer who has made abortion the focus of his extensive pro bono work and who represented the St. Louis abortion clinic in the 1989 Supreme Court hearings on *Webster v. Reproductive Health Services*; B. J. Isaacson-

Jones and the other women who work at Reproductive Health Services; Randall Terry, the politically ambitious, charismatic leader of Operation Rescue; Moira Bentson, a poor, single mother who serves as a "foot soldier" in Operation Rescue's battle against abortion; Vernice Miller, a black pro-choice activist and the developmental director for the Center for Constitutional Rights in New York City, who has worked hard at getting women of color involved—and heard—in the abortion debate; and Frances Kissling, head of Catholics for a Free Choice and one of the few activists who believes that the abortion issue can be satisfactorily resolved. Based on extensive personal interviews as well as outside research, the portraits are vivid and interesting, though clearly colored by the author's views.

Paige, Connie. **The Right-to-Lifers: Who They Are, How They Operate, Where They Get Their Money.** New York: Summit Books, 1983. 286 pp. Index. ISBN 0-671-43180-3.

The Right-to-Lifers is a detailed look at the pro-life movement—its roots; its growth and development through the early 1980s; its strategies and tactics; its politics; and its key players, supporters, and allies, from the hierarchy of the Catholic Church to the organizers of the New Right. Paige, an investigative journalist, shares few, if any, beliefs with her subjects, and she does not hesitate to expose their foibles and gaffes while at the same time giving them credit for their considerable skill and accomplishments. Rich in anecdotes, quotations, and descriptions of people and events, this book paints a vivid portrait that feminists, liberals, and abortion rights supporters are likely to find both disturbing and reassuring, since it will reinforce their beliefs about their opponents. Those it portrays and their allies, on the other hand, will probably find it biased and condescending.

Scheidler, Joseph M. **Closed: 99 Ways To Stop Abortion.** Rockford, IL: TAN Books, 1993. 377 pp. Index. ISBN 0-89555-493-3.

Closed is a new edition of a classic handbook of political activism, written by one of the country's most prominent, visible, and vocal opponents of abortion. The 99 brief "chapters" in this book offer practical, detailed guidance that would prove useful to almost anyone with a cause. The tactics range from "sidewalk counseling" of abortion patients to infiltrating "enemy" organizations. Included is a chapter on "Why Violence Won't Work." Although Scheidler's language may alarm and anger his opponents and those with less radical convictions, people on both sides would agree that his advice has proven extremely effective.

Staggenborg, Susan. **The Pro-Choice Movement: Organization and Activism in the Abortion Conflict.** New York: Oxford University Press, 1991. 229 pp. Bibliography, index. ISBN 0-19-508925-1.

This is a useful, if dry, sociological study of the abortion rights movement from its inception in the 1960s through 1990. It looks at three major types of organizations involved in the struggle for abortion rights: single-issue organizations such as the National Abortion Rights Action League (NARAL), population organizations such as Zero Population Growth, and women's movement organizations such as the National Organization for Women (NOW). In addition to national groups, Staggenborg also studied state and local chapters and independent groups in order to examine grassroots local activism as well as more widespread activity. The book is divided into four parts: Part I examines the origins and development of the movement before abortion was made legal by the 1973 *Roe v. Wade* decision. Part II discusses the impact of the 1973 victory on the movement, including the trend toward formalization and the "professionalization" of movement leaders. Part III describes the growth surge of the movement following the first major "countermovement" victory, the passage of the 1976 Hyde amendment banning Medicaid funding of abortions. Part IV examines the movement from 1983 to 1989, which the author describes as a period of stalemate between movement and countermovement forces, and following the 1989 *Webster* decision, which marked a critical turning point in the abortion conflict. The book concludes with an assessment of the implications of the pro-choice movements for general social movement theories.

The Ethics of Abortion

Burtchaell, James Tunstead. **Rachel Weeping and Other Essays on Abortion.** New York: Andrews and McMeel, 1982. 383 pp. Index. ISBN 0-8362-3602-5.

James Burtchaell is a Catholic priest and former university provost at Notre Dame who has written at length on abortion. This collection of essays holds firmly to the official Catholic Church view that the embryo is fully human from the moment of conception and that abortion is therefore murder. In one lengthy essay, Father Burtchaell draws parallels between abortion, the slaughter of Jews in Nazi Germany, and the depersonalization of American black slaves. In another, "What Is a Child Worth?," he extends the debate to infanticide and euthanasia. In yet another, he reflects on what he sees as a lack of character among women who choose to abort: "story after story [tells] how unborn young lives have been the wastage of an incoherence, disaffiliation, self-indulgence, and repugnance for truth that afflicts their parents." Well written and carefully researched, *Rachel Weeping* is an eloquent, if wordy, presentation of the classic arguments against abortion.

Crum, Gary, and Thelma McCormack. **Abortion: Pro-Choice or Pro-Life?** Washington, DC: American University Press, 1992. 149 pp. Bibliography. ISBN 1-879383-05-5 (cloth); 0-879383-04-7 (paper).

This is the first volume in a series on important controversial issues regarding public policy. It is set up as a "debate" between the two authors. Crum, a professor in the health sciences, has been active in the pro-life movement since the 1970s. He argues for a "no-compromise" position in which an unborn child's right to life outweighs any interest the mother might have in aborting it. McCormack, a sociologist and feminist, places the abortion controversy in a wider social and political context, comparing it to other issues related to women's rights, such as suffrage. She asserts that, like larger social movements that favor equality and liberation, the pro-choice movement is valuable because it places confidence in ordinary citizens to make important decisions about their own lives and futures. Both arguments are dispassionate, well documented, clearly written, and easy to understand, avoiding the overly academic tone of many similar essays. As such, this book provides a succinct and useful comparison of the two primary positions on abortion.

Grobstein, Clifford. **Science and the Unborn: Choosing Human Futures.** New York: Basic Books, 1988. 207 pp. Index. ISBN 0-465-07295-X.

Embryologist Clifford Grobstein is professor emeritus in biological science and public policy at the University of California, San Diego, and a member of the Ethics Committee of the American Fertility Society. In this book, he seeks "to dispel the darkness of the womb and to illuminate what is within" in an attempt to stimulate the development of public policies that address the status of the unborn with respect to such issues as abortion, in vitro fertilization, and medical research. Within the context of human development from fertilization to birth and beyond, he discusses the progressive development of individuality—genetic, developmental, functional, behavioral, psychic, and social. He then explores the issues and considerations underlying the status of the unborn at each stage of development—preembryo, embryo, and fetus. In conclusion, he calls for a concerted effort to address the questions of status of the unborn. Both scientific and philosophical, and totally free of polemic, this book is a valuable addition to the literature and a persuasive call for a national commitment to seeking consensus on issues that can only become more complex and troubling as time goes on.

Harrison, Beverly Wildung. **Our Right To Choose: Toward a New Ethic of Abortion.** Boston: Beacon Press, 1983. 334 pp. Index. ISBN 0-8070-1508-3 (cloth); ISBN 0-8070-1509-1 (paper).

Beverly Wildung Harrison is a Christian theologian and ethicist. In *Our Right To Choose*, she examines the ethics of abortion within the context of the attitudes of western culture in general and Christianity in particular toward women, medicine, religion, and the law. Most discussions of abortion ethics center around the moral status of the fetus, but, Harrison argues, the reasoning behind such arguments is intrinsically sexist. Instead, "the well-being of a woman and the value of her life plan must always be recognized as of intrinsic value in any appeal to intrinsic value in a moral analysis of abortion." Placing the abortion controversy within the broader context of procreative choice, Harrison examines the theologies behind the moral debate and presents a new view of Christian teaching on abortion, arguing that the latter has been distorted by patriarchal ideology and ignorance of newer methodologies of social and cultural history. She proposes a liberal theological and feminist perspective on procreative choice and abortion, finally challenging "those who support both procreative choice for women and respect for fetal life [to work] together to simultaneously reduce the necessity of frequent resort to abortion and to enhance women's well-being in society." This is a bold, passionate, and often difficult work, a classic in the field.

Abortion History

Garrow, David J. **Liberty and Sexuality: The Right to Privacy and the Making of** *Roe v. Wade.* New York: Macmillan, 1994. 981 pp. Bibliography, index. ISBN 0-02-542755-5.

Historian David Garrow received the Pulitzer Prize and the Robert F. Kennedy Book Award for his biography of Martin Luther King, Jr., *Bearing the Cross.* In this massive work, he chronicles the chain of people and events that culminated in the *Roe v. Wade* decision, beginning with the first attempts, early in this century, to overturn Connecticut's stringent anti–birth control law. Based on hundreds of interviews and nationwide archival sources, including previously secret files kept on the *Roe v. Wade* case by Justices William Brennan, William O. Douglas, and Thurgood Marshall, *Liberty and Sexuality* provides a vivid and detailed account of the long struggle to establish what many saw as a fundamental truth— that the right to privacy, including sexual and reproductive privacy, is inherent in the constitutionally guaranteed right to liberty.

Keller, Allan. **Scandalous Lady: The Life and Times of Madame Restell, New York's Most Notorious Abortionist.** New York: Atheneum, 1981. 191 pp. ISBN 0-689-11213-0.

This is a lively biography of the most famous—or infamous—abortionist of the nineteenth century, Anna Lohman, better known as Madame Restell. Restell had a thriving abortion practice in New York City for more than three decades, until she was finally brought down in 1878 by antiobscenity crusader Anthony Comstock. Comstock used his favorite trick of posing as a poor, desperate father to fool Restell into offering him "medicine" for his pregnant wife, whereupon he and his vice squad raided her house. Restell, whose income was rumored to be in excess of $1 million a year, escaped justice and provided a dramatic exit by slitting her throat in her bathtub the night before the trial was to begin. Keller, a newspaper reporter, writer, editor, and columnist who served for 23 years on the faculty of the Graduate School of Journalism at Columbia University, unearthed an abundance of detail that enriches this vivid portrayal of one of the more notorious episodes in abortion history. Includes illustrations.

Lader, Lawrence. **Abortion II: Making the Revolution.** Boston: Beacon Press, 1973. 242 pp. Bibliography, index. ISBN 0-8070-2180-6.

Abortion II is the inside story of the early abortion rights movement, told by Lawrence Lader, an author and activist whose crusade for abortion rights stretches back more than 30 years. His first book on the subject, titled simply *Abortion*, was published in 1966. With it, Lader launched a public campaign in which he realized he had "perilously few allies." Only two small groups had made any kind of organized protest against restrictive abortion laws: the Association for the Study of Abortion, a New York group made up mostly of doctors and lawyers, and, in California, the Society for Humane Abortion, which was "little more than a loyal band of partisans drawn to an incandescent rebel named Patricia Maginnis." Lader describes the growth of the abortion rights movement from this handful of protesters and lawbreakers—including clergy members and others who participated in referral services, as well as doctors who provided abortions at the risks of their careers and their freedom—to a series of judicial challenges, legislative debates, and mass protests that eventually shifted attitudes and finally laws about abortion. Though Lader can hardly be called objective, *Abortion II* stands as a classic and thorough account of the people and the events involved in the struggle for legalized abortion.

Messer, Ellen, and Kathryn E. May. **Back Rooms: Voices from the Illegal Abortion Era.** New York: St. Martin's Press, 1988. 224 pp. ISBN 0-312-01732-4.

This is an "oral history"—a collection of interviews about people's experiences with abortion prior to *Roe v. Wade*. Most of the brief stories are told by women who had abortions, or who wanted abortions and could not obtain them, during what the authors call the "dark years" when abortion was illegal. The women's current ages range from late thirties to mid-eighties; their stories include descriptions of abortions conducted without anesthetic in filthy apartments by leering "doctors," of shotgun marriages ending in divorce, or of handing infants over for adoption. One or two were pregnant as a result of rape, some were "good girls" who "made a mistake," others were married and felt for various reasons they could not add another child to their families. Also included are interviews with a psychiatrist who helped women qualify for therapeutic abortions, a doctor who performed a few carefully disguised illegal abortions, and abortion rights activists Bill Baird, Lawrence Lader, and Rev. Robert Hare.

Miller, Patricia G. **The Worst of Times.** New York: HarperCollins, 1993. 328 pp. ISBN 0-06-019034-5.

This is a collection of stories gleaned from interviews with people whose lives intersected with abortion in the days when it was illegal. The interviewees include women who had illegal abortions, practitioners who performed illegal abortions, adult children whose mothers died as a result of illegal abortions, and an assortment of people whose work brought them into contact with both the providers and their clients. These include a coroner who worked in a large city hospital during the 1950s and 1960s and who recalls seeing "three or four" deaths a year from illegal abortions, police officers who investigated and arrested abortionists, and an attorney who represented a doctor wrongly accused of performing an abortion that led to a woman's death. Also included is an interview with the wife of Robert Spencer, the small-town Pennsylvania doctor who quietly provided abortions for thousands of women from 1923 until his retirement in 1967. Miller lets her subjects speak for themselves, telling their stories in their own words. The result is a concrete, vivid portrayal of real people dealing with real and painful situations, far removed from the abstract slogans and rhetoric that generally characterize the public debate. Also included are a brief history of abortion laws and a brief overview of "underground abortion," including its estimated frequency, techniques, and complications.

Mohr, James. **Abortion in America: The Origins and Evolution of National Policy**. New York: Oxford University Press, 1978. 331 pp. Index. ISBN 0-19-502249-1.

This is the classic historical study of abortion and abortion policy in the United States. Mohr, a history professor, traces the roots of current attitudes and policies toward abortion through a detailed historical picture of abortion as it evolved throughout the nineteenth century. In 1800, abortion was a legal and accepted, if not openly acknowledged, practice. By midcentury, it had become increasingly common, particularly among married, native-born, Protestant women, and abortion practitioners and producers of abortifacients advertised openly in the everyday press and even in religious journals. By 1900, thanks in large part to the concerted efforts of the newly formed American Medical Association, abortion had been outlawed virtually throughout the United States. Mohr provides a fascinating and impartial analysis of the unique social, legal, and historical factors that led to this turnaround. Perhaps the most-cited book in abortion literature, *Abortion in America* provides essential background for understanding contemporary abortion policies, practice, and conflict.

Nathanson, Bernard. **Aborting America.** New York: Doubleday, 1979. 320 pp. Bibliography, index. ISBN 0-385-14461.

Bernard Nathanson is an obstetrician and gynecologist who is one of abortion's most visible and vocal opponents. In the late 1960s and early 1970s, however, he was a staunch advocate of legalized abortion and was a cofounder of the National Association to Repeal Abortion Laws (now the National Abortion Rights Action League). This book chronicles his early experiences with abortion, including his stint as director of the Center for Reproductive and Sexual Health ("the largest abortion clinic in the world"), his political involvement, and his gradual realization that his feelings about abortion had undergone a dramatic change. In the latter part of the book, Dr. Nathanson conducts a broader examination of the issues surrounding abortion. He critiques the "specious" arguments for and against abortion, discusses fetal development, and explores some of the philosophical, medical, and legal questions surrounding the issue. Finally, he suggests that it may soon be possible to transplant an unwanted fetus out of one womb and into another, or into some sort of artificial uterus—raising, but not answering, the question of what would be done with all those unaborted babies. This is a classic in the field, interesting both for its historical content and for its unique—and provocative—perspective.

Olasky, Marvin. **Abortion Rites: A Social History of Abortion in America.** Wheaton, IL: Crossway Books, 1992. 318 pp. Indexes. ISBN 0-89107-687-5.

This book might more accurately be called "a history of the anti-abortion movement in America." Olasky, a journalism professor at the University of Texas, set out to challenge the prevailing view of abortion history, which is largely based on the work of James Mohr [see above]. He begins by offering evidence that abortion, rather than being widely accepted in early America, was actually strongly disapproved of, and that the lack of legal consequences for abortion had more to do with the difficulty of proving it had taken place than with an attitude of tolerance. Unlike Mohr, who portrayed abortion as a largely mainstream phenomenon, Olasky asserts that women who sought to end their pregnancies belonged primarily to three groups: young women, often servants, who had been "seduced and abandoned"; prostitutes; and married spiritists, whose religion included sexual freedom among its covenants. Olasky also presents a different perspective on the nineteenth-century movement to criminalize abortion. He disputes Mohr's claim that the doctors who led the movement were motivated by a desire to gain a monopoly on the health care market by driving out "irregulars," such as midwives and homeopaths, saying that they were instead driven by a belief in the humanity of the fetus and a horror of killing carried over from the carnage of the Civil War. In the last third of the book, Olasky documents the gradual "breaking out" of abortion as American attitudes shifted and proponents of legal abortion gained ground. Meticulously researched, intellectually honest, and engagingly written, *Abortion Rites* provides a useful counterpoint to more widely known historical accounts.

————. **The Press and Abortion: 1838–1988.** Hillsdale, NJ: Lawrence Erlbaum Associates, 1988. 200 pp. Index. ISBN 0-8058-0199-5 (cloth); 0-8058-0485-4 (paper).

This book traces the history of abortion in the United States as it has been portrayed in the print media, with the emphasis on coverage by "broad-based, general interest print media" rather than that by religious, political, or special-interest magazines and newsletters. From the early advertisements of Madame Restell to the current controversy over fetal tissue transplants, the book presents an array of articles, editorials, and advertisements gleaned from newspapers and newsmagazines—primarily New York–based— as well as excerpts from a few popular books. Over the 150-year period, the author notes, attitudes toward abortion as expressed in the media have gone through a number of shifts. Restell and other abortionists used the press to promote abortion and build a lucrative business, but, in the later part of the nineteenth century, papers such as the *New York Times* and *National Police Gazette* "helped to turn the tide" against abortion. Coverage waned in the first part of the twentieth century, but since the 1960s, Olasky alleges, the press has shown an increasing bias in favor of abortion, in response to "the strategies of masters of abortion public relations." Despite its admitted bias, this book is an interesting and thorough account of the media's role in shaping attitudes and arguments about abortion over the last century and a half.

Solinger, Rickie. **The Abortionist: A Woman against the Law.** New York: The Free Press, 1994. 250 pp. Bibliography. ISBN 0-02-929865-2.

In this sympathetic biography of flamboyant Portland abortionist Ruth Barnett, Solinger also provides a more general history of illegal abortion as it was practiced in the decades preceding *Roe v. Wade*. Barnett performed some 40,000 abortions between 1918 and 1968, most of them in her well-appointed and antiseptic suite of offices in a downtown Portland business building. Her patients, many of whom were referred by doctors unwilling to perform the service themselves, came from all walks of life. For most of her career, Barnett worked without interference from the law, but as antiabortion sentiment increased following World War II, she was subjected to repeated arrests, prosecution, and jail time. Solinger's portrayal of the abortion business and its changing social status, from tacit acceptance to sometimes brutal suppression, goes well beyond the stereotypical stories of abortions performed on dirty kitchen tables in dark "back alleys." Throughout, Solinger argues that it was not the abortionists who endangered women's lives, but the laws that "created opportunities for individuals—sleazy entrepreneurs and ambitious politicians—who did not perform abortions, but positioned themselves to benefit from women's desperation, at women's expense. The story of the illegal era provides a glaring example of how, when an activity is simultaneously illegal, culturally taboo, and perceived as one of life's necessities by women, the opportunities abound for exploiting women while enhancing the power of men."

Weddington, Sarah. **A Question of Choice.** New York: G.P. Putnam's Sons, 1992. 306 pp. Index. ISBN 0-399-13790-4.

This autobiographical account depicts the events leading up to and following Weddington's famous victory as the novice lawyer who successfully argued *Roe v. Wade* before the Supreme Court. Beginning with her illegal abortion in a Mexican clinic in 1967 and her experiences as a graduate student at the University of Texas in the turbulent years of the late 1960s, Weddington describes the forces and people that led her to challenge Texas's restrictive abortion laws, then goes on to describe in detail the development and outcome of *Roe v. Wade*. The latter portion of the book is a narrative of the events surrounding abortion following the *Roe* decision and Weddington's continuing involvement in the struggle to keep abortion both safe and legal while maintaining a high-powered career that took her from the Texas state legislature to a job as an assistant to President Jimmy Carter to her ongoing role as a speaker and activist. The book concludes with a "plan for action," detailing what readers can do to support reproductive rights. Also included are a listing of pro-choice groups and information sources, as well as a brief bibliography.

Medical and Legal Aspects of Abortion

Abortion in the United States: A Compilation of State Legislation. Buffalo, NY: William S. Hein, 1991. Vol. 1, 632 pp.; Vol. 2, 751 pp. ISBN 0-89941-753-1.

In a succession of rulings, beginning with *Webster v. Reproductive Health Services*, the Supreme Court has shifted much of the power to regulate abortion back to the states while upholding abortion as a constitutional right. As a result, state abortion laws now represent a widely varied and ever-changing landscape, and a compilation of state laws provides a valuable research tool. This two-volume set, compiled by the Institute for International Legal Information, gathers in one place state laws that deal specifically with abortion or "a closely related matter." Also included are summaries of cases on abortion law, most of them dealing with the constitutionality of a particular statute. The first volume lists the laws by state. The second volume divides the laws under 11 subject headings, including legality of abortions; abortion patients (including consent and notification); aborted fetus or aborted infant born alive; health care facilities; health care personnel; use of public funds, facilities, or personnel; abortion referral, counseling, or encouragement; records of legal abortions; abortifacients; private insurance coverage; and miscellaneous. Because of the continuing onslaught of new legislation, readers are advised to check the currentness of statutes through such sources as supplements to state codes and electronic databases; the editors plan to revise the publication as new statutes are enacted.

Boston Women's Health Book Collective. **The New Our Bodies, Ourselves.** Rev. ed. New York: Simon and Schuster, 1984. 352 pp. ISBN 0-671-22145-0.

Abortion is the topic of chapter 16 of this well-known and highly acclaimed volume on women's health and self-care. The chapter packs a great deal of information and commentary into a relatively brief number of pages. It discusses both the physical and emotional aspects of abortion, including deciding whether to have an abortion, abortion techniques, finding and choosing an abortion facility, risks and complications, and what actually happens during an abortion. Included are firsthand accounts by women who have had abortions, as well as a brief resource list of organizations, readings, and films.

Drucker, Dan. **Abortion Decisions of the Supreme Court, 1973 through 1989: A Comprehensive Review with Historical Commentary.** Jefferson, NC: McFarland, P.O. Box 611, Jefferson, NC 28640, 1990. 206 pp. Index. ISBN 0-89950-459-0.

This slim volume offers clear and precise summations of Supreme Court cases dealing with abortion (with the somewhat puzzling exclusion of the 1980 *Harris v. McRae* case), from *Roe v. Wade* through the 1989 *Webster* decision. For each case, Drucker includes the disputed law in its entirety, followed by discussions of each contested provision and lower court rulings. These in turn are followed by paraphrased versions of the Court's opinion and concurring and dissenting opinions that retain the originals' "substance, tone and memorable diction." Each chapter ends with a brief summary of the Court's decision. The book also includes a brief historical overview of abortion, a description of the Supreme Court itself, a chapter on the "new era" of conservatism on the Court, and a short review of pending cases (which have since been decided). This invaluable reference work clearly shows the changing tone of the Supreme Court as it moves further away from the right-to-privacy precept of *Roe v. Wade* and toward upholding states' interest in the protection of fetuses as potential citizens.

Faux, Marian. *Roe v. Wade:* **The Untold Story of the Landmark Supreme Court Decision That Made Abortion Legal.** New York: Macmillan, 1988. 370 pp. Bibliography, index. ISBN 0-02-537151-7.

This book focuses on the events and the people behind the landmark *Roe v. Wade* decision: Linda Coffee and Sarah Weddington, two women fresh out of law school and looking to make their mark on the world; Norma McCorvey, alias "Jane Roe," an itinerant young Texan who "had a naive enthusiasm that occasionally made her a too willing party for the wrong opportunity and sometimes . . . for the right one"—in this case, acting as the plaintiff for a suit challenging Texas's restrictive abortion laws; John Tolle, the trial lawyer who defended Dallas County's right to enforce the laws; Jay Floyd, who defended the laws' constitutionality on behalf of the state; and a host of characters—judges, lawyers, feminists, activists, and others—who played parts in the case. Much of Faux's book is based on interviews with the principals (with the exception of McCorvey, who would not agree to be interviewed unless she was paid), on personal observations, and on Dallas and New York newspaper accounts of the period. Despite occasional factual errors, Faux has produced a vivid and often dramatic account not only of the events leading to the decision but of the social and legal context in which they took place.

Friedman, Leon, ed. **The Supreme Court Confronts Abortion: The Briefs, Arguments, and Decision in** *Planned Parenthood v. Casey.* New York: Farrar, Straus and Giroux, 1993. 502 pp. Indexes. ISBN 0-374-272-3-4.

The fragmented 1992 *Planned Parenthood v. Casey* Supreme Court decision was the culmination of the shifts that have taken place over the two decades since *Roe v. Wade*. Like that earlier case, it has come to be seen as a fundamental dividing line in the history of abortion. This volume contains the basic legal documents involved in the *Casey* decision, including the text of the oral arguments held on April 22, 1992, 3 (of 11) amicus curiae (friend of the court) briefs submitted by groups supporting the right to abortion and 3 (of 24) briefs submitted by abortion opponents, and the text of the decision itself. The latter includes the plurality joint opinion by Justices O'Connor, Kennedy, and Souter, as well as the dissenting opinions: individual ones by Justice Stevens and Justice Blackmun, and two joint dissents: one by Chief Justice Rehnquist and the other by Justice Scalia. These documents provide insight into a decision that has significance well beyond its effect on abortion laws and policies. As Friedman points out in his introduction, "The various opinions issued by the Justices presented a theory of constitutional adjudication that had not previously been articulated by members of the Court—what the Supreme Court's role is in our constitutional scheme, when it should overrule laws passed by a vote of the majority, and when it is appropriate for the Court to change its mind and overrule precedents."

Glendon, Mary Ann. **Abortion and Divorce in Western Law.** Cambridge, MA: Harvard University Press, 1987. 197 pp. Index. ISBN 0-674-00160-5.

Mary Ann Glendon is a Harvard Law School professor who has written extensively on family law, particularly from the perspective of comparative law, which compares how laws in different societies shape and are shaped by those societies. In this book, she compares abortion and divorce laws in the United States, Canada, and 18 Western European countries. Pointing to other nations that have achieved legal compromise in the face of fierce national debates over abortion, she offers suggestions for using foreign models to find both the substance and the expression of laws that combine compassion for unwillingly pregnant women with "affirmation of life." She argues that, in taking abortion regulation away from the states, the Supreme Court halted a process that would eventually have brought about compromise legislation in most states. If the issue were returned to the states today, "it . . . seems likely that a very few states might return to strict abortion laws, a few more would endorse early abortion on demand, and the great majority would move to a position . . . reflecting popular sentiment that early abortions should be treated more leniently, but that all abortion is a serious matter." Glendon's compromise proposals are not likely to please activists on either side, but they may find a receptive audience among the many Americans who find themselves caught in the middle of the current polar debate.

Harrison, Maureen, and Steve Gilbert, eds. **Abortion Decisions of the United States Supreme Court: The 1990s.** Beverly Hills, CA: Excellent Books, 1993. 298 pp. Bibliography, index. ISBN 0-9628014-6-1.

This is the third in a series of books on abortion-related Supreme Court decisions (not associated with the book by Dan Drucker [see above]). The first two books covered the abortion-related decisions of the Supreme Court in the 1970s and 1980s, respectively. This book consists largely of the actual text of decisions rendered during the first years of the 1990s, edited to remove "legalese" and make them comprehensible for the lay reader. Included are the texts for five decisions: *Hodgson v. Minnesota, Ohio v. Akron Center for Reproductive Health, Rust v. Sullivan, Planned Parenthood v. Casey,* and *Bray v. Alexandria Women's Health Clinic.* Each decision is preceded by brief excerpts and an overview that lists the question at issue, the lower court(s) involved, the law being challenged, the parties and their counsels, the dates of the arguments and the decision, the justices in the majority and the minority, and the author(s) of the decision and any concurring or dissenting opinions. Also included is the text of the U.S. Constitution.

Hern, Warren. **Abortion Practice.** Boulder, CO: Alperglo Graphics, 1990. 368 pp. Index ISBN 0-9625728-0-2 (paper).

Warren Hern is a physician, anthropologist, and epidemiologist who owns and operates an abortion clinic in Boulder, Colorado. A pioneer who has been responsible for a number of innovations in abortion practice, Dr. Hern is also an activist who has worked diligently to preserve abortion rights and to help make abortion both safe and available. Designed as a textbook for practitioners, *Abortion Practice* provides a comprehensive treatment of all aspects of providing abortion services, including public health aspects of abortion; counseling; operative procedures and techniques; day-to-day clinic operation and management; management of complications; legal aspects of abortion practice; long-term risks of abortion; and the role of the abortion provider in the community. Abortion, Dr. Hern writes, "takes place in a context of public controversy and private anguish. . . . A commitment to provide this kind of care in an excellent fashion is more than a decision to practice a certain medical specialty or participate in a certain kind of health care for women. It is a commitment to the expansion of choice." Written for the most part in clear, nontechnical language, this book offers thorough, practical, and detailed advice for counselors, nurses, and other clinic personnel as well as for physicians. This book was originally published in 1984 by J. B. Lippincott.

Imber, Jonathan B. **Abortion and the Private Practice of Medicine.** New Haven, CT: Yale University Press, 1986. 164 pp. Bibliography, index. ISBN 0-300-03554-3.

This well-written book examines abortion from the perspective of physicians in private practice. Sociologist Imber begins by looking at the history of abortion from a medical perspective. He then examines the medical profession's "search for its proper role" with respect to abortion, a role that "depends on far more than an ethics of choice." Imber spent two years observing and interviewing the 26 obstetrician-gynecologists practicing in "Daleton," a medium-sized city whose lack of an abortion clinic forces doctors to decide whether, when, and how to provide abortions to their patients. Looking at characteristics that may affect the doctors' choices, Imber examines their reasons for refusing or agreeing to perform abortions and the feelings and opinions underlying those reasons. What he finds is a "haunting ambivalence," with many doctors approving of women's right to choose abortion but reluctant to perform abortions themselves. This ambivalence, along with a moral legacy of opposition to abortion, is an important factor in the failure of the practice of medicine to accommodate legal abortion. "As long as abortion continues to occupy a controversial place in American life," Imber concludes, "its acceptance and discouragement will go hand in hand. This is its cultural legacy and the doctor's dilemma."

Judges, Donald. **Hard Choices, Lost Voices: How the Abortion Conflict Has Divided America, Distorted Constitutional Rights, and Damaged the Courts.** Chicago: Ivan R. Dee, 1993. 334 pp. Index. ISBN 1-56663-0160-9.

In this book, University of Arkansas law professor Donald Judges attempts to fill what he sees as a serious information gap in the public furor over abortion: despite the intensity of opinion and emotion that surrounds abortion, few people seem to have any clear idea of the social, medical, and, in particular, the legal issues involved. Judges begins by offering some facts about the nature of the debate and outlining its demographic, social, medical, and historical contexts. He then focuses on the constitutional issues surrounding abortion and on the increasingly divisive and confused actions of the Supreme Court in this arena, concluding that the Court's current approach offers "perhaps the worst possible resolution of the conflict in constitutional terms from either side's perspective." Finally, he offers a possible solution based on what he calls the "repugnance hypothesis"—that there is a point in pregnancy, somewhere between the fifteenth and eighteenth week, beyond which abortion "feels wrong" to most people because of the increasingly human appearance of the fetus. This point should replace viability as the legal threshold for determining whether or not a woman may have an abortion. Acknowledging that any "bright-line" test is susceptible to criticism, Judges points out that any resolution, other than total prohibition of abortion or abortion on demand throughout pregnancy, involves such a test. "The trouble with the current state of abortion law is not that its bright-line viability test produces arbitrariness at that boundary, but rather that the application of that test produces arbitrariness *throughout* pregnancy." The real test of a policy, he concludes, is its workability and practicality. "We are now so far from any real common-ground resolution of the abortion problem that it would be cynical to be more demanding of a new approach than we are of the current one. The repugnance hypothesis does not promise complete harmony, it merely asks whether we can do better."

National Abortion Rights Action League (NARAL). **Who Decides: A State-by-State Review of Abortion and Reproductive Rights.** 5th ed. Washington, DC: NARAL, 1995. 181 pp. No ISBN.

This is the fifth annual edition of NARAL's useful compilation of state laws and policies related to abortion and reproductive rights. Listings for each state and the District of Columbia provide information on availability of abortion services; positions of key elected officials and legislative bodies; selected legislative activity for 1993–1994; current statutes and regulations; state constitutional protection for abortion; policies on education regarding sexuality and sexually transmitted diseases; family planning services; and major party platforms. Also included are overviews of statutes and regulations in U.S. territories, an analysis of key findings, and tables showing how the states compare with respect to different aspects of abortion and reproductive rights; for example, mandatory waiting periods and public funding for abortion.

Roe v. Wade: **The Complete Text of the Official U.S. Supreme Court Decision.** Annotated by Bo Schambelan. Philadelphia: Running Press, 1992. 133 pp. ISBN 1-56138-202-7.

This slender but useful volume provides the complete text of the Supreme Court's majority and minority opinions on *Roe v. Wade*, annotated by lawyer Bo Schambelan. To make the text more readable, most of the legal citations have been moved to an appendix, along with sections that contain legal language not accessible to lay readers (the removed language is summarized in brackets within the text). Following the opinions are brief "postscripts" summarizing subsequent Supreme Court decisions relating to abortion through *Planned Parenthood v. Casey*. Also provided are brief biographies of the justices who participated in the *Roe v. Wade* decision, the preamble and the relevant amendments to the Constitution, and a glossary of legal terms used in the decisions.

Rubin, Eva. **Abortion, Politics and the Courts.** Rev. ed. Westport, CT: Greenwood Press, 1987. 254 pp. Bibliography, indexes. ISBN 0-313-25614-4.

Eva Rubin is a professor of political science and public administration who has also written on the Supreme Court and the American family. In this book, she examines the use of litigation as an avenue for effecting changes in public policy—specifically the campaign by women's organizations to use the courts to overturn state criminal abortion laws. She also attempts to "assess the impact of [*Roe v. Wade*] to see what we can learn about the consequences, intended and unintended" of Supreme Court "megadecisions" that cause "indirect changes across a broad spectrum of activities: political, governmental, medical, social, religious, moral, organizational." In clear, understandable language, Rubin explains the background of abortion law reform and early litigation efforts; the backstage negotiations and reasoning behind *Roe*, especially the concepts of trimester and viability; the political battles that followed the decision; and the state legislative response and corresponding judicial responses to new laws through 1985. Although she agrees with many critics that the Court took a legislative role in *Roe*, she interprets that role differently: "the decision making . . . is often legislative in that it is prospective and affirmative, rather than historical and negative." The Court's reasoning in *Roe* may have seemed inadequate, she proposes, because it failed to reconcile the doctrines of liberty and privacy with the real constitutional principle at issue in the case—"gender equality, the proposition that only with the right to accept or reject responsibilities for procreation could women choose to play roles as free, autonomous, participating citizens in a democratic system on an equal basis with men." Includes a detailed chronology of abortion-related legal, political, and judicial events from 1980 to 1986.

Psychological and Health Aspects of Abortion

American Psychological Association. **Testimony on the Psychological Sequelae of Abortion.** Paper presented to the Office of the U.S. Surgeon General, December 2, 1987. Washington, DC: American Psychological Association, 1200 17th Street, NW, Washington, DC 20036. 39 pp. Bibliography. No ISBN.

Over the last 20 years, American Psychological Association members have conducted research on the psychological sequelae of abortion and published several comprehensive reviews of the literature. This testimony represents their consensus views. Given the large numbers of women who have had abortions, the report states, "if there are widespread, severe psychological sequelae of abortion, we would expect them to be readily detectable." However, "because there is no reporting system in place to track the number of visits of patients for post-abortion psychological sequelae, no statistics with known measurement error are possible." The report discusses the problems with existing research, including (among others) inadequate methodology, researcher bias, lack of consensus in defining psychological sequelae and on selecting comparison groups, lack of standardization in data collection methods, lack of preabortion comparison data, small sample size, and the fact that "studies of women's response to abortion do not all examine the same event or medical procedure." Given these limitations, the majority of studies indicate that although "at some level, abortion is a stressful experience for all women . . . psychological sequelae are usually mild and tend to diminish rapidly over time without adversely affecting general functioning." The report goes on to cite apparent risk factors for negative abortion sequelae and concludes with a recommendation for a theoretically sound, multivariate approach to investigating postabortion psychological reactions. An extensive bibliography of journal articles is included.

Committee on Government Operations, 101st Congress. **The Federal Role in Determining the Medical and Psychological Impact of Abortion on Women.** Washington, DC: U.S. Government Printing Office, 1989. 30 pp. House Report 101–392.

In 1987, President Ronald Reagan directed U.S. Surgeon General C. Everett Koop to prepare a comprehensive report on the health effects of abortion on women. The report was prepared in 1988, but the surgeon general decided in January 1989 not to release it. Consequently, the Subcommittee on Human Resources and Intergovernmental Relations of the House Committee on Government Operations conducted an oversight investigation of the surgeon general's report. This report is a summary of the committee's findings. Both Reagan's and Koop's opposition to abortion are well known, and abortion rights groups interpreted Koop's refusal to release the report as evidence that its findings did not favor the antiabortion point of view. The congressional report would tend to back this accusation, citing discrepancies between the report and Koop's letter to the president as well as testimony from various experts and information from the report itself. In a strongly worded dissent, however, six representatives accuse the report of "[painting] a misleading and inaccurate picture of the abortion issues" presented before the subcommittee and of having an "unambiguous proabortion bias" that fails "to acknowledge the health effects on the pre-born child."

Francke, Linda Bird. **The Ambivalence of Abortion.** New York: Random House, 1978. 261 pp. Index. ISBN 0-394-41080-7.

This oft-cited book consists primarily of personal stories of individuals who have been involved in abortions—not only the women themselves, but their husbands, lovers, and parents. In their own words, people describe how an abortion—whether pending, just over, or years in the past—has affected their lives and their relationships. Of all ages and from all walks of life, the storytellers run the gamut of emotions, from anger to regret to relief. The book is divided into chapters according to whose story is being told: single women, married women, men, couples, teenagers, and parents, plus a chapter on women who had abortions 30, 40, or even 50 years ago. A classic in the field.

Reardon, David C. **Aborted Women: Silent No More.** Chicago: Loyola University Press, 1987. 373 pp. Index. ISBN 0-8294-0578-X.

This book purports to be an objective, research-based report on the physical and psychological effects of abortion, based on answers to a questionnaire sent to about 250 members of Women

Exploited by Abortion (WEBA). (It is worth noting that the author never states how many women actually responded to the questionnaire—all results are shown in percentages rather than numbers.) Although Reardon goes to some pains to explain that the respondents are representative of all women who have had abortions, based on factors such as age, marital status, and socioeconomic background, the self-selected nature of the survey group and the small sample size fatally flaw the results. Nevertheless, the book offers a well-written, sympathetic, and thought-provoking portrait of women who consider themselves victims of abortion. Most of the respondents report they were pressured into having abortions; they cite such aftereffects as severe depression, alcoholism, drug abuse, and physical abuse. Additionally, many of the women felt that the treatment they received in abortion clinics was cold, uncaring, and coercive. The book includes a foreword by Nancyjo Mann, founder of WEBA.

Rogers, James L., George B. Stoms, and James L. Phifer. **"Psychological Impact of Abortion: Methodological and Outcomes Summary of Empirical Research between 1966 and 1988."** *Health Care for Women International,* Vol. 10 (1989), pp. 347–376.

This is a review of articles on the psychological impact of abortion published in English between January 1966 and April 1988, written in an endeavor to provide policymakers and clinicians with "a reliable method [for deciding] how much confidence to place in statements seemingly supported by quantitative references from this literature." Only articles that reported original empirical data were included; articles "motivated only by theoretical, philosophical or moral considerations" and those that presented case studies of patients in clinical practice were excluded. Out of 280 articles located that dealt with psychological sequelae of abortion, 76 met the review criteria. Of these, 31 were defined as prospective studies (subject measurement first occurred prior to abortion) and 32 as retrospective studies (subject measurement first occurred after abortion), while 13 were comparison studies that compared a post-abortion group with a group of women who had given birth. The bulk of the report consists of tables that summarize data from the articles in order to provide a synopsis of study demographics, methodological limitations, and gross statistical features (such as sample size, attrition rate, type of outcome measured, and outcome incidence). Also included is a table of definitions of methodological limitations, such as contradictions, interviewer bias, lack of baseline comparison, small sample size, and unclear criteria. The report concludes by noting that outcome incidence and methodological profiles vary substantially across the studies: "Both advocates and opponents of abortion can prove their points by judiciously referencing only articles supporting their political agenda." A list of investigations summarized is included.

Sachdev, Paul. **Sex, Abortion and Unmarried Women.** Westport, CT: Greenwood Press, 1993. 321 pp. Bibliography, index. ISBN 0-313-24071-X.

This is an in-depth examination of the psychological impact of abortion on a group of women representative of the majority of women having abortions—white, between the ages of 18 and 25, unmarried, and undergoing an abortion in the first trimester of their first pregnancies. Sachdev, a Canadian social work professor who has edited four previous books on abortion, conducted lengthy, one-on-one interviews with 70 women in Ontario, Canada, who fit the profile and whose abortions had taken place in major hospitals six months to one year earlier. The women also completed detailed questionnaires designed to provide internal checks on the consistency of their information and self-reported emotional responses to their abortions. Among the areas Sachdev explored in the study were the women's "sexual and contraceptive dossiers," how they reacted to becoming pregnant, how they came to choose abortion, their experience of the abortion itself, and their reactions following abortion. Sachdev's findings supported those of several recent studies: overall, while many of the women felt guilt or depression immediately following the abortion, the reactions were mild and tended to dissipate over time. Serious and prolonged psychological consequences were rare and tended to coincide with problems not related to the abortion. Women who identified with the pregnancy, who had moral or religious objections to abortion, who had difficulty with making the abortion decision, and who received insufficient support from key people (such as husbands or parents) were the most likely to experience psychological problems. Other factors included the attitude of the service providers and the woman's ability to cope with life stresses. Also included are a succinct overview and comparison of abortion in the United States and Canada and a review of earlier studies on the psychological effects of abortion.

Shostak, Arthur B., and Gary McLouth. **Men and Abortion: Lessons, Losses, and Love.** New York: Praeger, 1984. 333 pp. Index. ISBN 0-03-063641-8.

This poignant and insightful book addresses a gaping hole in the literature on abortion—its impact on men, the "co-conceivers" who are mostly ignored in what is often perceived to be solely a women's issue. Using questionnaires completed by 1,000 "waiting room men" and a small number of interviews, including several with male abortion counselors, the authors explore the thoughts, behavior, and emotions of men who were, willingly or unwillingly, abortion participants. The study reveals that many men, rather than being unfeeling villains who get women pregnant and then abandon them emotionally if not in fact, are deeply and permanently affected by the experience of abortion. It also shows the importance of involving men in both pre- and post-abortion counseling and offers suggestions for "[helping] men *and* women make the best of an experience which tries them as few others may in their lifetimes."

Zimmerman, Mary K. **Passage through Abortion.** New York: Praeger, 1977. 222 pp. Bibliography, index. ISBN 0-03-029816-4.

In this book, Zimmerman, a sociologist with a particular interest in women and health, examines women's abortion experiences within the context of their relationships to "significant others" and to society in general. In a study that began soon after the 1973 Supreme Court decision legalizing abortion, Zimmerman conducted in-depth interviews with 40 women about six weeks after each had had an abortion. She found, among other things, that the ways in which the women experienced their abortions, and how well they assimilated the experience, were strongly affected by their relative "affiliation" or "disaffiliation." Those women with secure relationships, a sense of direction, and well-defined societal roles fared much better than women whose social ties were more tenuous. Zimmerman also found that, despite the legality of abortion, virtually all of the women regarded abortion as a deviant and nonmoral act and disapproved of it—even after having had abortions themselves. In order to retain their concepts of themselves as moral persons, therefore, the women attempted to deny responsibility for their abortions, saying that they had been "forced" by circumstances to abort. It is important to note that this study, while valuable, is now some 15 years old; it would be interesting to see it repeated in the context of the current social climate.

Social and Political Aspects of Abortion

Condit, Celeste Michelle. **Decoding Abortion Rhetoric: Communicating Social Change.** Champaign: University of Illinois Press, 1990. 236 pp. Index. ISBN 0-252-01647-5.

This difficult but fascinating book explores the impact of rhetoric ("the use of language to persuade") on social change and vice versa through a detailed examination of changes in attitudes, policies, and perceptions about abortion since 1960 as revealed through public discourse. "Explanations of the path through which America has arrived at its current abortion laws, practices, and understandings must include the study of discursive forces, because only through public discourse can material realities be expressed and ideas materialized." Through in-depth analyses of the language and imagery of books, articles, speeches, media coverage, court decisions, laws, "educational" and political campaigns, and television programming, Condit shows how elements of both the pro-life and pro-choice viewpoints have been assimilated into public views and practices concerning abortion. Combining rigorous scholarship with the attitude that "studying meaning-laden human activities requires not detachment from competing sides but full empathetic engagement with all positions," *Decoding Abortion Rhetoric* is a valuable addition to the literature on abortion.

Cook, Elizabeth Adell, Ted G. Jelen, and Clyde Wilcox. **Between Two Absolutes: Public Opinion and the Politics of Abortion.** Boulder, CO: Westview Press, 1992. 236 pp. Bibliography, index. ISBN 0-8133-8287-4.

This useful book fills an important gap in abortion literature by providing an in-depth analysis of public attitudes on abortion. Based on media coverage, Americans would seem to be gathered on one side or the other of the distinct boundary separating the public pro-choice and pro-life positions. Based on numerous surveys over the last two decades, however, the boundary is not nearly so sharply defined. Instead the evidence indicates that "a majority of Americans do not support either an unlimited 'right to life' or an unlimited 'right to choose.' Rather, a majority of Americans

appears to believe that the status of the embryo and the preroga-
tives of the mother must be weighed and balanced in some fashion." In clear, easy-to-understand fashion, the authors explore the
evidence to support this view. Beginning with a brief overview of
the debate, they go on to introduce the survey data on which the
book is based and perform some preliminary data analysis. Subsequent chapters focus on different aspects of the data: one chapter looks at the reasons people have for supporting or opposing
legal abortion; one investigates the role of religion in shaping abortion attitudes; another examines the characteristics of pro-life and
pro-choice supporters as well as those who are more ambivalent;
and another explores the effects of abortion politics on election
outcomes. The book concludes with some "cautious predictions"
about the future of the debate and an attempt to project how abortion politics might change if *Roe v. Wade* were overturned or further modified.

Craig, Barbara Hinkson, and David M. O'Brien. **Abortion and
American Politics.** Chatham, NJ: Chatham House Publishers, 1993.
382 pp. Bibliography, indexes. ISBN 0-93450-88-8 (cloth); 0-934540-
89-6 (paper).

This thorough and interesting book could (and probably does)
serve as a textbook for political science classes at the high school
or college level. The authors, both professors of government, have
written extensively on Congress, the presidency, constitutional law,
and the legislative and judicial processes. Their aim in writing
this book is not to resolve the abortion debate or to present arguments in favor of either side. Rather, it is to "use the abortion controversy as an illustrative portrait, even if in some ways a
disappointing reflection, of the American governmental and political process." Because abortion politics has affected every level
and every branch of American government, "few issues more viv-
idly illustrate how our political institutions actually operate in
governing a nation of over 250 million diverse individuals." The
first five chapters analyze abortion politics as played out between
Roe v. Wade in 1973 and the 1989 decision in *Webster v. Reproductive
Health Services,* focusing on the various actors involved—courts,
interest groups, the states, Congress, and the president and executive branch. Chapter 6 discusses the roles played by all of the actors in *Webster.* Chapter 7 provides an excellent analysis of public
attitudes on abortion, in particular the uses and misuses of opinion polls. The next two chapters analyze post-*Webster* abortion

politics at both the state and national levels. The final chapter addresses the court cases that followed *Webster* and considers abortion politics following the election of President Clinton (but preceding the 1994 congressional election).

David, Henry P., Zdenek Dytrych, Zdenek Matejcek, and Vratislav Schuller. **Born Unwanted: Development Effects of Denied Abortion.** New York: Springer Publishing, 1988. 143 pp. Bibliography, index. ISBN 0-8261-6080-8.

The abortion debate as it is currently framed focuses primarily on either the fetus or the pregnant woman, while psychological studies have dealt primarily with the effects of abortion on the women who have them. Another body of work exists, however, that deals with the psychological and social repercussions for children whose mothers, at least initially, did not want them to be born. This international anthology presents detailed examinations of several longitudinal studies of children born from unplanned, unwanted pregnancies, including the oft-cited Swedish study by Forssman and Thuwe of children born to women denied abortions between 1939 and 1942. The findings consistently show that such "unwanted" children are at a developmental disadvantage—they do less well in school, are more likely to have mental health problems, are more likely to get into trouble with the law, and are less likely to be satisfied with their lives as adults than "wanted" children. The authors go to some pains to clarify both the methodologies used and the weaknesses in each study and to explain the concepts of "wantedness" and "unwantedness" as viewed in the research. Clearly written, well organized, and thoroughly documented, this slim volume helps to fill a significant gap in the literature on abortion.

Davis, Nanette J. **From Crime to Choice: The Transformation of Abortion in America.** Westport, CT: Greenwood Press, 1985. 290 pp. Index.

In this far-ranging and complex work, sociologist Davis analyzes the evolution of abortion from criminal act to legal option within the broader context of social transformation. She examines the slow, nonlinear process of change in abortion attitudes, laws, policies, and practices since the nineteenth century, from granting "exceptions" to the laws, through gradual liberalization, toward full legality. Abortion, she writes, has yet to evolve into a woman-centered procedure that benefits women themselves rather than the doctors and clinics that provide abortion services. Further, the "medicalization" of abortion has made the medical profession, rather than the church, family, or state, the primary agent for regulating abortion. Davis's discussion places abortion and the struggle for a "free, rational and just reproductive policy" at the center of a feminist vision of the transition from patriarchal control to a society in which neither responsibilities nor choices are constricted by gender. "In the framing of a moral outlook that proceeds from women's needs and experiences, the human values that women have historically been assigned to preserve expand out of the confines of private life and become the organizing principles of society. Such a gender-free society does not obliterate differences, but opens up to each person the fullest expression of both masculine and feminine attributes."

Devereux, George. **A Study of Abortion in Primitive Societies.** New York: International Universities Press, 1976. 414 pp. Bibliography, index. ISBN 0-8236-6245-4.

This oft-cited book was first published in 1955, when abortion was a topic rarely spoken of or discussed in public forums. Devereux's primary focus, however, was not abortion itself but a desire to link the "social and psychological sciences" by performing a comparative study that linked cultural studies with an in-depth psychoanalytical approach to understanding human behavior. In Part One, Devereux examines data on abortion as practiced by some 400 primitive tribes, as well as 20 historical and modern nations. He looks at a variety of factors, including conscious and unconscious motivation for abortion; alternatives to abortion; frequency and timing of abortion; techniques and physical consequences of abortion; attitudes toward and treatment of aborted fetuses; abortionists; attitudes toward abortion; and social action, including penalties and nonpunitive measures taken toward abortionists and women who aborted. Part Two takes a psychoanalytic approach, discussing such factors as "trauma and unconscious motivation in abortion," "the flight from parenthood," and abortion as "castration of the father." Also included are descriptions of abortion as practiced by each of the tribes studied and tables comparing the occurrence of various abortion-related traits among the tribes. Whether or not one agrees with its heavily Freudian interpretations, the book presents a fascinating array of comparative information on the motives, methods, and attitudes regarding abortion in so-called primitive societies, some of which provide remarkable parallels with our own.

Francome, Colin. **Abortion Freedom: A Worldwide Movement.** London: George Allen & Unwin, 1984. 241 pp. Bibliography, index. ISBN 0-04-179001-4.

Colin Francome is a British sociologist who has done extensive research and writing on abortion, birth control, and teenage pregnancy. This book examines recent widespread changes in abortion laws, policy, and practice—in the 15 years preceding the book's publication, more than 40 countries liberalized their laws. Francome examines the ideas and strategies of the forces promoting and opposing legal abortion, focusing particularly on Britain, the United States, and Europe. From early debates over birth control, through legalization of abortion, to the debates following such legalization, Francome follows the course of the legal and political battles over abortion as they have been waged in different nations. He concludes that birth control education and availability have the best potential for reducing the number of both legal and illegal abortions, and notes that although "developments in rights of control of fertility will obviously not solve the deep economic and social problems facing the world . . . they will give people greater control over their lives and more opportunity to have the number of children they want and at a time of life when they are best able to care for them."

Ginsburg, Faye D. **Contested Lives.** Berkeley: University of California Press, 1989. 315 pp. Bibliography, index. ISBN 0-520-06492-5.

This is an anthropological case study of the response of a middle-American community (Fargo, North Dakota) to the opening of the state's first abortion clinic within its borders. Within the context of a local conflict between pro-choice and pro-life activists, Ginsburg explores the much larger cultural drama of women's social movements in the United States. In her analysis of the life stories of the Fargo activists, Ginsburg found that although the women represent polar opposites in their stance on abortion, their involvement grew out of a shared belief that something is very wrong in the way American society treats women and families: "Whether pro-life or pro-choice, activists express their motivation for social action as a desire to alter the meaning and circumstances of procreation in order to make conditions better for the next generation. In other words, they are concerned, as female activists, with their role in reproducing the culture, but in terms different from the present." The fact that the two sides have distinctly contrasting views of what it means to "make things better" is at the heart of the abortion debate. This is a difficult but fascinating work.

Jaffe, Frederick S., Barbara L. Lindheim, and Philip R. Lee. **Abortion Politics: Private Morality and Public Policy.** New York: McGraw-Hill, 1981. 216 pp. Index. ISBN 0-07-032189-2.

This is an examination and analysis of public policy on abortion from the 1973 *Roe v. Wade* decision through the late 1970s. The book does not attempt to assess the rightness or wrongness of abortion but asserts that since women have throughout history sought abortions and will continue to seek them whether they are legal or not, all women should have access to legal, safe abortion services. The authors present various findings on the social, emotional, demographic, and health benefits of legal abortion and note the failure of the American health care system to respond adequately to the Supreme Court's decision as of the late 1970s. They also draw strong parallels between the battle over abortion and earlier battles over contraception, which is still opposed by the Catholic Church and a number of antiabortion groups. Though somewhat dated now, this book provides valuable in-depth historical and political analysis of public policies and private practices in the area of abortion services and birth control.

Joffe, Carol. **Regulating Sexuality: The Experiences of Family Planning Workers.** Philadelphia: University of Pennsylvania Press, 1987. 208 pp. ISBN 0-87722-423-4.

This book is based on a sociological tradition of studying conflicts in social policy by examining the experience of "front-line" workers—those in service bureaucracies who interact directly with the public. In the case of abortion and birth control services, these are the counselors, doctors, nurses, and other staff members who work at family planning and abortion clinics. Although much of this book is dedicated to the ways in which such workers directly and indirectly influence ("regulate," in Joffe's terms) sexuality in America, the chapters dealing with abortion counseling provide an interesting portrait of people who are involved with abortion on a daily, or at least weekly, basis. Abortion work qualifies as what Everett Hughes described as "dirty work"—"it can be physically disgusting; it can be symbolically degrading; it can involve morally dubious activity. Yet, under certain circumstances, such work can also take on a heroic or 'charismatic' character." Although their work was often difficult and emotionally draining, and although they found abortion morally troubling, the counselors perceived their jobs as satisfying and important, and all but 1 of the approximately 75 counselors involved believed firmly that abortion must remain a legal option.

Luker, Kristin. **Abortion and the Politics of Motherhood.** Berkeley: University of California Press, 1984. 324 pp. Bibliography, index. ISBN 0-520-04314-6.

This is an unusually balanced and compassionate study of how the practice of and attitudes toward abortion in the United States have changed over the last 200 years. Much of the book is based on lengthy, in-depth interviews with activists on both sides of the issue. Luker, a sociologist who has spent much of her career studying abortion, concludes that abortion activists (as opposed to the general population) hold diametrically opposed worldviews that affect their attitudes on a wide range of issues, most notably the roles of women and men in the family and in society. Thus, for both sides, the abortion conflict is a win-lose situation that allows little room for compromise. Luker sees little chance that the debate will be resolved any time in the foreseeable future.

————. **Taking Chances: Abortion and the Decision Not To Contracept.** Berkeley: University of California Press, 1975. 207 pp. Index. ISBN 0-520-02872-4.

Although some women seek abortions as a result of contraceptive failure, many more seek abortions because of a failure to use contraception at all or to use it effectively. These women are often stereotyped as irresponsible, disturbed, or neurotic. Luker, however, examined women's own reasons for not using contraception despite having access to contraceptives and the skills to use them. She conducted a study of 500 women seen at an abortion clinic in California in the early 1970s, when the state's relatively liberal law made abortions fairly easy to obtain. Fifty women also participated in a series of in-depth interviews, along with ten women who obtained abortions from a private physician. Luker places contraceptive risk-taking inside a social and cultural context of complex relationships, going well beyond the simplistic psychological explanations usually given for women's "irresponsible" risk-taking behavior. She concludes that women's decisions about contraception are part of an ongoing process and are based on weighing perceived costs and benefits of contraception against the perceived risks of pregnancy—perceptions that do not necessarily coincide with those of family planning and abortion practitioners.

Petchesky, Rosalind. **Abortion and Woman's Choice: The State, Sexuality, and Reproductive Freedom.** Boston: Northeastern University Press, 1990. 412 pp. Index. ISBN 1-55553-075-3.

This is an updated edition (the first edition appeared in 1984) of what is perhaps the most comprehensive and well-known feminist work on abortion. In her far-ranging, thoroughly researched, and well-written analysis, Petchesky seeks to determine (1) why abortion has become so politically and socially controversial; (2) what are the historical developments and social and cultural conditions that have led to increases in abortions and the development of state policies and moral ideologies related to abortion; (3) how these conditions and policies affect the changing position and consciousness of women; and (4) what are the elements of a feminist vision of abortion and its relation to the total conditions of women's reproductive freedom. A "feminist morality of abortion," she writes, "would [address] the issues that 'right-to-lifers' raise in human, social terms and [move] well beyond them." It would "contain within it the possibility of transcending and transforming the existing sexual division of labor *at the same time* as it recognizes women's specific situation in reproduction. Ultimately, this means rejecting 'maternal thinking' as a gender-specific practice while persistently defending abortion as a gender-specific need."

Periodicals

Most of the organizations listed in chapter 4 publish periodic news-letters. Many also publish journals or other periodicals. The following are periodicals that either have wide circulation independent of organization membership or that are not associ-ated with an organization.

Bernadell Technical Bulletin
P.O. Box 1897
New York, NY 10011
Bimonthly. Free; write to be placed on mailing list.

The *Bernadell Technical Bulletin* is a newsletter published by abortion-provider-turned-abortion-opponent Dr. Bernard Nathan-son and his wife Adelle. The newsletter consists of abstracts and reviews of articles published in the medical literature concerning abortion and other "life issues." Each abstract or review is followed by commentary written by Dr. Nathanson that interprets the ar-ticles in terms that are "easily understandable by the reader" and that strongly support the pro-life point of view.

Family Planning Perspectives
111 Fifth Avenue
New York, NY 10003
Bimonthly. $42 per year for institutions; $32 per year for individuals; $52 per year for foreign subscriptions.

Established in 1968, *Family Planning Perspectives* is a professional journal published by the Alan Guttmacher Institute, an inde-pendent nonprofit research institute that has become a leading source of abortion statistics and information. The journal con-tains in-depth, peer-reviewed articles by medical and social science professionals, scholars, and researchers on new research, policy positions, and other topics related to reproductive health services in the United States. Highly regarded in the field, *Family Planning Perspectives* features frequent articles on various medi-cal, social, and legal aspects of abortion, along with other top-ics such as teenage pregnancy and sexuality, prenatal and maternity care, sex education, unintended pregnancy, infertil-ity, sexually transmitted disease, birth control, and abortion. Three monthly departments, "Update," "Special Report," and

"Digest," report on new developments in areas of special interest. Back issues are available for $10 a copy.

Human Life Review
Human Life Foundation, Inc.
150 E. 35th Street
New York, NY 10016
Quarterly. $20 per year; $25 per year for foreign subscriptions.

Established in 1975, the *Human Life Review* is a journal dealing primarily with abortion and related issues from a pro-life point of view. Some of the articles and essays are original; others have been reprinted from newspapers and other periodicals in an attempt to "bring our readers the best of what has appeared elsewhere, if we think it belongs in our 'permanent record' of the Abortion War and related battles." Contributors have included such luminaries as Nat Hentoff, Patrick Buchanan, William F. Buckley, Jr., and Malcolm Muggeridge. Sample article titles include "Feminism and Abortion," by Martha Bayles; "Bioethics and the Holocaust," by Richard Neuhaus; "Rape and Abortion," by Mary Meehan; and "The Lie of Pro-Choice," by James Bowman. Back issues are available for $4 per copy; library-bound volumes and microform are also available.

Studies in Pro-Life Feminism
Feminism and Nonviolence Studies Association, Inc.
811 E. 47th Street
Kansas City, MO 64110
Quarterly. $39 per year, $72 for two years for libraries and institutions; $32 per year, $59 for two years for individuals. Discount for subscriptions ordered in groups of three or more.

Studies in Pro-Life Feminism is the brainchild of Rachel McNair, founder of Feminists for Life of America. This multidisciplinary journal is intended to serve those needing or wanting to know about feminist thought and the consistent life ethic. Each edition contains analyses of current topics and trends related to abortion and other life issues (such as the death penalty), along with original research, commentary, and critical reviews. The premier issue, which came out in January 1995, included an essay on "Feminism, Self-Estrangement, and the 'Disease' of Pregnancy," an article on the politics of research on the relationship between abortion and breast cancer, and a copy of the amicus curiae brief filed by Feminists for Life of America in the case of *Bray v. Alexandria*, as well as previews of forthcoming books.

News Service

The Abortion Report
3129 Mt. Vernon Avenue
Alexandria, VA 22305
(703) 518-4600
(703) 518-8701 (FAX)
Daily. Cost varies according to type of subscription.

The Abortion Report is a daily (Monday–Friday) briefing of abortion-related political, judicial, and legislative events occurring around the country. Established in 1989 following the *Webster* decision, *The Abortion Report* draws on a nationwide network of information sources, including local newspapers, activists, journalists, researchers, elected officials, and others. Included in each report is a "Spotlight Story" focusing on a particular event; "State Reports" on court actions, demonstrations, polls, etc.; "Legislative Outlook" on current legislative actions in the states; "National Briefing" on events of national scope; "Insider Commentary," interviews with politicians, activists, scholars, and other individuals; and coverage of upcoming state and national political races. The report averages 9 to 12 pages per day. Items are brief, to the point, nonpartisan, and wholly factual, making this a valuable source of up-to-the-minute information for journalists, researchers, and activist organizations. Three methods of delivery are offered: downloading to computer via modem, FAX, and mail, although mail delivery is discouraged because of the timeliness of the information.

Selected Nonprint Resources 6

Computer Database Search Service

The Abortion Report
3129 Mt. Vernon Avenue
Alexandria, VA 22305
(703) 518-4600
(703) 518-8701 (FAX)

The publishers of *The Abortion Report* [see chapter 5] maintain a database that contains all information previously published in the report. A full-time staff person is available to search the database for information on any topic related to abortion; a full print-out will then be delivered, sent by FAX, or mailed to the inquirer. Subscribers to *The Abortion Report* receive a discount for database search services.

Resources on the Internet

Because the Internet is constantly growing and changing, trying to pin down resources on any individual topic is a challenge, and abortion is no exception. Several of the organizations listed in chapter 4 maintain World Wide Web sites, including the Feminist Majority (http://www.feminist.org), National Right to Life Committee (http://www.clark.net/nrlc/), the National Organization for Women (http://now.org/now/issues/abortion/abortion.html), and the Population Council (http://www.popcouncil.org/council/programs/programs.htm), with new ones being added all the time. Call or write the organization to see if it has an e-mail or World Wide Web address.

Following are some of the more stable and informative abortion-related sites maintained by individuals or groups.

The Abortion Rights Activist
http://www.cais.com/agm/index.html

The *Abortion Rights Activist* is a treasury of abortion-related information maintained by Adam Guasch-Melendez. Especially useful are a list of "Tools for Activists," including hypertext links to abortion-related sites on the Internet (both "pro-choice" and "anti-choice") and a copy of the National Abortion Federation's *Community Action Guide*; news summaries of recent events (updated weekly); a comprehensive list of incidents of violence against abortion clinics; and "Action Alerts," information on upcoming legislation, court cases, and other abortion-related issues. In 1996, Guasch-Melendez planned to add sections on mifepristone (RU 486) and the methotrexate/misoprostol drug combination currently being tested for nonsurgical abortions. Send e-mail to agm@cais.com.

ProLife Infonet
infonet-list@netcentral.net

The College Right to Life Connection
crlc-list@netcentral.net

These moderated, one-way discussion lists are provided as a public service by NetCentral, Inc. ProLife Infonet distributes legislative alerts, newsletters, noteworthy news items, and other information from various national, state, regional, and local organizations within the pro-life movement. The College Right to Life Connection distributes information submitted by college pro-life organizations at the national, state, regional, and local levels, as well as providing a forum for discussion about ideas and strategies for college right-to-life organizations and individuals. Interested parties can subscribe over the web to these and the other mailing lists that NetCentral sponsors; send e-mail to listserv@netcentral.net.

The ProLife News
plnews-info@netcentral.net

The ProLife News is (normally) a bimonthly electronic publication of news and comment on pro-life issues, mainly abortion and euthanasia. The free newsletter consists mainly of contributions by readers, supplemented by articles that the editor summarizes from other publications. Each issue is typically 300 or more lines (80 column format). In addition to news and announcements, regular features include "On the National Front," "What Works?," "Reader Questions," "Across the Pond," and "Quote-of-the-Month." The newsletter has been distributed since January, 1991, with readers worldwide, but mostly in the United States and Canada. Beginning with Volume Five (1995), all issues have been available on the web (HTML format), as well as in ASCII and PostScript formats.

The ProLife News maintains archives of back issues, as well as a list of other pro-life resources on the net. Readers can subscribe to the ProLife News directly from the web (requires a forms-compatible web browser). For information on subscribing, send e-mail to plnews-info@netcentral.net or contact the moderator at plnews-mod@netcentral.net.

The Ultimate Pro-Life Resource List
http://www.prolife.org/ultimate/

The Ultimate Pro-Life Resource List is maintained by college student Steve Ertelt, a self-described "libertarian pro-life feminist" who "wish[es] to convey that a number of groups of people from very different backgrounds, cultures, beliefs, and opinions support the right to life. The list does not support a religious or political viewpoint and we will promote information from folks who support the right to life regardless of their views on those issues." The Ultimate Pro-Life Resource List publishes only materials that depict the "positive right to life ethic" and therefore does not include information that "is overtly graphic in nature or promotes illegal or militant activities."

Videos and Films

Abortion: For Survival

Type:	16mm film, videocassette
Length:	30 min.
Date:	1989
Cost:	Purchase, $29.95 each for 1–9, $19.95 each for 10–29, $14.95 each for 30 or more (video); rental, $250 per week (16mm film)
Distributor:	Feminist Majority Foundation

The primary message of this video is that making abortion illegal causes women to die. Citing international evidence that criminalizing abortion does not cause the rates of abortion to decrease, *Abortion: For Survival* argues forcefully not only for keeping abortion legal in the United States, but for changing U.S. funding policies that restrict family planning programs in other countries and that even in some cases prohibit treating women for the effects of botched abortions. The video, which includes footage of a suction abortion and interviews with social scientists, medical professionals, population experts, and Third World government officials, also addresses such issues as the decline of contraceptive research in the United States, the plight of unwanted and abandoned children, and the effects of uncontrolled population growth in the world's poorest countries. An accompanying booklet contains statistical information cited in the video, which was produced by a coalition of abortion rights advocates.

Abortion: Past, Present and Future

Type:	Videocassette
Length:	18 min.
Date:	1989
Cost:	Purchase, $40; rental, $20
Distributor:	Educational Video Center

This brief video was researched, filmed, and edited by a group of teenagers in New York City. Much of the video consists of interviews with passersby, who are asked, "What do you think of abortion?" "Do you know anyone who has had an abortion?" "Do you think abortion should be illegal?" "What do think would happen if abortion were illegal?" More in-depth interviews feature two women who describe their abortion experiences ("How did you feel when you had the abortion?")—one of which took place in 1946—and two clergymen, one a Catholic priest who reiterates the church's stand against abortion, the other a black Baptist minister who asserts that choice is a God-given right and one that must be supported. Also included are footage of abortion rights and antiabortion demonstrators. The filmmakers provide some background information, but for the most part they let their subjects speak for themselves. Other than the audio, which sometimes makes the speakers difficult to understand, the production quality is quite acceptable. What makes this video outstanding, however, is the open-minded, nonbiased way in which the filmmakers approached their subject and the wide range of viewpoints they were able to include. These qualities make the video an excellent starting point for discussion, particularly for high school classes and various youth groups. Also included is a teacher's guide with questions and activity suggestions designed "to motivate students to read, write, discuss, and ultimately act responsibly when confronted with the issue of abortion."

Abortion: Stories from North and South
Type: 16mm film, videocassette
Length: 55 min.
Date: 1984
Cost: Purchase, $895 (film), $595 (video); rental, $100
Distributor: The Cinema Guild

This film was produced by Studio D, a special mostly woman unit of the Canadian Film Board that was founded in 1974 to create films from the perspective and experience of women. Explaining that each year throughout the world 30 million to 50 million women have abortions, more than half of them illegally, and more than 84,000 of these women die as a result of abortion complications, *Abortion: Stories from North and South* presents personal stories, interviews, and case studies from six countries—Ireland, Canada, Peru, Colombia, Japan, and Thailand. These stories—of desperation, resourcefulness, and, sometimes, tragedy—provide vivid documentation of the film's central premise: abortion is, and always has been, a fact of human existence. "Only the laws and conditions under which abortions are performed vary from place to place, and time to time." In Peru, women who survive abortion complications are taken by "abortion police" straight from hospitals to jails where they, and their children with them, will serve sentences of two to three years. In Thailand, a village abortionist massages her pregnant daughter's belly in an unsuccessful attempt to dislodge the placenta and cause a miscarriage. In Japan, women who have had abortions bury the fetuses in expensive crypts meant to capture the unborns' drifting souls. This visually beautiful film has a detached, unemotional, "just-the-facts" tone, but its content packs an emotional wallop. *Abortion: Stories from North and South* won the grand prize at the 1985 Golden Gate Awards film and video competition of the San Francisco International Film Festival and received first place in the Contemporary Social Issues category from the National Council on Family Relations Seventeenth Annual Film Awards Competition.

The Answer
Type: 16mm film, ¾" broadcast tape, videocassette
Length: 12 min.
Date: 1987
Cost: Purchase, $198 (film), $49.95 (¾"), $23.90 (video), discounts for quantities of ten or more.
Distributor: Bernadell, Inc.

This film, which was produced in response to criticisms of Bernard Nathanson's *The Silent Scream,* consists of voluntary testimony from Jay Kelinson, the doctor who performed the abortion documented in that film. Seated at a desk, Dr. Kelinson answers an unseen questioner as if he were indeed giving testimony at a legal trial. Yes, says the 38-year-old obstetrician and gynecologist, he learned to do abortions as a medical resident; no, there was no discussion of ethics in the lessons. From 1979 to 1982, he performed perhaps 10,000 abortions, working in three or four different clinics, and during that time he noticed "personality changes" in himself. No, he is not pro-life; in fact, he still does abortions "for medical reasons," though since seeing the film used in *The Silent Scream* he no longer performs them "on demand." Kelinson goes on to say that he himself made the ultrasound tape used in the film, that there was no manipulation of the tape or its speed, that there is "no doubt in my mind that there was some perception of impending doom," and that the fetus did indeed pull away from his instruments as claimed in the film. As Kelinson points out, he has "nothing to gain" by making this film, which, although it does indicate the veracity of the ultrasound tape made during the abortion itself, does not answer many of the other criticisms made of *The Silent Scream*. [See also *Planned Parenthood's Response to the Silent Scream, The Silent Scream,* and *The Silent Scream: Responding to Critics*].

Are You Listening: Women Who Have Had an Abortion
Type: 16mm film, videocassette, audiocassette
Length: About 28 min.
Date: 1972
Cost: Purchase, $450 (film), $300 (video), $30 (audio); rental, $65 (film), $50 (video)

Are You Listening: Women Who Have Not Had an Abortion
Type: 16mm film, videocassette, audiocassette
Length: About 28 min.
Date: 1977
Cost: Purchase, $450 (film), $300 (video), $30 (audio); rental, $65 (film), $50 (video)

Are You Listening: People Who Have Struggled with Abortion
Type: Videocassette, audiocassette
Length: About 29 min.
Date: 1984
Cost: Purchase, $300 (video), $30 (audio); rental, $50 (video)
Distributor: Martha Stuart Communications

These three videos, produced with the aid of the Ford Foundation, span a period of 12 years. *Women Who Have Had an Abortion,* produced in 1972, and *Women Who Have Not Had an Abortion,* produced five years later, feature informal discussions among groups of women of different ages, races, and marital status. One group is made up of women who, faced with an unwanted pregnancy, chose to have abortions; the other group is made up of women who chose to carry their pregnancies to term. The third film, *People Who Have Struggled with Abortion,* was produced in 1984. It also features an informal discussion, this time among a group of men and women from widely varying backgrounds, including a doctor, a rabbi, a counselor, a nurse, a legislator, a nun, a black activist, and others, all of whom have struggled with abortion in some way. In each of these films, people talk candidly about their experiences with abortion, their beliefs about its rightness or wrongness, the politics associated with it, and their feelings about whether it should be legal and available. As one man points out, people on both sides of the debate have a tendency to view each other as "the worst people in the world"—mainly because in looking at their opponents, they see what they are afraid to see in themselves. These films are an attempt to cut through the polemic and show, as Stuart remarks, that "it's not that simple." Although interesting separately, the films are best viewed together, so that viewers can clearly see both the contrasts and the similarities among people who have struggled with the same issue, but who have emerged with different, and very individual, answers.

Assignment: Life
Type: Videocassette
Length: 52 min.
Date: 1980
Cost: Purchase, $49.95
Distributor: American Portrait Films International

This "docudrama" about a fictional journalist's exploration of the abortion issue made its debut at the 1980 convention of the National Right to Life Committee. Ann Sommers, a writer for "The Daily Press," is assigned to do a story on abortion and to cover both sides of the debate. Although she initially feels that abortion should be a woman's personal decision, Ms. Sommers comes to believe that abortion is, indeed, murder. During the film, she interviews a doctor who owns and operates a chain of family planning clinics, an administrator for the Birth Control Institute, several women who have had abortions and several who have chosen to have and keep their babies, a former prostitute and topless dancer who nearly died from abortion complications, the parents of an adopted child, the mother of a baby allegedly born at 23 weeks gestation, a lab technician who processed fetuses from abortions, and a number of well-known antiabortion activists, including Jack and Barbara Willke, Bernard Nathanson, James Dobson, Congressmen Henry Hyde and William Dannemeyer, Don Smith of Crusade for Life, and Cardinal Manning, the archbishop of Los Angeles. She also witnesses, along with the audience, a suction and a saline abortion, and attends a right-to-life rally in Washington, D.C. The viewer is left wondering why, if she is supposed to be covering both sides of the issue, Ms. Sommers gives such lopsided attention to people on the antiabortion side of the debate. This lack of balance diminishes the film's effectiveness. Includes study guide.

Back Alley Detroit

Type: Videocassette
Length: 47 min.
Date: 1992
Cost: Purchase, $445; rental, $75
Distributor: Filmmakers Library

In this historical documentary, doctors, nurses, health care and women's rights activists, law enforcement officers, and women who had illegal abortions talk about their involvement with abortion prior to *Roe v. Wade.* Among the speakers are doctors who describe some of the methods used to induce illegal abortions and their results; the owners of an abortion referral service that sent women to London where they could obtain legal abortions; the founder of the Michigan Clergy Counseling Service, a network of sympathetic clergy members who helped women obtain abortions; members of the Jane Collective, a clandestine, self-taught activist group that safely performed more than 10,000 abortions in the Chicago area; an assistant to a doctor who performed illegal but safe abortions in his office for 30 years; and a woman who served as an undercover agent from 1958 to 1968 for the Detroit Police Department, posing as a pregnant woman wanting an abortion. Interspersed with and accenting the interviews are film footage, photographic clips, and period popular music. Simply told and tastefully produced, the video provides a vivid picture of what it was like in the decades before abortion was legal, without being graphic or attempting to manipulate the emotions of the audience.

A Better Way

Type: Videocassette
Length: 30 min.
Date: 1986
Cost: Purchase, $39.95; rental, $5 per week through National Right to Life Educational Trust Fund
Distributor: American Portrait Films International, Boone Productions, Inc., National Right to Life Educational Trust Fund

Host Pat Boone talks with people who have chosen alternatives to abortion in this upbeat yet low-key film. Included are the 18-year-old mother of a 3-year-old, along with her parents and the child's father; a woman who was raped in her own home and her now

22-year-old daughter; an obstetrician who works to match unwanted babies with caring parents; a couple who have adopted
three "special-needs" children, including a boy who suffered severe abuse and two girls with Down's syndrome; a woman who
became pregnant at age 40 and who had her son, now a 16-year-
old law school graduate, against her doctor's advice; and the
mother and therapist of a cerebral palsy victim who died at age
31. Boone reads a passage written by the latter, who eloquently
states his opposition to abortion, while affirming that it is a "question of personal morals." What to do about a "crisis pregnancy,"
Boone concludes, is "a matter of personal choice," but "once those
choices are made, they're final." And, he adds, with the thousands
of parents wanting to adopt, "there is no such thing as an unwanted child." Boone is a relaxed and congenial host, and his
interviewees are warm and attractive people. This film's
nonjudgmental and positive tone has a great deal to do with its
success in promoting its message.

Eclipse of Reason
Type: 16mm film, ¾" broadcast tape, videocassette
Length: 27 min.
Date: 1987
Cost: Purchase, $309 (film), $85.90 (¾"), $44.90 (video),
               discounts for quantities of ten or more
Distributor: Bernadell, Inc.

Like its predecessor, *The Silent Scream, Eclipse of Reason* aims for—
and achieves—maximum emotional impact. The film features
graphic footage of the dilatation and evacuation abortion of a 20-
week-old fetus, interspersed with interviews with several former
abortion providers and two women who say they have suffered
physical and psychological damage as a result of their abortions.
The film is intended to supplement *The Silent Scream*, which
showed an early abortion, by showing an abortion late in the second trimester (when fewer than 1 percent of all abortions are performed). Introduced by Charleton Heston and hosted by Bernard
Nathanson, the former abortion provider who has become one of
the antiabortion movement's most vocal activists, *Eclipse of Reason* uses a fetoscope to show the fetus in utero before and during
the abortion procedure. Included is a step-by-step guide for pre-
senters, including a script of introductory remarks. Not for the
faint-hearted.

From Danger to Dignity: The Fight for Safe Abortion
Type: 16mm film, videocassette
Length: 57 min.
Date: 1995
Cost: Purchase, $95 (libraries and institutions, includes
               public performance rights), $49.95 plus $5 shipping
               and handling (individuals and reproductive rights
               groups); rental, $45 (film), rent may be applied to
               purchase price
Distributor: Concentric Media

This documentary by award-winning director Dorothy Fadiman provides a comprehensive and in-depth look at the struggle to legalize abortion, beginning in the early 1960s and culminating in the 1973 *Roe v. Wade* Supreme Court decision. The film opens with a dramatization and account of Fadiman's own nearly fatal illegal abortion in 1962, then moves on to highlight the activists, doctors, legislators, clergy people, and others who helped women obtain safe abortions even as they fought to overturn abortion laws. Fadiman and her crew unearthed a wealth of archival footage for the film. In one scene, we see New York Assemblyman George Michaels cast the decisive vote on the bill to repeal the state's abortion laws, painfully aware as he does so that he is ending his career. In another, Arizona "Romper Room" hostess Sherri Finkbine speaks to reporters on her return from Sweden, where she had gone to obtain an abortion after learning that thalidomide, which she had been taking for morning sickness, caused severe birth defects. Also included are recent interviews with many of the people who were in the forefront of the movement. Among them are California activist Patricia Maginnis, who repeatedly risked and even invited arrest to keep her cause in the courts and before the public; Minnesota physician Jane Hodgson, who openly defied that state's laws by performing an abortion in a hospital; the Reverend Howard Moody, founder of the Clergy Counseling Service; members of Chicago's Jane Collective, the network of housewives and students who performed some 11,000 abortions during the late 1960s and early 1970s; and Sarah Weddington, the attorney who at age 26 successfully argued *Roe v. Wade* before the Supreme Court. Only the interviews are in color. The remainder of the film, including eerie shots of hospital corridors and dark, deserted streets, as well as the archival film clips, is in black and white. Masterfully filmed and edited, *From Danger to Dignity* provides an excellent overview of an important era in abortion history, whatever one's opinion of the outcome. *From Danger to Dignity* is the second of a planned three-part series. The first, *When Abortion Was Illegal* [see below], focused on the "untold stories" of women who had illegal abortions prior to *Roe v. Wade*. The third, tentatively titled *The Fragile Promise of Choice,* will deal with current threats to legal abortion.

Girl on the Edge of Town

Type: 16mm film, videocassette
Length: About 30 min.
Date: 1980
Cost: Purchase, $85 (video); rental available
Distributor: Paulist Productions

This film demonstrates the power of a good story well told to make a point without preaching or exhorting. Gina and her boyfriend Wayne get "carried away" one night, and inevitably she discovers she is pregnant. Gina and her parents live on the edge of town; her father hauls wood and does odd jobs, and her mother runs a fruit stand. Her mother is harsh and bitter, and when Gina tells her the news she finds out why—her parents married because they "had to," and they have been struggling ever since. Her mother urges her to have an abortion and save herself from the same fate. Wayne raises the money, but in the clinic Gina changes her mind because "if my mother had done it, there wouldn't be any me." The two plan to marry, but then Wayne gets the news that his Navy scholarship has come through—and he is required to remain single until he graduates. How Gina makes, and accepts responsibility for, her final decision, becoming stronger and more mature as a result, and how she finally triumphs, make for an engrossing and audience-involving story. The characters in this film are multidimensional, and they act and talk like real people. The result is far more effective than other films that work much harder at getting their message across. Included is a study guide with excellent thought- and discussion-provoking questions.

Holy Terror

Type: 16mm film, videocassette
Length: 58 min.
Date: 1984
Cost: Purchase, $895 (film), $595 (video); rental, $100
Distributor: The Cinema Guild

This is a fascinating inside look at the radical elements of the pro-life movement who seek to stop abortion by any means possible, including violence. Using a minimum of narration, the film offers footage of activists praying, meeting, demonstrating, confronting clinic workers and women seeking abortions, testifying at congressional hearings, being loaded into police wagons, and rallying in a prison yard. At a mock Nuremberg trial held in a hotel ballroom, the jury convicts the defendants (represented by papier-mâché heads)—"the Feminists," "the Courts," "the Doctors," "the Lawyers," "the Providers," "the Celebrities," and "the Politicians"—of "crimes against humanity." At a right-to-life convention, attendees display name tags decorated with tiny sticks of "dynamite" and the phrase, "Have a blast." At an abortion clinic, protesters lock arms to block the entrance and yell at a frightened and dismayed teenager as clinic workers attempt to comfort her. Interspersed with these often-dramatic moments are statements by clergymen, politicians, pro-life and pro-choice leaders, and abortion clinic staff members, as well as scenes of clinics destroyed by bombs or fire. Although the filmmaker is an abortion rights supporter, the film is subject to multiple interpretations—pro-choice advocates will find it horrifying, while pro-life activists may very well be cheering. This film received a blue ribbon from the American Film & Video Festival and a certificate of merit from the Chicago Film Festival, and it was named the Nonprint Editors' Choice for *Booklist* magazine.

Leona's Sister Gerri

Type: Videocassette
Length: 57 min.
Date: 1995
Cost: Purchase, $275 (educational institutions), $175 (nonprofit organizations), $149 (libraries), $90 (individuals or pro-choice groups), add $10 shipping and handling to all orders
Distributor: New Day Films

In 1973, *Ms.* magazine published a grisly black-and-white photograph showing the naked body of a woman crouched face down on a motel room floor. There was blood on the floor behind her, and her purse lay discarded a few feet away. The photo had come from "police files," and the woman had died from an illegal abortion in 1964. Over the years the photograph became an icon for the abortion rights movement, appearing repeatedly in the media and on posters at numerous demonstrations. The woman who came to symbolize all those who died in dirty motel rooms and "back alleys" from illegal abortions was Geraldine Santoro, called Gerri. In 1964, she was 27 years old and living with her parents and two young daughters in Connecticut after fleeing her abusive husband. When she got pregnant by a man she had met at work, she kept it a secret, though she talked to her sister and friends about "someone she knew" who was pregnant and didn't want to be. She was six-and-one-half months' pregnant when she learned her husband was coming from California to get her and the girls. Desperate, she asked the baby's father for help. Following instructions obtained from an acquaintance, he attempted the abortion. When it was obvious she was dying, he fled, leaving her to be found by the police the next day. (He later pled nolo contendere to attempted abortion and manslaughter and was sentenced to a year and a day in prison.) In 1992, Gerri's sister Leona decided it was time to tell her story and asked a family friend, filmmaker Jane Gillooly, to help her. The result is an intensely personal and moving portrait, told primarily by Gerri's family and friends and revealed in old photographs, mementos, and scenes of her hometown and the farm where she grew up. In addition to making a poignant case for abortion rights and against domestic violence, the film raises provocative questions about the conversion of a private tragedy into a public symbol. *Leona's Sister Gerri* has won several awards, including "Best Television Documentary" from the National Women's Political Caucus and a Bronze Apple from the National Educational Film and Video Festival. In 1995, it was aired as an episode of public television's POV (Point of View) series, generating a huge response.

Life and Choice after *Roe v. Wade*

Type: Videocassette
Length: 87 min.
Date: 1992
Cost: Purchase, $69.95
Distributor: PBS Video

This video was produced as part of "That Delicate Balance II: Our Bill of Rights," a PBS television series on the Constitution. It consists of a panel discussion centering around a hypothetical state that has passed restrictive abortion laws and how the state would handle challenges to the laws based on the Constitution and the Bill of Rights. The panelists, who include doctors, lawyers, activists, judges, members of Congress, and journalists, discuss the practical legal consequences of making dramatic changes in United States abortion laws. The well-moderated discussion avoids the polarization into pro-choice/pro-life camps that happens in most so-called television debates, and in doing so provides a thoughtful, informative examination of a highly complex topic. The discussion, which was taped in 1991 in front of a live audience, assumes a good understanding of the Constitution and the legal system, which could restrict its usefulness for teenage audiences.

Living Forward, Looking Back

Type:	16mm film, videocassette
Length:	30 min.
Date:	1993
Cost:	Purchase, $400 (film), $250 (video); rental, $50
Distributor:	Cinema Guild

In this documentary, six women tell their stories about being unwillingly pregnant in the years before abortion was legal. The film uses old photographs, film footage, and magazine illustrations to portray a time when sexuality was shrouded in secrecy, being unwed and pregnant was the greatest of shames, and a girl who "got into trouble" had limited choices: go to stay with relatives or in a home for unwed mothers until she had a baby who would be given away to strangers, or risk her life at the hands of an illegal abortionist. Three of the women discuss the humiliation of being forced to carry their pregnancies to term and what was, for them, the wrenching loss of their children: "My shame was that I gave her up," says one woman, close to tears. "My parents' shame was that I had her." The others describe their experiences with illegal abortion, including a woman who was raped by a friend of her father's at age 16, then nearly died after having her uterus perforated in an abortion in which the "anesthesia" consisted of being punched in the head. Also interviewed is an obstetrician-gynecologist who describes what it was like treating women who developed sepsis after botched abortions and compares the prelegalization and postlegalization eras. This film won several awards, including a Gold Apple from the National Educational Film and Video Festival, a Gold Medal from the Student Academy Awards, and a Silver Plaque from the Chicago International Film Festival.

s: A Legacy of Loss from Illegal Abortions

Videocassette

Length: 30 min.
Date: 1993
Cost: Purchase, $295; rental, $55
Distributor: Filmmakers Library

In this poignant video, four Philadelphians tell what it was like to lose a mother as a result of an illegal abortion—though none of them knew at the time that was what had happened. One is a 69-year-old woman whose mother died in 1929 at the age of 30 after trying to self-abort with a knitting needle. Another is a woman in her thirties, who was 4 when the body of her 26-year-old mother was dropped off at a hospital emergency room by two men who sped away without a word. Another woman describes being brought up during the 1950s by her grandmother, who hovered over her in fear that she would meet the same fate as her mother. A man in his seventies describes how he hid in a closet and refused to let his father out of his sight after his mother's death; she had tried to abort after a doctor told her that having another child could be medically dangerous. All four chose to speak out in hopes of preventing the same thing from happening to another generation of children. Their stories are skillfully interwoven, and straight interview footage is broken up with tours of their old neighborhoods and photographs taken before their childhoods were disrupted by sudden and, at the time, unexplained loss. Also included is testimony from a doctor who worked at Philadelphia General Hospital during the 1950s and 1960s, when an entire ward was reserved for the victims of botched abortions. Well produced and at times wrenching to watch, this video provides stark evidence of some of the possible consequences of illegal abortion.

No Alibis

Type: Videocassette
Length: 38 min.
Date: 1986
Cost: Purchase, $39.95; rental, $5 per week from National Right to Life Educational Trust Fund
Distributors: American Portrait Films International, Boone Productions, Inc., National Right to Life Educational Trust Fund

The jacket for this video calls it "a fast-paced drama on abortion designed especially for teenage audiences." The design incorporates an MTV-style rock video—which includes images of Nazi soldiers shooting down the musicians—interwoven with the linked stories of three people: a television journalist whose assignment to do a story on abortion coincides with her dismayed discovery that she is pregnant, a high school teacher who takes his crusade against abortion into the classroom, and a pregnant student who was one on a long list of conquests by an arrogant jock. These stories could indeed provide high drama—but they, and the message they attempt to promote, are trivialized by the presentation, which is awful. Some of the characters spill over into caricature, particularly the doctor/owner of an abortion clinic—a leering, cigar-smoking sleaze who lives in a palatial mansion complete with a foreign maid and a wife and friends who prattle on about animal rights while he says with a sneer that he "leaves the moral and ethical problems [about abortion] to theologians." The high school students preach at each other obnoxiously, and the teacher uses a class "discussion" as a forum to ram his views down students' throats. The slick production, vivid imagery, and catchy music are not enough to compensate for the poor quality of the writing.

No Easy Way Out

Type: Videocassette
Length: 20 min.
Date: 1992
Cost: Purchase, $19.95, quantity discounts available
Distributor: American Portrait Films International

This relatively low-key video uses dramatization and testimony to deliver its message that there is "no easy way out" of an unintended pregnancy. In the dramatization, a pregnant high school girl is urged by her boyfriend and others to get an abortion; she does, but is haunted by the decision. When she becomes pregnant a second time, she decides to have the baby and give it up for adoption, writing in her diary that "I know there will be pain, but I can deal with this." Her story is interwoven with brief segments of people talking about their experiences with abortion: a young man who compares his feelings after the birth of his son to his anguish over his girlfriend's earlier abortion, a young woman who says that she "didn't feel bad" about her abortion until a year later, another who describes the "cold, tight feeling" of the abortion and the sound of the suction machine. A recurring theme in the testimony is "I really didn't want an abortion. I just didn't know what else to do." Also included are a brief look at embryonic and fetal development, neatly inserted into one of the dramatization segments as part of a high school health class, and a doctor who discusses the difficulties of helping patients deal with unplanned pregnancies, emphasizes the physical risks of abortion, and describes what happens in suction and dilatation and evacuation abortions. The film's uplifting ending shows the jubilant teenager hugging her father after being notified that she has been admitted to college. This video does an effective job of portraying the dilemma faced by people who believe that abortion is wrong but feel trapped by an unwanted pregnancy. It would be even better if it also explored the subjects of contraception and/or abstinence as possible means of avoiding repeat abortions.

Operation Rescue

Type: Videocassette
Length: 30 min.
Date: 1988
Cost: Purchase, $49.95
Distributor: American Portrait Films International

This film pays tribute to the radical organization that has received considerable media attention for its use of civil disobedience in its campaign to stop abortion—a campaign that the film leaves no doubt is indeed a holy crusade. Footage of demonstrations and "rescues" is interspersed with pictures of fetuses or unborn children (depending on your perspective), both postabortion and in utero, and abundant biblical quotations. Randall Terry, Operation Rescue's founder and leader, exhorts his followers to repent of their apathy and atone for their "blood guilt" by doing whatever is necessary to stop the "legalized child killing" and save the nation, which is "increasingly staggering under the weight of God's judgment." When man's law and God's law conflict, he says, Christians must act to change man's law, not from a position of judgment but from a "platform of repentance." *Operation Rescue* provides a vivid portrait of the passion and purpose behind the pro-life movement; whether it inspires or dismays will depend on the audience's point of view.

The Other Side of the Fence

Type:	Videocassette
Length:	28 min.
Date:	1993
Cost:	Purchase, $295; rental, $55
Distributor:	Filmmakers Library

This unusual video portrays a woman who "lived, ate, and breathed" the antiabortion movement, becoming one of its most outspoken and militant leaders, until a life crisis forced her to reexamine her beliefs and loyalties. Nancy O'Brien grew up with a burning desire to "make a difference" and eventually found her cause in fundamentalist Christianity and the movement to eliminate abortion. She and her husband, a church leader, moved to Cincinnati in 1985, the same year filmmaker Lynn Estomin began working at Planned Parenthood. The O'Briens formed Project Jericho, with the goal of making Cincinnati an "abortion-free city." Estomin's task was to videotape the actions against the clinic, which included a firebombing and weekly confrontations, almost always with O'Brien at the forefront. In 1987, however, Nancy O'Brien abruptly disappeared from public view. Five years later, Estomin tracked her down and made this film portrait. The film is most effective when O'Brien is telling her story—she is articulate and forthright as she describes how she threw herself into the movement, only to be betrayed and abandoned first by her husband and then by her church, and her subsequent search for new answers to replace her shattered beliefs. The filmmaker's attempts at symbolism, such as a dimly lit dancer freeing herself from the cords that entwine her or a faceless woman shredding a copy of *Cosmopolitan*, fall a little flat. Overall, however, this is an interesting depiction of one woman's transition from passionate conviction to a more sober, if sometimes bitter, awareness.

Our Right to Abortion

Type:	¾" broadcast tape, videocassette
Length:	28 min.
Date:	1986
Cost:	Purchase, $250 (¾"), $195 (video), discounts available to pro-choice activist groups; rental, $60
Distributor:	Women Make Movies

This video aims to inspire viewers to join the struggle to keep abortion both safe and legal in the face of continuing legislative and judicial challenges. It opens and closes with footage of the March 9, 1986, rally for reproductive rights in Washington, D.C., and features such prominent spokespersons as Gloria Steinem, Eleanor Smeal, and Karen DeCrow, along with the powerful vocals of singer/songwriter Holly Near. Also included are interviews with both advocates and opponents of legal abortion, including several New York State legislators and the respective directors of the Syracuse chapters of the National Right-to-Life Committee and Planned Parenthood, as well as women who discuss their own abortions and a doctor who describes women who come to him saying, "I don't believe in this, I really don't believe in this—but I don't want this pregnancy." Although it breaks no new ground, the film is well produced, and it shows respect for all of its subjects, including those who express opposing points of view.

Personal Decisions

Type: 16mm film, videocassette
Length: 30 min.
Date: 1985
Cost: Purchase, $395 (film), $295 (video); rental, $50
Distributor: The Cinema Guild

Personal Decisions presents the stories of seven women who chose to have abortions at particular times in their lives: a woman who in 1954 became pregnant as a result of a brutal rape; a 16-year-old girl who took two weeks to decide, with the full support of her parents, that she was not ready to have a child; a couple looking forward to the birth of their second child who chose abortion after amniocentesis showed a severe defect in the fetus; an obstetrician and mother of four who became pregnant during medical school as a result of contraceptive failure; an immigrant mother of three whose fourth pregnancy threatened her plan to leave her abusive husband; a single teenage mother of two who became pregnant just as she had completed her high school degree and was about to enroll in a job-training program; and a woman whose best friend was beaten to death by her father when he discovered she was pregnant and who, 40 years later, supports her daughter's decision to have an abortion despite her strong Catholic beliefs. Interspersed with these stories are segments of an interview with Dr. Kenneth Edelin, an obstetrician and gynecologist who at one time was convicted as a result of performing an abortion (the conviction was subsequently overturned). The women and their families and partners represent a wide range of socioeconomic, cultural, and religious backgrounds; they are frank and open as they discuss their decisions, which they feel were both intensely personal and right for them. The film is well produced and the stories sensitively portrayed; nevertheless it would be more balanced if it had included women who chose not to abort as well as those who did.

Planned Parenthood's Response to the Silent Scream

Type: Videocassette
Length: 24 min.
Date: 1985
Cost: Not available for purchase
Distributor: Arrange for viewing or rental through local Planned Parenthood affiliates; see white or yellow pages for affiliate nearest you

This film was produced by Planned Parenthood of Seattle as a rebuttal to *The Silent Scream*, which it says presents only one dimension of abortion, with "deliberate distortions of film and fact." Several stories of women who had abortions are presented, along with testimony from specialists in the areas of pediatrics, neonatology, embryology, obstetrics and gynecology, family medicine, ultrasound, and medical ethics. They list the "five most alarming inaccuracies" in the film, including inaccurate statement of fetal age; use of a plastic model of different gestational age; use of different cameras for the ultrasound imagery, beginning with a sophisticated camera and changing to one that shows less detail; alterations in film speed; and the description of the fetus's sensing danger and attempts to avoid it, which could not occur at this gestational age since the brain is too undeveloped to sense danger or pain or to perform purposeful movements. The doctors also criticize the terminology used in the film, such as "rip apart," "tear," and "crushed," as manipulative. Other criticisms include a lack of sympathy for the woman or others involved and the implication that "everything will be fine" if every pregnant woman carries her pregnancy to term. This film is simply produced, with no music or special effects. The interviewees are direct and straightforward and use nontechnical language to present their case. *The Silent Scream*, they say, will not change a woman's decision to have an abortion; it will simply cause her to feel more guilt about doing so. [See also *The Answer, The Silent Scream,* and *The Silent Scream: Responding to Critics.*]

Roe vs. Wade

Type: Videocassette
Length: 92 min.
Date: 1989
Cost: Rental
Distributor: Available at many video rental stores

This Emmy award-winning made-for-TV movie stars Holly Hunter as Ellie Russell, alias "Jane Roe," and Amy Madigan as Sarah Weddington, the Texas attorney who successfully argued the *Roe v. Wade* case in front of the Supreme Court. The movie is loosely based on the events leading up to the now-famous 1973 decision legalizing abortion. Ellie Russell, an itinerant, poor Texas woman who has reluctantly agreed to let her own mother raise her young daughter because she is unable to, discovers that she is pregnant. In the course of her unsuccessful attempts to gain an abortion, she meets Linda Coffee and Sarah Weddington, two fresh-out-of-law-school attorneys who have been searching for a plaintiff to challenge the constitutionality of Texas's strict abortion laws. Thinking that she might be able to win her abortion, Ellie agrees—only to learn that the case will take many months to wind its way through the courts. The movie then follows the separate stories of Ellie, who goes to stay with her father while she awaits the birth of the child she cannot afford to keep but cannot bear to give up, and Coffee and Weddington, who are moving the case ever closer to the ultimate forum, the Supreme Court. An important minor character is Jay Floyd, the attorney who is given the task of arguing for the state and who finds himself increasingly convinced that abortion is in fact murder and that "children's lives are depending on me." The movie is satisfyingly dramatic, although the dialogue suffers from an occasional lapse into exposition and the writer has taken a fair amount of artistic license. The acting, particularly from Holly Hunter, is first-rate, making this an entertaining and absorbing, if not precisely accurate, portrayal of a pivotal period in abortion history.

The Silent Scream

Type: Videocassette
Length: 28 min.
Date: 1984
Cost: Purchase, $49.95
Distributor: American Portrait Films International

This is probably the most famous abortion film ever made; it is certainly the most controversial. Its release provoked a storm of outrage among abortion rights supporters and galvanized pro-life activists, who saw in it documentary proof of their claim that abortion is murder. *The Silent Scream* is artfully produced and written, making maximum use of music, emotional language, and props to deliver its message. Hosted by Dr. Bernard Nathanson, *The Silent Scream* begins by showing a high-resolution ultrasound exam of a fetus inside the belly of an obviously pregnant woman—though it is never stated, she is certainly not the same woman whose uterus is shown in the abortion segment of the film. Then Dr. Nathanson states that we are going to see an abortion "from the victim's viewpoint." After a discussion of fetal development and a description of the abortion procedure, both explained with the aid of plastic models, Dr. Nathanson appears seated in front of a large-screen television. As the ultrasound tape is shown, he uses a plastic model of a fetus and actual instruments to explain what is happening in the fuzzy pictures on the screen—now the baby is pulling away from the instruments inserted into the uterus, now the mouth is open in a "silent scream," now the forceps are being used to crush the head. He describes the "secret language" used by the abortionist and the anesthesiologist ("did you get 'number one'?"—meaning the head) and talks about abortion clinics that are "franchised out like fast food." As the camera alternates between shots of grieving women and discarded fetuses, he talks of victimized women who are sterilized and "castrated." "The destruction of a human being," he says, "is no solution to what is basically a social problem," and he calls for a better solution that would have "decent regard for the overriding priority of human life." [See also *The Answer; Planned Parenthood's Response to the Silent Scream* and *The Silent Scream: Responding to Critics.*]

The Silent Scream: Responding to Critics

Type: Videocassette
Length: 29 min.
Date: 1985
Cost: Purchase, $15
Distributor: National Right to Life Educational Trust Fund

In this video, Kay James of the National Right to Life Committee interviews Dr. Bernard Nathanson, the former abortionist turned antiabortion activist, about his controversial 1984 film *The Silent*

Scream, which critics claimed contained inaccuracies and deliberate distortions. James questions Nathanson about each of the criticisms leveled at the film; whether his answers are satisfactory or not will probably depend on the audience's point of view. For example, in response to denials that a 12-week fetus can perceive pain, as is asserted in the film, Nathanson says that he was not claiming that "pain is recognized on a cognitive level" and that cortical development is not necessary for the perception of pain. Further, the point of the film was not that the fetus felt pain, but that viewers witnessed "the cold-blooded destruction of a living human being." Nathanson also delivers a scathing attack on the "high cash, low-visibility [abortion] industry," which he estimates takes in over $1 billion annually, and decries the victimization of women who "have not been told the truth" prior to obtaining abortions. In conclusion, Nathanson, who attributes his change of mind to his experience in perinatology, concludes by saying that he is working on a new technology that will "finally decide the abortion issue"—possibly a reference to *Eclipse of Reason*, reviewed above. [See also *The Answer, Planned Parenthood's Response to the Silent Scream*, and *The Silent Scream*.]

So Many Voices: A Look at Abortion in America
Type: 16mm film, videocassette
Length: 30 min.
Date: 1982
Cost: Purchase, $450; rental, $50
Distributor: Phoenix Films and Video (Order #22169)

Hosted by Ed Asner and Tammy Grimes, this film opens with a montage that nicely illustrates the poles of the abortion debate. "One in ten women has had an abortion," say the hosts, who cite polls showing that the majority of Americans believe that abortion should be legal—but only in certain circumstances. Some of those circumstances are described by people who have experienced them directly—a couple whose first daughter was born with Tay-Sachs disease and who would not have risked a second child without the option of abortion; a rape victim; a police woman whose own mother died from an illegal abortion and who deals daily with unwanted children; a doctor who recalls a ward filled with women suffering complications from illegal abortions; a mother of four whose own mother died from an illegal abortion 51 years earlier; a doctor who changed his mind after 30 years of opposition to abortion; a former president of the National Abortion Federation; a former antiabortion volunteer who speaks positively of her decision to have an abortion and the experience that followed; and workers at an abortion clinic in Ft. Wayne, Indiana, which has been subjected to harassment and threats. Although it claims to look at both sides of the debate, this film comes down clearly on the side of "the right to make our own choices"—the antiabortion viewpoint is represented primarily through segments of public speeches by antiabortion leaders Mildred Jefferson and Carolyn Gerster.

Stand Up for Choice

Type: Videocassette
Length: 3 15-min. cassettes
Date: 1993
Cost: Purchase, individual episodes, $39.95, all three
              episodes, $99.95
Distributor: The Cinema Guild

This three-part series is intended primarily as a training tool for teaching pro-choice activists how to defend abortion clinics and patients from antiabortion violence. The three episodes—*The Blockade, Escorts,* and *From Vigilance to Violence*—show footage of actual clinic confrontations, highlighting tactics used by Operation Rescue and other groups to attempt to shut down or deny access to clinics, as well as methods that can be used to defend clinics, shield patients, and deter violence. Also included are interviews with antiabortion protestors and "rescuers," pro-choice activists, clinic workers, abortion providers, and women who encountered demonstrations when they showed up at the clinic for abortions. A training booklet is available free with purchase.

Supreme Court Decisions That Changed the Nation:
Roe v. Wade

Type: Videocassette
Length: 15 min.
Date: 1989
Cost: Purchase, $69 (home use)
Distributor: Guidance Associates

This brief video is one of a series on significant Supreme Court decisions. It provides some historical background on eighteenth- and nineteenth-century attitudes toward abortion and the role of medical doctors and medical science in making abortion illegal. It then delves into the cultural and medical aspects of questions involving the right to privacy and the parts the Ninth and Fourteenth Amendments played in the *Roe v. Wade* decision. Because of its brevity, the video is valuable mostly for raising questions and encouraging viewers to seek more information on the many and complex issues involved in the abortion controversy.

When Abortion Was Illegal: Untold Stories
Type: 16 mm film, videocassette
Length: 28 min.
Date: 1992
Cost: Purchase, $495 (film with public performance rights), $95 (video with public performance rights), $29.95 (video for home use only), add $5 shipping and handling to all orders; rental, $45 (film only), rent may be applied to purchase price
Distributor: Bullfrog Films

This documentary garnered an Academy Award nomination for Best Documentary Short Subject in 1992. Intended to open a "sealed chapter" of women's history, *When Abortion Was Illegal* skillfully weaves together old photographs, engravings, news clippings, and recent interviews to present a poignant account of the physical, emotional, and legal consequences of illegal abortion in the United States prior to 1973. To make the film, director/producer Dorothy Fadiman drew on dozens of interviews with people from all over the country. Her subjects include women who had illegal abortions, medical practitioners who dealt with the consequences of botched abortions or who risked their careers and freedom to perform abortions, and individuals who broke the law to help desperate women find safe abortions. Also included are accounts drawn from old newspapers and other documents, including statements made by dying women who had yielded to police pressure to reveal their abortionists' identities. Fadiman, who nearly died from an illegal abortion in 1962, made *When Abortion Was Illegal* as a way of reaching a generation that has no memory of an era when abortion was shrouded in secrecy, shame, and fear. The documentary, which was produced in association with San Jose, California, public television station KTEH, is the first of a planned three-part series. Part two is *From Danger to Dignity* [see above]. The third segment, tentatively titled *The Fragile Promise of Choice*, will examine current threats to safe, legal abortion, including barriers to abortion access, the continuing decrease in abortion providers, and harassment and violence directed at abortion providers and patients.

Who Broke the Baby?
Type: Videocassette
Length: 28:30 min.
Date: 1987
Cost: $19.95
Distributor: American Portrait Films International

This visually attractive and well-produced film is aimed primarily at teenagers. It is based on the book of the same title; both were written by Jean Garton, a self-described former abortion activist who tried to have an illegal abortion in 1971 and who changed her mind after researching abortion slogans and finding "that they lied." The title comes from a question asked by Garton's son at age three, on seeing a picture of a dismembered fetus. As the film opens, the attractive young narrator explains that our minds are conditioned by "image-distortion and double-speak" to not think of the fetus as human. Like building contractors who avoid numbering the thirteenth floor in order to "avoid the reality of its existence," society has made "the unborn child . . . the thirteenth floor of the human family." The rest of the film is a brisk-paced examination of the best-known abortion rights slogans. The segment on "Every woman has a right to control her own body," compares the risks of sexual activity to the risks of driving. "Abortion," states the narrator, "is evidence of a body that has been out of control." In response to the claim that women will seek abortions even if they are illegal, she asks "Should we legalize car theft and shoplifting" because some people will do them anyway? Saying that women have abortions because of "convenience, expediency, and economics," she concludes with a plea to viewers to "be the person who will help [a pregnant woman] want her baby to live."

With a Vengeance: The Fight for Reproductive Freedom
Type: 16mm film, videocassette
Length: 40 min.
Date: 1989
Cost: Purchase, $600 (film), $225 (video), discounts
               available to pro-choice activist groups; rental, $75
Distributor: Women Make Movies

Filmmaker Lori Hiris has used some deceptively simple techniques to make a powerful film about the expansion of the abortion rights movement to a broader struggle for full reproductive freedom. Filmed completely in black and white, the film has a deliberately rough, old-fashioned feel that emphasizes its blend of past and present. Throughout, Hiris combines sound and pictures in unusual and provocative ways to juxtapose different periods and aspects of her subject. Interview segments intersect with cartoon drawings, still photos, footage of demonstrations and speeches, newspaper headlines, and printed words to reveal the historical, political, and personal underpinnings of the women's movement and its continuing struggle to win not only reproductive freedom but freedom from racism, sexism, and poverty, along with full access to health care and support for having and raising children. No single voice tells the story. Instead we see and hear numerous women and men—old, young, black, white, Latina, Asian—from early abortion rights activists such as Patricia Maginnis, Lawrence Lader, and the Redstockings, to present-day leaders like Byllye Avery and Flo Kennedy, to young college students concerned that a right they have grown up with may be taken away. This is a radical film that will almost certainly not win converts among those who oppose abortion. Abortion rights activists, however, will find it both an absorbing portrait of their history and an inspiration to continue their struggle.

Distributors

American Portrait Films International*
P.O. Box 19266
Cleveland, OH 44119
(216) 531-8600
(800) 736-4567
(216) 531-8355 (FAX)

---

* In addition to the films listed here, American Portrait Films International has a number of other pro-life films, including several tailored for teenage audiences and some intended specifically for use in crisis pregnancy counseling. American Portrait Films International produces and distributes films based on traditional Judeo-Christian values, primarily to activist groups, churches, and Christian schools and bookstores. All videos are inexpensively priced ($15 to $30) and available for purchase by individuals. Write or call for catalog.

Bernadell, Inc.
P.O. Box 1897
Old Chelsea Station
New York, NY 10011
(212) 463-7000

Boone Productions, Inc.
2600 West Olive, Suite 930
Burbank, CA 91505
(818) 841-6565

Bullfrog Films
P.O. Box 149
Oley, PA 19547
(800) 543-3764

The Cinema Guild
1697 Broadway
New York, NY 10019
(212) 246-5522

Concentric Media
1070 Colby Avenue
Menlo Park, CA 94025
(415) 321-1533

Educational Video Center
87 Lafayette Street
New York, NY 10013
(212) 219-8129

Feminist Majority Foundation
1600 Wilson Boulevard, Suite 704
Arlington, VA 22209
(703) 522-2214

Filmmakers Library
124 E. 40th Street
New York, NY 10016
(212) 808-4980

Guidance Associates
90 S. Bedford Road
Mt. Kisco, NY 10549
(914) 666-4100

Martha Stuart Communications
147 W. 22nd Street
New York, NY 10011
(212) 255-2718
Cable: Listening NY
Telex: 508937 Stuart

National Right to Life Educational Trust Fund
419 7th Street, NW, Suite 500
Washington, DC 20004–2293
(202) 626-8809

New Day Films
22-D Hollywood Avenue
Hohokus, NJ 07423
(201) 652-6590
E-mail: tmcndy@aol.com

Paulist Productions
P.O. Box 1057
Pacific Palisades, CA 90272
(213) 454-0688

PBS Video
1320 Braddock Place
Alexandria, VA 22314-1698
(703) 739-5380

Phoenix Films and Video
468 Park Avenue S.
New York, NY 10016

Women Make Movies
225 Lafayette Street, Suite 212
New York, NY 10012
(212) 925-0606
(212) 925-2052 (FAX)

Other Sources

A number of the organizations listed in chapter 4 have produced videos that are available for purchase or rental; see individual listings.

Glossary

abortifacient a substance, such as an herbal mixture, used to cause abortion

abortion delivery or removal of a fetus before it becomes viable

abortion, failed an abortion that does not successfully terminate a pregnancy

abortion, incomplete an abortion in which a portion of the embryo or fetus remains in the uterus

abortion, induced an abortion brought about by the use of drugs or by mechanical or surgical means

amniocentesis introduction of a hollow needle into the uterine cavity to withdraw amniotic fluid or to inject a drug

amniotic fluid liquid within the membranous sac that surrounds the fetus within the uterus

anencephaly a congenital malformation of the skull in which all or part of the brain is absent

aspirator a device that removes material by suction

317

cannula   a tube that is inserted into the uterus and through which the contents of the uterus are withdrawn

catheter   a hollow cylinder or tube placed into the vagina and threaded into the uterus, through which drugs are administered

cervix   the neck or opening of the uterus, which extends down into the vagina

cesarean section   removal of a baby from the uterus through an incision in the abdomen. Also spelled cesarian, caesarean.

life begins

conception   alternatively defined as: (1) the moment at which an egg and a sperm come together to create a zygote and (2) the implantation of a fertilized ovum in the lining of the uterus

fertiled egg before it plants its egg along in uterine wall

contraception   the prevention of conception or impregnation through any of several methods; also called birth control

contraindication   a reason for not using a procedure

curette   a spoon-shaped instrument used to scrape tissue from inside the uterus

D & E abortion   dilatation and evacuation. A procedure where the cervix is dilated, after which the fetus and pregnancy tissue are grasped with a forceps and removed from the uterus.

DIC (disseminated intravascular coagulation)   a condition that prevents blood from coagulating properly

dilation   stretching or enlarging the cervical opening. Also called dilatation.

dilators   tapered metal or plastic rods of progressively larger diameters, which are inserted one at a time into the cervix in order to stretch the opening so that a cannula or other instruments may be inserted

Down's syndrome   a genetic disease, characterized by the presence of 47 chromosomes rather than the normal 46, which causes mental retardation and physical abnormalities

echogram   see **sonogram**

ectopic pregnancy   a pregnancy that occurs outside the uterus, most often in a Fallopian tube, and that can be fatal to the mother

embolism   an obstruction in an artery caused by a blood clot, air bubble, or foreign material

embryo   technically, the term given to the fertilized zygote after it has attached to the wall of the uterus and through the eighth week of development

ergonavine   a drug used to contract the uterus

Fallopian tubes   the two tubes leading from the ovaries to the uterus. Each month an ovum passes from one ovary through the Fallopian tube to the uterus. The Fallopian tubes are where fertilization takes place.

fertilization   the union of a spermatozoan and ovum to form a zygote

fetus   technically, the term given to the developing human organism from the end of the eighth week of development through the completion of pregnancy

forceps   an instrument used to grasp tissue

gestation   the period of a pregnancy from conception to birth

gravida   a pregnant woman

HCG   human chorionic gonadotropin, a hormone produced during pregnancy

hysterectomy   surgical removal of the uterus

hysterotomy   technically, an incision into the uterus; also used to describe a method of abortion where the fetus is removed from the uterus through an abdominal incision

implantation   attachment of the fertilized egg to the lining of the uterus about one week after fertilization takes place

infertility   the inability to conceive and bear offspring

instillation abortion   an abortion accomplished by placing a chemical substance in the uterus that subsequently causes contractions, or labor, so that the fetus is expelled

IUD   intrauterine device, a small metal or plastic object that is placed in the uterus to prevent implantation of the fertilized egg

laceration   a tearing of tissue

laminaria   the stem of a Japanese seaweed that, when inserted into the cervical os, causes the cervix to dilate over a period of several hours or overnight

laparotomy   an incision made through the abdominal wall

lithotomy position   the standard position for pelvic exams, pelvic surgery, or childbirth, in which a woman lies on her back with her knees bent and her legs apart

LMP   last menstrual period. Length of pregnancy is usually calculated from the first day of the last menstrual period. In actuality, however, fertilization usually takes place in the middle of the menstrual cycle, so that length of pregnancy LMP is actually about two weeks less than the gestational age of the fetus.

menarche   the onset of menstruation at puberty

menstrual extraction   removal of the contents of the uterus by suction before pregnancy has been confirmed

molar pregnancy   an abnormal mass in the uterus that is often mistaken for a pregnancy in the early stages of gestation

mucus   the material secreted by the cells lining the body cavities

multigravida   a woman who has been pregnant more than once

multipara   a woman who has given birth two or more times

nulliparous   never having given birth to a child

organogenesis   the origin and development of organs

parity   having given birth to one or more children; often used with a number to indicate how many times a woman has given birth (a multiple birth delivery is defined as a single parous experience)

primigravida   a woman pregnant for the first time

primipara   a woman who has given birth to a child or children for the first time

oral contraceptive   a pill that contains hormones that simulate early pregnancy and prevent ovulation, thereby preventing pregnancy

osmotic dilator   a compressed sponge containing a chemical that dilates the cervix by absorbing fluid from it and expanding

ovary   the female reproductive gland that contains the ova, or unfertilized eggs

oxytocin   a drug used to stimulate uterine contractions

perforation   an opening or tear in the uterine wall

peritoneal cavity   the abdominal cavity containing the pelvic and abdominal organs

peritonitis   inflammation of the lining of the abdominal cavity, usually as a result of infection

PID   pelvic inflammatory disease. An inflammation involving the fallopian tubes, ovaries, and peritoneum.

placenta   the organ that transmits nourishment from a woman's bloodstream to her fetus; also called afterbirth

placenta previa   a condition in which the placenta blocks the cervical canal during childbirth

pregnancy test, radioreceptor   a blood test that can detect very early pregnancy

pregnancy test, urine slide   a test performed on the urine to detect pregnancy

pro-choice   a term used by persons who favor legal abortion to describe themselves

pro-life   a term used by persons opposed to abortion to describe themselves

prostaglandin   a fatty acid found in many body tissues and a substance used in some methods of second trimester abortion to stimulate uterine contractions

psychotropic drugs   drugs used to relieve anxiety by affecting the brain

quickening   the first perception of fetal movement by a pregnant woman

quinine   a plant extraction used to treat malaria; sometimes used as an ineffective abortifacient

retained tissue   tissue that remains in the uterus after an abortion.

Rh factor   a substance found on the surface of red blood cells in individuals who are Rh-positive. Those who do not have the substance are called Rh-negative.

Rh-immune globulin   a substance containing a specific amount of Rh antibodies, which protect against the Rh-positive red blood cells of an Rh-negative woman after an abortion, miscarriage, or childbirth

right-to-life   the belief that human beings have a right to live that begins at conception and ends at natural death

rubella   also known as German measles. A viral infection that, when contracted in the first three months of pregnancy, can cause such defects as mental retardation, blindness, and/or deafness in the child.

saline   a salt solution

saline abortion   a method in which amniotic fluid is withdrawn through a needle inserted into the amniotic sac and replaced with a saline solution, which causes the fetus to die and to be expelled by the uterus.

septic abortion   an abortion associated with high fever (100 degrees or more) caused by uterine infection; may lead to septic shock and death

septic shock   a severe loss of blood pressure caused by certain infections. Usually accompanied by high fever, it will be fatal unless treated promptly.

sickle-cell anemia   a genetically transmitted disease of black and Mediterranean people that can cause disintegration of the red blood cells

slippery slope   an argument claiming that once society has have taken the first step along a given path, it will inevitably go the rest of the way "down the slope." In the context of abortion, the slippery slope argument is used most often by those who believe that legal abortion will lead to such societal abuses as involuntary euthanasia and elimination of "defective" or "useless" people such as the physically or mentally disabled or the elderly; it is used less frequently by those who claim that criminalizing abortion will lead to a revival of restrictions on birth control and increased repression of women.

sonogram   also called echogram. An image or picture created by sound waves, similar to an X ray.

sound   an instrument used to measure the depth of the uterus

speculum   an instrument that is inserted into the vagina and opened so that the vaginal walls and cervix are visible

sterilization   surgery to permanently end reproductive capacity

suction curettage   see **vacuum aspiration**

Tay-Sachs disease   a genetically transmitted disease of Ashkenasic Jews that causes mental retardation and early death

tenaculum   a grasping instrument used to hold the cervix in place during an abortion

thalidomide   a psychotropic drug that, if taken during pregnancy, can cause severe limb deformities in the fetus

trimester   one third of a full-term pregnancy (about 13 weeks)

ultrasound   see **sonogram**

urea   a natural liver by-product that can be produced synthetically. Used in abortion in conjunction with other agents to induce uterine contractions.

uterus   the hollow, muscular, pear-shaped organ in which the fertilized egg implants and grows into a fetus

vacuum aspiration   evacuation of uterine contents by vacuum suction

vacuum aspirator   a hollow tube through which the contents of the uterus are removed in a suction abortion; also the suction machine to which it is attached

vagina   the canal that extends from the uterus to the vulva

viability   the point at which a fetus can survive outside the uterus, with or without artificial life support

vulva   vaginal lips

womb   see **uterus**

zygote   the fertilized egg before it implants itself in the uterine wall

Index

325